Red Shirts and Roses

The tale of the
two Old Traffords

By Eric Midwinter

The Parrs Wood Press
Manchester

First Published 2005

THE PARRS WOOD PRESS
St Wilfrid's Enterprise Centre
Royce Road, Manchester, M15 5BJ
www.parrswoodpress.com

ISBN: 1 903158 59 1

Printed by Compass Press Ltd of London

ACKNOWLEDGEMENTS

E.W. Horning, the creator of 'Raffles, the Amateur Cracksman' and amateur cricketing 'crack', was a wicketkeeper, if, according to his brother-in-law, Arthur Conan Doyle (whose only first-class wicket was that of W.G. Grace), a shortsighted and asthmatic one. Andy Searle, the Editorial Director of The Parrs Wood Press, energetically sustains that rare convention of wicket-keeper-publisher/writer, without the myopia and the breathlessness. He keeps a splendid wicket for the descendants of the old Metro Vicks team, a company that figures not infrequently in the following story. They still play, with considerable success, on the old Metros' ground in Ashton-on-Mersey.

Andy Searle, whose father and I were at school together at much the same time, brings that same cricketing flair and enthusiasm to his publishing duties and it has been a delight to produce a book for so sympathetic and encouraging a publisher. Like several other authors of sporting prints, I owe him a substantial debt.

He whom Beryl Reid's Monica might have termed my 'super-special chum', John Rennie, generously agreed to read, verify and correct the proofs for me. It is a generosity not to be dismissed lightly, for his lifelong commitment to the sacred cause of Manchester City is as devout as mine to their rivals. Asking him to read this text was tantamount to inviting a vegetarian to manage a butcher's shop. Thus he was gallantry itself, his mission eased by our joint and fervent worship of Lancashire County Cricket Club. He grudgingly admits to having enjoyed half the book. Away from his sporting ties, John Rennie, a bustling, extrovert Mancunian of warm-hearted geniality and abidingly strong social values, practically single-handedly pursued the arduous task of embedding the concept of Community Education into the British consciousness, whilst now, in a mode that makes the ill-natured think of poachers and gamekeepers, he is the much-respected Chairman of the Warwickshire Police Authority.

His zealous, encouraging and extremely perceptive undertaking of this proofreading role was roughly the thousandth kindness he has solicitously tendered me in the near forty years of our profound and cordial friendship.

Both Andy Searle and myself would like to express our keen appreciation of the generous help given by the ebullient Keith Hayhurst, the smiling face of Lancashire cricket, in providing most of the illustrations, including the front cover picture. Another human dynamo, Eric Hughes, contributed the two photographs of immediate post-war football at Old Trafford, and John Dawson, Lancashire's official photographer, was kind enough to provide the picture of Andrew Flintoff. Affectionate thanks are also due to them both.

3

Red Shirts and Roses

Finally, the text is based on almost 70 years remembrance and a not much shorter time of reading about these matters, an experience that would have made the task of providing a full reading list extremely laborious and invidious. Four works have, however, been utilised for special reference and it is appropriate to include an acknowledgement of those. They are B. Bearshaw *From the Stretford End; the Official History of Lancashire County Cricket Club* (1990); R. Brooke & D. Goodyear *A Who's Who of Lancashire County Cricket Club 1865-1990* (1991); G. Dykes *The United Alphabet; a Complete Who's Who of Manchester United FC* (1994); M. Wylie et al. *The Official Manchester United Illustrated History* (2001).

Eric Midwinter
April 2005

CONTENTS

Front cover image: George Best strides forth with Jack Crompton to open the batting at Old Trafford cricket ground... in a charity match.

PART ONE:

THE BEGINNING

1.

OT Squared; The Twin Temples

LANCASHIRE were playing back to front, or rather sideways on, so it must have been versus Pakistan in 1967. That was the only time they ever played a match west to east, end on to the pavilion. Old Trafford has been criticised in that the upper drawer pavilionites have to watch sideways on, unlike most Test grounds, but, at least, it does not suffer the dire embarrassment of a clumsy sightscreen being manhandled awkwardly back and to and generally getting in everyone's way. There was a quiet passage of play and my friend, Norman Garner, with whom I watched a lot of football and cricket at that time, spoke thoughtfully. He nodded towards the footlights of the nearby football ground and glanced around the cricket arena. 'These are your twin temples, aren't they?' he asked, somewhat rhetorically and with a characteristic sniff.

I had perforce to agree, although it was to be another quarter century before I faced overtly the strength of that sentiment and came readily to acknowledge that Lancashire County Cricket Club and Manchester United played the role and satisfied the niche in my life that religion does for others. Some vestige of intellectual snobbery had stopped me from daring to equate the red rose and the red shirts with the ancient majesty of the great world creeds that seemed to bring such succour to millions, but, increasingly, not least as respect for these global faiths waned, I more boldly recognised that, outside of family and private ties, this was the nearest I had to emotional props and intelligent beliefs.

Born and bred a minute's walk from Sale Station, with but a six minute electric train journey to Warwick Road Station, and not much longer on what was then the 49 Manchester Corporation bus along the Stretford Road, the two Old Traffords were quickly in my sights and proximity was an important issue. Even more significant, my father was a keen sports follower, with 'Lanky' and 'the Reds' his rooted preference, so that there was about as much chance of my becoming, say, a Manchester City and Yorkshire fan as a child born in Kabul has of becoming a Particular Baptist. Let us assume that nature and nurture conspired to bring about this dispensation.

Red Shirts and Roses

Unluckily, the Second World War intervened just as I was becoming sentient of these matters. This meant that my first properly remembered visits to the twin temples occurred in peculiar circumstances. Because of bomb damage both in December 1940 and March 1941, Manchester United were playing at Maine Road, home of Manchester City. In the autumn of 1941 my father, known as Ack, took me thither. He was in the fire brigade and we were joined by one of his mates, Jackie Hulme, in peacetime a saxophone player with the orchestra of one of the big cruise ships like the Queen Mary, itself recruited for wartime service. It was a bus ride and then a tram ride to Maine Road. The two men bought meat and potato pies, although one expects they found precious little of the former therein, while, the scarce sweets coupons having been raided, I was presented with a Mars Bar as we arrived at the ground. As befitted a war-child and in honour of the occasion, I ate it very slowly. I assumed this was some form of ritual and, 30 years later, I gave my son, Matthew, a Mars Bar when I first took him to see United.

We queued at the turnstiles - I, of course, ducked in through the schoolboy entrance for a tanner - and entered the huge ground. My father grinned. 'Run up those steps', he said, temporally removing from his mouth the near permanent cigarette, 'and take your first look at a football ground'. I scampered up the broad stairs at his bidding and looked over the great expanse of green, over to the players' tunnel and the rising flights of concrete terracing, already filling with servicemen and be-mufflered workers, almost all of them emulating my father in the nicotine stakes. Although I did not find these words then, what impressed most was the sheer organisation of it all, what with the perfect white lines and the neatly rigged goal nets. The only football I had seen to date had been mainly pick-up stuff on parks, with never a net and not always a post in view, and not much by the way of uniform costume. Primary schools then did not include sport on the curriculum

The closest I had been to such orderliness in football matters was when I had played for the local wolf cubs against the cub pack of a nearby preparatory school. Here there were goal posts and touch lines and the prep school boys all ran out in natty blue shirts, whereas we were wearing our rather dowdy cub uniforms, with not many of us even properly shod in football boots. They swamped us nine-nil, one of my first cruel lessons in how an efficient bourgeoisie will always exert control over a proletarian rabble.

Now I was at Maine Road and excitement mounted as the teams emerged, a great cheer welcoming United, a hollow groan depressing the visitors. 'You can always tell which is the home team', commented Ack, this time through the side of his mouth, thus avoiding having to remove the Player's cigarette, for he was a formidable chain smoker who blamed the long nights on duty awaiting fire calls for his addiction. For the first of a thousand times I enjoyed the thrill of viewing those startlingly red shirts. The visitors were Blackburn Rovers, clad in their famed blue and white, with their key player at centre half, Bob Pryde. The match began, and, in order quickly to brush away the bad news under the carpet of sorrowful history, Blackburn won something like three-one.

Two aspects stand out. One was the wide spatial distribution of the players, each with his own assigned role and ambit of operation. When I commented on this, my father smiled, as best he could with his lips clenched around a rapidly diminishing cigarette. He recognised again the distinction between the order and formality of the professional experience over and against the park games I had endured, in which two goalies, as they were invariably labelled, shivered between a couple of coats or school bags, while the rest hunted the ball like a pack of ravenous wolves, with not one child more than about four yards from what Victorian sports journalists called 'the leather'. 'A bit like the Premier League today', do I hear an old-timer acidly observe? It is true that nowadays fluidity is all and it is not uncommon to see 21 players congregated in one penalty area. One often wonders what an attacking side would do at a corner kick, if, as in 1941, the defending team were to leave four or even five players upfield. Would they dare to leave them at liberty to gather up the kind of ricochet out of the goalmouth that often occurs at a corner kick, free to romp home to steal that winning goal?

The other memory is of the crowd - and it was quite a large one - becoming disillusioned with United's puny efforts. A chant began: 'Put Carey in the forwards', repeated over and over, and increasing in volume. The majestic Johnny Carey was playing at right half and the fans wanted him up front to mastermind the attacks. In an intriguing example of wartime democracy at work - after all, it was the citizen's war - whatever then passed for the management of the team acquiesced. John Carey moved to inside right; there was a distinct shift in the tempo and United did pull themselves back, if a little too late, into the game. Curiously, my first sighting of Manchester United coincided with my only witnessing of such a demotic piece of decision-making. It is scarcely likely that Sir Matt or Sir Alec, Caesars both, would have bowed so tamely to the spoken will of the unwashed hoi poloi. Curiously, for all the sharpness of that memory, I cannot recall the end of the game or the journey home.

As for the players, and apart from the cultured Carey, destined to play a major part in United's post-war Renaissance, there were, in 1941, a group of regular players who became very familiar to us. There was the captain, Billy Porter, a very industrious fullback; another rugged fullback, George Roughton, who also captained United and whom we used to see walking his Red Setter near our school; the brave goal keeper, Jack Breedon, released on Saturdays from his war-work as rate-fixer at nearby Metrovicks, and another effective fullback, poor Hubert Redwood, who died of tuberculosis later in the war while on active service. There is something unfair about dying in such an anti-heroic way on military business, rather like Lord Byron, who died of rheumatic fever at Missolonghi in 1824, as he lent his support to the insurgents in the War of Greek Independence, or Rupert Brooke who died of blood poisoning in 1915 en route to the Dardenelles. Jack Smith was the big, dark-haired, lumbering centre forward, occasionally a butt for the crowd, although he did bang in a few goals every season, whilst there was also Bert Whalley, who remained on the coaching staff after the war and, sadly, perished in the Munich Disaster; the long-serving right winger, Billy Bryant, like Jack Breedon and Billy Porter a war-worker at Metros, and, another who found himself at work in Trafford Park, the dour wing half, Bill McKay.

Those homely figures might not have been Schmeichel, Cantona and Beckham, but they were childhood heroes and they don't come more heroic than that. After all, I actually lived with someone who rubbed shoulders with Jack Breedon among the lathes of Metros. We lived with my grandmother and she was the perfect citizeness of the war, obeying every official call to save this or salvage that. In obedience to the strictures of one of the many pamphlets thrust through our letterbox by an importunate bureaucracy, she even transformed our front room into a gas shelter. Frankly, it was not much deployed for other functions; like some sort of sanctified chamber, it was used only for high days and there were not many of those in the darker phases of World War II. A delicate seamstress, she produced beautifully designed excluders for the fireplace and doorway, which added to the atmosphere of reverence; she located her commode sensitively in one corner; flung open the windows daily, whatever the temperature, to air the room; changed a couple of water bottles each day, and kept some precious tins of food in the bookcase. It was probably the only such shelter in the Manchester area and it was always a matter of some regret to me that this haven was never put to the test. I could have been sat on my granny's commode, tucking into a tin of pineapple chunks, while the district's equivalent of unprepared foolish virgins were dropping like flies.

So it was no surprise when, official notification having been posted at the town hall, off trotted my grandmother thereto, returning home with a young woman who, under the Direction of Labour laws, found herself drafted from being an assistant in a sweet shop in Barrow-in-Furness to working on Lancaster bombers at Metros. Winnie Wharton lodged with us for the rest of the war - and I almost dropped my copy of the *Rover* comic (Nick Somebody in 'It's Goals that Count' and Rob Somebody-else in 'It's Runs that Count', according to the season) when she casually mentioned that Jack Breedon was a rate-fixer where she worked. 'What's he like?' I managed to gasp, once sufficiently recovered from the shock of such profane acquaintance. The answer was, of course, noncommittal. He was just another rate-fixer, with whom workers negotiated over the prices of jobs and, thereby, the amount in one's weekly pay-packet. He might even have been mortal.

Soon, with school-friends, the journey to watch the Reds at Maine Road became a familiar trek. The first visit to Old Trafford itself was postponed until the first season after the war, when, in 1945, the Central League resumed and the Reserves - the 'Stiffs', as my father termed them - played there on alternating Saturdays. The place was a wreck. The entire main stand had been demolished and it was, in the theatre style of the day, 'standing room only', although another bomb had smitten one of the end terraces and smashed the roofing. The playing area itself had been badly scorched. What had been the main stand was simply a mess of broken concrete and tangled metal and overgrown weed. Just above and to the right of the players' tunnel grew quite a substantial bush - there was a press photograph of George Roughton holding one of its branches and staring in some awe upon its intrusive foliage. It would be some time before temporary and uncovered seating would be erected. So, in the autumn of 1945, I paid my first visit to the demolition site that was Old Trafford, stood on the terraces facing the panorama of rubble, enjoyed every minute and felt at home.

This text seeks to scrutinise the contrasts and comparisons of football and cricket in this Mancunian setting. An early and personal one is that my own introduction to cricket was much more urbane than the inchoate shambles of pick-up football on the local park, ere that opening sight of United at Maine Road. I had played cricket in our bit of a back garden with Ack and my older brother, Bryan. As a four-year-old, I can distinctly remember being caught out for the first time and having to learn the harsh lesson that the cricketing Gods set many more snares than, as I had naively believed, the single one of the tumbling stumps. Nonetheless, in general terms, I watched proper cricket before I really played it.

My father was the scorer at the local Sale club, then a power to be reckoned with in the Manchester Association. Occasionally on those pre-war weekends my mother or my brother would escort me on the short walk to the ground. We would make ourselves known to Ack, although, armed with his coloured pencils within his little timbered hut and keeping an eye on the scoreboard operator, he was, for about the only time in his existence, disinclined to chat volubly. We would shift ourselves some yards away and sit on one of the wooden benches, constructed from superannuated railway sleepers. Through the watery sunshine of memory one is able to discern quite a pastoral picture of white-clothed figures moving softly across a large expanse of greensward. It was all quite calm and polished, compared with the hullabaloo of children's football.

There is one vivid, noisy remembrance - and I can even recollect the name of the cricketer. It was Eric Greenhalgh, who played a few games for Lancashire in the 1930s. His father had been the professional at Sale; during the war he was to act as groundsman, coach and talkative savant. He had another son, Edwin, whom I came later to know quite well, for - somehow it is difficult to keep this going concern out of the narrative - he was the captain and groundsman and general organiser of the Metrovicks cricket team that played in Sale. It must have been 1936 or 1937. We were sitting quietly, enjoying the stately pick-pock of ball on bat, when, abruptly, there was violence. Eric Greenhalgh pulled a ball powerfully down into the ground about ten yards from the boundary; it flew past our ears, only inches away and with the players' cry of warning too late had it been that morsel closer; it smashed through the thicket hedge and there was a satisfying crunch of glass, as the whirling ball smashed into one of the greenhouses in the nurseries that then backed the ground on two sides. One began to realise that this sophisticated pastime could, of a sudden, be brutal.

Come the war, the postponement of first-class cricket before I had a chance to witness it. Old Trafford cricket ground was, like its footballing counterpart, bombed in the blitzes of December 1940 and March 1941. Although the former assault, a four-night aerial bombardment just prior to Christmas, was the worst phase of the Manchester blitz, it was the March attack during which both grounds sustained the most damage. The top of the pavilion, some of its amenities, the groundman's residence, a couple of the stands and the Warwick Road End score box were damaged and there were craters on the playing area.

Part of the Old Trafford football ground had been used from 1939 by the military, as had the training ground at the Cliff, Lower Broughton. The cricket ground was utilised as a transit camp, initially for troops returning from Dunkirk in 1940, while a Royal Engineers unit was stationed there and the Ministry of Supply made a large storage area of the ground. Obviously, this gave it some martial import and guards had to be posted. On the night of the 1941 attack a sentry was killed at the main gate.

Red Shirts and Roses

It is puzzling what adheres to the surfaces of memory and what does not. I have thought about that sentry a thousand times over the last 60 years. Part of the explanation is perhaps that he probably thought he had what used then to be called 'a cushy number', keeping watch over provisions, while others were flying sorties against the German raiders, criss-crossing the cold Atlantic in constant fear of u-boat torpedoes or shipped out to the Far East to face the Japanese menace. But this was total war and, along with the 61,000 civilians killed in air raids, there were military casualties and he was one of them. The counterpoint to that is illustrated by the tale of the talented England inside forward, Raich Carter, who dutifully joined the fire service in Hull. Jeered at during the 'phoney war' for shirking the colours, he signed up with the RAF and was given a safe as houses posting as a physical training instructor in the lonely middle of Scotland, while his ex-mates in the fire brigade were hammered by the ferocious bombing of Hull.

However, there is another silly crumb that sticks in the craw of sentiment. It is merely the concept of being killed violently at a great cricket ground. There is a poignancy about so displeasing a juxtaposition. One is reminded of Arthur Mailey's chilling thought when he had the exquisite Victor Trumper stumped: he shiveringly 'felt like a boy who had killed a dove'.

I went past the ground often enough, peeping out of the train to and from Manchester, observing what, if anything, was happening. Once there were sheep grazing on the holy turf. Next door, on the spare land to the north, there was the bulbous silver-grey envelope of a barrage balloon, anchored and swaying in the breeze. But there was no cricket.

Nevertheless, there was local cricket and it took on a heady significance. The authorities in World War II, their psychology a little more advanced than it had been in World War I, encouraged sport, in part to raise money for the needy war charities but mainly to offer some succour to weary troops and tired munitions and allied workers. Cricket matches were very much part of this minor carnival of sport, with local clubs hosting matches featuring their own local talent alongside famous first-class names. If my father were free from his fire brigade duties, he was often called upon to score for these games, usually ones that pitted the grandiloquently titled Lady Kemsley's Daily Dispatch War Fund XI against some other assembled faction. A rising nine-year-old, I was judged competent to help staff the scoreboard. Off we went, with self-importance mounting as I was allowed in for nothing on such occasions because of my official function in this war-winning exercise.

The upshot was that I watched most of the Lancashire players, recruited for these events, before I actually saw Lancashire. Thus, in parallel with seeing Manchester United for the first time on alien terrain, I saw, informally, the best part of the Lancashire team before I had visited Old Trafford. There was Eddie Paynter, composedly nursing the ball over the bowler's head for sixes into the tennis courts; he was now around 40 years old but he was making tons of runs in the Bradford League and he was still playing with his distinctive lateness. There was Cyril Washbrook and Winston Place; Buddy Oldfield and Albert Nutter; Jack Iddon, still looking slim and debonair; George Duckworth, the hanging judge of stumpers, his characteristic cock-a-hoop appeal less a plea for justice than a delivery of sentence; even the veteran Charlie Hallows, his hair yet sleekly dark.

12

OT Squared; The Twin Temples

There were others, like Jim Smith, the big Middlesex quick bowler and tail-end slogger, or, from even more exotic climes, Learie Constantine, the first black man I consciously remember seeing, the left hand spinner Ellis Achong, the first person of Chinese descent to play in a Test match, and E.A.Martindale, an attacking West Indian player with bat and ball. Local club players would be allowed a run or two to please the fans, while local worthies would offer half crowns to the kitty for every six struck. 'Manny' Martindale caused many half-crowns to be plucked from the trouser pockets of those grocers and shoemakers. On the Sale ground he would, after the fashion of Eric Greenhalgh, create work for the glaziers of the district, as the glass of the nursery greenhouses was splintered by his terrifying blows.

On one occasion a knot of batsmen, dismissed early, were strolling round the ground and stopped to chat with my father. Not only did I have intimate contacts with someone who knew Jack Breedon at work, I had a father who hobnobbed with Lancashire cricketers. These included Leading Aircraftsmen Norman Oldfield and Albert Nutter and Sergeant Cyril Washbrook, all of the RAF, wearing blue serge tunics over their whites, not the usual blazer. Cyril Washbrook had given his square cut and towering hook shots an airing before tapping the ball meekly to first slip and the others had gone cheaply. They explained that Martindale, angered by what he felt to be an unfriendly LBW decision, and one so early in his innings that it had certainly disappointed the crowd, was bowling at an alarming pace on so natural a pitch. They had deemed it wiser, in the phrase beloved of the Sunday papers' crime reporters of the day when interviewing ladies of easy virtue, to 'make an excuse and leave'. The precept of yielding up one's wicket willingly fell oddly on the infant ears of one who normally required strong men to prise the bat from his protesting hands, even if the stumps were demolished. It was a lesson in professional self-reliance long remembered these 60-plus years.

Then one Friday evening in July 1944 I happened to be crossing the station approach on the way home. I bumped into a schoolfellow, Peter Lane. He was a year or two older than me and he was an energetic cricketer; he was just finishing his paper round. An affable youth, with whom I occasionally chatted, we were not intimates and, a year or two later, when he left school and started work, I more or less lost contact with him. He had just spotted a notice in one of the Manchester Evening Newses he had been delivering about a cricket match at Old Trafford the next day. He had determined to go and, on the spur of the moment, wondered if I would like to accompany him. I was very keen - and thus, by dint of this minor and accidental conjunction, I found myself journeying for the first time to the other Old Trafford.

Next morning, Saturday 22 July 1944, tomato (with sugar sprinkled on) sandwiches at the ready, I met Peter Lane and we took the electric train those six minutes to Warwick Road Station. We paid our sixpence at the half-price entrance and took up a place on the tiers of benching just inside the boundary, in front of the higher stands. We were facing the pavilion, at about square leg. Strangely, we were in about the same location as I had been on that first visit to Maine Road. I gazed incredulously at the lush turf and across to the pavilion, looking reasonably majestic despite the depredations of bombing. One was used to walking about and coming across blitzed sites in Manchester and its environs and, having now visited Old Trafford football ground several times, bedraggled sports arenas seemed de rigeur.

Apparently there had been a couple of small scale games already in 1944, the first since 1939. Western Command had played an RAAF Unit XI and an RAF North-Western XI. But this was the first big fixture and, one was later to learn, it came about through an appeal from Australia House to the Lord Mayor of Manchester for the Royal Australian Air Force XI to play at Old Trafford for the benefit of the Red Cross and the RAAF Welfare Fund. They were to receive £250 each. The RAAF played the North of England, captained by Herbert Sutcliffe.

The opening was macabre. A posse of officials and players took the field and proceeded to spread Cecil Parkin's ashes where the Test wicket usually was. The Grock of English cricket had died in 1943 and his last grim jest was a request that his remains be thus disposed of when first there was a major match at Old Trafford. Something of a brisk north-easterly breeze, helpful to Dick Pollard's outswing from the Stretford End, ensured that the white dust blew up and back into the startled countenances of the mourning party. Years later it was a bleak event that Pilot Officer Keith Miller would recall in his own memoirs, for he was playing, just on the cusp of his flamboyant fame. He made only 2 and his score line - stumped Duckworth, bowled Constantine - makes for exciting reading.

The video tapes of memory have not become snagged or snarled in respect of this blessed Saturday. The Australians batted first and made 220 for 5, declared. Learie Constantine took three wickets, racing in with that characteristic glance upwards at his arm as it reached the apex of his delivery wheel. He bowled Flying Officer Ross Stanford, who made 71, and the wicket keeper, Flight Lieutenant S.G. Sismey for 36. His fielding was equally compelling. In spite of the relative unimportance of the fixture, he was a coiled spring of concentration, holding his arms forward in readiness, his fingers long and prehensile; he took a blinding catch to get rid of Sismey, off the bowling of Ellis Robinson, the Yorkshire off-spinner. There was also a pleasant half-century from Flight Sergeant C.P. Calvert. In the coming December, aged but 21, he was killed in a mine-laying expedition over the Baltic Sea. A cricket match was just a stolen interlude for these airmen, most of them facing such ultimate peril in the days before and after.

My only glimpse of Herbert Sutcliffe was very limited. He was plumb LBW for 3. However, our schoolboy champion, Cyril Washbrook, was at his imperious best. He blasted and struck to some purpose, making 133 not out, in something over two hours. How magical that, on this, my first visit to Old Trafford, 'Washy' should strike so belligerent a century. He added 140 with his faithful compadre, Winston Place and then 52 in a bewildering 30 minutes with Learie Constantine. Batting at the Stretford End, Constantine, in a delectably saucy dish of 25 runs, lifted his left leg and tapped the ball underneath it. The ball sped down towards us at square leg and his face lit up in an expansive grin at the devilment of it.

North of England won by 7 wickets with three minutes to spare. Peter Lane bought a *Manchester Evening News* so that we might read about what we had watched so far and catch up with other pieces of local news. And, yet again, I have no memory of the short homeward journey. But what a lucky first trip it had been. All those names: some, like Herbert Sutcliffe and Jack Iddon, not to be witnessed again; some, like Keith Miller, destined for immortality, all of them rapidly committed to memory. It had, meteorologically speaking, been a dullish day, but I already knew enough of Mancunian lore to understand that a rain-free day was a bonus and that many a youngster's maiden outing to Old Trafford had been ruined by what Portia called 'the gentle rain from heaven'.

These were my introductions. I saw Manchester United before I saw Old Trafford; I saw Old Trafford before I saw Lancashire, although, courtesy of Lady Kemsley, I saw most of the Lancashire pre-war staff before I saw Old Trafford. The rites of passage were also quaint. The opening ceremony on first watching United was the presentation of a Mars Bar. The opening ceremony on first visiting the cricketing Old Trafford was the spreading of Cec Parkin's ashes.

I was up and running, dedicated to the twin causes. Time, then, to begin to ask questions about what had gone before and how it had all happened. How did these two sacred sporting cathedrals come to be erected and in such close proximity?

2.

The Advent of Old Trafford Cricket Ground

THE BUILDING of the two Old Traffords, indeed the formation of the two great clubs that play in them, illustrates perfectly the process by which professional sport in Britain was inaugurated. Cricket, along with horse racing, some athletics, and boxing, was in the first generation of sports that adopted a format of rational discipline on a countrywide basis. This happened during the 18th century and the early years of the 19th century. Football, along with the rugby codes, hockey, tennis and a dozen other games, reached the same degree of formality in the, for sport, inventive years of the last third of the 19th century. It is no accident that Old Trafford and Lancashire preceded Manchester United and Old Trafford.

Anxiously sentimental antiquarians have attempted to push back the origins of their particular sporting interests, keen to bring a vintage aura of longevity to their chosen pastime. The oldness of wine rather than the freshness of chicken is the selected analogue. A passing mention in an aged script or the sighting of a medieval drawing has, in the past, given rise to hoots of recognition. Alas, there have been incidents of this where, for instance, golf and cricket have both been identified as having the same source.

One major aspect of this understanding is the modern preoccupation with fixtures. There was plenty of 'play' in pre-industrial Western Europe, just as there have always been what Johan Huizinga, in his masterful account of these matters, called 'interludes'; passages of respite, in the often toilsome existence of all societies. Except for the rich and blue-blooded - hence the incidence of elaborate Real (that is 'royal', as in Madrid) Tennis courts in stately dwellings and meeting places - this 'play' was narrowly localised. Groups of servants or villagers would devise, adapt and pass down their own parochial diversion, using whatever terrain, instruments and objects were to hand; there would be adaptations, as incomers, visitors or returning natives suggested elements they had seen on their travels, but, basically, there were probably as many variations as there were communities. After all, there were over 15,000 parishes in Britain in the 18th and 19th century. This meant that, leaving the few large towns out of the equation, the average community was no more than 400 or 500 strong.

Critically, few had the time or the means to visit other locations and play against another group. Before 1830 Britain was well-nigh immobilised. It was a largely pedestrianised society. Most people walked everywhere, maybe pushing a cart for vocational reasons. Horses were not so widely available for leisure purposes. Even where they were, six miles was regarded as a reasonable limit for an outing and fifteen miles the very extreme restriction. As late as 1803, the Prime Minister, William Pitt the Younger, legislating for the training of local militia

16

during the threat of Napoleonic invasion, insisted that no man should be expected to travel more than six miles for two weekly parades for such martial instruction; 'not more', he proposed, 'than the sturdy English peasantry are in the habit of going when led to a cricket match or other rural diversion'. (The 'led' is revealing; it suggests a note of control, of such happenings only occurring at the behest of the local squirearchy.)

Of course, people then were fine walkers. The likes of William Gladstone and Charles Dickens, deep into the 19th century, thought nothing of the 30-mile stroll. The point is that it took them a very long time. Extensive walking cannot defeat time. In 1830 only 75m public transport journeys were negotiated in Britain, a beggarly four per head of population. The populace was, as Charles Pearson wrote as late as 1846, 'chained to the spot'.

There was precious little sportive intercourse between towns and hamlets, thus there was no sensible motive for having national rules for games. People assembled locally and played their own game, pick-up style, rather as people today might arrive at their golf or badminton club and make up a foursome. It is possible that they did not much care about playing anyone else. We are so snarled up in our mentality with the idea of sport as contest that some of that wholesome precept of disportment has perhaps been lost. As we shall have cause to notice, the origins of both Lancashire cricket and Manchester United football have some vestiges of that ancient convention.

Indeed, the very complex nature of cricket indicates it was something of a late developer, for it is an amalgam of several versions of ball, club and target diversions. In its original 'underhand' format, it resembled 'bowls' ('bowling' is still retained to describe an act that many would have regarded as its opposite) and other skittles-like games. The primitive cricket bat was shaped more like a hockey stick and, of course, as in hockey, the target had to be defended by the stick. The search for runs resembled the rounders and baseball genre, while, until 1787, charging of fielders *à la* the football codes was permitted. Perhaps the main oddity was the use of two targets, as opposed to the single board or butt of most similar sports. Given that there were originally only two stumps - and, in some versions, they were wider than they were high - there is something of the two 'ends' of the football or hockey formula. Cricket seems to be the only sport where, as opposed to single, dual or team combat (or one person, as in baseball, facing the whole of another team) two players face the opposing squad. It is all very confusing, but it is typical of the condition of 'gameness', of hundreds of variations on a score or more themes, that prevailed until quite late on in British sporting history.

It was gambling that led directly to the formalisation of sports. When, during the 18th century, the wagering fad grew apace, as, after the political ructions of the 17th century, there was some economic settlement of the nation. Hambledon, for romantics the cradle or Bethlehem of cricket, was, in effect, a sort of Las Vegas come to Hampshire, given the heavy betting on 'matches' - for 'games' was the term used to distinguish contests where betting was not involved. The noble and well-to-do found in horse racing, boxing and cricket yet more outlets for their passion, but gambling without rules leads to undue dispute.

Red Shirts and Roses

The earliest surviving cricket rules are, in fact, 'articles of agreement' between the Duke of Richmond and Mr A. Brodrick of Surrey in 1727, for a match between teams they had raised and on which significant stakes rode. The 'London' code, printed in 1744 and the forerunner of the laws of cricket, was probably designed with much the same peaceful end in view, for there had been cricket matches that had ended precipitately in bitter argument and violence. There were parallels for this, for instance in The Jockey Club, founded at much the same time by the likes of Sir George Bentinck and Admiral Rous for the stricter control of racing. In boxing, there were the 1743 Broughton Rules (after Jack of that ilk, whose Tottenham Court Road Amphitheatre in London was the chief locus of that unruly sport), these being the precursors of the Queensberry Rules of the mid-1860s.

Gentlemen's cricket clubs began to be established, especially in the London region, and they were constitutionally based on the kinds of gentlemen's clubs that were, during these decades, set up for other social purposes. Gradually, they spread outward from that south-east fastness. Historians have suggested that the slowness of cricket - and other sports - to reach the north-west was because of the tight regimes of mills and warehouses that reduced leisure time to the minimum. Cultural barriers may also have existed, in that communications were so dilatory. What the historian G.M. Trevelyan called 'the unremedied badness of the roads' made even the shortest journey something of a lottery. Until the improved roads, thanks to the work of men like Thomas Telford (who died in 1834) and John McAdam (who died in 1836 and who travelled 30,000 miles of roadway, experimenting with the road surfaces that came to take his name) and the flying coaches of the late 18th century, the journey from London to Manchester took three days. Even with such upgrading, it was a 24 or 30-hour trek. The journey from Manchester to Liverpool by road was a five-hour slog, while the canal trip from Manchester to Southport was of a tedious twelve hours duration.

It was the advent of the 19th century, then, before there were any cricket clubs in Lancashire. Liverpool, in the introductory guise of Mosslake Field Society, has good claim to be the first, dating from 1807, while, especially during the 1820s, there was quite a crop of new clubs from Preston to Rochdale, though not all of them prospered. Although there was some inter-club activity, these were often places where members went to play cricket among themselves, just as they might have attended one of their political or social clubs and played whist or billiards. It was regarded as the manly thing to do. It was not surprising that Manchester businessmen determined to join together for cricketing purposes.

The Manchester club dated from 1818, although there is some evidence that it might have got under way in 1816; some of the necessary written formularies may have been lacking, for those who start famous institutions do not always have the future chronicler as their prime motivator. Whichever of the years, it fell between the Battle of Waterloo in June 1815, which concluded the Napoleonic Wars that, with their demand for uniforms and other cotton goods had been a propitious time for the rising Lancashire textile trade, and the satirically named Peterloo Massacre, which came in the post-war period when trade was poorer and political tempers raised. This occurred on 16th August 1819, when some 60,000 working people from the surrounding mill towns had processed into St Peter's Fields (where St Peter's Square and its environs are today), some of them - for they saw it as a kind of holiday - in their Sunday finery. They were paraded to listen to William 'Orator' Hunt, a leading spokesman of the day on parliamentary reform. The Tory magistrates attempted to arrest him and disorder broke out; the local volunteer Yeomanry and regular hussars dispersed the huge gathering with drawn sabres; eleven were killed and at least 400 were injured. It is strange to think of cricket being played in the vicinity of such proceedings.

John Rowlandson, obviously a busy bee in the Tony Blair mould, was Manchester's first President, Secretary and Treasurer. There were fixtures, including games against the local army garrisons and also, despite the travel problems, regular fixtures with Liverpool. However, a good deal of the cricket continued to be internally generated. Manchester remained largely a 'sides' club, with, for instance, the married playing the single or with games based alphabetically according to surnames.

The Manchester club first played in the Adelphi, a verdant meadow in Salford, close to the River Irwell and opposite the Salford Crescent. There was played what, in the annals, is regarded as the first 'Great Match' to take place in Lancashire. This was in 1826, when Manchester beat Liverpool by 39 runs. Typically of the age, a two innings match was negotiated comfortably in the day, the scores being 55 and 83 against 65 and 34. Batsmen had not yet come to that dominance, which, barring rain or a monumental display of hitting, delayed a two innings game for more than a day.

In 1834, the cricketers moved to a field on Moss Lane, near Chorlton Road, Hulme, not far from where Maine Road would much later be built. Soon professionals were being deployed to strengthen the amateur talent. In 1845, when, oddly, the separate innings were fought out on either ground, rather like a modern European football cup-tie, Manchester and Liverpool both fielded professionals. Manchester's choice of the famous Kent and All-England star, Fuller Pitch, was a shrewd move: he had match figures of 15 for 37.

However, Manchester cricket had suffered, in 1842, a grave humiliation at the hands of the Marylebone club, a clear illustration of the cultural chasm that, in sport and in one or two other fields, separated the metropolis and its region from the provinces. On this first visit to Lord's, Manchester were ousted for 59 and then, according to press reports, the Mancunian bowling 'was very deficient, it being of the old-fashioned underhand school, which afforded the MCC gentlemen much amusement in hitting it away' to the tune of 200 or so. Although round arm bowling had been legalised in 1835 and practised substantially hitherto, it had not spread much to the north-west and the Manchester eleven had neither the technique nor the experience either to defend against or promulgate it. Greatly discomfited, the Manchester team forfeited the game at this point and skulked home.

Manchester was to benefit, like much of the country, from the itinerant efforts of the 'Exhibition' elevens, those bands of seasoned professionals who, before the counties had matured and come to exert control over cricket's chief paid employees, beat tracks to the remotest parts of the kingdom, spreading cricket's gospel and garnering some decent pickings at the same time. In the molten crucible of primitive industrial existence they were part of a motley bunch of nomadic entertainers roaming the country, as cheerfully represented by Charles Dickens in Mrs Jarley's travelling waxworks in *The Old Curiosity Shop* and Mr Vincent Crummles' fit-up theatre company in *Nicholas Nickleby*.

The leading and most successful cricket promoter was Nottingham's William Clarke, who ruled the All-England XI with some authority, paying off the players after each match, before sweeping the rest of the coins on the table into his tall hat for his own often handsome profit. Their visit to Hulme in 1846 was without doubt the most important cricket match to have been staged in Manchester to that date. This time Fuller Pitch was in command as a batsman and for the other side. He made 61, not out, and the Manchester XVIII - for the Exhibition teams normally played against such odds - was vanquished by an innings and 31 runs.

In 1847 Manchester made an honourable draw with their erstwhile conquerors, captained by Kent's Alfred Mynn, the game ending, somewhat controversially, on the evening of the third day with the home team in a reasonable position. Non-members wishing to watch from the pavilion 'house' were charged half a crown (12.5p); the band of the 69th Regiment of Infantry blared and trumpeted, and goodly crowds were in attendance. Betting was still exerting its influence, with 'very heavy sums' resting on the results: it was estimated that up to £40,000 was riding on the outcome of that second encounter.

The following year, 1848, saw the Manchester club on the move again. Building development, that constant bane of settled urban life, was the cause, as housing and apposite amenities spread over the Hulme area. The club was pushed out into Stretford, to the south-west, where the de Trafford family ruled the roost. Reputedly their antecedents stretched back to the time of King Canute or Cnut, a monarch, of course, celebrated in such place names as Knott Mill, at the southern end of Manchester's Deansgate and, of course, Knutsford. Certainly Randolph, Lord of Trafford, swore allegiance to William the Conqueror and the family basked in the respectable luxury of this large estate until modern times. The New Ground, Stretford New Road, was a piece of this domain. Decently cultivated, it was hard-by the Botanical Gardens and was later to be the site of the rather less calming pastime of greyhound racing, when the White City Stadium was built.

It was drained, 'a huge roller' was utilised and a 'commodious' pavilion erected. There were now 230 members; the fixtures with Liverpool and the All-England XI were pursued, while in 1849 there were a couple of games described as a Lancashire XI versus a Yorkshire XI. Manchester had issued the challenge to the Yorkshire faction: the unfailing co-identification of Manchester and Lancashire was taking root. Nonetheless, only about eleven games were played each season, so that, even allowing for a modicum of purely social members and supporters, one may clearly assume that plenty of 'sides' matches, probably seen as practice games, were played among the Manchester members.

The success of the 1851 Great Exhibition had whetted the appetite of many for that kind of expansive show, and in 1856 plans to hold an Arts Treasures Exhibition in Manchester were put in hand. It was the Prince Consort who persuaded the organisers to concentrate entirely on the arts, and this exhibition is said to have been the first in Britain to display for public gaze pictures from private collections. A committee was formed whose first task was to find a site, preferably one away from the smoky, filth-strewn nucleus of the town. The cricket ground was ideal. It was held only on lease by the Manchester club from the current de Trafford lordling, Sir Humphrey, and thus was easily transferable to a prestigious undertaking with regal backing. Close to the Botanical Gardens, the three-acre site, with an entrance on Stretford New Road, was tailor made for the 'Arts Treasures Building'. In marked contrast to some of the dilly-dallying over construction in the next century, the negotiations were speedily resolved and up went the artistic edifice. Prince Albert, that energetic doyen of such expositions, opened the Exhibition, probably the largest of its kind outside London at that time, and Queen Victoria and the Prince of Wales, later Edward VII, were among the million visitors over the five months the fair was open. The celebrated arts pundit, John Ruskin, was one of the lecturers recruited.

Such an aesthetic triumph was little consolation to the evicted cricketers, who were homeless from June 1856 and played little that summer. There was much-expected bitterness and the threat of official eviction was mooted. Some Manchester members stormed off in a huff and started the Western club in Eccles. The longer-term compensations were, however, immense, so much so that one is bound to ponder whether some of the Manchester club authorities were willing co-conspirators in their own removal. The monetary recompense of £1300 was modest, given the previous expenditure on the ground, but a major condition was that the de Trafford estate would provide a replacement field. The proposed land was just 400 yards from the Exhibition site and consisted of seven or eight acres of level, gravelly, sandy turf, where informal cricket had already been played. The compensation money was put to good use in the building of a fine pavilion, with groundsman's quarters, dressing rooms for 'members' and 'strangers', a central turret and a dining room of some 90 square yards dimension. There was also a wine cellar; 'no unimportant acquisition in a cricket pavilion', mused the *Manchester Guardian*, presciently foreshadowing the time when John Arlott would act as both cricket and wine correspondent for that great newspaper. To add to these bucolic flavours, the main entrance to the ground was through the premises of the Trafford Arms Hotel, although a path was also opened from the Exhibition site.

The first of the two wondrous Stretfordian cathedrals was now in place. Traditional rivals Liverpool obliged by providing a happy outcome to the opening fixture. In June 1857 they managed, in rainy weather, only 78 and 89 against Manchester's 152 and 46, leaving the home side winners by 31 runs. A sign of the eminence of the new ground were matches organised between George Parr's Exhibition team, just returned from its visit - the first-ever overseas cricket tour - to America, against Another England XI in 1859; All-England and United All-England in 1861 and North against South of England in 1862. These fixtures provided a stage for the leading professional cricketers of the day and attracted much attention, so much so that the fragile wire fencing - there was only wooden palisades on the pavilion side - was soon replaced by solid wood railings all the way around, so worried were the organisers by the receipts lost because of freeloading onlookers.

Red Shirts and Roses

The auspices were good but it was not all plain sailing. Manchester cricket club had nearby rivals in the shape of the Broughton club in Salford, formed in the mid-1820s. Broughton had had a smallish field in Lower Broughton Lane but had moved on to a more luxurious meadow provided by the Clowes estate in Higher Broughton. When there was that year's hiatus in the Manchester saga - and when recalcitrant members shifted to Eccles - there was just the merest chance that Manchester might have lost its local and regional pre-eminence. Broughton had already commendably hosted some Exhibition matches. It is an intriguing fact that, a decade or so later, W.G. Grace would play eight games in each of the seasons 1870-77, without, admittedly, much personal good fortune, at the Broughton club. He raked in the coinage as the leading light of the United South of England Exhibition XI, before he made his first-class debut in Manchester, for Gloucestershire, at Old Trafford in 1878. There was too the focus of Liverpool, a worthy club in its own right, for the cricketing allegiance of the region.

Nonetheless, the Manchester club thrived. There were straws in the wind. The usual achievements of the Exhibition XI, which normally thrashed XVIII of the natives, caused press comment and local thinking about the benefits of a wider selection to face such daunting opponents, while the occasional hiring of professionals continued. County cricket was beginning to emerge in a more recognisable form. For instance, the strong Surrey team was welcomed to the Western ground on Eccles Old Road during the summer of exile of 1856. The 'Manchester' side that vanquished a Surrey combine that had been unbeaten all summer was, in fact, a 'district' team, with Broughton and Western as well as bona fide Manchester players, plus three professionals, two of whom - the renowned John Wisden and Fred Lillywhite - did most to procure the victory. It was in such conditions that the notion of a county club began to be considered.

Before turning to an account of how the Lancashire county club was established in the wake of the creation of its famous ground, it might be opportune to take a glance at the social character of Manchester during the first forty years of the Manchester club's existence. This is a matter of some import, for it was then that Manchester became what the gifted social historian, Asa Briggs, was to call 'the shock-city of the 1840s'. It was the world's first primarily industrial city, with all the dire flaws of such a regimen, but replete with bustle and energy.

Population, of course, was the key. When the Manchester club was formed, the inhabitants of Manchester, Salford and its environs numbered less than 100,000; when Old Trafford cricket ground was opened, the figure was nearer 500,000. Rising birth-rates and labour migration, drawn by the siren call of industrial jobs, were the causes. Placing that in some perspective, the total population of Lancashire had been 673,000 in 1701, a mere fortieth of the national sum; in 1831, with Manchester and Liverpool contributing mightily, it had jumped to 1.4m, now a tenth of the whole. In the same period, the 1700s to the 1830s, the national total had more than doubled from something less than 6m to 13m: Lancashire's population had shot up astronomically nine-fold in the same period. For all its expanses of wild and agricultural land, Lancashire's population density, at 1,003 per square mile was, after London, the highest in the kingdom. 250,000 of the inhabitants of Manchester and Salford were packed into one square mile.

The Advent of Old Trafford Cricket Ground

What were all these people doing? Most of them were finding work in the new power-driven cotton industry. Lancashire, centred on Manchester, was the fount of the new industrialism that would gradually sweep the world. Not long before, spinners and weavers had operated domestically or in small groups, often in remote spots, close to fast running streams; the huge, many-storied, gaunt brick mills of the 19th century took their name from the relatively small water-driven 'mills' of that former time. In 1800 there were only 500 steam-powered looms in the whole of the country. In 1833 there were 100,000 in Lancashire alone. In 1789, eventful occasion of the start of the French Revolution, the first steam-powered loom to be commercially operated began to whirr and zoom in Manchester, announcing that the other Revolution, the Industrial one, had definitely arrived. In the 1780s there were only two cotton mills of any stature in Manchester; by the 1800s, not only were there 52 substantial mills in the town, there were 61 machine shops and iron foundries. By the 1840s there were 185 cotton mills, plus 28 silk mills and a plethora of dye works, bleaching shops, calico printing premises, as well as more iron foundries, millwrights' and machine makers' workshops.

There was a clue here as to future developments that would have a beneficial side-effect on the prowess of Manchester's sporting institutions. Manchester had fast become the financial and business centre for this formidable engineering and chemical revolution in the production of cotton goods. Manchester served the region as supplier and marketer. It had enjoyed an advantageous start. Its 18th century linen-drapers and other merchants had 'put out' raw material to the hundreds of small scale craftsmen and women across the county, providing credit, warehousing and the sinews of trade. The first Exchange, the hub of the Lancastrian cotton trade, was constructed on classic lines in 1729 and the first bank was opened in 1771. Soon came the more specialist manufactures. In 1824, not without a delicate irony, Charles Macintosh, he of the eponymous raincoat, often to be seen in prominent use at Old Trafford cricket ground, opened his waterproof fabrics outfit in Cambridge Street. Manchester was a full-blown commercial centre of enormous standing.

One of the factors responsible was transport, both of people and freight. There was a tiny paradox at the heart of this civic development. People of all classes needed, with twelve-hour working days and poor transport, to be close to their work-places. One of the reasons club-life prospered was because of the close alignment of home, work and, necessarily, leisure - the club could be visited on the way to and from the warehouse or office. The cramped housing did mean that, conversely, there were open spaces. St Peter's Fields, scene of the notorious massacre, was some 14,000 square yards, the acreage of more than a dozen football grounds, which pushed down near where the Midland Hotel now stands. The Free Trade Hall was consciously built on the site as, in part, a memorial, in 1838. Of course, building moved on apace and we observed how the Manchester club were pushed off their Hulme field.

Conversely, there was no shortage of land a mile or so away on the de Trafford estate - and now the other side of the equation told. One of the difficulties for members, let alone spectators, was getting to the ground. It was in the middle of farming land and there were few houses or shops nearby. A dilatory horse-drawn omnibus meandered down the tree-fringed thoroughfare of the Chester Road as far as Trafford Bar, leaving one with quite a stroll to the cricket ground. Much fewer people than are sometimes imagined had a horse for riding or a private carriage, so Shank's Pony remained the chief means of locomotion.

It was to be the transport component of the Industrial Revolution that would unlock the conundrum. There had been some improvements. The Turnpike Trusts, with their wooden toll-gates (wagon and four horses were charged about 1s6d, that is 7.5p) not unlike the motorway tolls of a later epoch, had helped mend the roads; the road through Stretford was one of ten or so main routes out of Manchester that had been 'turnpiked'. In 1754 a Manchester flying coach was advertised in these exciting terms: 'however incredible it may appear, this coach will actually (barring accidents) arrive in London in four days and a half', at a cost, incidentally, of £2.25p, plus food and lodgings en route. This journey time had been, by the early 19th century, rather reduced.

Then there were the canals, although of course, they were more involved with freight than passengers, if not exclusively so. Although there had been canalised rivers, like the Mersey and Irwell Navigation, dating from mid-18th century, the Bridgewater Canal was the first British waterway built independently of rivers. It was opened in 1761 and enabled the young Duke of Bridgewater, retired to his Worsley estates after disappointing love affairs and trips abroad, to shift his coal from his mines to Manchester and sell it for less than half the usual price, at 4d per hundredweight. James Brindley, his self-taught engineer, was then to be responsible for an entire network of British canals. At first, the canal reached only Longford Bridge, Stretford, but soon moved on to Deansgate, where extensive wharves and warehouses were built, and then pushed westwards to Runcorn, providing a valuable water link with Liverpool.

The point of stressing this development was that the Bridgewater Canal obviously passed close to Old Trafford cricket ground. This had two linked bonuses. First, there was some passenger traffic - two hours from Castle Quay to Altrincham - and, second, more significantly, the canal had the effect of opening up these southern and western districts to population growth, as trade and residences followed the canal route. Quite a lot of Lancashire cricket support would emanate from these newly growing townships of Cheshire and South Lancashire.

However, it was the railways that plainly had the most profound influence, and their construction was observed by the Victorians with an awe little short of religious. It is not surprising. The application of steam power to locomotion was an invention as astounding to people then as putting a man on the moon in the modern era - and, because it affected everybody's daily life in some form, it was even more remarkable than that rather hollow lunar landing. When little green men, clutching ray guns in their seven-fingered hands, failed to leap out from behind the rocks to repel astronautical boarders, it all fell a little flat. Not so with the railways. They were at once the culmination and the glory of the Industrial Revolution, and they transformed lives.

The Liverpool to Manchester railway, opened in 1830, was the first line to use mechanical power on a public facility intended mainly for passengers, and its terminus, Liverpool Road, Manchester, was the world's first passenger railway station. By 1850 there were 6,000 miles, and by 1860 16,000 miles of railway criss-crossing the nation. By the 1840s there were 1,200 trains running daily, against 500 coaches, taking half the time and at a third of the price; 25m rail passenger journeys were undertaken in 1842. Manchester already had five main lines carrying goods and passengers to all points of the compass.

Suddenly London was only a few hours away from Manchester. For the first time people had to contemplate a national clock, legalised by the creation of the Greenwich Mean Time statute of 1880. Before the railways no one had ever contrived to arrive from one place to another so quickly that having the same time mattered, and thus times had varied from one town to the next, rather after the manner of 'lighting up' times.

The most direct effect on Old Trafford was the construction of the South Manchester Junction and Altrincham railway. From 21st July 1849 an hourly service operated between Oxford Road Station and Altrincham. The express took 20 minutes and the stopper 30 minutes, with the fare for the full journey on the latter costing 4d for first-class, 3.5d second-class and 2.5d third-class, suddenly presenting people with about the cheapest public transit ever known in Britain. The line soon boomed and carried substantial numbers of passengers. Again, the effects were twofold for the cricket grounds, old and new. Building and commercial development followed the railway, while it was also able to deposit and pick up cricketing customers. It is true that Old Trafford station still left one with a dreary walk across the mainly agrarian terrain, but it was an enhancement on the previous fate of likely spectators, namely, a hike all the way from Manchester. And, to be helpful, the railway staff would ring a bell at Old Trafford station to warn folk that the train would shortly be leaving. Warwick Road Station, yards from the ground, was added in 1931 and that made Old Trafford cricket ground one of the most accessible sporting arenas by train in the country.

There was some amelioration of the harsh conditions. The Anti-Corn Law League, its headquarters the Free Trade Hall, led the struggle to abolish the tariffs that halted the importation of grain, kept the price of bread artificially high and protected the farming and landowning interest. Richard Cobden and John Bright, the chief proponents of the free trade and laissez-faire theories that came to be termed 'Manchesterism', ensured that the cotton interest was properly represented. It did not suit hard-working Manchester mill-owners and merchants that they had to pay higher wages to textile workers to pay over the odds for bread, in order to cosset farmers and idle, rich landowners. The Prime Minister, Sir Robert Peel, with his strong Bury connections, recognised the logic, inaugurated the abolition of the corn laws from 1846 to 1849, wrecked his own career and witnessed a destructive schism of the Conservative Party he had done so much to build.

With food cheaper, with technology improving all the time and with the industrial scene very much in Lancashire's favour, it was high time for working hours to be addressed. The 1833 Factory Act, partly aimed at child labour in the Lancashire mills, had been something of a damp squib and easily evaded. The upshot of much pressure and industrial strife was to be the 1847 Factory Act. A complicated law, it tried, by reducing the hours of women and children, to lessen the hours worked by skilled men, reliant on the others for the processes they sustained. At bottom, it produced a situation where a ten-hour, instead of a twelve- hour day, became the norm in the mills and workshops of Manchester and its hinterland, and where, as a means of reducing the overall weekly hours to a more reasonable proportion, work stopped early on a Saturday. This was the embryo of the Saturday half-day, of much importance to workers who wished either to play or watch sport. The introduction of a handful of 'bank holidays' - the name was dreamed up by Lord Salisbury but the idea was Sir John Lubbock's - in 1871 was another boost to such needs. The very first was 19th May 1871; Mondays were the obvious choice, for Saint Monday, as in the mining industry, was the day when workers most commonly feigned illness and pinched an extra day. In 1879 the term 'weekend' was first used.

About this time textile wages ran out about 12s (60p) for an unskilled and £1.15 (£1.75p) for a skilled worker. It was a reasonably stable income and, as food prices dropped, a trifle might have been more readily available for leisure, such as the odd day at a cricket match. These advances were relative. As we shall have immediate cause to observe, social conditions were, for the working population, unbelievably filthy and noisome, cramped as they were into hurriedly thrown up back-to-back hovels, that had been built higgledy-piggledy to accommodate the incoming work-force.

The factory discipline was also very severe, the rule of the clock like a rod of iron. The control of agricultural labour was stricter than romanticists would have one believe, for animals had to be tended and crops nurtured, even if there were seasonal rhythms. It had been the self-employed outworkers, domestically based - weavers like George Eliot's Silas Marner - who had enjoyed some liberty. It was from among their ranks that the first generation of professional cricketers had chiefly arisen, including lace workers in the Nottinghamshire area. They had more easily combined a day's cricket with their labours at home. Nonetheless, this slight freeing of industrial workers, with a shilling or so to spend, was the first step towards the hordes that would later crowd into the sporting stadia such as the two Old Traffords, first for county cricket and then for league football.

3.

The Coming of County Cricket

RIDING ON the 50 bus into Manchester on the easterly Wilmslow Road route, one wondered idly, whilst passing Platt Fields on the left, why there was a large statue of the tall, gaunt Abraham Lincoln perched there. Later studies revealed the connection. During the American Civil War the ports of the Confederacy states were blockaded, so that raw cotton, vital to the mainspring of Manchester's wealth, was unavailable. This threw the textile industry into the throes of slump. Now, although the crux of that internecine struggle was whether a member state could thus disrupt the federacy, its emotional and overt feature was the argument over slavery. Lincoln's victory ensured that slavery was abolished - and also that the securely centralised United States became the world's first superpower. The rest, as they say, is global history.

The cotton workers took the slavery issue very seriously. It would be their pennies that contributed towards old Abe finding a plinth in Platt Fields. Despite their suffering and that of their families, they held true to the federal northern cause. It was a show of adherence to principle in the face of grim despair that makes some of the attitudes of later years, such as worries over job losses with the onset of immigration, a little wanting in idealism. The stolid and thoughtful behaviour of the textile workers at this time impressed many, not least William Gladstone, who provided some unemployed spinners and weavers with work at his Hawarden residence.

Surat cotton from India proved to be an unsatisfactory substitute and, although the last pre-war American crop had been the heaviest on record, the stock did not last long. By the winter of 1861/62 and thereafter there was much distress. At this stage 530,000 workers were directly involved in the varied cotton businesses and trades, while there were many others who played peripheral or indirect roles. Soon 250,000 Lancastrians were reliant on the poor rates and as many again on private charities, organised by such noblemen as the Earl of Sefton. The Poor Law services, predicated on the theory that there was work aplenty and that lazy individuals should be pressed by the short official commons of the workhouse into taking up these opportunities to earn an honest crust, were hopelessly overwhelmed by one of the first examples of international markets being distorted by political events. They had no answer to the sober problem of an entire mono-economic region being flung into grief with, it has been estimated, £10m lost in profits and wages. Efforts were made to make the machinery of relief more flexible; £1.5m of state funds was loaned for public works, and private subscriptions realised another £2m. £1m then would roughly correspond to £100m today.

Poverty has evil side effects. Working in enervatingly heated and dusty conditions and living in overcrowded, damp homes, many workers and their families were in no fit state to withstand famine. During the 1850s 12 per cent of the working population lived in cellars; six or seven sharing a bed was not uncommon; the accumulation of human ordure was such that, for instance, in Ardwick and Old Hulme Road, the dung-hills were re-christened 'dung-mountains', given that they were upwards of 25,000 tons in volume. Half of Manchester's 600 streets were clogged with refuse and sewage, and even the rain was 'the colour of ink'. The dramatic construction of the Longendale water supply scheme, which would not only bring ready provision of fresh water but also drive the new egg-shaped terracotta piped sanitary programme, was only just bearing fruit by the 1860s.

Sickness was rife, not more so than during the Cotton Famine. Typhus enjoyed a changing series of sobriquets. Once it had been 'gaol fever'; in the 1840s, during the massive emigration from Ireland during its very much more dreadful famine, it became 'Irish fever'; now it was 'famine fever'. Manchester and Salford, along with the larger mill towns, were badly hit. During those years some 5,000 died annually in Manchester and its districts of typhus, scarlet fever and smallpox. Cholera still lurked and there would be a major outbreak in 1866. Such was the incidence of bronchitis, diphtheria and tuberculosis in the textile areas that special inquiries were instigated in the early 1860s. Infant mortality was twice the national average.

Yet 34 gentlemen gathered together on Tuesday 12th January 1864 in Manchester's Queen's Hotel, in the midst of this unprecedented disaster and almost within sight of crowded soup kitchens, and established Lancashire County Cricket Club.

Eleven of them were from the Manchester club and ten from the local Broughton, Western and Longsight clubs, so that, predictably, the Manchester area was well-represented. There were four gentlemen from the Liverpool club and, in all, thirteen clubs sent representatives, with the north of the county fielding hardly anyone. Resolutions to form a county club and request founding donations from Lancashire clubs were passed. It was, of course, a wholly bourgeois enterprise; there was no thought of providing amusement, either by way of playing or watching, for the thousands suffering in the surrounding famine areas. It was to be a subscription club like, for example, the Manchester Athenaeum, where Charles Dickens presided over a magnificent soirée in 1843.

Lancashire's first game was against Birkenhead Park. It was played at Warrington and they found themselves on the poor side of a draw. Eight matches were played in 1864 and 43 gentlemen were used, in part, perhaps, to ensure most interested parties had a look-in, and also because, especially for away fixtures, these busy merchants and mill-owners found it difficult to find sufficient leisure time. Lancashire's first ever win was at Liverpool, where the Gentlemen of Shropshire were defeated by an innings. In the return match against the strong Birkenhead Park combine, they included professionals - Hickton, Holgate and Nicholls - for the first time, but still only managed to draw.

In July of 1865 came the first genuine county match, when an under-strength Middlesex team were welcomed to Old Trafford and beaten by 62 runs. Three professionals, Roger Iddison, Fred Reynolds and Bill Perry, eked out the Lancastrian forces, the first two bowling out Middlesex in their second innings. The first innings scores were tied and V.E. Walker took all ten Lancashire second innings wickets with his accurate underarm bowling. Some 300 or 400 spectators made their way on foot or on omnibus to the ground, yielding a gate of only £25. The amateur eight on this momentous occasion were R. Blackstock, E.J. Bousfield, F.J. Crooke, J.F. Leese, J. Makinson, E. Whittaker, Sam Swire (who was Lancashire's Secretary from 1873 until his death in 1905) and Alexander Rowley, who probably skippered this inaugural 'county' side and who was one of seven cricketing Rowley brothers, one of whom, Edmund, was normally to be Lancashire's captain throughout the county's first fifteen seasons.

Lancashire lost the return match at Islington heavily; the pattern of weak visiting sides was sustained. They played a couple of other matches that summer and this established another pattern. Each season a tiny number of county matches and minor fixtures was arranged. In 1866 Surrey were added to the fixture list and it was at the Oval that Roger Iddison made Lancashire's first ever century; his 106 contributed hugely to Lancashire saving the match after being over 200 behind on the first innings. In 1867 the first 'Roses' match was played at Whalley and with a distinctly distressing result; emotion must not be the hurdle to the dispatch of information - Yorkshire won by an innings and 56 runs.

The Liverpool club had played a main part thus far, to the point of being the central organisers, but the loss of money, such as in the Surrey fixture at Wavertree in 1866, led to a rethink. Manchester CC agreed to adopt full financial responsibility, some £120 per annum, for the basic expenses of the county club, provided home matches were played at Old Trafford and the Manchester committee picked the teams. The club subscription was raised to two guineas and the county subscription reduced from a guinea to ten and then five shillings (25p) but finance was tight and, as A.N. Hornby, who first played for Lancashire in that sorry 1867 affair at Whalley, was later to remark, 'an annual deficit was customary' for the entire club-cum-county venture. The hat was passed round at the annual general meeting or otherwise individuals paid for specific items, as when A.B. Rowley personally met the cost of improvements to the pavilion.

It was tough going for the Manchester cricketing mafia, for spectators were not numerous and the 'great matches' - there was a popular clash at Old Trafford in aid of the Cricketers' Fund for down-and-out professionals in 1867 - were not synonymous with county matches, as was later the case. There were the usual curios consequent on a new team being launched. The professional, James Ricketts, made one of the most theatrical debuts ever when, in 1866 against Surrey at the Oval, he became the first Lancastrian to carry his bat at county level in making 195, not out. He also set something of a more familiar Red Rose precedent: he did not live up to his early promise. Frank Wynward Wright, a man of the cloth who had attended that inaugural meeting at the Queen's Hotel, became in 1869 at Old Trafford against Sussex the first amateur centurion, with 120, not out. The professional, William Hickton, was the first Lancashire bowler to take ten wickets in an innings: in 1870 he dismissed Hampshire for 46 runs in their second innings, although cricketing theologians have disputed the first-class status of that game.

The Manchester club was not showered with thanks for taking on the burden. There was envy and suspicion. There were complaints that they only picked Manchester members and, the reverse, suggestions that some talented amateurs refused invitations out of 'petty jealousies' - that Yorkshire match at Whalley was allegedly one such occasion. The notion of playing all home fixtures at Old Trafford also came in for criticism, but again there was a counter-complaint that local clubs chose to arrange fixtures when Lancashire were at Old Trafford, including one or two of Broughton's continuing list of 'Exhibition' matches. With middle-class amateurs so unwilling to travel to away games, results remained very uneven. In 1871 Derbyshire, in their first-ever county match, dismissed Lancashire for 25, the lowest total in the county's lengthy annals.

He who pays the piper…Manchester were finding the money to pay the bills, at a time when the club would be lucky to find 200 turning up for a day's cricket. Liverpool had had its chance and had failed; in so far as there was a contest for the mind and soul of Lancashire cricket, Manchester had triumphed beyond a peradventure. In 1872 Lancashire played half a dozen county matches and Manchester, with enormous success, played 32 games. The team-sheets were often indistinguishable. Like exploitative humans and politicised pigs in George Orwell's *Animal Farm*, one could no longer tell the difference.

Why was the shire ticket so meaningful and necessary? At this point in the century Manchester had sprung to challenge even the supremacy of London by dint of its creation of national wealth and its vigorous political attitudes. By the time Lancashire CCC came into existence, Manchester's gross population was 350,000. With a dozen mainline banks, it had the best financial facilities outside London and the Royal Exchange moved into its third building just following the birth of Lancashire cricket, its main hall the largest room devoted to commerce in Europe, very needful for its 3,000 members.

Everything came in a rush. Manchester was incorporated as a borough in 1838, thereby obtaining the semblance of some modernised local government. The townships of Ardwick, Chorlton-on-Medlock, Hulme, Cheetham and Beswick were embraced by the new and ambitious borough. Seventeen years later, in 1853, it was a city. Its first bishop, James Prince Lee, oversaw the erection of 110 new churches in his diocese in the years following his appointment in 1847. The retail co-operative movement having started in T'Owd Lane, Rochdale, in 1845, the first wholesale co-operative society was established in Manchester in 1862, and thereafter the town housed the headquarters of that splendid enterprise, the Co-Op. In 1864, as Lancashire first took the field, the new assize courts were opened, while, as we have noted, fresh water and sanitary provision was being supplied. A modern police force, fire brigade and prison were other civic attributes.

Manchester was, in 1850, the first provincial town to take advantage of the Free Libraries Act; it was equally early in laying out three municipal parks; Owen's College was the first constituent college of the new northern university; the scholarship of its leading scientists, men such as John Dalton, J.P. Joule and Osborne Reynolds gave practical boosts to industrial development; the *Manchester Guardian*, launched in 1821, had by now become the national bugle of the self-confident cottonopolis. Charles Hallé's orchestra and choir had entertained at the Arts Exhibition of 1857, when the Manchester club had been driven from one field to another. They were prevailed upon to remain and the famed Hallé concerts began in 1858.

The Coming of County Cricket

The orchestra would soon play in the Free Trade Hall, already in its third, its Venetian, refurbishment. The Free Trade Hall was to Manchesterism as the Vatican is to Roman Catholicism. The tenets of untrammelled commerce, alongside a civil dignity, mixed with pragmatism that yearned for a clean, orderly ambit in which trade could be really free, as free, as one of its exponents Benjamin Heywood cried in nonconformist mood, 'as the winds of heaven'. Soon after Lancashire was formed, up went Alfred Waterhouse's mock-Gothic town hall, baroque symbol of Manchester's surging potency.

The parliamentary reform movement, of which the Peterloo Massacre had been so tragic a part, had been rewarded by the mild Reform Act of 1832. It had had the overall effect of enfranchising the middle classes and suddenly giving large towns like Manchester their own first chosen representatives - and the Manchester club arranged a cricket match to celebrate its passage. Prior to this time, Lancashire had fourteen MPs, the same as in Tudor times; now it had 26, not many more, but at least they were more sanely distributed. Newton-le-Willows, where the lords of the manor, the Leigh family, had nominated two MPs (this was sometimes called, by the 'pig-tailed Tories', 'virtual representation' for Manchester), lost both. The other developing cotton towns were also constitutionally recognised. The sensible and sober attitude of the textile workers during the Cotton Famine was a factor in the case for extending the vote to the urban working class, which found successful resolution in the 1867 Reform Act.

Men like Richard Cobden and John Bright brought an abrasively radical edge to British politics: the building of the Reform Club in Pall Mall, London, deliberately bigger than the Tory and Whig political clubs, was their sanctum in the capital. Manchester was the chief provincial political centre in mid-19th century. Of course industrialism, in the words of Friedrich Engels, an observer of the Mancunian scene, 'forced to the surface the problem of class'. Few could avoid, as the novels of Mrs Gaskell (wife of the minister of Manchester's Unitarian church in Cross Street) depicted, the extreme juxtaposition of masters and men. The 'shockability' of Manchester lay in this strange and intensely close alignment of abject poverty and gleaming wealth. Queen Victoria, having visited the town in 1851 (the year, incidentally, the adjective 'Victorian' was coined) came near to realistic assessment in her diary entry, where she wrote of 'the good order and behaviour of the people' who were 'painfully unhealthy looking'.

Alexis de Tocqueville, the perceptive French commentator, had spotted the socio-economic dichotomy early on: in 1835 he wrote of the 'homes of vice and poverty, which surround the huge palaces of industry and clasp them in their hideous folds'. Charles Dickens - whose novel of factory life and its allied political creed, *Hard Times*, published in 1854, used Preston as a model for the fictional Coketown - was mesmerised by Manchester. Just as he was fascinated by the villainy of a Fagin or a Quilp, the satanic dwarf of *The Old Curiosity Shop*, so did he find the light and shade of Manchester life strangely exhilarating. It was, he wrote, 'every whit as wonderful, as fearful, as unimaginable, as the oldest Salem or prophetic city'.

Something of that startling dualism may be perceived in the picture of 34 well-to-do gentlemen walking or riding to the Queen's Hotel in the January of 1864, the chill wintry climate intensifying the suffering of the thousands of famine victims, in order almost nonchalantly to start a county cricket club. Like the Renaissance city-states of Florence and Venice, the brash vigour of Manchester made it the first prominent English provincial city of the modern dispensation. Given this pushy assurance one might wonder why, the Liverpool rivalry vanquished and the other local clubs none too friendly, Manchester did not revert to its former and more realistic title. After all, the Lancashire team was chiefly the Manchester side sailing under a different flag. The club might have seized the chance to broadcast itself nationally as 'Manchester', just as, in later years, two of the local football teams were only too pleased to adopt the city's grand name.

There were probably two general reasons why this did not happen. Firstly, the shires had an impressive lineage as administrative units. As late as the time of Jane Austen, there was a proclivity to elide 'county' and 'country' and the shrewd - and Manchester-based - historian of 18th century England, Lewis Namier, referred to 'county commonwealths'. Even in the 19th century the counties remained 'the matrix of local society in which political opinion was formed'. The earliest cricket games with the 'county' tag attached were between sides raised by county bigwigs; there was some cachet in using the shire's name and, as the landowner in question owned large tracts of the given county, it perhaps had some proprietorial justification. The administrative device of the county club is chiefly a 19th century manifestation, as Lancashire's own story demonstrates. The motive was usually the same as well, namely, to widen the net and raise the standards. There had been press and allied comment about the weakness of individual clubs, especially when faced with the overwhelming might of the Exhibition XIs, who rather erased their own rationale by stimulating the organisational concept of a wider domain. This was, by tradition, identified with the shire, one of the most persistent of English institutional forms.

The formation of the county clubs in England and Wales is remarkably similar in pattern, particularly when one compares this with the variable ways in which Football League clubs came into being. Gentlemen foregathered to start a cricket club, or, as in the cases of Nottinghamshire and Yorkshire, to defray match expenses through a subscription list. Eventually, in all cases, the emphasis was on members paying a subscription and thereby having voting rights to elect a committee to run affairs. It was the parochial club writ large; it had its parallels in a dozen other sorts of Victorian gentlemen's clubs, political, commercial, engineering, artistic, literary, professional and so forth.

Walter Boden convening a meeting in Derbyshire in 1870; a meeting in, very properly, the Shire Hall, Chelmsford, Essex in 1876; a meeting in the Angel Hotel, Cardiff in 1888; a meeting at the George Hotel, Winchester, in 1879, when district representation for the Hampshire club was agreed; a meeting in 1870 at the Bull Inn, Rochester, Kent, with the autocratic Lord Harris in the chair; an inaugural meeting, following the formation of a provisional committee for Middlesex, at the London Tavern in 1864; a meeting at Sidmouth in 1875, chaired by the Rev. A.C. Ainslie, resolving to form a Somerset club; the Horns Tavern in 1845 hosting meetings that determined to set up the Surrey club; Colonel Jervis calling a meeting in Leamington

The Coming of County Cricket

in 1882 from which Warwickshire sprang to fitful life...even unto the beneficent choice of a comfortable hotel, as with Lancashire, for that opening assembly, the salient originating points are very akin.

The same might also be said about the prominence of a particular club, like Manchester, such as Montpelier for Surrey, or the usage of, for instance, 'the Gentlemen of Warwickshire', for early games around about the coming of the official county club. It is, with one or two exceptions, an astonishingly uniform tale. It is, then, not altogether surprising that Manchester and the Gentlemen of Lancashire chose the same path. Indeed, in 1880 the two clubs, Manchester and Lancashire, acknowledged their common law marriage with the official nuptials of amalgamation, and were henceforward known as 'The Lancashire County and Manchester Cricket Club'.

It was 1884 before, in response to the challenge of the rise of conurbations like Manchester, the rather contradictory formula of the 'county borough' was introduced, at the same time as there was a radical overhaul of shire administration. Had that enactment been passed twenty years earlier, we might have had a Manchester CBCC instead of a Lancashire CCC. The London County Cricket Club was formed in 1899 in the wake of London County Council's establishment. It was a brave experiment, with W.G. Grace very actively in charge and the Crystal Palace as its prestigious base. It played many first-class matches and, by and large, held its own, but it did not command massive support. It lingered on until 1908, when the cricket ground was turned over, to W.G. Grace's outrage, to the more profitable pursuit of tennis. Its real problem was that Middlesex and Surrey were already too well-established as the London 'County' clubs.

Another ground for utilising the persistent heritage of the shire may have been linked to the discomfort and guilt many felt about the onset of a vital industrialism. Throughout the 19th century a resolute determination to enjoy the proceeds of manufacturing labour was matched by a somewhat hypocritical shunning of urban and commercial life. This was marked by a chaste affection for a heavily fanciful rural past. Eric Hobsbawm has written of 'the characteristically mythical Britain of the travel poster...the heavy incrustation of British life with pseudo-medieval and other rituals, like the cult of royalty, dates back (only) to the late Victorian period, as does the pretence that the Englishman is a thatched-cottager or a country squire at heart'.

This cult has been termed 'the medieval dream'. The colourful pageantry of the Young England movement and, later, the Primrose League, with both of which Disraeli was cleverly associated, are political testaments to this notion. The Primrose League, which peaked at a million members in 1910, had the arcane nomenclature of 'habitations' - such as the 'King Athelstan habitation' at Malmesbury - for branches, while subscriptions were 'tributes'. The radicals were not to be outdone, conceiving of an Arcadian past despoiled by a rampantly commercialised present. 'The Norman Yoke' theory had the Norman Conquest destroying the Saxon freedoms won by Alfred the Great, and their heroes were Hereward the Wake and Robin Hood. In 1893/94 Robert Blatchford's socialist tale - with its significant title - *Merrie England* sold 750,000 copies in its penny edition in its first year. His left-wing Manchester journal, *Clarion*, launched in 1891, sold

40,000 copies a week, while his Clarion cycling clubs soon had 7,000 members, their wheels carrying them out to the very countryside that was purportedly their rightful heritage.

It was, unsurprisingly, the age of folklore - the word itself a Victorian coinage - with, by Edwardian times, Cecil Sharp the salient collector of rustic tales and songs. They were suitably bowdlerised. Maid Marion, the sexily sensuous witch of pre-industrial legend, was transformed into the trusty tomboy of Victorian lore. When we primly sang, at Springfield Council School in the 1930s, 'As I was going to Strawberry Fair', the teacher never explained, or rather herself was not aware, that the succulent fruit was an analogy for the female pudenda and that fair was deployed as an adjective not a noun. Heaven knows what was meant by the ballad's refrain, 'Rifle-trifle-fol-de-diddle-dido'.

In literature Sir Walter Scott weighed in with the nascent historical novels, like *Ivanhoe*, with its classic tournament at Ashby-de-la-Zouch and its public school sportsmanship, and these were followed by stories such as Charles Kingsley's *Hereward the Wake* and Charles Reade's *The Cloister and the Hearth*. Charles Dickens conducted his love-hate relationship with teeming London, often counterpointing the idealised serenity of rurality, even with occasional cricketing snippets, to the unease and anomie of urbanism.

In architecture and the arts there was a restoration of what has been called 'vibrant medievalism'. Augustus Pugin was a prime influence in this respect. St Pancras Station and the Houses of Parliament are examples of the resultant mock-Gothic style - and so is Manchester Town Hall. Even Britain's first venture into the full-scale light music industry (and the word is used advisedly), with the Savoyard operas of Gilbert and Sullivan, took note of the mood. Although accurately described as 'urban folk-ballad operas', they frequently chose the bucolic woodland ethos of *Iolanthe* or the mock-Tudorbethan splendours of *The Yeomen of the Guard* to attract the customers and sell the sheet-music.

This rural yearning, this clinging to rustic vestiges, may go some way to explaining the English obsession with gardening, once said by a well-known sociologist and rose gardener to represent the only fascist element in the British working class make-up. (Some of us admire the man who claims to carry a Gardeners Anonymous card at all times: if the urge to garden overtakes him, he rings their number and they try to talk him out of it - 'My name's Eric; I'm a gardener.')

Academically, the Victorian historians strove to seek out medieval foundations and derivations. The great constitutional historians, like William Stubbs and E.W. Maitland tracked down legal and institutional origins in Anglo-Saxon and Anglo-Norman sources. It is not surprising that early cricket chroniclers followed suit, finding outlandish testimony to show that cricket had a medieval fountainhead, with shepherd boys romping - the ancestors of Cyril Washbrook and Cec Parkin - on the Downs. In *Tom Brown's Schooldays*, published in 1857 (the year Old Trafford was opened), Thomas Hughes, most muscular of the 'Muscular Christians', has Arthur, Tom's intellectual other, define cricket incorrectly and anachronistically as 'the birthright of British boys, old and young, as habeas corpus and trial by jury are of British men'.

The Coming of County Cricket

It was all something of a preposterous conceit but the inalienable concretion of the county championship proved to be one of its most enduring images. Paradoxically, this pastoral dream was largely to be played out in great cities like Manchester, for rural heartlands could not support such an expensive reverie. The pretence of a sylvan idyll was largely and increasingly to be enjoyed amid the smoke and grime of the industrial and commercial centres.

There was a second reason. Manchester, or at least its politics, had mellowed. The working classes had grown more respectable and the middle classes more conservative. It was said that the Manchester gentry had 'cooled down to a genteel tone'. The somewhat bumptious style of John Bright (the smug and self-opinionated mill-owner, Mr Bounderby in *Hard Times* is said to be his conscious likeness) was distinctly set back by his defeat as one of Manchester's MPs at the 1857 hustings. He blamed his loss on ingratitude and snobbishness. In 1872 he was probably even more scandalised by the appearance of the Conservative leader, Benjamin Disraeli, arch-defender of the corn laws, on the platform of the Free Trade Hall. An oration by Saddam Hussein to the American Congress might be the nearest to a modern parallel.

Richard Cobden, calmer and more astute, was disappointed but analytical. His humane hope had been that Manchester would be a latter-day Athens, its trading success creating a stage for cultivated progress. In his considered opinion, the Mancunian tycoons had opted to mimic the feeble-minded landowning elite. He dismissed Manchester businessmen, of whom he had once been the champion, with the scornful epitaph of 'glorying in being the toadies of a clodpole aristocracy'.

The parvenu merchants of Lancashire's textile districts were seeking a place in the old sun of English patrician life. The sort of uneasy visit that Manchester had paid to Lord's, when they were humiliated by MCC in 1842, was a straw in this sociological wind. Maybe it is the same reason. Maybe this self-revulsion at being Johnnies-come-lately was merely another aspect, along with those neo-Tudor house fronts and those unnatural gardens, of that craving for the rustic blessings of yesteryear.

As the volcanic intensity of Manchester's upheaval simmered and cooled, so too did the tempo of its leading citizens. A county cricket club was an apposite illustration of this rejection of fiery revisionism and embracing of conventional values. In that a county cricket club was the emblem of a pastoral, allegedly ancient and decidedly anti-intellectual tradition, they seized upon it as a mark of their upward mobility. It was one of the fashions that they could choose to clothe their bourgeois bodies in upper-class mantles.

Manchester Men had become the Gentlemen of Lancashire.

4.

Birth of a Football Club

THE PATIENT wait for football to catch up with cricket in these pages is reflective of the time lag between the national consolidation of the two sports. Well over a hundred years separated the publication of the first formal rules of either game, both of them only genuinely acknowledged at first in the south-east. 38 years divided the birth of Lancashire CCC and Manchester United. 52 years separated the openings of the two Old Traffords.

Like cricket, football had a pre-history of scrappy, fragmentary, parochial pieces of action. An image is conjured up of milling hordes of people in Whitby on Shrove Tuesday or in Devon on Good Friday, a pig's swollen bladder obscurely associated with this formless mob action. As with cricket, the localised nature of the pastime militated against the adoption of agreed national rules; indeed, one is bound to presume that a restrictive code would not have been welcome. As with cricket, the breakthrough had much to do with the sudden enthusiasm in the Victorian public school for physical exercise.

Thomas Arnold is famously remembered for his part in transforming the public schools from 'essentially self-governing republics, run by a prefectorial elite, in which the teachers rarely intervened' to agencies based on, in Thomas Arnold's own text, 'Godliness and good learning'. It was his wish to turn sinful boys into 'Christian gentlemen'. By evolving as expensive boarding establishments, many of the large number of public schools formed in his wake robbed either local and/or poor boys of the chance for which some of these benefactions had been intended, but that is another and sadder story. Thomas Arnold himself, although not adverse to wholesome exercise, was not too enthusiastic about what came to be called Athleticism, but his disciples were. The Muscular Christians and Christian Socialists, such as Thomas Hughes and Charles Kingsley, author of *The Water Babies*, constructed the ethic of 'manliness', the essence of which was the stiff upper lip and the straight left elbow. George Cotton, Tom Brown's 'the young master' (who would have married Thomas Arnold's daughter, Jane, had his mum not been a heavy drinker) as head of Marlborough; Charles Vaughan at Harrow; Edward Thring at Uppingham; H.H. Almond at Loretto - these were the type of head teachers who sanctified the adoration of games. H.H. Almond is held responsible for inaugurating the depressing regime of open windows, cold baths and long runs as part of these educative delights.

It was extremely shrewd. 18th century and Regency boyhood was a violent, brutish affair, as Henry Fielding's picaresque novel, *Tom Jones*, testifies. What the rash of new and reformed public schools did was to channel this disruptive energy into regulated play. Moreover, the field sports of the previous generation, which had often led to barbarous disorder among the boys, were replaced by school-based games under pedagogic control. Vigour and courage were still the emblems of youthful probity, but they were now carefully monitored. It was - hence Thomas Arnold's anxieties - well-nigh anti-intellectual. One head determined, in his own words, to avoid producing 'a nation of effeminate, enfeebled bookworms'.

These schools, of course, were the forcing-houses for the teachers, soldiers, vicars and colonial officers who would, in time, spread the creed of Athleticism quite sincerely as an adjunct of Christianity, a tendency that would have immense ramifications for sport both at home and abroad. Initially however, football was chiefly played internally. Cricket had already taken up something of a national stance. There is no more dramatic illustration of the strides school cricket had taken than these events of 1796 and 1861. In the former year the Eton authorities banned a match the pupils had arranged with Westminster school on Hounslow Heath - and the Westminster pupils were notorious for debauched roughness as they made their way to and from their playing fields. The returning Eton team were each and everyone vigorously flogged for their defiance and probable misbehaviour on their travels, which, as they had suffered a heavy defeat, was a distinct case of adding injury to insult. In the latter year, that of 1861, 700 carriages and 7,000 spectators processed to Lord's for the first day of the Eton and Harrow match, already a must on the fashionable calendar. Did not Soames Forsyte, in 'The Man of Property' volume of *The Forsyte Saga*, spot the hauntingly lovely but aloof Irene among 'six thousand top hats, four thousand parasols' at Lord's during the Eton and Harrow match?

Football, the winter alternative, when travel was more difficult, remained internalised. Although William Webb Ellis famously 'first took the ball in his arms and ran with it' at Rugby School in 1823, not many, so to speak, ran after him. It was 1841 before the schoolboys at Rugby played anything like recognisable rugby, not least because William's presumptuous gesture was frowned upon by his betters, and the first Rugby school rules are dated 1845. Few matches were played against other teams; indeed it would be the 1890s before Rugby played another school at its eponymous game. It remained a primarily intramural activity and such was true of other schools. Sometimes the architecture of the school (this also applied for diversions like the Eton Wall Game or Rugby Fives) led to distinctions, with the more confined city schools, such as Westminster, favouring the less expansive stratagem of dribbling to the more nondescript booting at schools, like Rugby, with larger grounds.

The drive towards uniformity came as, with the wider acceptance that sport should be maintained in adulthood so that the healthy mind and body might stay in concert, these energetic youths went up to Oxbridge or took up employment. They were keen to continue playing both football and cricket but the difficulty with football was the same obstacle that had faced cricket decades before: there was no standard format.

Hostelries play a wholesome role in sport's saga. In December 1863 there was a meeting of interested parties at the Freemason's Tavern in London's Great Queen Street, consequent on what, in effect, had been the formation of the Football Association in the previous October, its express purpose the resolution of this poser.

These first laws of football were issued as 'The Rules of the London Football Association'. In fact, they were based on the Cambridge University rules, outlined about 1848 under the auspices of a group of practitioners led by George Sault and

H.C. Malden. They were little more than guidelines, with teams restricted to 20 players, with the pitch limited to the ample size of 200 by 100 yards, with the goals eight yards wide by eight feet high, and with a primitive veto on offside.

It is of some interest that, when the ball went out of play, there was a hectic rush to see who might 'touch' it down and claim the (often prodigious one-handed) throw; hence touchline and touch-judge. The virtues of omission were as surprising as those of commission. There were no crossbars, although tape might have been used, and no nets; there were no sanctions by way of free kicks and penalties. In the sporting climate of the day, it was assumed, in what were in any event rough exchanges, that infringements would be accidental, with rival captains settling disputes quickly and politely. When the penalty kick was introduced after 1891, there were negative reactions; well into the 20th century it is said that the Corinthians team kicked penalties wide and instructed their goalkeeper to stand aside for a penalty, regarding it at a badge of shame that they should be associated with opponents who were, or themselves be, guilty of such heinous behaviour. To add to the cricketing allusions there were, in these later years, two umpires and a referee to whom decisions could be 'referred', as with the third umpire of modern times. Gradually, the referee reigned supreme and the umpires were downgraded to linesmen.

The so-called London Football Association did not at first quite command the same authority in football as did the MCC in cricket. The foremost alternative faction was based on the Sheffield Association, which already probably had rather more artisan support than the primarily 'old boys' teams of the London region. Its rules, extant as from 1870, include, for example, a more liberal outlook on the still vexed question of offside. In any event, there was almost immediately a clash, the result of the London/Cambridge axis forbidding of handling. When William Webb Ellis ran with the ball, it was not the handling but the motion that mystified his fellows. It was carriage forward, with the possibility of passing the ball by hand, that caused upset. Moreover, as dribbling and foot-rushes increased, there was a tendency to object to handling in principle. The pretty tale is told of a group of Old Harrovians, foregathered and playing in Yorkshire, who gave their opponents a pair of white gloves and two silver coins to hold as a prophylactic - showing some insight into Tyke psychology - against them touching the ball with their hands.

Hacking provided another dilemma. Mr Campbell of the Blackheath club argued hotly in its favour. The call for its abolition, he protested, 'savours more of those who like their pipes or grog or schnapps than the manly game of football' and he offered to 'bring over a lot of Frenchmen who would beat you with a week's practice'. Shades of Eric Cantona.

The upshot was an early rift among the footballing fraternity, one that cricket mercifully escaped. Blackheath led the charge away from the Association game, with Oxford University and Richmond next in line. Two other main renegades from the FA were the Manchester and Liverpool clubs, important in this study in that these premier Lancashire football combines opted for rugby. Incidentally, the club that, by the end of the 20th century, was the chief rugby union flag-carrier, Sale, was formed in 1861 by members of the Sale Cricket Club, itself formed in 1854. That was a setback for association football in the Manchester and Merseyside areas. The Rugby Union was established, with these three clubs enlisted, and the Blackheath rules largely adopted in 1871, the Pall Mall Restaurant in London being, for those noting these Egon Ronay listings, the venue. In 1875 the XX became the modern XV. Because rugby and football were soon to be perceived as class-bound, it must be emphasised that the schism was not. It was two lots of middle and upper-class public schoolboys in fierce debate; the schoolboy slang terms 'soccer' and 'rugger' should always remind us, after the argot of 'champers' for 'brekkers' and 'starkers' at 'Twickers', of these decidedly plummy origins.

The next element in the national football equation was the launch of the FA Cup competition, itself based, at least in part, on the Harrow Cock House trophy. Charles Alcock, 'the father of modern sport', was, *inter alia*, Secretary of the FA from 1870 to 1895. An Old Harrovian, he, like his committee colleagues from Eton, Charterhouse and elsewhere, thoroughly understood the concept of the knockout tourney. In fact, one aspect was quickly dropped. This was the process of elimination to find a challenger (hence FA Challenge Cup) to face the existing champion, who had a bye into the final round. Boxing was to sustain this device, for, as Marlon Brando mumbled in *On the Waterfront*, 'I coulda been a contender'.

The famous cup was planned in London in 1871 by a sub-committee of seven and first fought over in the 1871/1872 season, with fifteen teams participating. Eight of them were London-based and only one, Queen's Park, from far away Glasgow, could be classified as northern. Wanderers - all of Oxbridge or celebrated public school stock and captained by Charles Alcock - beat Royal Engineers, two captains and nine lieutenants, one-nil, at the Oval, where Alcock doubled up as Secretary of Surrey CCC.

Alongside and as an essential component of these attempts at unification was the crusade to spread football among the working classes. The motives were plentiful. It was in 1863, the year the FA was formed, that according to *The Oxford English Dictionary*, the word 'sport' was first defined to convey the sense of participation of an organised game, usually collectively and in the open air. There was a shift to the idea of what the Victorians called 'rational recreation', with organised games intended, amid other leisure pursuits, to keep the young healthy in mind and body, away from the taverns and avoiding - with the extra time granted them by the factory acts - sloth. The devil who made work for idle (factory) hands must be thwarted. Britain's was a very young population. The average age was 26; it is 38 today. Over half the population were under 20 and less than a quarter were over 45; three-fifths of the population was unmarried. The populace was bigger and many of them were crammed into dreary factories and corralled into grim towns.

The reasons of religious value; public health and medical needs; prevention of social unrest; a ready willingness, as we have observed in the enthusiastic rigour of social betterment in Manchester, to organise civic and municipal existence more rationally; even a crude gloss ('social Darwinism') on evolutionary theory and the 'survival of the fittest' - all coalesced in firming up this campaign to take sports to the working classes. The moral aspect of the crusade was uppermost. Drink was more or less outlawed in football clubs, which never, by and large, gained the same repute for bonhomie as did rugby and cricket clubs. It is no coincidence that

William Booth left the Methodist pulpit in the early 1860s, very close in time to the establishment of the FA, to begin his work in the slums of London that led to the formation of the Salvation Army. Alcock and Booth were driven by very similar motives.

The diaspora of football in the last third of the 19th century saw the proliferation of football clubs all over the country. It must not be forgotten that cricket played its part too. Jack Williams, the Liverpool-based social historian, has calculated, as one example, that as late as 1900, 97 of the 111 cricket clubs in the Bolton area and 59 out of the 81 in Burnley and district had church affiliations. So many games were, in the late 19th century, scheduled for Liverpool parks that play commenced at 5.30am to accommodate them all, while in 1860, when the Macclesfield silk mills closed, as many as 40 matches were being negotiated on that town's newly laid park.

Football however, had three beneficial advantages over cricket. With a discreet reduction in the 1863 dimensions, it took up less room. It took less time. It took up less resources, for unless you were lucky enough to belong to a church or a work-place that subsidised the team, cricket was more expensive. I have a photograph of my father, Ack, in the neatly kitted out team line-up of Sale Holmfield, a useful local league team, dated round about 1916. That was manageable, but he could not have afforded to join the rather expensive local suburban cricket club (as opposed to the more accessible teams in the industrial townships) and play the other game he loved: he rarely played organised cricket until, in early middle age, he played some wartime civil defence cricket.

Of course, there were outlets for working-class youngsters in the world of cricket, not least in the leagues that came into prominence in the Northern and Midlands industrial areas towards the end of the 19th century. Gradually, however, the sheer number of football clubs grew and grew.

Newton Heath, the progenitor of Manchester United, was among this miscellany of football teams. The momentous year was 1878. Benjamin Disraeli was Prime Minister; the Great McDermott was singing his resonantly imperialist 'Jingo' song at the London Palladium and William Booth's following formally adopted the title of the Salvation Army. The club was officially known as the Newton Heath (Lancashire and Yorkshire Railway) Cricket & Football Club. The railway company had built one of its depots, including a carriage and wagon works, at Newton Heath. About the time Old Trafford cricket ground was opened Newton Heath had, like the de Trafford estate, been fairly open land, but now it had become fully urbanised.

The Lancashire and Yorkshire Railway company, formally the Manchester and Leeds Railway, had been among the early railway runners, specialising in what would now be called commuters - they were among the first railway businesses to sell large amounts of season tickets - and holidays - they promoted many of the excursion trains to Blackpool and elsewhere. This was the company that, in 1847, had persuaded the Manchester Town Council to adopt 'standard' time, more than thirty years before the national agreement. So it was not a firm lacking in initiative. The railways companies were among the most paternalistically progressive in the country, being the first major concerns to offer, in the 1870s, a week's holiday with pay and later to lead the way with occupational pensions for tradesmen.

40

Birth of a Football Club

It is, then, not surprising that the Dining Room Committee at the Newton Heath plant was made responsible for 'classes of improvement' and supervision of physical activities. The employers were anxious to bind the employees into loyalty to the company by such means; they were eager to present a more emollient face of capitalism to thwart the peril of red agitation; they were keen to keep workers in good health for legitimate economic reasons, and they wished to offer some counter to the temptations of drink. They had a point. The 1870s marked a peak in alcohol consumption, with up to a quarter of working class wages spent on liquor. In 1876 the average consumption of beer for the year was 35 gallons, four times what it would be in the 1970s.

As the artisan crafts, among which railway employment was regarded as being most estimable, grew in respectability, this bonding of tradesmen to the company name was intensified. Brass bands, several of whom would be destined to parade around Old Trafford football ground, were another method utilised by employers. By the end of the 19th century there were 50,000 brass bands blowing and tooting, with company sponsorship - Black Dyke Mills; Hammond's Sauce; Foden's Motor Works - prominent. As well as many 'Temperance' bands, there were a thousand Salvation Army bands. As with football there was competition, its national foci being the Crystal Palace, also home to the FA Cup for a spell, and Belle Vue Gardens, Manchester, where, in 1908, 2.5m people listened to 500 bands in contest. Many choirs, dramatic groups and horticultural societies had similar occupational roots.

The sportive railwaymen of Newton Heath were given a clayey parcel of land close to the works on North Road and there, among the puddles, they splashed and gambolled. Cricket must have been difficult, but cricketers were less fastidious about climatic conditions in those days. It was just a bare, wet field, without any changing or other accommodation. 'The Three Crowns', a pub on the Oldham Road a half a mile away, and later 'The Shears Hotel' were used for this purpose, although it is a moot point whether this connection was supportive of the temperance motif. At a later date 33 Oldham Road became the club's office.

It must be emphasised that, at the onset, this was primarily a 'sides' club, with the workers using this rather primitive facility for their own games, the Mancunian stillness doubtless rent by the equivalent of cries such as 'you can't have David Beckham two nights running'. Probably there would be teams based on departments of the works or matches arranged with other railway combines. By the 1880s ambition had led Newton Heath further afield to a host of friendly matches with other Manchester 'soccer' teams, among them West Gorton, later, in merger, to be known as Manchester City. Nor did the new club want for gravitas in its administration. It had a president, predictably the works superintendent, Mr F. Attock, who was able to enlist prestigious vice-presidents, including local MPs, among them A.J. Balfour (soon to be Prime Minister), and C.P. Scott, the most distinguished editor of the *Manchester Guardian*.

Thus the origins of Manchester/Lancashire and Newton Heath/Manchester United could hardly have been more different. The former was set up by gentlemen for gentlemen; the latter by gentlemen for workers. Both perfectly exemplified the manner in which top-class cricket and football came to England. In cricket a relatively small number of counties, no more than eight at this stage, had imposed their weight and influence on the scene, their only likely emulators another set of county clubs that would either climb the steep ladder into the carefully controlled County Championship, or form what would become the Minor Counties grouping. With football, the tadpole theory was in evidence. Hundreds of clubs were started in dozens of fashions, principally but not exclusively through the habit of middle class do-goodery, and then eventually a few frogs emerged from the spawn to form the Football League.

Indeed, the origins of the current Football League incumbents testify to this. Although, of course, many were started just as football clubs, not a few of these of a later vintage, when the idea of running a football club in a town became the vogue, there is much variety in these beginnings.

There are other successful works teams, like Manchester United. Arsenal, originally Dial Square, arose, of course, from the Royal Woolwich Arsenal munitions complex, while Coventry City (Singers' Cycle Works), Millwall (Morton and Co., the jam and marmalade specialists) and West Ham United (the Thames Ironworks shipbuilding concern) are others. The churches and Sunday Schools have something for which to answer. Bolton Wanderers, Bury, Mansfield Town and Fulham all began life under clerical monitorship. Everton were originally St Domingo's New Methodist Connection Church Sunday School, something of a challenge if one embarks on the football chant of 'Give us an S…'

Schools and teachers played their part, either as old boys, such as the then rather lordly Blackburn Rovers, or as elementary teachers, as with Sunderland and Northampton Town. However, as we have already seen with Newton Heath, cricket was to the fore. Several famous football teams either began as cricket teams or as joint cricket and football teams, among them Middlesbrough, both the Sheffield clubs and Derby County. Bradford City, Ipswich Town and Burnley, alternatively, had early rugger connections.

In this maelstrom of sources it is scarcely surprising that several Football League clubs had hybrid roots. Southampton (schoolmasters and church), Stoke City (old boys - Old Carthusians - and works - another railway company, the North Staffordshire), Wolverhampton Wanderers and Aston Villa (both church and cricket) are among these. Leyton Orient contrived to have three sponsors for the price of one when, in 1881, the Homerton Theological College's Glyn Cricket Club opted for football as well. Needless to say, almost all Football League club birthdays fall into the pressure cooker time for modern British sport, the period from the 1860s to the beginning of the Great War in 1914.

Newton Heath became parochially well-known in a city where, as yet, football was not substantially established. The properly financed teams like Bolton Wanderers, Blackburn Rovers and Preston North End were way out of their sights, as they concentrated from 1884/85 on a lengthy run of success in the newly founded Manchester Cup, including, in the second round of the 1886/87 tourney, an 11-1 licking of the soon-to-be Manchester City.

It was 1886/87 that 'the Heathens', to give their nickname a judicious airing, entered the FA Cup for the first time. There were now over 120 entries and the roster has, for the modern eye, a zany look about it, what with Glasgow Rangers in the semi-final and teams like Old Carthusians, Old Westminsters, to say nothing of Darwen, all having enjoyed strong runs into the quarter-finals. Aston Villa beat West Bromwich Albion in the final in front of 16,000 spectators at the Oval. Newton Heath did not threaten the top-notchers, subsiding to Fleetwood Rangers in the first round. It was a draw at full time and, Newton having refused to play extra time, the referee awarded the tie to Fleetwood. One could conclude that better times would, in the future, attend the club's attempts to grasp the coveted FA Cup.

The rise of spectatordom and professionalism, as they jointly affected both Lancashire and Manchester United, will be reviewed in chapter six; suffice it to say that, in the closing decades of the 19th century, it had an immense impact on football. Legitimised, with limitations, by a grudging FA in 1885, in a desperate attempt to avoid the even worse sickness of 'veiled professionalism', as Charles Alcock, who (wearing his cricket hat) understood some of the repercussions of 'shamateurism', termed it. In 1888 William McGregor, 'the father of the League', invited twelve of the strongest professional combines to play a contest of home and away fixtures. The Football League was born. It soon enjoyed much success and, with the old-style amateur clubs languishing under the pressure, London was at something of a discount, the twelve founding clubs coming from the industrial North and Midlands.

The FA Cup Final of 1883 was a benchmark in this change. In what the football writer Geoffrey Green called 'a battle between two worlds', Blackburn Olympic became the first northern, indeed the first non-public schoolish side, to win the trophy, as they defeated Old Etonians, despite their six internationals, 2-1 after extra time. They had had a break at bracing Blackpool and undertaken systematic training; both rather frowned upon by the metropolitan elite. Olympic included five textile workers, an iron foundryman, a plumber, a dentist's assistant. a picture framer and two, one of them the coach, Jack Hunter, who may only be described, in the Victorian patois, as 'professors', surreptitiously paid for their efforts.

Newton Heath were frantically keen to obtain a place in the Football League. The club applied the first year and many times thereafter, but they were always spurned. Crucially, they lacked a decent ground and decent amenities, nor could they guarantee an average gate of 4,000. Even more to the point, they were not much good. Even playing in the lower leagues that were immediately scheduled, first the Football Combination and then the Football Alliance, they did not set the Irwell on fire.

Then luck changed. The year the Football League decided to expand the First and also form a Second Division, Newton Heath had its best year yet, finishing runners-up in the Alliance, the Vauxhall Conference of yesteryear, and leaping straight into the First Division. The first league game, at princely Blackburn Rovers in the autumn of 1892, was a close-fought 3-4 loss, with Bob Donaldson scoring the first-ever league goal, while the first home league game, before a then record crowd of over 10,000, brought the first league point from a 1-1 result against Burnley. Luck changed again. Despite a 10-1 win (still the club record league winning margin) over that season's FA Cup winners, Wolves, Newton came last. In those balmy days, with another nod to cricket, Test matches were played between the top of the second and the bottom of the first tables for the ultimate accolade. They managed to salvage themselves one year, beating Small Heath, but, failing again the next season, they succumbed to rising

Liverpool. The Heathens went the path of the ungodly into the depths of Division Two and there they slumped never to lift themselves again. Beset by continued financial worries and dubious organisation, these were to be difficult years.

One important step had, however, been taken. The increasingly tenuous links with the railway company were, in 1892, with that first dreamed of sortie into league football a reality, sundered. A new limited company, Newton Heath FC, was listed. A secretary, Alfred Albut, late of Aston Villa, was appointed, and even if costs rose and the Stock Exchange remained unimpressed, it was typical of the moves being made by the senior football clubs across the nation.

It is difficult to exaggerate the importance of this decision either in specific or general terms. At a stroke it altered the whole conspectus of a Football League club, especially in comparison with a County Cricket club. Against a background of continuing demographic growth and urban development, the provision of leisure facilities for spectators was in the ascendant. It was, in historical time, an abrupt switch. Newton Heath shifted from being a paternalistically run works team to a limited company and business in fourteen years. It was par for the course of many Football League clubs, which, whether their roots were clerical or vocational, very swiftly found themselves gazetted as limited companies. The County Cricket club, with its strong and often vocal membership and with its longer years maturing, was for many years not so vulnerable to the siren voices of big business. The county clubs, among them Lancashire, continued to look back to the early 19th, even the late 18th century, and endured as gentlemen's clubs, despite the changes of purpose and character. The Football League clubs, among them Newton Heath, took their cue from the profitable businesses they saw thriving in the fruitful decades of Victorian commerce. It was a monumental distinction.

One symptom of that distinction was soon evident. When Manchester-Lancashire cricket club had found themselves under the fiscal cosh, a discreet passing around of the hat at the AGM normally did the trick. The Duke of Devonshire - 'What's the damage this time?' was his yearly query - would annually bail out neighbouring Derbyshire CCC, and that degree of landowning support was true of several counties. The football club company found itself in the hands of shareholders who, on the whole, preferred to make a profit and were aghast when debits, not credits, accrued.

Slumming in the Second Division, the Heathens evinced an accurate reverse Victorian image of the Christians; they were fallible, unkempt and savage, where the others were proud, godly and well-behaved. Anecdotes abound of unpaid bills, badly paid players, dubious deals and disastrous results. Only in 1896/97, when only Test matches were their renewed undoing, did Newton Heath flirt with promotion.

By the end of the 1901/02 season, with hefty debts and winding-up orders in the offing, there was a meeting at the New Islington Town Hall, at which the shareholders sat in louring gloom.

Then there was a miracle. Miracles tend to be associated with the birth of great religions, and Manchester United was no exception. Up bravely spoke the captain, Harry Stafford. He revealed that he had found financial benefactors; not three, but four, wise men were the saviours. Their names - Messrs Davies, Jones, Brown and

Taylor - may lack the lustre of Melchior, Gaspar and Balthazar, but their decision to toss £200 each in the kitty was as welcome as the gifts of gold, frankincense and myrrh.

Like all the best nativity legends, this had an animal playing the lead role, like the wolf with Romulus and Remus in the founding of Rome or, indeed, the donkey, sheep, ox and ass of Bethlehem specification. During a previous fund-raising bazaar, Harry Stafford's St Bernard had worn on its back a collection box, but had wandered off and was lost with, one presumes, Manchester City supporters numbered among the suspects. Imagine Harry Stafford's surprise when the dog and collection box, both intact, were found and returned by J.H. Davies. The fairy tale continued. J.H. Davies was a wealthy man and his daughter, deviating slightly from the Hans Christian Andersen model, had taken a shine, not to Harry Stafford, but to his dog. And when Harry Stafford recounted the woes of the Heathens, Davies' heart was moved and, in turn, he moved the hearts of Messrs Jones, Brown and Taylor - the condition being that the dog become the property of the young and - here one tries a bow at a venture - beautiful daughter.

No doubt bidding a tearful farewell to his valiant pet, Harry Stafford made the canine sacrifice for the greater cause. No other St Bernard, not even one of those with a keg of monkish brandy about its neck in the Alpine snows, has ever effected so spectacular a rescue. Quite simply, a dog bought United lock, stock and barrel.

J.H. Davies, as he went on to prove, was not all sentiment. A condition of his agreeing, with his fellow Mancunian Magi, to invest in the club was that the old board should be swept aside, like the ugly sisters in panto, in order that the Cinderella of Newton Heath be transformed into the Princess Crystal of Manchester United. There was much enthusiasm for this, the ugly sisters themselves being probably quite relieved at this miraculous turn of events.

This fundamental change of ownership prompted thoughts of a change of name, for, ambition flying forward propelled by such nascent energy, there was a feeling that a second Manchester team was a viable option. Several suggestions were made, including, apparently, Manchester Celtic. Louis Rocca, a distinguished servant to the club as chief scout for many, many years, is sometimes credited with proposing United - and United it was.

The original Newton Heath team had played in the gold and green hues of the Lancashire and Yorkshire company livery; later these were changed to green shirt with golden trimmings; later still, it was to be white shirts and blue knickers (to employ the rather ambivalent usage of the age). A new destiny under a new name called for a new robing: red shirts and white shorts were determined upon and so has it blessedly remained.

The FA was only too pleased and relieved to give a benediction to the fresh regime. On 28th April 1902 Manchester United celebrated its birthday.

5.

Old Trafford Bound

THE OMENS were promising. Manchester United won their first league game on 6th September 1902; they beat Gainsborough Trinity 1-0, away. Charlie Richards still awaits canonisation for scoring that first ever United goal. Then they won their first home league match, against Burton United, on 13th September, again, 1-0. Those unlikely Second Division opponents should remind us of the ephemeral nature of this sporting life. Manchester United had been narrowly saved from joining, *inter alia*, Bootle and Darwen in the non-league knacker's yard. Having finished close to the bottom of the table in the last Newton Heath season, they managed a creditable fifth place in the 1902/03 competition.

The North Road ground had been developed, with stands built in 1887 and 1891, but it was still something of an undrained morass. When Newton Heath FC was officially formed in 1892, the last of the linkages with the railway company were severed. This brought two additional financial burdens. One was a hike in the rental demanded by the railway landlords; the other was an end to concessionary travel for the players-cum-railwaymen. In fact, the land was sub-contracted, for the railway company let it for a nominal sum from Manchester Cathedral, the Church of England being one of the country's richest landowners. Despite the wintry ravages of the Heathens, the cricketers among the railway employees still struggled to ply willow against leather on that unkindly terrain, while the practice of charging for entry for football matches offended the lease and possibly the susceptibilities of the Anglican proprietors. In any event, because the now divorced football club had total winter use of the ground, it effectively excluded any railway staff in search of exercise. Newton Heath were faced with eviction.

Hurriedly the club sought about them, the 1893/94 season being close at hand. They had to abandon their precious new stands, receiving less than £100 recompense for leaving them in the hands of the Lancashire and Yorkshire Railway Company and, all the while, other debts mounted. Newton Heath faced the same problem that had puzzled Manchester cricket club when forced to leave their first ground on the de Trafford estate, but without the corollary of anyone finding them a replacement.

A home was found at Bank Street, Clayton, about three miles from North Street, still to the north-east but closer to the city centre. The field was leased by and belonged to the Bradford and Clayton Athletic Company, so there was obviously some kindred spirits to welcome the footballers. There were already stands on two sides of the pitch, one side-on and one behind a goal, and a cinder terrace was speedily added behind the other of the goals. Where the de Trafford estate in the 1850s provided some hint at least of sylvan moments, with both art treasures and cricketing gems unsullied by too much industrial spoilage, Clayton by the 1890s was a locus for grime and stench. The ground was surrounded by industrial buildings, with chemically noxious fumes belching from encrusted chimneys. In this respect it was typical of the Football League arenas of the day, many of them poking upwards from densely packed working-class terraced housing and ugly, smoky factories.

Newton Heath did contrive to steal a 3-2 win over Burnley on their first outing there at the beginning of the 1893/94 campaign, before a crowd of 7,000, but apart from winning the Lancashire Cup, by dint of beating Blackburn Rovers, in the late 1890s, the move to Clayton had not been the happiest of precedents. Although the sums were in hundreds rather than millions of pounds, Newton Heath's situation was not unlike that of several football clubs today. There was a viciously spiralling downward circle of investing in not-so-good and selling good players, and trying to offer not only success on the field but with something nearer to comfort around it - all coupled with the fickle jade of the precarious gate, then basically the sole source of income.

The switch to Manchester United and the input of new monies was a critical moment. It heralded a change of mood and an influx of verve on the part of the new board. J.H. Davies sorted out some of the financial mayhem that had characterised the ancient regime, while Harry Stafford and James West, following in Alf Albut's footsteps as secretary, tried to improve the playing side. Crowds, perhaps lured by the new sense of zest and the new all-embracing Manchester branding, almost trebled from an average of 4,000 to nearly 11,000. 20,000 watched that first home match of the newly named Manchester United against Burton United in 1902.

Financial stability was resolved, but, despite Herculean labours, the reward of First Division status proved elusive. J.H. Davies had donated some funds for players and transfer fees, one or two of them touching the extravagant £150 mark. Professional football has always been an uneasy world in terms of its financial transactions. The 1900s were rife with problems of illegal payments and other fiscal irregularities. The ramifications of these across the city at Hyde Road, home of Manchester City, were to benefit United, but they themselves were also beset with FA inquiries. Both Harry Stafford and James West received four-year bans in 1903 following charges of financial impropriety.

In 1908 J.J. Bentley, journalist, businessman and Secretary of Bolton Wanderers, became chairman, charged with the task of restructuring the club. He came from Tufton, where an Old Harrovian had started one of Lancashire's first football teams in 1872. With his briskly clipped moustache and autocratic bearing, he also later acted as United's Secretary and enjoyed something of a national reputation in football circles. J.J. Bentley, naturally anxious to cleanse then refurbish the Augean stable of his club's administration, strongly recommended James Ernest Mangnall as the next secretary. An old boy of Bolton Grammar School, but more of a cyclist and a harrier than a footballer, he had been involved with Bolton Wanderers and then Burnley before moving to the noisome climes of Bank Street. A sharp-featured man, with foxy, astute eyes and a dark moustache that pre-empted that of Mein Führer, he was exactly the official required to make good the promise that the business input of J.H. Davies offered. Moreover, his was a broad sweep. Apart from reducing the backroom staff to one, thereby having himself take on even some of the groundsman's duties, this hermit of an administrator became what later would be called team manager. He was one of the first secretaries to embrace football affairs directly. Hitherto, with yet another glance cricket-wards, the team captain, acting as a species of player-coach, had shared these responsibilities with the secretary, in the style of the Stafford and West double act.

The rather different partnership of Mangnall and Davies was rewarded with a return to the First Division, but only after a couple of frustrating campaigns that left Manchester United just short of the pace. Then, in 1905/06, with crowds of up to 40,000 crammed into Bank Street and, in complementary style, United's best-ever cup run - defeat by Woolwich Arsenal in the quarter-finals - promotion was gained, after twelve disappointing years in the lower division. It was the beginning of the first of several purple patches in the club's glamorous history.

1907/08 was to be the seminal season in that dramatic saga. Having developed a strong defensive barrier, Ernest Mangnall recruited, in consequence of troubles at Manchester City, four players, including the legendary Billy Meredith and the prolific scorer, Sandy Turnbull. City, having won the FA Cup in 1904 when a brilliant individual effort by 'the Welsh wizard' had secured victory over Bolton Wanderers, had been wracked from top to bottom by scandals relating to illegal payments and match-fixing. There were sweeping bans on officials and tough suspensions of first team players, but this is no time to pause and enjoy the troubles of others.

For now United, Ernest Mangnall having snapped up the miscreants to the fury of other clubs anxious to sign them, had an attacking edge - and it was immediately in focus. An enthused crowd of 40,000 gathered at Bank Street on 1st January 1907 and watched transfixed as the dream started to come true: a Meredith cross led to a Turnbull goal, and Aston Villa were felled.

With this well-balanced side available for the whole of the 1907/08 campaign, the sights of ambition were raised. Sandy Turnbull shot and nodded a record number of goals for a season - 25 in 30 appearances - that stood while two global conflicts were negotiated, until the iron-cased left foot of Jack Rowley struck well and truly in the early Busby years. Not only were United First Division champions for the very first time, they outdistanced their nearest rivals, Aston Villa, by a convincing nine points. It was the first of fifteen such major successes, as of 2004, but that initial taste of the main dish retains its savoury flavour close to a century on. For those involved there might have been murmurings that the club's guardian angel or patron saint - St Bernard, perhaps? - had produced another miracle. After all, it was but a few years since, with the collapse of Newton Heath, the club had teetered precariously on the very brink of closure.

This great campaign was notable for one other event. Just at the beginning of that season, Manchester United resolved to begin the search for a new ground. Bank Street, with its pitch denuded of grass and its walls pressed hard against an industrial plant, was considered too impoverished a setting of so grand a club - and the cavalier manner of winning the title must have underpinned that sense of glorious aspiration. The ground did not seem big enough. There were occasions when the thousands packed inside could see little and the thousands locked outside could see nothing.

Old Trafford Bound

The Old Trafford site was chosen fairly quickly; perhaps someone had spotted it prior to the public announcement about a likely move. It was a parcel of land on the other side of the main road from the cricket ground and, in a move symptomatic of the business connections of league football, it was the Manchester Brewery Company, of which J.H. Davies was chairman (as he also was of the Walkers and Homfrays Brewery) that actually purchased the land. They then leased it to the club. Renting from an industry rather than a landed estate was another of those subtle differences between the ways of league football and county cricket. J.H. Davies himself paid for most of the costs of constructing the new ground, an expenditure of £40,000, or £2m at today's prices.

Archibald Leitch, who had something of a reputation as an architect specialising in football stadia, was hired and the plans, for the times, were quite excessive. Indeed, the original scheme for 100,000 spectators was reduced to 80,000, but this still made it the most modern of footballing arenas. Gates were still relatively modest. Charles Alcock, sitting in his Oval office, would smile over the couple of thousand or so who meandered in for the first Cup Finals at the Oval, reflecting on the 20,000-plus spectators for, say, Surrey and Nottinghamshire, let alone a Test match. Even by the 1890s the crowds had only reached something over 20,000; in fact, the biggest Cup Final crowd thus far was at the Manchester Athletic Club, Fallowfield, when 45,000 saw Wolves lose out 1-0 to Everton in 1893. After the 1894 Final had been played at Everton's ground (Notts County being the winners), the event returned to London, taking up residence at Crystal Palace until the outbreak of the Great War. Even then there were only three gates in excess of 100,000 in this period, the first being the 111,000 who bore witness in 1901 to a drawn encounter between Spurs and Sheffield United.

So the prospect of a large league ground was extravagantly ambitious, as were the plans to include offices, with telephones (from its beginnings about the end of the 1870s, the telephone was now much more common; there were 6m trunk calls in 1898 and 36m in 1913), a laundry and plunge baths, de luxe changing accommodation and such modern-sounding amenities as a gym and fitness rooms. Nearly 13,000 could be accommodated under the covered grandstand, which also boasted 750 upholstered tip-up seats, theatre style, for the dignitaries. It was then the most commodious grandstand in British football.

An important aspect was the coherent design of the ground. The 1893 Cup Final at Fallowfield had been a social disaster. J.J. Bentley had proposed the venue, as being one of the few outside London where a goodly assemblage could be catered for, but a totally unexpected 45,000, to say nothing of hundreds more who could not affect an entry, overran the frail wooden palisades that were the sole barriers, occupied the reserved seating and hugged the touchline, so much so that the game was almost abandoned. Goodison Park, the site of the next replay, proved to be a more practical solution, making a case for the larger, purpose built enclosure. Moreover, while optimistic of providing accommodation for over 70,000, Old Trafford was planned skilfully enough to permit reasonably close sightlines for everybody. The constant complaint of utilising cricket and athletics fields - the Oval, Crystal Palace - for soccer was that the action was too far removed from the majority of the customers.

49

Red Shirts and Roses

Not unexpectedly, Old Trafford was used for the 1911 FA Cup replay, when 58,000 watched as Bradford City disposed of Newcastle United, before the great honour was bestowed of using Old Trafford for the 1915 Cup Final. The 'khaki Cup Final', so-called because of the number of servicemen among the crowd, saw Sheffield United beat Chelsea on a rainy April day and with the 50,000 crowd in the most sombre of moods, given that the Great War was already well into its lethal sway.

The building of Old Trafford completed a gradual movement away from the north-east of the city where the original fan-base resided. The new base was five miles from Bank Street and in an almost exact diagonal from the Oldham Road, where Newton Heath pointed, via Failsworth, to Oldham. At the same time, J.H. Davies and Ernest Mangnall were eager to conceive of United as a city-wide club - and there were certain other interlocked factors to be considered.

The first was the success of the Manchester Ship Canal. The merchant, Daniel Adamson, was one of the chief protagonists of this significant engineering feat, and the canal was suggested at a time when there had been a serious decline in the use of Manchester's warehousing and mills, because of the distance from the ports. Fuelled by the irritation caused by the exorbitant rates charged by the Port of Liverpool and the rail and canal carriers, but inspired by an imaginative leap of confident minds, work began in 1887. It was opened in 1894, in the presence of Her Majesty the Queen and that other imposingly regal personality, my grandmother.

For I am a child of the canals or, at least, a great-grandchild. My great-grandfather, Joseph Clare, was a chief ostler, stationed between Lymm and Oughtrington on the Bridgewater Canal. A respectable artisan, he had a house, free coals and two guineas a week in the 1870s, much the same, incidentally, as my father earned, minus the house and coals, in the 1930s. Joseph Clare, enfranchised by the 1867 Reform Act and lured by the astute Disraeli with his joint temptation of imperialism abroad and sanitation at home, was a member of the Conservative-inspired Primrose League, a devoted low Anglican and one of the first of a never-ending queue of working-class Tory voters, deluded by the snare of confining respectability.

In 1892 he was, to use an apt footballism, transferred to the Bridgewater Department of the Manchester Ship Canal Company, who shelled out £1.7m for the Bridgewater Navigation. He lived in a Canal Company house in Little Edward Street, hard by the stables. This was off Quay Street, Deansgate, part of the site now occupied by Granada Television Studios. I visited that little family home, with its stone-flagged floors, aged four in 1936, that being the first time I had ever attended a wedding and, on the occasions I have since had cause to visit the TV studios, I have always felt some sense of restoration. This sentiment was enhanced when, on the early credits of *Coronation Street*, remaining brickwork of that ancestral abode could fleetingly be observed. When in turn his wife, Margaret Clare, and then he himself died, their coffins were ceremoniously conveyed in barges for burial in Oughtrington.

Let not that gloomy thought overwhelm the headier emotion evoked by the picture of the old Queen declaring open the Ship Canal, constructed at a cost of £15m. In a pen provided for the workers and their families watched my grandmother, Ada Margaret Clare, then seventeen and a handsome wench, already being assiduously courted by Harry Midwinter. She was an apprentice, later a mistress milliner and an

50

impeccable needlewoman - recall, from chapter one, ours being the most aesthetically elegant anti-gas chamber in the Northwest Civil Defence Region. Although a devout monarchist, the chief memory she had of the glittering occasion was the dreadful hat worn by Queen Victoria.

Within two years 35 steamer lines were using the new waterway; not only raw cotton and the subsequent finished textiles, but also many foodstuffs, especially dairy products, and other goods were conveyed along the canal. By 1902 it was the fifth port in the kingdom, assessed by value of imports. In general, it meant that Manchester had rid itself at a stroke of its dependence on the cotton trade, for, at the turn of the century, it could be boldly claimed that Manchester Docks offered the nearest ocean terminals to a body of 8m people, a fifth of the British population. In 1909, even as Old Trafford was being built, Edward VII opened the largest of the docks, Number Nine Dock, and the minimal depth of the canal was increased to 28 feet. In its first year of operation, this 'elongated harbour' carried 1m tons of cargo; soon it would be twenty fold that figure.

The Manchester Ship Canal ran to the west of the de Trafford estate. The estate's northern border was Trafford Bar and its southern frontier was the edge of the townships of Stretford and Barton-on-Irwell, approximately marked off by the Bridgewater Canal. Trafford Hall stood majestically towards Trafford Bar and now the Ship Canal, following the original bed of the Irwell, pursued the path of the northern boundary. Sir Humphrey Francis de Trafford, head of that noble family, was disconcerted to find the big ships sailing down the Ally-ally-o right past his bedroom windows. It did not sit well with aristocratic self-esteem. Running deer and Capability Brown landscaping would have been preferable to a slow-moving boat carrying a cargo of, say, some of the 300,000 tons of grain that annually was carried down the canal.

Disturbed by these nocturnal nautical visions, and doubtless tempted by the prospect of filthy lucre, he was moved to sell off the estate in 1896. The Trafford Park Syndicate, spearheaded by E.T. Hooley, a nimble speculator, bought the estate and a new combine, Trafford Park Estates Ltd, was founded. It is worthy of note that the first impressions included a balanced complex of factories, workers' cottages, suburban villas and leisure facilities, including parks and a racecourse. There was a hint of the Saltaire, Bournville or Port Sunlight experiments about these first plans; in fact, it sounds more like the present Salford Quays than what did transpire.

It was an understandable musing. Apart from the cricket ground, there were the Royal Botanical Gardens, while in 1887, in the footsteps of the 1857 Exhibition that had disrupted the activities of Manchester Cricket Club, Queen Victoria's Golden Jubilee was celebrated by a National Exhibition of Arts, Science and Industry. It was sited between Talbot Road and the railway, with its entrance near Old Trafford station. It was a major success. 4.5m attended over 166 days, with 74,600 passing through the clicking turnstiles on one day alone. Sports, mainly athletics and cycling, were included, while the cricketing enthusiast might have played truant from the serious consideration of the worthy exhibits in mid-July and watched admiringly as the Lancashire of Hornby and Barlow beat the Gloucestershire of W.G. Grace by an innings and 88 runs.

The eventual outcome did not match this happy dream of a harmonious mixture of work and play. The Managing Director of the new Trafford Park company, the hard-headed Marshall Stevens, recognised that the industrial potential was vast. Apart from Trafford Hall becoming a hotel and the laying of a golf course, it was industry, industry, industry. The estate was vigorously marketed. In 1897 the Royal Agricultural Show, complete with gas-powered tramcars and performances by the Barnum and Bailey Circus, was used, paradoxically, to lease out industrial land, with W.T. Glover being the first of the big companies to take root. The Manchester Ship Canal was an enormous booster. There was space for grain storage elevators, for oil depots and refineries and for factories treating incoming foodstuffs and timber.

In 1900 the British Westinghouse Electric and Manufacturing Company arrived in Trafford Park, forerunner, in 1919, of Metropolitan Vickers, producers of electrical and automotive goods and employer of one of the largest work-forces in Britain. That focus, which naturally attracted smaller similar companies as feeders and sub-contractors, ensured that by early in the 20th century, Trafford Park was probably the largest engineering complex in Europe. A further feather in the industrial cap was the advent of the Ford Motor Company in 1911; Trafford Park was chosen as the British site for the assembly of the Model T 'tin lizzie'.

Manchester, the Cottonopolis, was transforming itself into a more complete industrial regional capital. When one talks of the Industrial Revolution, London is often left out of the picture, as mining, shipbuilding and textile areas are emphasised. But London underwent a massive change of commercial tack during the 19th century, with industries developing to serve the needs of a hugely expanding metropolis. Now Manchester had to offer the same services to its hinterland.

The appearance of Ford motorcars reminds us that transport was hurriedly keeping pace with the rapid expansion of industry. As well as the railways that soon served the Manchester and Salford Docks and the new industrial estate so well, and as well as the little aerodrome that was built on Trafford Park in 1911, road transport was improving. Manchester's famous setts had made almost all its roads infinitely more passable and, as well as the horse-drawn omnibuses, some of them around from the middle of the century, there were the trams. Cheap and cheerful, these brightly lit 'gondolas of the people', as Richard Hoggart lucidly described them, were the heaven-sent vehicles of the working classes, for whom the omnibuses had been a trifle expensive. Trams completed the circle of urban transit: railways took passengers on the longer journey, and the trams, usually radiating outwards from the rail centres, covered the shorter distances.

Horse-drawn trams arrived in the major cities, such as Manchester, in the 1870s, the usual practice being for the municipality to own the tracks and lease them to private operators. The electrification of the trams was a major blessing and, like other authorities, Manchester in 1901 took the trams into public ownership. The use of tramcars, rattling along with their rackety, but strangely comfortable, seats and stately ambience, rose astronomically. During 1901/02 Manchester's electric trams conveyed 24m passengers; it was 206m during 1913/14. It did not escape the notice of J.H. Davies that the tramcars bowled along the road towards Stretford, Sale and Altrincham, passing within yards of the chosen site for the football club, a pleasing complement to the nearby train service. Nor did it escape his notice that, on Saturdays, the gates of the engineering works of Trafford Park and the dockyards of Salford would be flung open and thousands upon thousands of manual workers would be only too ready to be mesmerised by the skills of Billy Meredith.

The first phase of the Saturday half-day had been in place for a generation. Initially, this involved - it being a twelve-hour day that was under consideration - a 2 o'clock finish, although, over the years, this gradually contracted to high noon. The traditional Football League kick-off time of 3pm was thus timed opportunely to allow the workers to leave their lathes and looms, have a pie and a pint, and stream to the football ground. Mr Davies possibly dreamed of such a stream of engineers, leaving their Trafford Park work-benches, joining together with others journeying by tram and train and all cramming into his envisaged new stadium.

Much had altered in the 50 years since the Saturday half-day and the Old Trafford cricket ground had been developed. It is true that county cricket is, contrariwise, an urban phenomenon. Indeed, given the varied legislation concerning local government, many cricketing counties either do not, as concrete administrative entities, exist (for instance, Yorkshire, Glamorgan, Sussex, now split in twain, and Middlesex) or find their cricket headquarters are no longer officially in the dedicated county ambit (for instance, Lancashire, Warwickshire, Surrey, Gloucestershire, Leicestershire and Derbyshire), usually because the relevant conurbations have become autonomous local governmental authorities.

Equally, first-class cricket was the creature of the railways and no county could, until the late 20th century development of the motorways, undertake a first-class programme unless it had a top-ranking rail link. This was not so much to ensure that the spectators could attend, as to guarantee that the teams could honour a tight fixture list. Paddington is as important as Lord's in the W.G. Grace story. So one cannot gainsay that senior cricket is more about city termini than village greens.

However, the earlier momentum of cricket allowed it to shroud itself, as we observed in chapters two and three, in middle-class, even upper-class, values, the device of the subscription club and the 'gentleman' cricketer being symptoms of this. Cricket was, then, urban but not industrial. Football, at this uppermost level, was more uncompromisingly industrial and commercial in character. J.H. Davies and his ilk hoped to make profits out of football, although like their descendants today, they probably were less prudent in their investments when it came to football and enjoyed the buzz of involvement with an exciting sport. They deliberately targeted the working-class community as their potential audience. Where the cricketers came to their Old Trafford because it retained some pastoral illusion, the footballers came to theirs because it didn't; rather it was the proximity of Metros and Salford Docks that appealed. The long generation gap between the two Old Traffords resulted in textiles and railways being the midwife of the one and engineering and tramcars that of the other.

A curio was the status of Stretford, then a township of a few thousand souls occupying less than six square miles, that found itself housing what were to become two of the most famous sports venues on the planet, rather one suspects to the occasional resentment of the mighty Manchester Corporation. Stretford supposedly derives its name from the 'strata' the Romans had flung across the Mersey, the better for the Frisian troops who defended the Mancunium fort at Castlefield, to communicate with their XXth legion headquarters at Deva or Chester, for Mancunium was an outpost on the important Chester-York road. The Romans arrived in 79 AD and remained for 350 years. Their thankless task was to preserve the peace imperilled by the fierce Brigante tribe to the north, rather as today a line of uniformed police might keep at bay a howling mob of football hooligans.

The 'strata', known as Crossford Bridge, separated my confrères and myself from Old Trafford. The Mersey is so much associated with Liverpool that it is sometimes forgotten that it has to start somewhere inland before making its leisurely way westward. Its banks were something of a playground for we local youngsters. It did have one historical claim, although it was not on the cinematic scale of *The Bridge at Remagen* or *The Bridge on the River Kwai*. During the 1745 Jacobite Rebellion Bonny Prince Charlie was made welcome in Manchester, where a rebel battalion was raised. It is true the staid citizens of Manchester had found disturbing two Scottish practices, viz., stealing boots (many of the advancing army were poorly shod) and urinating in the streets. Yet their sympathies were so aroused as to cause the tearful song 'Farewell Manchester' allegedly to be composed by the Young Pretender himself, an air later warbled by my fellow choristers and myself at Springfield School, when we were done risking our innocent souls with *Strawberry Fair*.

The Hanoverian authorities had demolished all the Mersey bridges as a stratagem to halt or deter the Jacobite march, and Bonny Prince Charlie's men made an ostentatious show of repairing Crossford Bridge and pushing troops forward through Sale and Altrincham. It was an adept feint, of which Billy Meredith might have been proud, to gull the Duke of Cumberland and his advisers into believing that the invasion was taking a westerly route. Instead the main force crossed the Mersey at Stockport and pressed onward in a south-easterly direction. The insurrection, however, ran out of steam at Derby; the Jacobites retreated back to Scotland to be routed at the Battle of Culloden. Apart from that colourful incident, Stretford had had little entitlement to be listed among the centres of civilised discourse. Now, 150 years on, it quite suddenly found itself bound north and south by famous waterways, housing Britain's first planned industrial estate and playing host to First Division football and county and Test cricket.

Old Trafford opened for business on 19th February 1910. Liverpool were the visiting party-poopers, beating United 4-3, who yielded a two-goal advantage.

6.

Playing Up at the Two Old Traffords

AT LAST BOTH Lancashire County Cricket Club and Manchester United Association Football Club are both *in situ* at their respective and hallowed residences. Such was the half a century time lag between the construction of the two grounds that we must now practise the literary equivalent of football's 'keepy-uppy' to update the cricketing situation.

For about fifteen seasons Lancashire's exploits among the 'octarchy', the eightsome reel of major county teams, were fitful. The problem of persuading amateurs to play in what were regarded tellingly as 'foreign' - that is, away - fixtures remained, while Lancashire's 'professors' were not as settled or, indeed, as proficient as, say, those of Yorkshire or Notts. The virtuoso leg spinner and attractive batsman, A.G. Steel, played only intermittently, although the briskness of his delivery, especially in his youth, and the crispness of his hitting place him among the elite of amateur all-rounders. However, this nerveless Liverpudlian found his professional legal duties prevented him from managing more than 47 appearances for the county.

Attempts were made to build an improved supportive force of paid aides. Alec Watson, a Scot from Coatbridge, was the 'pro' at the Rusholme club before embarking on a solid 23 summers' career with Lancashire. His offspin had the pertness of his rather Frenchified look, with his wispy beard, baroque moustache and wavy locks, but, despite his slight build, he bowled with the relentless pressure of one of the power-looms in the nearby mills. He took 1,308 wickets at an average cost of 13 runs for his adopted shire. Bedford-born Richard Pilling, 'the Prince of wicket-keepers', stood up to every bowler, one or two of them, like John Crossland, of tempestuous pace, on decidedly natural pitches and wearing flimsy protection, certainly compared with the *Star Wars*-esque apparel of the present era. From above the unlucky horseshoe of his drooping moustache, he gazes patiently, mournfully from his photographs, his shrunken features and deep-sunk eyes indicative of the consumption - said to have been contracted playing football - that caused his death at 35. He died at his home in Manchester in 1891 and was buried in Brooklands Cemetery, having stumped and caught a sum of 446 victims in 137 Lancashire matches. Moreover, around his neat efficacy did A.N. Hornby develop one of the first really proficient English fielding combines, rather more after the Australian fashion.

The obdurate Richard Barlow joined 'the Boss', A.N. Hornby, in an opening partnership of classic character. Tall, heavily bearded and imposing in build, he was the Roundhead professional, pick of the stonewallers in an age when 'castled' was a synonym for 'bowled'. Hornby was the Cavalier amateur, careless of risk and sprightly in assault. Together in 1875 they compiled an unbroken 148 against

Yorkshire to harvest a ten wicket victory; it was Lancashire's first century opening stand. Richard Barlow drove bowlers to the verge of lunacy with his indefatigable concentration. He carried his bat 50 times, eleven of those exercises in placid resolve being on behalf of Lancashire. Once against Nottinghamshire he was 5, not out, out of a total of 69; he batted for 150 minutes and, having not scored in the first 80, the last 70 minutes were positively riotous. Modern players noted for adhesive defence look passionately profligate by comparison.

Thankfully, there was a chink in his armour. Although his wife helped in his shop on Stretford Road and faithfully brought him his dinner each day he played at Old Trafford, theirs was not the most blissful of relationships and she seems to have suffered from some mental ailment. Later in life he was enjoying the breezes of Blackpool's North Shore when he met and fell in ardent love with a winsome lady on the staff of the nearby Imperial Hotel. They had a love child. This romance is restorative of the juices of human nature; one might expect your dapper amateur to be falling in love, not your stolid professional. It was as if Jeeves had found himself in emotional turmoil, with Bertie Wooster the studied counsellor. Barlow, a cricket obsessive, died in 1919 and his tombstone in Layton Cemetery, Blackpool, reads 'Bowled at Last'.

1878, that fateful date for the caterpillar of Newton Heath that would become the butterfly of Manchester United, was also a significant year for Lancashire. Two consecutive games in July constitute a watershed between the ancient and the modern. First, Gloucestershire visited for the first time, fielding the 'all-resistless' Graces. It is the match immortalised by the poet, Francis Thompson. When that restless mix of drugs, illness and religiosity rendered him unable, because of emotional tumult, to join friends at Lord's to watch his favourites in 1907, he stayed at home and wrote cricket's most idyllic poem, *At Lord's*, with its haunting refrain of 'My Hornby and my Barlow long ago'. Messrs Hornby and Barlow inspired with a 100 first-wicket stand, Hornby made exactly 100 and W.G. Grace weighed in with an undefeated half century, in a rain-affected match that ended in a draw, just favouring Lancashire.

It was, however, the crowd that took the immediate eye. There were 4,500 on the Thursday, 10,000 on the Friday and 14,000 on the Saturday, with according to some estimates, 2,000 more people who evaded the frail entrance gates. This total of around 30,000 was unprecedented. There were four turnstiles but these were insufficient. Turnstiles incidentally were invented in 1871, the same year that, rather appositely, bank holidays were introduced. The ground was overrun; the farm wagons deployed as temporary stands proved inadequate; there was ugly encroachment onto the field of play; and the quick-tempered Hornby himself plunged in among the truculent spectators and delivered some 'hard knocks'.

The next match was the first visit of an Australian team to Old Trafford. Grandstands were erected; policing was increased; stout roping was provided; refreshment kiosks and tents were supplied; popular admission was doubled for this one fixture, amid outraged yelps, from sixpence to a shilling (5p, for the post-decimally illiterate). About 15,000 attended another rain-interrupted occasion, during which Charlie Bannerman impressed for the visitors with his hefty hitting, while, in the home interest, Rev Vernon Royle, first in a long list of swoopingly rapid Lancastrian cover points, was the star.

Playing Up at the Two Old Traffords

The two games netted the club approximately £1,500. The spectre of financial distress was lifted. It was a turning point, there was a realisation that the future lay with spectator interest. Hitherto it had been a matter of pleasing the members, both playing and watching, with some paid help if it was at all affordable. Henceforward the mood leaned more to spectators as the motive force, their sixpences and shillings, even their florins (10p) to stand on the polite pavilion side, funding a more welcoming and functional stadium in which a more efficient and better-waged squad of professionals would, in harmonious balance with the top amateurs, accomplish itself so competently that the crowds would expand and the cycle of money, gates and results be further sustained.

In these early years of championship cricket, there was no official table. It was left to the sporting press to oblige, usually with the defiantly Victorian yardstick of fewest losses, and, with the number of fixtures played by each county very variable, there was occasionally confusion and argument. Lancashire proceeded to win or share this unofficial Championship, as judged by many pundits, four times in the next few years. In 1879, in Edmund Rowley's final and very moist summer as captain, they shared the title with Nottinghamshire, having lost only once, although some contrary voices, including W.G. Grace's, insisted that Yorkshire should be named the champions. In 1880 Albert Neilson Hornby brought his martial and autocratic mien to bear on the captaincy, a position he was to hold for many years, after which he was an authoritarian President for many more. Lancashire won the title again in 1881 when they went undefeated through the summer, winning ten of their thirteen county matches. They shared the Championship with Nottinghamshire after a rumbustious campaign in 1882, and with Surrey, when the 1889 season produced the peculiarity of three out of eight counties being winners.

Money was spent on the playing surface, including a sound drainage scheme, and on stands, a ladies' pavilion, refreshment rooms, press and telegraph accommodation and other amenities. Amateurs now had their rail and later their hotel expenses met, while the professionals, although still separated from their purported betters, had improved changing rooms that, at least, were situated on the same side as the pavilion, where the amateurs prepared themselves for the fray. Ladies were banned from the pavilion, but they did now have special facilities for 300 of their gender and class; there were 600 lady subscribers at this point. By the 1890s there were nearly 2,000 members, while crowds of 5,000 were regarded as minimal and commonplace and 10,000 no rarity. On the second day of the Australian match in 1884 there was a ground record of 19,000, although it would be wrong to suggest that all had an ideal view. Handsome profits accrued. There were cultural shifts. It was about this time that 'luncheon' replaced 'dinner' at Old Trafford, what some might believe to be a retrograde and effeminate step.

The third Test match ever held in England was played at Old Trafford. The first, in 1880, was at the Oval, organised, ineluctably, by Charles Alcock, who was also chiefly responsible for the first rugby and association football 'home' internationals. The second, in 1882, was also at the Oval. Old Trafford's first was in July 1884, a week or so before the first ever Lord's Test. It was the fourteenth meeting of the two Test playing sides and the match was drawn. Hornby, Pilling,

Barlow and Steel represented the red rose. An umbrella may be metaphorically raised to hide the ominous fact that the first day of Test cricket at Old Trafford was wiped out by rain. Manchester was thereafter a regular centre for Test cricket; the 1888 affair was one of the shortest on record, England winning by an innings before the second day's lunch, while Nottingham's William Gunn scored the first Test century at the ground in 1893.

Jack Crossland, always struggling with accusations of throwing, and Arthur Mold were the main quick bowlers over this decade or so, with Frank Sugg, Arthur Paul and Albert Ward bolstering the batting. Aside from Alec Watson, there was the tragicomic figure of Johnny Briggs. He is Lancashire's leading all-rounder, quite simply by dint of being the only Lancastrian to score over 10,000 runs and take over 1,000 - in fact, over 1,500 - wickets, while he was another who adorned the covers with speed and adeptness. He was the most cheerful of cricketers, his chubby features twinkling with happiness and his plump frame full of bounce as he plied his left-hand spin for England and Lancashire, cavorted at cover point and struck handsome blows with the bat. Brian Statham is his only rival as the most popular player in Lancashire's saga. Beset by severe epilepsy, he also had mental problems and died in Cheadle Asylum in 1902, like Richard Pilling, in his 30s.

He was replete with a child-like guile; he was a delightful prankster and, without cricket to occupy him, he could seem wayward and distracted. His funeral was watched by over 4,000 people, almost like an average gate at Old Trafford. It was timed at the dinner (let us persist with the old convention) break, so that workers could flock by tram and a special train to Stretford Cemetery for the interment of 'Boy' Briggs. It was as if a benignly amusing child had been viciously struck down.

Johnny Briggs was the first - and best - of the popular heroes, which the great hordes in attendance at the football and cricket arenas, and the many more who heard and read of their exciting exploits, were taking to their hearts. It may seem a far cry from Johnny Briggs to David Beckham, but hero-worship was to mark the ascendancy of the spectator element that now dominated both the County Championship and the Football League.

County cricket was becoming more aware of its potential and moves were made to organise it more competently. A County Cricket Council met in the late 1880s, one of its jobs, under strong media pressure, to resolve the knotty issue of the Championship. The Council duly proposed three divisions of eight counties each, with promotion and relegation, and with a points system based on subtracting losses from wins and ignoring draws. 1890 was thus the first officially recognised championship and Surrey won it. Somerset, the best of the second-class counties, arranged first-class fixtures for 1891 - but the bottom club, Sussex, stayed put. The process of expanding the first-class roster began, with six more counties enrolling before the century's end, making fifteen at that stage. In other words, there was promotion but not relegation. In 1894 the MCC, with the counties' approval, proclaimed that in future there would be first-class counties and non-first-class counties, without further sub-division. The weaker brethren formed the Minor Counties Association in 1895.

Similarly, an attempt to establish a cup competition for county cricket floundered miserably in 1873. It was not easy to transfer football's winning mechanisms to county cricket. One reason was the open-endedness of cricket. Most sports either assess the position after a given time, as in the football codes or hockey, or agree a target, as sets for tennis, 501 for darts or the most economic completion of a golf round. Cricket, perhaps jerked quite quickly by improved pitches and batsmanship from a period when four innings were normally comfortably negotiated on a fine day to a more long-drawn out affair, chose neither option. With rain increasingly accepted as a hazard in more effete days, the threat of the abandoned or abjectly drawn match undermined the competitive ethic. It would be nearly a hundred years before, by a drastic and, for many, unhappy reconstruction of the sport, this question would be realistically addressed.

As for Lancashire, their first official championship came in 1897, although they had successfully retained top-of-the-table positions for most of the decade. In 1897 Arthur Mold and Johnny Briggs found more stalwart help on the bowling front, while Archie MacLaren, averaging a mighty 56, together with a durable display from his professional colleagues, ensured the batting was in good fettle. They just scraped ahead of the powerful Surrey team in an exciting end to the season. The membership mounted to over 3,000 and 200,000 were now paying annually at the turnstiles, yielding frequent crowds of 20,000, with even the occasional assemblage of 28,000, as for the Australian match in 1899. Finances were stable and the county committee took a deep breath and forked out £24,732 to purchase the ground outright, together with some adjoining packets of land. It transpired to be a sensible piece of property marketing.

Over the next ten years, during the time when Manchester United was formed and moved to be Lancashire's near-neighbours, the county eleven usually stayed close to the top of the table. They won the championship once more before the outbreak of the 1914-1918 war. This was in 1904. Lancashire were undefeated. The legendary S.F. Barnes had played a couple of grudging seasons for Lancashire before removing his genius back to the leagues, where the ratio of monetary gains to work-rate was more acceptable to that irascible figure. Lancashire's bowling looked a little bereft, but the spinner and useful bat, Willis Cuttell and the left-handed Jim Hallows (another sickly but valiant specimen and epileptic, who died aged 36) combined with the fizzy pace bowler, the whole-hearted amateur Walter Brearley, to take lots of wickets. Other amateurs, like the Australian medical student, Leslie Poidevin, and the breezy left-hander, Harold Garnett, contributed helpful runs, while Jack Sharp, a brave all-rounder and, as an impressive right-winger for Aston Villa and Everton, one of that tiny band of double internationals, also made commendable efforts in the county's cause.

These were the mainstays. Yet, when all respect to their hearty contributions has been appreciatively paid, they were as journeymen compared with the team's three masters. Rather like the Middlesex success of 1947, with Bill Edrich and Denis Compton in rampant form, this was a rare title in which world-class batting rather than world-class bowling was the dominant factor. With Archie MacLaren, Reggie Spooner and J.T. Tyldesley in their brave pomp, the daily destruction of opposition bowling adopted the remorseless yet swift character of a pounding blitzkrieg. Runs were scored freely and quickly, the panache of these batsmen perhaps more reminiscent of the colourful cavalry charge than the grey panzer advance.

Reggie Spooner, next in the sublime lineage of Lancashire cover points, had wrists that were as fondly observed as David Beckham's right instep. Distracted from overmuch cricket because of his soldiering duties, his sinuous arms dispatched the ball with the crack of a pistol shot, as reporters raided dictionaries and jostled over adjectives like 'majestic' and 'regal', struggling to convey some cue as to his imperious fluency. In idle moments at a cricket match, one of my favoured reveries is to daydream of MacLaren and Spooner, who, with 368 at Liverpool in 1903 in 210 minutes, raced to Lancashire's first-wicket record, opening the batting for Lancashire in a limited overs match, with a perfect pitch, regulation 70-yard boundaries, restricted fielding and bowling rules, and one of today's anonymous county 'attacks', if that is not too robust a word. And then for Johnny Tyldesley to come in, should either of those Ivanhoes fall perchance in tourney, as a kind of Robin Hood replacement. One might predict an average of 400 an innings.

If the Golden Age of cricket was a classical one, then Neville Cardus was right to apostrophise Archie MacLaren as the Brutus figure, 'the noblest Roman of them all'. Given, in absolute contrast to his noble grandeur on the cricket field, his flawed character and his inept business transactions, Mark Anthony might have been an even more accurate Roman appellation. Nonetheless, the exaggerated hoist of his left leg and the extravagant curl of his back-lift, preparatory to the straightness and potency of his drive and the grandiose flourish of his follow-through, made him the most thrilling of batsmen to watch. His 424 for Lancashire at Taunton in 1895, still the highest first-class score by an English-born player, was the acme of the Golden Age and Archie MacLaren was one of its most magnificent protagonists.

John Thomas Tyldesley, deemed to be the 'Player' who batted like a 'Gentleman', was one of only a few professionals who, in the late Victorian and Edwardian epoch, could stand with pride beside Ranji, C.B. Fry and that amazing group of dazzling amateur batsmen. With nearly 38,000 runs in all first-class cricket, he simply butchered bowling, his bad wicket play and his obliteration of leg spin being especially notable. Of medium but athletic build, with the conventional tribute to Mexican banditry adorning his upper lip, he was the diffident assassin. Sportsmen, like murderers, do not always reveal their character during business hours. Disarming, if quietly assured and withdrawn away from the crease, he was, rather like the mild-mannered Dr Crippen once he had decided to slay his bumptious wife, brutally homicidal when he reached it. Possibly his delight - J.T. Tyldesley that is, not Crippen - in whirling what he called 'buxom Lancashire lasses' around the dance floor gave him the agility, and his taste for the calming doctrines of Independent Methodism the composure, to commit such lethal deeds day in and day out. One morning in 1930 he ate his breakfast, sat down to pull on his boots and died. He left the world in civilian mode; had he chosen to leave it in his contrariwise cricketing character, he would have leapt from the roof of Manchester Town Hall in Albert Square.

Playing Up at the Two Old Traffords

As Lancashire enjoyed this purplish patch, adding their own sheen to the essential glory of cricket as it peaked on the spacious greenswards of Edwardian England, Manchester United, awaiting and then newly arrived at Old Trafford, were eager to add laurels to their solitary First Division title.

This they did, twice over. Still at Bank Street, and with Old Trafford under construction, they delighted the fans by a gratifying success in the FA Cup. Brighton, Everton and Blackburn Rovers were removed with varying degrees of assurance, before United faced Burnley in the sixth round. With Burnley in the lead and with less than 20 minutes remaining, a bitter snowstorm swept over the Pennine fastness of Turf Moor, leaving the markings hidden and the referee on the verge of hypothermia. The match was abandoned; United won the replay; a Harold Halse goal denied fancied Newcastle United in the semi-final - and the Reds were in the Final for the first time of many.

Their opponents were Bristol City, built around the indefatigable England centre-half, Billy Wedlock. The match was at Crystal Palace and the attendance was 68,000. United stayed at Chingford overnight, travelled to London by train on Saturday morning, then took a bus to the ground like everyone else. Truth to tell, it was a disappointing and rugged encounter, with the two centre-halves, Wedlock and Charlie Roberts, defending commandingly and, predictably, Billy Meredith the only attacker of exceptional noteworthiness. He created scenes of alarm among the Bristol defence and, after 22 minutes, he crossed the ball deliberately into the path of Harry Halse. His shot struck the bar forcibly and Sandy Turnbull, although carrying a thigh injury, was the one with the smartest reflexes. His goal was the only one of the match. Vince Hayes retired with a broken rib but United clung on to their goal, as the game grew increasingly scrappy and United, wearing white shirts with a scarlet trim for the occasion, were scolded by the referee for time-wasting.

Charlie Roberts gratefully accepted the cup from Lord Charles Beresford; after dinner, the players and officials relaxed at the Alhambra Music Hall, and then it was the train back to Manchester. The supporters thronged on to Manchester Central Station and lined the short distance from there to the town hall and then to a hotel close to Bank Street. The band played triumphant melody and there was a torchlight procession for the players as they were transported back to the city centre for dinner at the Midland Hotel. It would be a long generation before there would be such another night.

Over the winter of 1910/11, the first full season at the brand-new stadium, United remained in authoritative command. Enoch West, signed from Nottingham Forest and invariably addressed affectionately as 'Knocker', formed a dual spearhead with Sandy Turnbull. Their shared darting strikes rivalled the lightning salvoes of Archie MacLaren and Reggie Spooner. United enjoyed a phenomenal run but Aston Villa were also in surging form. In the penultimate game, Villa caned United and all hung on the last match of the campaign. United, at home to Sunderland, romped to the solace of a 5-1 win, and then the crowd gathered patiently to wait for news from Anfield, where Villa were the visitors. It was tremulously announced that Liverpool had won - and Manchester United enjoyed their second First Division title.

Red Shirts and Roses

Just as Lancashire, in the years around the turn of the century, had bid fair to produce the first of their several great sides, so had Manchester United responded in kind. The bi-partisan supporter had much to cheer, with the summer spent gasping at the hussar-like assaults of MacLaren, Spooner and Tyldesley, the winter employed in admiring the resolute balance of the Reds.

Just as one might have been instructed, as I was as a child at St Paul's Sunday School, to memorise and chant the names of the Twelve Apostles, should it not be equally obligatory for the issue of Manchester United fans to be able to recite in suitably hushed tones the names of that first-ever cup-winning team?

Moger; Stacey and Hayes; Duckworth, Roberts and Bell; Meredith, Halse, J. Turnbull, Sandy Turnbull and Wall. These were the heroes of Crystal Palace and the nucleus of the team that won United's first three trophies. There was the immense figure of Harry Moger the reliable custodian, as journalists of the day might have called him, and George Stacey (the uncompromising miner's sobriquet of 'Silent' is not much in vogue among 21st century footballers) and Vince Hayes (a Miles Platting lad, cheerful in the face of plentiful injuries, who, surprisingly, coached the Norwegian team in the 1912 Olympics) formed the tough full-back partnership.

The backbone of the team was the half-back trio and, as late as the 1950s, most of United's fans could roll off those three names as effortlessly as they might those of Freeman, Hardy and Willis, claiming them as the finest ever such threesome. Dick Duckworth, consistently sharp; Charlie Roberts, tall and quick-thinking, and an attacking centre-half; and Alec Bell, unfussy and neat in all he did - it was probably, and allowing for that soupçon of prejudice that may creep into the most disinterested analysis, the most effective half-back line-up in club football until half-back line-ups disintegrated in the 1960s.

Billy Meredith, like his gifted descendant, Stanley Matthews, bonded skill to stamina, understanding that perspiration and inspiration are the co-partners of genius. With 48 Welsh caps, a profusion of millinery for that age, his gauche bandy gait belied his exceptional pace and dribbling magic, the exhilarating prelude to his exquisite crossing of the ball, and unlike Stan Matthews, he was also a valued goal-scorer. With something of Sherlock Holmes about his lanky frame and sharp, knowing features, he gripped a toothpick between his clenched teeth, an aid to concentration and a unique personal emblem. An anecdote testifying to his perfectionism tells of, having kicked a corner behind on the Saturday, he broke into Old Trafford on the Sunday to practice corner kicks, muttering the while, 'there are 120 yards to aim at'.

His fellow forwards greedily gobbled up the spicy treats he fed them. Sandy Turnbull, stocky, deliberate, his widow's peak gracing that deadly forehead, was the main recipient, but Harold Halse, slightly built but extremely confident, was a superb opportunist striker at inside-right. James Turnbull, who gave way to 'Knocker' West, was the ideal foil for the more contemplative Sandy, his energetic dash discomforting many a central defence, while the England outside-left, the sleek George Wall, tormented opponents with his tricky pace on the other side of the park. What is more, he was still playing in his 40s - for the Manchester Ship Canal FC, representing his post-football employers across the bridge from Old Trafford.

Playing Up at the Two Old Traffords

For an amalgam of reasons, both Lancashire CCC and Manchester United FC failed to cheer their fans very much in the last years before World War I. Nevertheless, under the generalship of Archie MacLaren and Charlie Roberts, they had set high competitive standards. Both teams were nationally known and their star players household names.

7.

Team Building Exercises
in Stretford

TWO CLUBS on two neighbouring grounds producing the initial two of their series of celebrated teams and making two sets of national headlines in the two decades before the First World War…that was the position as the curtains were drawn on the Edwardian age. Despite the self-evident dissimilarities, there were some striking resemblances in the building of the MacLaren and Roberts' task-forces. This arose from the two clubs having made corresponding compromises with the challenges set by the fused elements of spectatordom and professionalism.

Allowing for some of the shifting cultural conditions that accompanied the changes, the professionalisation of cricket and football pursued roughly the same route, with Lancashire and Manchester United illustrating the process clearly enough. The first cricket professionals had often been employed on the estates of the propertied toffs who assembled teams to play for wagers: Thomas Waymark, 'the father of cricket professionals', was reputedly hired as a groom at Goodwood, the Duke of Richmond's place in Sussex, whilst Thomas Aylward was a bailiff for the Kentish patron Sir Horace Mann and, allegedly, 'a poor one', maybe indicating that it was something of a sinecure. As the county clubs struggled into existence, and particularly as the travelling circus of Exhibition elevens faded, one finds, as with Manchester and Lancashire, that professionals were hired, usually to reinforce the bowling

In the world of football, jobs were offered to likely players, the works teams obviously well placed for that purpose. The pre-United Newton Heath's 'professors' were of this ilk. In the 1880s several Welshmen arrived, one or two of them, like the hefty full-back Jack Powell, of international calibre. Scotland though was the major source of reinforcements. In 1887, so the tale runs, Pat O'Donnell walked all the way from Glasgow and obtained employment with the railway company and a place in the football team. The semi-professionalism - to use a charitable epithet - of the clubs, such as Preston North End, Blackburn Rovers and Bolton Wanderers, in the textile belt created much stress on the FA. In 1882 that controlling body had sought to outlaw payment other than legitimate expenses, itself ever a running ulcer of difficulty. However, in 1885, with certain limitations, professionalism was legitimised and in the same year J.H. Forrest, the Blackburn Rovers teenager, became England's first paid international, amid a battery of conservationist squeals.

Part of the antagonism was to do with the import trade in players. When Major, later Sir Francis, Marindin - an Old Etonian who played in goal for and skippered the Royal Engineers in the first FA Cup Final and was now President of the FA - refereed the 1886/87 semi-final, he entered the winners' dressing room. It was West Bromwich

Albion. They had beaten the Preston North End 'Invincibles', inclusive of what would now be called a 'foreign legion'. 'Are you all Englishmen?' he cried. 'Yes, sir' returned the Throstles in loyal and lusty voice, whereupon he presented them with the ball and wished them luck in the final, where, sadly, they lost to Aston Villa. Sir Francis would receive a dusty answer were he to raise that non-politically correct query in some Premiership dressing rooms nowadays. Even the tolerant *Manchester Evening News*, in 1887, apropos the Newton Heath line-up, asserted 'we do not recognise a local man in the team'.

Parochialism may have a wider ambit now than then, but the same complaints are today made about 'overseas' players in cricket and European and South American stars in football. There are other modern features that are redolent of late Victorian and Edwardian musings on professionalism. Most of these were to do with either control or corruption. The first was an anxiety about reserving the services of a paid servant of the football or cricket club and the second concerned a raft of ways in which illegalities crept into the economic equation.

The cricket professionals, having enjoyed the sturdy independence of the Exhibition elevens, did not always take kindly to the encroachment upon their liberties of the county system. S.F. Barnes, perhaps the best bowler ever to have played, was the supreme example. A story is told that testifies both to his intransigence and to Archie MacLaren's true-blooded phlegm. Spirited almost from nowhere by MacLaren to tour Australia in 1901/02, his incipient Scargillism was already in evidence by the time the leaking tub in which they sailed was shaken by tempest in the Bay of Biscay. Archie MacLaren consoled a terrified young amateur with the soothing speculation that, were they to drown, 'that bugger Barnes' would drown alongside them.

Professionals plied their trade from county to county. Roger Iddison, for instance, contrived to play for both Lancashire and Yorkshire, and also Cheshire, as well as being the principal organiser of the United North of England XI and a member of the United Yorkshire XI. Their first loyalty, in a precarious trade, was to their pocket.

Here beginneth the saga of birthright. The desire to use players born in the county was really motivated by the perceived need to halt poaching and excess mobility among these jobbing professionals. Amateurs were rarely requested to present their birth certificates to sceptical committees. They may have had family or property connections in the shire or they may have taken up some career posting, a clerical living or a schoolmastership, in the area. It was enough that they lived locally and were subscribing county members. It is a matter of quiet and satisfying enjoyment that Lord Hawke, the autocratic tsar of the successful Yorkshire teams for many years from 1883 onwards, was born at Gainsborough, Lincolnshire and not on God's acre.

In 1873, after close debate, with, yet again, Charles Alcock taking a hand in the proceedings, a regulation was agreed by the counties and endorsed by MCC insisting that one county per season was sufficient and that it might be determined by birth or residence, based on a two year domicile. This honoured a long tradition in county cricket and remained the foundation of qualification for many years. As we have observed, the FA, under concerted pressure mainly from the Lancashire elite clubs, legalised professionalism in 1885. It is of interest that, still with Charles Alcock at the

FA's helm, the 1885/86 rules for cup contests included a clause that competing professionals should have been born or resident for two years within a six mile radius of the club ground or headquarters and the one-club/one-season condition was also included. It was not long before the southern clubs, led by Arsenal, signed on professionals.

However, the chief difference lay in the business-like character of the footballer's contract, arising formally from the FA's decision to enforce an annual registration of professionals. This eventually created the 'wage-slave' mentality, as it came to be pejoratively termed. In any event, both first-class County and Football League clubs benefited from the strong class element in the bargaining process, with, in the culture of the time, the master having the whip-hand socially and economically as well as legally over the servant. In any event, most paid cricketers and footballers, given the relatively reasonable lifestyle and payment, were only too pleased to forego the drudgery of the collier's pick or spinner's loom.

Both games, in their professional dispensation, were subject to the usual pitfalls that seem to lie in wait for the monetarily inclined. In its gambling era, cricket had been haunted by scandals that make the antics of the late W.J. Cronje seem like harmless flutters. The 'Green Man and Still' in London's Oxford Street had, in the late 18th century, been the centre for professionals both to hawk their talents and to consider alluring bribes. As late as 1817 the Nottinghamshire and England game at Lord's is said to have been sold on both sides, suggesting the implausible vision of bowlers trying not to take wickets and batsmen just as urgently attempting to get out. Until the coming of spread betting in the 20th century, with the artificial formalism of limited-overs cricket, bribery was an imprecise art in cricket, where fortune is notoriously fickle. The simpler, quicker formula of football was more vulnerable to corruption.

Thus the Football League, even after the reluctant acceptance of professionalism, found itself caught up in all manner of corrupt practices. In 1904 both Manchester United and City were among several clubs punished for financial malpractice by the FA, while it was the near destruction of Manchester City in the 1904/07 period (riven by FA investigation into illegal wage payments and transfer irregularities, to say nothing of alleged match-fixing by players, including Billy Meredith) that led to the strengthening of their neighbours, courtesy of the adroit negotiations of Ernest Mangnall, already discussed.

Next the exorbitant investment of J.H. Davies attracted the attention of the FA. Manchester United became a limited company in 1907, a status that had been or would be adopted by all Football League clubs. However, the FA was worried about the paucity of the published accounts and felt that Davies treated the concern as his personal fiefdom, rather like some pre-incarnation of Chelsea's Russian owner, Roman Abramovich. A report in 1910 proposed that United be more strictly managed and that shares be made available on the public market.

It was about the same time that, on the labour side, United players, led by Charlie Roberts and Billy Meredith, campaigned vigorously for the rights of the Players' Union. They tried to revive the dormant carcass of an ailing association, started in 1898, by affiliation with the Federation of Trades Unions, but the FA and the Football League combined to quell the agitation. The United squad, almost 30 players, cup medallists and all, were suspended and forced to train at the Manchester Athletic Club at Fallowfield. Charlie Roberts, the fearless and principled leader in this dispute, refused to be swayed, but a settlement had to be reached, otherwise the start of the 1909/10 season would have been wrecked. Perhaps his militant reputation was a factor in Roberts' transfer in 1912, for £1,500 to Oldham Athletic, whom he led the next season to their best-ever league placement, runners-up in Division One. Charlie Roberts was later to found a successful tobacconist's business.

Worse was to follow. The Great War obviously encroached on the 1914/15 season, although the various competitions were completed under grave difficulties. Some players felt that, with the likely end of football and their own involvement in the hostilities, it was time to make whatever flimsy hay was available while the sun still wanly shone. The home fixture with Liverpool, which United won 2-0, attracted abnormal gambling on the exact score and a match-fixing scandal ensued. As a consequence, eight players were banned for life, among them Knocker West and Sandy Turnbull, who had emerged as a bit of a hothead during the union strife. It should be observed that Sandy Turnbull gave his life for his country, being killed in the Arras sector of the Western Front in 1917, having enlisted with the Footballer's battalion in 1915. Arthur Whalley, a tough half-back who was also involved in these betting shenanigans, served with the Middlesex Regiment, reached the rank of Sergeant and was badly wounded at Passchendaele, but he recuperated well and played post-war.

In the world of cricket the nearest to such problems, as far as the Lancashire club was concerned, were comparatively mild issues to do with the residential qualification and with shamateurism. There was considerable acrimony between the Nottinghamshire and Lancashire hierarchies in the 1880s because of the latter's recruitment, among them Johnny Briggs of Sutton-in-Ashfield, of the former's offspring. Similarly, recollecting that his business acumen was in inverse proportion to his batting prowess, Archie MacLaren received a testimonial of over £1,200 in 1905 and was appointed player-coach for the 1922 summer at a fee of £550. Typically, he asked for advances of £350 before the season opened. J.T. Tyldesley, who became the quietly competent coach the following year, was paid only £300, while MacLaren received £105 severance payment. And A.C. MacLaren heartily detested being regarded as an employee.

Archie MacLaren's ineptitude as an economic man underlines the fact that the 'Gentleman and Player' distinction was a social, rather than an economic one, although as J.T. Tyldesley might have added, had he not been a reticent Independent Methodist, the two often go hand in hand. MacLaren, like W.G. Grace and some other misnamed amateurs, fell between the sociological stools: they came from a social class that made it difficult, if not impossible, to become professionals, but their family circumstances made it difficult, if not impossible, to play as pure amateurs. It was a problem that was to haunt first-class cricket for many years. The Manchester sports outfitters where every Mancunian of a certain age probably shopped - Alec Watson and Mitchell; Tyldesley and Holbrook - provided branding evidence that canny professionals sometimes could make appreciable headway in the sordid world of commerce, where some amateurs were unable to shine.

Red Shirts and Roses

There were occasional rifts in the world of cricket, the chief one being the strike of 1896, when five senior Test players asked for their fee of £10, plus expenses, to be doubled for the Australian match at the Oval. It is intriguing that the nearest to cricketing militancy and the struggle to legitimise the footballer's trade union came during the years when the fierceness of workers' campaigns had been raised more than a notch. There was the Match Girls' strike of 1888 and the London Dock strike in 1889. 1911 was marked by a brief railway shutdown, a noisy strike of seamen and dockers and the start of extensive mining disputes, extending into 1912. The number of trade unionists sprang from 1.5m in 1892 to 4.1m in 1914. There is a plausible case that suggests that, had it not been for the outbreak of World War I, the British state could have been radically crippled at worst and radically transformed at best by collective industrial action.

The football and cricket actions were gentle stuff, but the cricketers did have an argument. In 1896 the amateurs, including Ranjitsinhji and F.S. Jackson, would receive £25 expenses for a Test match, with W.G. Grace on £40, while the amateur Australians were expecting to rake in £500 each from the tour. The strikers were faced down, although their wages would soon be increased, but it did publicise the oddity of a situation where cricket professionals earned, on average, £150 a season and amateurs often received £20, even £30 or £50 per game. Moreover, the 'pros' had to pay for travel, meals - including lunches - and accommodation, often amounting to £4 a match. Bonuses were paid to both groups by some counties, with the amateurs maybe getting £100 to the professional's £50. It might be added, in parenthesis, that one or two jockeys were already being paid in thousands, where footballers and cricketers were lucky to make hundreds. Jockeys were among the best-known sports personalities of the hour: in the 40 years before World War I a handful of top riders, like Fred Archer, earned as much as £75,000 in a career.

By 1914 there were almost 5,000 football professionals mostly earning £3 or £4 a week, and about 500 cricket professionals earning a little more, with top players perhaps making perhaps £6 or £7 a week. Benefits helped, with J.T. Tyldesley netting a substantial and record £3,111 in 1906. In any event, both sets of professionals were earning more than their brothers in the working classes that they had left behind in the mills, pits and foundries. In the years before the First World War the average manual worker's annual income wage was £100; the average paid cricketer would now have made over £200.

The middle class and working class gulf was more apparent in county cricket than in the Football League, simply because the middle-class and working-class representatives were combining in the same activity. Archie MacLaren and J.T. Tyldesley would share a massive stand at Old Trafford and then go their separate social ways, like Officer and Sergeant Major. This exemplified the enduring difference between the Football League, as represented by Manchester United, and the County Championship, as represented by Lancashire. With one or two exceptions, the football teams were all professional and thus working class in origin, while the cricket teams made an accommodation to compound the social classes.

Team Building Exercises in Stretford

However, the peculiarly cosmopolitan cauldron of urban and industrial existence in Lancashire caused the pre-1914 teams at the two Old Traffords, despite this glaring social anomaly, to be developed on a much closer parallel. It was here that the factor adjacent to professionalism, that is, spectatordom, came into its own. Under the pressure of their urban surrounds, both clubs had rather abruptly become a part of the entertainments industry.

First, they had shifted swiftly from being a playing club, be it for cricketing merchants or footballing railwaymen, to clubs offering a leisure facility - concomitant with going to the theatre - to the city and its environs. With Lancashire, there was an intermediate stage whereby it was recognised that many members would prefer to watch than play, although there may have been something resembling that step in the old Newton Heath Locomotive work-place. Once into that mode, the circle of enticing more spectators to pay for improved players and facilities rolled on relentlessly. In their best years before 1914 Lancashire would have 200,000 shelling out their sixpences at the gate, a matter of 5,000 a day, rising to 15,000, plus members, on a good Saturday, whilst Manchester United were attracting an average of well over 20,000 per home game, with a seasonal tally approaching 500,000.

The model of Preston North End and Blackburn Rovers, with their emphasis on training and team-building, much of it to the sniffy disgust of the southern amateur factions, obviously affected neighbouring Manchester United. They quickly adopted the mould of professionalism, with all the corresponding aspects of transfers and the like. With cricket, the amateur ethos had endured more strongly. Many counties adhered strongly to the amateur convention, using professionals sporadically and, come summer vacations, ditching them for the returning schoolteacher or vicar. This was apart from the rather different approaches of Nottinghamshire and Yorkshire, where the professional ethic had been cultivated in the more flexible trades of wool, lace-work and hosiery, and the county elevens had remained strikingly powerful but in a consistently parochial tradition. Lancashire were the protagonists, along with Surrey, of what, to pre-empt a later coinage, might be called a 'third way'.

This was founded in a resolution to create a team of which Lancastrians would be proud and for which they would be willing to pay. The intention, probably only half-consciously at the onset, was to produce a team for the area, not of the area. Of course, were the requisite players to be available, as often they were, from the Lancashire terrain, then all was well and good, for it heartened the members and spectators that much more warmly. Indeed, it might be argued that the success of the county team encouraged cricket in the region, not least in the growth of competitive league cricket. This was to have an always slightly ambivalent relation with the county club, but the dates of formation - the Bolton and District League, 1889, what became the Lancashire League, 1890, and what became the Central Lancashire League, 1892 - suggest that there was some cause and effect.

The industrial districts of south and east Lancashire were, from the early industrial era, attuned, as London had always been, to incomers. The inward migration of mill workers from across the country, the lively influx of Welsh and Scottish contingents (onto Merseyside as well as into Manchester) and then the Irish immigration of the 1840s were examples of this cosmopolitan disposition. With cotton proving to be the first of the global staples, there was an awareness of peoples across the planet, with, for instance, a pertinent German presence in Manchester: Charles Hallé is one example; another is the one my grandmother worked for, who had his windows xenophobically smashed when the Great War broke out.

With, those broken panes aside, its mental set less chauvinistic than some other regions (where the attitude of 'here's a stranger; throw a brick at him' still ruled) the extended Manchester region, not unlike a smaller version of the United States at much the same period, was something of a melting pot, and anxious to flex its cultural muscles with music, with theatre, with the arts, with sport. It was an approach that caused some unrest in sporting circles, whether it was Scots playing for United or Nottinghamshire lads playing for Lancashire. Like United, Lancashire soon applied the yardstick of the best available for the job, so that, unlike in other counties, there was little compassion shown to amateurs who were not talented enough to displace incumbent professionals.

As Marriott Edgar wrote in his epic poem, *The Runcorn Ferry*, when the Ramsbottom family were locked in severe disagreement with old Ted the Ferryman over his uncompromising regime of twopence per trip:

> *The further they paddled the deeper it got,*
> *But they wouldn't give in once begun;*
> *In the spirit that's made Lancashire what she is -*
> *They'd sooner be drownded than done.*

Both Lancashire and Manchester United were charging hard cash at the gate; they were rightly obliged to assemble the best repertory of players they could. It was, then, the Lancashire and Manchester United supporters that characterised the teams, not necessarily the players.

Now that every day we hear evidence of how the genetic endowment of a human being and, say, a banana only differs three-fifths, the sacred claims of birthright look even more preposterous than they did. Humans share 66% of the genetic make-up of a chicken and 88% of that of a rat. Moreover, being born in a particular place must be one of the most arbitrary ways of human assessment ever invented and, as we saw, the driving force was chiefly to stop pragmatic professionals from shifting camp too often. How pathetic were those tales of heavily pregnant women being rushed inside the frontiers of Yorkshire, so that, were they have to have a son and were he to be a top-rate cricketer, he would qualify for that inward-looking shire. Did they - do they - believe that some metaphysical cloud hung precisely over the broad acres and that, by arcane process, it breathed Yorkist fumes into the lungs of the newborn babe?

The residential qualification had more logic to it, in that it challenged the sportsman to associate himself with the relevant district and become immersed in its culture. In that regions have a cultural persona, it is certainly created and passed on by learning rather than genes. No St Cecilia's virus or third tonsil is invested in the physiological make-up of the Welsh: because of a particular combine of social features, singing became an important attribute in parts of Wales, and accomplishment in that field a mark of great self-esteem. This led to an intense association of music and 'Welshness', but it was never hereditary in any biological sense.Thus, in so far as Manchester or anywhere else has 'characteristics', they are a matter wholly of nurture and not nature. The example of poor Richard Pilling may be cited. He was born of Lancashire parents in Bedford in 1855 and they soon moved back north and settled in Church, near Accrington, when he was but an infant. Inducted into that society, he was very soon substantially more 'Lancastrian', in so far as the term has any meaning, than someone born in Accrington who moved as a toddler to Bedford.

The case of William Evans Midwinter springs to mind. He was born in St Briavels in the Forest of Dean in 1851 and ten years later his family emigrated to Australia, his father, John Midwinter, fancying his chance in the gold rush. He became a valuable all-round cricketer and played in the very first Test match in 1877, taking 5 for 28 in England's first innings. Known picturesquely as 'the Sandhurst Infant' and 'the Bendigo Giant', it came to the wily Dr Grace's attention that he had a Gloucestershire birth qualification. He soon became the world's first transoceanic cricket commuter, steaming backwards and forwards, chasing, with Victoria, the Australian season and, with Gloucestershire, the English summer. He also contrived to be the only man to have played for Australia against England and England against Australia at cricket. Battered by a series of domestic tragedies, he died in the Kew Lunatic Asylum, Melbourne, in 1890 aged only 39. Whatever else, it is difficult to envision him as some sort of rubicund-cheeked, rustic Gloucestershire figure.

My family tradition has it that he was my great-grandfather's cousin. The Midwinter clan foolishly reversed the Cinderella story, tumbling from riches to rags over the centuries. They were originally wool broggers or brokers of some eminent stature in the medieval south-west - one diary entry of a rival woolman in the middle ages reads bitingly, 'Thomas Midwinter; would to God we were rid of him'. My feeble branch, with the wool trade in decline in the south-west and cotton booming in the northwest, trekked to Manchester in 1835 and the rest is anything but history. With some 40 great aunts and uncles, many of them with issue of their own, I was, as a child, very familiar with the eclectic usage of 'cousin', or of 'aunt' and 'uncle', to cover a multitude of kin. It was generational. If they were close to us in age, they were cousins, whatever the degrees of consanguinity. So I was not taken aback by the thought of someone being my great-grandfather's cousin. Just to be on the safe side and, although I have actually visited Cherry Tree Cottage in St Brivels, where 'Mid' was born, I have never checked up on the family tradition just in case, like many a family tradition, it happens to be false.

Another family tradition was that, during his sportive perambulations, he visited my grandfather's family when playing at Old Trafford. I like to think it was either the 'my Hornby and my Barlow' match with Gloucestershire in 1878 (when, seeing you ask, he scored 22 and 25 in a low-scoring encounter) or that very first Test match at Old Trafford in 1884, when he top-scored with 37, representing, seeing you ask, Australia.

Attending an Australian Test at a somewhat later date in 1961, I bumped into a friend and his son and, in a dull passage of play, I attempted to beguile the little boy with this tale of my ancestor with the unique international record. He patently did not believe me, but his father encouraged him to rummage in his satchel, among the crisps and lemonade, for his cricket annual. He looked up the facts and figures; he looked at me with incredulous awe. 'Next time you tell that story', advised my wise friend, 'make it your grandfather'.

It was certainly my grandfather's counsel, on the subject of raconteur-ship, of which he was something of an artist, that, while one should never lie, one might embellish the truth. However, the exploits of Lancashire, under the captaincy of A.N. Hornby and A.C. MacLaren, and of Manchester United, under the powerful leadership of Charlie Roberts, need no refinement. Teams had been built to satisfy the emotional hunger of the Manchester crowds.

Every creed requires its St Paul, its organiser and consolidator. The progenitors, men like Sam Swire and Harry Stafford, had toiled splendidly at the two clubs, but the death-rate among sports clubs was high and there came a moment when that confirmation was needed to guarantee stability and survival. The two Pauline figures in this piece of history-making were, for Lancashire, A.N. Hornby himself, and, for United, the promoter J.H. Davies.

John Henry Davies had experienced, courtesy of Harry Stafford's dog, something of a Damescean conversion on the road to Newton Heath. Until that startling juncture, he knew nothing of football, having previously funded cycling and bowls in the Manchester area. He had, however, two traits beloved of ailing football clubs: enormous wealth and spontaneous generosity. His success in business had rendered him wealthy in his own right, but he had also heeded the strictures of the old Northern injunction that one should always marry for love and always love where there is money. His wife, and the mother of the new owner of Harry Stafford's dog, was Amy Tate, daughter of Henry Tate who, in partnership with Lyle, had built the sugar refining concern. Their major base, given the need for a convenient port for their precious import from the West Indies, was Liverpool. My father, summoned thence from Manchester during the Liverpool blitz, would tell us of fighting the scary fire there, with bubbling syrup and crackling sugar.

With such terrors still 50 years in the future, J.H. Davies was happy to pour money into Manchester United and Old Trafford. As President of Manchester United, with hard cash and equally hard business discipline, he transformed the club from a district to a city-wide team, one that was recognised nationwide. Bespectacled, walrus-moustached and gently smiling, he looked like a slightly chubbier version of Hawley Harvey Crippen, already tangentially introduced as an analogue for the dual J.T. Tyldesley character.

Crippen, one of those criminal curiosities whose name echoes horrendously down the corridors of time, was not much of a monster and, indeed, recent findings have thrown doubt on the safety of a conviction blown up melodramatically by the tabloid press and, in particular, the *John Bull* magazine. A medico of sorts, he allegedly poisoned his wife, the third-rate music hall performer, Belle Elmore, an act justified by Marie Lloyd as a piece of legitimate theatre criticism, and was executed in 1910, just as United started their first full season at Old Trafford and went on to win the Championship. According to the private view of his counsel, Crippen was merely trying to quieten with drugs the overwhelming ardour of his large-bosomed, broad-flanked spouse, the better to preserve his amorous zest for his demure mistress, Ethel le Neve.

Team Building Exercises in Stretford

It might be added that, although born in North America, Crippen, having lived in what is now London NW5, had a Middlesex cricket residential qualification.

We may assume that John Henry and Amy Davies had no such domestic problems, as they reclined in the luxury of spacious Moseley Hall, Cheadle, a mansion where the United players, doubtless abashed by the opulence of it all, were invited to celebrate the winning of the FA Cup or the taking of a Championship. Of course, in Ernest Mangnall Davies had a competent aide, as administrator, coach and motivator. Mangnall was also the grey eminence behind the formation of the Central League for the reserve teams of northern Football League clubs. Whisper it in shocked wrath, he suddenly shifted in 1912 to Manchester City, where he was responsible for the kind of changes in City's fortunes that he had engineered with their rivals.

Where J.H. Davies was a second-generation businessman, making a fortune from a prominent service industry to the thirsty working classes, Albert Neilson Hornby was a successful first-generation industrial child. His family made a pile in Blackburn, where he was born, out of textiles and he joined, somewhat sporadically, the business and lived off the proceeds. It was this sort of new money that underpinned the sudden growth of the Victorian public schools. Desiring a social place among the upper classes, off he went to Harrow, where his unfailing energy made him natural clay for the Harrovian cricketing mould of orthodoxy matched by heroics. A.N. Hornby's biography follows a classic pattern for the age. Having flirted momentarily with Oxford University he returned to Lancashire and, apart from cricket, played football occasionally for Blackburn Rovers, won nine rugby caps for England, boxed (and fearlessly took on rowdies both in Australian and Manchester crowds) shot - he was a Captain with the East Cheshire Militia - and, above all, hunted with the same dash and ferocity which he batted and fielded.

It is said that it was his brisk fielding at Lord's, scattering the spectators and injuring one of them, that led to MCC fixing on formal boundaries. They had been in intermittent use but were not included in the laws of cricket until 1884. Aptly, given Hornby's influence on spectator-oriented cricket, they are an example, like touchlines in the football codes, of the way crowds alter sporting conventions. The long-time *sans frontières* of lacrosse, never a magnet for large gates, is the exception that proves the rule. In the past, cricket scoring had been mostly all running and there were those who regarded boundaries as having an adverse affect on fielding and fitness. When cricketers spoke, in those ancient days, of fielding 'in the country', they were not jesting. As in golf, local rules abounded. Even after World War II my father would, citing antique precedent, assert that a six had to land not over the boundary edge but outside of the Sale ground.

Tiny of stature - hence his nicknames from schooldays of 'Monkey' and 'the Little Wonder' - keen of countenance, with his clipped officer's moustache and short Imperial cut with its defiantly central parting, A.N. Hornby took cold baths that caused W.G. Grace, not the most hygienic of men, to shudder, and rode roughshod over Lancashire cricket for its critical generation. Hasty of temper, cutting in rebuke and generous by nature, he was, as Neville Cardus perceptively remarked, 'The Squire of Lancashire Cricket'. True to social form, this son of the cotton mills resided among the plush meadows of Cheshire, at Parkfield, Nantwich, with his country house cricket ground and his stable of prancing hunters - and, as at Moseley Hall, an occasional hearty and maybe embarrassing welcome for the professionals in his charge. He personified the Manchester man who became the Lancashire gentleman and he was 'the Boss' of Lancashire cricket from taking on the captaincy in 1880 until after the First World War.

Both A.N. Hornby and J.H. Davies, with their money and landed estates, represented the new industrial aristocracy with its re-discovery of old values and, certainly in both their cases, a heavy dosage of *noblesse oblige*. The introduction of the secret ballot in 1872 means that there can be no final assessment, but it is unlikely that either man, when in the polling booth, allowed his stubby pencil to hover long over the name of a candidate proposed by the Labour Party, originally, as from 1900, the Labour Representation Committee. It might be guessed that the Liberal Candidate caused them little further scrutiny of the voting slip.

Davies was a rich brewer. If, as was opined, the Church of England was the Conservative Party at prayer, it was the brewers, incensed by Liberal nonconformist attitudes to licensing, who were generous donors when the collection plate was circulated on behalf of the Tories. There were still over 90,000 on-licenses in 1911, one for every 400 of the population, but they had been severely curtailed. Hornby was a Jorrocks figure, that caricature, first published by R.S. Surtees, of an upwardly mobile grocer, given to huntin', shootin' and fishin'. Hornby was a more responsible and polished human than Jorrocks, but his upbringing had weaned him away from the Manchesterism of his forefathers.

Richard Cobden would have disapproved of them both. He would scornfully have judged them to be members of the 'clodpole aristocracy' into which, as we earlier noted, he believed Manchester and Lancashire individualists had descended. Yet, unlike many of their number, they had some perspective of modern shifts and, more significantly, the will to act accordingly.

The dissimilarities between the two mentors of Manchester sport reflect the differences in the format and dating of the games in which they were involved. The similarities reflect their awareness of how sporting clubs needed to be fashioned in response to the challenge of the urban environment. Another contemporary parallel is that of Annie Horniman, pioneer of provincial repertory theatre, who established her famous company at the Gaiety Theatre, Manchester, in 1907 and whose 'Manchester School' of dramatists, represented, for instance, by Stanley Houghton and his *Hindle Wakes*, was the 'kitchen sink' genre of its day. Her aim, according to the *Manchester Guardian*, was to make the theatre 'as much a part of the mental life of people here as novel reading is'. She was also a key supporter of the Dublin Abbey Theatre.

Like Annie Horniman, A.N. Hornby and J.H. Davies realised that a regional capital, such as Manchester, deserved its own theatre, be it of drama or sport, in its own image, rather than having to rely on crumbs from the metropolis, by way of touring companies or, for cricket, in the now dead practice of itinerant Exhibition XIs. It was all part of devising a regional culture for Mancunians and their near neighbours of which they could be proud and which would bring them high-class entertainment.

Team Building Exercises in Stretford

For all the jingling of cabs and the clanking of trams carrying masters and men to one or other of the two Old Traffords, the tale of Manchester United and Lancashire cricket club prior to 1914 has modern overtones. There were controversies, as there have been in the present era, about playing qualifications and incomers, about players' rights and wages, about dodgy payments and deals, about wealthy financiers, about the costs of plans for new stadia, about match fixing and other malpractice. Much of it sounds all too decidedly up-to-date.

One final and strange parallel concerned the continent. Having won their first Championship in 1908 and having drawn the first ever contest for the Charity Shield with Queen's Park Rangers (they won a replay 4-0 during the next season and thus United became first holders of that trophy), Manchester United toured Europe for the first time. They won every match during a tour of the Austro-Hungarian Empire. To underpin the analogies, their 7-0 drubbing of the Budapest League leaders, Ferencvaros, led to an outbreak of hooliganism, with the players attacked, with many arrests made and with the police drawing their swords to cope with the rioting. *Plus ça change...*

PART TWO:

THE MIDDLE AGES

8.

Life and Death in Wartime

THE DEADENING blots of the two World Wars fall darkly across the pages of the story of any 20th century British institution, political, cultural or otherwise. They halt some processes and accelerate others. Whichever the case, they act as sombre monuments, dividing time and action with unavoidable starkness. Nor may their proximity to one another be overlooked. Indeed, some historians, bearing in mind conflicts such as the Spanish Civil War and the Sino-Japanese struggles, speak of one war, stretching from 1914 to 1945. Just a score or so of football and cricket seasons separate the two World Wars.

Thus when one examines this 'medieval' period of any typical sports club, such as Lancashire or Manchester United, one must remark on its brevity. Lancashire had played in 45 official County Championships and Manchester United in 43 Football League campaigns before 1945/1946 heralded the long modern era. They have each played a round 60 seasons since that point. Nonetheless, that brief inter-war spell was very important in the history of both games, although, locally, the tale is an extremely mixed one. The 1920s and 1930s mark the zenith of Lancashire cricket and the nadir of Manchester United's exploits.

Both World Wars were, of course, traumatic - but they were traumatic in entirely and curiously differing ways. Despite the horrors of the Eastern Front and the sporadic hostilities in North Africa, British action in the 1914-1918 war was intensely concentrated on the Western Front, whilst the collateral damage to property across Europe was not extensive. Zeppelin airships and, later, Gotha bombers raided Britain, in particular London, although one or two strayed over Lancashire towns, such as Bolton, and lighting restrictions were imposed. To put that in perspective, 1,117 British civilians were killed as a result of all these enemy attacks, whereas, during the World War II raids on Manchester, as many were slaughtered in the two nights of 22nd and 23rd December 1940.

Life and Death in Wartime

Economically, there was full employment. The textile looms whirred away in a busy maze of uniforms, blankets, sandbags, bandages and much else, while the call for armaments and military vehicles was equally strong. Given heavy martial recruitment, there was even a shortage of labour, so much so that over 2m women adopted what had been male jobs. 800,000 of these were, to the consternation of many men, in the engineering trades, with the munitions and other war-orientated firms of Trafford Park - an industrial complex that grew significantly in response to the exigencies of war - among those to benefit from this form of recruitment. Apart from assisting in the emancipation of women, along with the vote and other emblems of equal citizenship that soon were granted, this also helped in the general increase in household income during the Great War.

There was a German blockade, sustained by the 390 U-boats that were built, of which the Royal Navy sank 178. This reached a critical moment in the first quarter of 1917, when 2m tons of shipping - some 1,500 ships - were lost, many of those cargo vessels en route for the ports of Liverpool and Manchester. The supply of sugar, the domain of John Davies' wealthy in-laws, was reduced by a half, and rationing, by registration with a particular retailer, was introduced towards the end of 1916. Otherwise provisions were in good order, although panic buying, one of those restless psychological disturbances one finds during the stress of war, led to lengthy queues and artificial shortages. The Government was reluctantly forced, early in 1918, to introduce rationing schedules for meat and fats; all demands were met and consumption actually increased.

These were minor side effects. The genuine horror of the First World War was the loss of military life. 9m men from Britain and the British Empire were mobilised; 900,000 were butchered; 2m were wounded, many of them seriously disabled, making casualties of a sad fraction of a third of that mobilised total. In the war years male mortality was eightfold the norm; of British males born 1892/95, that is, those who were between 19 and 22 at the onset of war, a third were killed. Not a street and scarcely a family were spared.

The Deansgate 'village', officially the St John's Ward of Manchester, and home to my grandmother's family, sent 586 men to war. Their names were inscribed on a Roll of Honour, solemnly fixed to the wall of the county court. At the top were separately listed the 148 who were left 'asleep on the field of honour', as those responsible sought to mask the sheer bloodiness of it all behind somewhat cloying euphemisms. My grandmother's nephew, Albert, was killed in France, but her favourite brother, Sam, survived. He was a regular soldier, having fled the tedium of apprenticeship with a wheelwright by the canal side to join up and find himself at the Relief of Ladysmith in the Boer War. Off he went to France as part of what the Kaiser called 'the contemptible little army', the British Expeditionary Force, that expertly and bravely delayed the early German offensives at Mons and Ypres. Great-uncle Sam was eventually the oldest of Manchester's 'old contemptibles'. He won the Military Medal, although this was not an event upon which he was prepared to elaborate. A Sergeant in the Royal Field Artillery, he was, he admitted, grooming his horse when his officer brought him the news, while the nearest we could ever approach the reasons was some mumbled hint about running with a coil of wire between lines of German riflemen to restore a communications connection.

His wife died of TB in a remote Irish village. Temporarily blinded by poison gas and given compassionate leave, he made his way from France to this isolated hamlet, at a time when uniformed British soldiers were not the most welcome sight in Ireland, and brought back his three-year old daughter for my grandmother to care for until he re-married. Apparently her only infantile assertion was 'Up with the Sinn Fein and to hell with the King.' It was on the occasion of her wedding in the 1930s that I recall making a visit to the family home in Little Edward Street, a marriage that endured over 60 years. One of her daughters, prompted by an old photograph, then sought out the Irish resting place of her erstwhile grandmother: all the village emerged to greet her. The legend of the blind, handsome English soldier who had travelled so valiantly to claim his daughter had been handed down these 80 years. There have been worse film scripts. As for great-uncle Sam, he did stalwart duty with the civil defence on Salford Docks during World War II, thus serving his country, silently as well as valorously, in three wars.

Many Lancashire and United players answered the call to the colours. A dozen or so cricketers were already enlisted by the Christmas of 1914, among them R.H. Spooner, one of the 'soldier-cricketers', who had seen service in the Boer War and was a captain in the Lincolnshire Regiment in the 1914-1918 War. Also A.H. Hornby, son of the 'Squire' and, a chip off the old hunting block, a War Office adviser on cavalry horses, and Archie MacLaren, Lieutenant, later Captain, in the Royal Army Service Corps, who, with Captain Gilbert Jessop, energetically organised recruiting campaigns. They were among the three-quarters of first-class cricketers who had enlisted by 1916, at which point over 2,000 MCC members were in the armed forces.

Several Lancashire cricketers died in the war. These included Bill Tyldesley, one of the so-called Westhoughton Tyldesleys and a promising bat, killed in action in Belgium in 1918; Harold Garnett, a cavalier left-hander who played for the Gentlemen and toured Australia without playing a Test, who was killed at Cambrai in 1917, and Alfred Hartley, killed in France, just weeks before the Armistice. Alfred Hartley was born in New Orleans, as was his brother, Charles, who also played for Lancashire: their father, George, Lancashire-born but an emigrant merchant in New Orleans, also played three times for the county. The Oxford blue, E.L. Wright, from Chorley, who played four games for the county, lost his young life in the trenches in 1918, while the rather anonymous figure of J. Nelson, from the Blackpool district, who made one Lancashire appearance, also died on active service.

Old Trafford itself was used as a British Red Cross centre, but, as the war heated up, the pavilion and its surrounds became a full-scale military hospital for 80 or so patients, with nearly 2,000 wounded soldiers being nursed there during the hostilities, until, in fact, February 1919, not long before the start of the first post-war season. Johnny Tyldesley, too old for war service, helped the Red Cross, meeting ambulance trains and taking the wounded to hospital, often using his own car for the purpose.

Manchester United also lost players, among them Pat McQuire, an amateur reserve, and Oscar Linkson, a full-back who had, in fact, moved into Irish football in 1913 and who was killed in France in 1916. We have already noted, with sadness, the notable loss of Sandy Turnbull and the wounding of Arthur Whalley; centre-forward Arthur Casman was also badly injured but he, too, recovered sufficiently to resume playing, while Josh Rowe, another amateur, was wounded serving with the East Surrey Regiment. Other United servicemen included Richard Holden, a full-back who joined the Royal Flying Corps in its infancy; James Hodge, a wing-half who, like great-uncle Sam, served with the Royal Field Artillery; the goalkeeper, Ezra Royals, who was whisked away with his Territorial Army unit and found himself on the front line within days of war being declared; George Hunter, a half-back who was born at Peshawar, near the Khyber Pass, and who served as a Company Sergeant Major in France and at Gallipoli; and, another who was quick to enlist, Birmingham-born George Travers, who served in Salonika. The half-back, Frank Knowles, served with the Royal Garrison Artillery and guested, during his training at Aldershot, with Arsenal, whilst the outside-left, Joseph Nolan, played for the 46th Division XI in France.

George Wall was another well-known star who joined the army, rising to the rank of Sergeant with the Black Watch, while two youngsters who would sign for United at the end of the war were also soldiers - the likeable Joe Spence was with the Machine Guns Corps and John Williamson, having played for Ancoats Lad Club, enlisted with the Manchester Pals Regiment. Over twenty footballers who had played or who would play for Manchester United were in the forces. There is the interesting tale of Frank Buckley, born in Urmston, who was a centre-half with United in the 1900s, who joined the 1st Footballers' Battalion and was wounded on the Somme, who rose through the ranks to become a Major, and who, adhering rigidly to that title, brought martial strictness to his success in football management, particularly with Wolverhampton Wanderers, for many, many seasons. Spare a passing thought too for goalkeeper Tom Wilcox, who was born at sea, on the sailing barque, *Grassendale*, and who served with the Royal Welsh Fusiliers, and for John Fitchett, a full-back who, in a mad burlesque of all this military zeal, became a member of Fred Karno's Army, touring with that theatrical company of comic mimes.

Such was the massive disruption of the ranks both of the cricketing and the footballing Old Traffords. Such was the destruction of the normality of British civilian life. There was, moreover, a further swathe of distress to add to these physical disturbances. The British people were psychologically overwhelmed by the stress of the war. There had been no major conflict since the Napoleonic Wars that had ended with the victory of Waterloo in 1815. The minor wars of the succeeding hundred years had been mainly imperial skirmishes, like the Zulu or South African Wars, involving only the regular army and the Royal Navy. The closest to home and the biggest conflict had been the Crimean War of 1854-56, when the British lost 22,000 men, only 3,000 more than on the first dreadful day of the Battle of the Somme in 1916. Only 4,000 were killed in action, the rest succumbing to disease.

Now suddenly a volunteer army of 2.5m answered Kitchener's famous call, chiefly in a mood of eager idealism. Conscription was introduced in 1916 but it had the perverse consequence of revealing how many men needed to be retained in essential civil occupation; one of the disbenefits of volunteering had been to rob necessary trades of craftsmen. After a century of military quietude at home the 1914-1918 War shook the nation to its cultural foundations. Some of the ramifications - the panic buying of foodstuffs; the attacks on shops bearing vaguely Germanic name-

Red Shirts and Roses

plates (the 1915 sinking of the Lusitania led to such riots that, in Liverpool, troops had to be summoned to quell the troubles); the harsh treatment of conscientious objectors and perceived cowards, such that key munitions workers wore badges to protect them from the white feather brigade - this hysteria spoke graphically of a people long inured from the fell practices of warfare.

Sport, ineluctably, responded according to the mores of the hour. Cricket took itself especially seriously. In the most negative sense, the nightmare of the First World War is the most important event in cricket's history. The 1914 season spluttered out soon after the declaration of war in the August of 1915, with Surrey awarded the title and with the Army already in residence at the Oval. W.G. Grace, in the only overtly political act of his life, wrote in *The Sportsman* on 27th August, calling on 'all first-class cricketers of suitable age' to 'come to the aid of their country without delay'. It was not, he said, 'fitting that able-bodied men should be playing cricket by day, and pleasure seekers look on'. The pugnacious Archie MacLaren from, it has to be confessed, the security of his Manchester recruiting office, was extraordinarily xenophobic, denouncing the Kaiser as 'that crowned madman' and 'that hog in armour' in his magazine, *World of Cricket*. Yorkshire made the enlistment of players in the services or on munitions 'a strict condition of their continued engagement'.

Although there was a little relaxation with games for charity in the last years of the war, top-class cricket was halted in its tracks. There were attempts to sustain league, services and schools cricket, but first-class cricket was stopped for the first time since its inception some 50 years hitherto. As cricket's Golden Age had dawned so brightly in the late Victorian and Edwardian era, it had been accompanied with intellectual confusion. Plainly, cricket had been over-egged as a moral and nationalistic tool, seen now as a preparation for 'those who play their game in the fields of France', with, in Rudyard Kipling's haunting phrase written in 1914, 'your English summer's done'. Imperialism, Christianity and Athleticism had become irrevocably befuddled in the minds of the upper classes. Cricket was 'the Holy Game', in Lord Harris' hushed whisper, 'God's Classroom', with Wisden 'the Cricketer's Bible'. According to the Rev Thomas Waugh, writing about death in 1894, 'the whole redeemed Church of God meets you with the words, 'well played, sir'. It becomes difficult to determine whether cricket was a metaphor for Christianity or vice versa.

Couple with this the Imperialist sentiment of the 'white man's burden' and the thousands who read the best-seller, *Deeds That Won The Empire*, written by W.H. Fitchett, an Australian, 400,000 of whose countrymen travelled to Europe to fight in World War I, of whom 80,000 were slain and a further 220,000 injured. 'Who dies for England, sleeps with God', asserted the Poet Laureate, Alfred Austin. It is a sentiment celebrated in Henry Newbolt's poem, its refrain still augmenting the exterior wall of Lord's, about the subaltern, recalling how he had faced 'a bumping pitch and a blinding light', who, when 'the Gatling's jammed and the Colonel dead', rallies the ranks with the cry of 'Play up, play up and play the game'.

The pages of the wartime *Wisdens* are dense with the brief memorials to some 3,000 slain cricketers. The majority of them were public schoolboys who had spent some afternoons in the nets, coached by gnarled old professional cricketers, and

80

some in the OCTU drill shed, instructed by hard-bitten ex-Army NCOs, the latter induction the avenue to almost instant commissions and a high risk of death in the trenches. The Germans were 'demon bowlers' firing their Krupps shells from 'a concrete grandstand far beyond the boundary'.

Consider these lines from a poem, *Lord's Leave 1915*, by E.W. Hornung:

> *Bigger than the cricket here; yet some who tried*
> *In vain to earn a colour while at Eton*
> *Have found a place upon an English side*
> *That can't be beaten.*

First-class cricket was stopped not because it was trivial but because it was important; it was not so much that one should not mix business with pleasure, as that one could not undertake two meaningful, God-given roles simultaneously. That sentiment was to have a long-term effect on English cricket.

The football authorities were more pragmatic. Football had always been viewed as more of a winter pastime for the upper echelons and a hardy diversion for the working classes; of late, it had, as Old Trafford football ground demonstrated, developed into as popular a spectacle as the summer game, if not more so. Where cricket at its top levels represented something of a pseudo-religious cult, first-grade football was a more matter-of-fact business. Where Lancashire made losses that left the club with debts of some £12,000 by the end of hostilities, Manchester United contrived to keep playing. The Football League organised a 'Lancashire' and a 'Midlands' division, with 'principal' and 'subsidiary' sections, plus a 'London Combination'. After the introduction of conscription, police attended games to keep a sharp lookout for backsliders. Old Trafford's mainstay was little Wilf Woodcock, born in Ashton-under-Lyne, who managed to make 132 appearances for United in wartime football and scored 69 goals.

As well as the 'Pals' regiments that were formed to appeal to parochial camaraderie, there were vocation-associated units, such as the Artists' Rifles. Two footballers' battalions were established, the first of which was officially entitled the 17th Service Battalion of the Middlesex Regiment. It first saw action in France just before Christmas 1915 and Major Buckley was its second-in-command. By hook and by crook, football enjoyed something of, in that dire time, the least worse of both worlds. It kept the flags flying both in some corner of a foreign field and also on the corners of its own football fields. These events, if in a more minor key than with cricket, prefigured the post-war practices of soccer.

Finally, the nightmare was over. Dappled sunlight filtered in through the shutters and cricketers and footballers peeped above the safety of the bedclothes. Demobilisation of such large numbers was not a rapid process but those in charge of sport had some time in hand. The County Championship was resumed in 1919, the authorities having had nearly six months to prepare, although they opted, not too successfully, for a two-day tourney. With almost a year in hand, the Football League ran its first post-war season in 1919-20.

Red Shirts and Roses

In April 1919 the Services cricketers reassembled at Old Trafford, now free of its wounded soldiery. They formed practically a full team. Flight Sergeant Harry Makepeace and Corporal Charlie Hallows, destined to form one of Lancashire's several famed opening partnerships were among them, together with Sergeant Ernest Tyldesley, a batting talent of impressive quantities and qualities. Sergeant Harry Dean, the quick left-hand bowler; Gunner Lol Cook, the medium-paced bowler from Preston, and Gunner Ben Blomley, an Oldham-born wicket-keeper, were also present. Absent were Captain Hornby, who retired to a huge estate near Cork where he maintained his father's interests in rural sports, and Captain Spooner, still recuperating from his wounds. A number of commissioned amateurs declared themselves available, among them Captains Frank Musson and C. Stowell Marriott, but none of them played much for Lancashire. J.T. Tyldesley, having journeyed thousands of miles in the succour of wounded soldiers, delayed his retirement to bring his vast experience to the needs of the team.

Myles Kenyon was made captain. He was made of the proper stuff of amateur skippers. Bury-born and the son of a former MP for that town, and educated at Eton and Cambridge University, he was commissioned in the Duke of Lancaster's Own Yeomanry, but was wounded when on attachment to the 9th Battalion of the South Lancashire Regiment in Macedonia. The hospital ship, *Dover Castle*, which bore him home, was torpedoed in the Mediterranean, but he was mercifully saved. Although not the most prolific of batsmen, he led Lancashire for four summers with a decent efficiency. Lancashire beat Northants by ten wickets at Old Trafford in their opening post-war match. What with the debts and the taxes, the price of admission was doubled from a tanner to a bob or in avant-garde money from 2.5p to 5p, a stupendous - and the very first - increase from the birth of Lancashire cricket fifty years before.

Over at Old Trafford football ground John Robson, appointed manager in 1914, turned to the vain task of reinvigorating a club that had declined steeply in the last pre-war seasons. He gathered about him a nucleus of players that would provide the spine of the eleven for years. The solid full-back pairing of Moore and Silcock made its joint debut in the first pre-war game, which was away against Derby County. They played for the first of many times in front of Jack Mew in goal. The stylish centre-half, Clarence 'Lal' Hilditch, and Joe Spence also played their first game for United. There will be more news of this quartet in the next chapter, but it was, on the day, Wilf Woodcock who rescued a point with the goal that secured a 1-1 draw.

The crowds reassembled in some numbers at both grounds as normality returned, but, in retrospect, one may discern some crucial differences. In workmanlike manner, football rolled up its figurative sleeves and knuckled down to the mundane job of providing reasonable fare, week in, week out, at some ninety or so venues. The original twelve of the Football League had grown substantially, with four divisions in the competition. There were few entirely new clubs; only two or three current League clubs, among them York City, Peterborough United and Colchester United, are of post-1918 formation. However, there was room for mobility; Tottenham Hotspur and Ipswich Town did not graduate into the Football League from the Southern League until after the First World War. Although the inter-war decades were not years of exhilaration in the footballing sense, they were steady enough. More importantly, the game was growing internationally, not least on the Continent. It is true that the conservative Football Association did not react very progressively to this fact, but fact it was. At least the roots were kept firm enough in the home soil, so that, come the later and more expansive post-1945 era, English clubs were in a position to take advantage of that broader conspectus of the sport and the technical and other changes with which it was associated.

On the other hand, cricket was, in the original connotation of the verb, petrified by World War I. Its sacrosanct quality rendered it untouchable. Many of those who ran cricket's affairs had fought the war to preserve what they cherished from the past, to return to the Edwardian calm and splendour of Hove and Worcester and Lord's. The idea of altering the treasured, sacred, stately measure was, in almost a theological sense, anathema.

The Victorians, mighty believers in progress and, relevantly, the formulators of the doctrine of evolution, would have had no truck with such stultifying nonsense. They were assured and ardent, ever ready to move onwards and upwards. Their more nervous descendants, paralysed, and understandably so, by the 1914-1918 bloodbath, looked back where their grandfathers would have looked forwards. Cricket was transfixed in a sort of cultural aspic. It was played from memory. The Victorian tradition of continuing revolution yielded to the 20th century tradition of...traditionalism.

The beautiful shape of cricket was artificially conserved and there was little, save a minor tinkering here and there with the laws and regulations, by way of radical change. Compared with any other major sport, the construct of cricket then and now is very similar. The Victorians' restless experimentation with bowling techniques and batting strokes and mainstream laws was at an end. Crucially, the County Championship became ever more concretised. After the flexibility of the late 19th century came the immobility of the 20th century; after Glamorgan's advance into the elite in 1921 (not least with friendly help from Lancashire) there was to be no other entrant until Durham in 1992, 71 years afterwards. Even more crucially, no one left. It was a closed shop, a cricketing cabal - and, until 1963, the Players and Gentlemen division was sustained. On the world stage, first-class cricket remained the province of Victorian English influence, that is, it only notably developed in imperial confines. Two dates epitomise the geopolitical distinction between football and cricket. In 1904 the International Federation of Football Associations (FIFA) was established. In 1909 the Imperial Cricket Conference (comprising England, Australia and South Africa) was formed.

It was not that playing cricket from memory was unattractive. What Gerald Howat has percipiently called 'the Second Golden Age' was a box of delights, with Don Bradman and Wally Hammond and many others in the 1920s and 1930s every bit as enthralling as their gifted forebears. The argument is that neither novel devices nor organisational stratagems emerged, as cricket existed in a kind of trance. There was nothing ugly about it. It was akin to the lovely but 'dead-pale' Lady of Shalott, of Tennyson's mournful poem, floating down the stream, 'till her blood was frozen over'.

Red Shirts and Roses

Somehow Manchester United and Lancashire exemplify these two attitudes. Manchester United had a dogged and unspectacular twenty years before the 1939-1945 war, yet it kept firm hold on a large band of eager adherents, as if in preparation, like the whole of world football, for the exciting advances of the second half of the 20th century. Lancashire, conversely, had its proudest hours, playing the fashion of triumphant, skilful and focused cricket that was characteristic of the mid-wars era, almost as if it might have been the last glorious flourish before English first-class cricket was faced with turmoil and crisis from the 1950s onwards.

9.

Red Shirts in the Sunset

SOME YEARS ago there was a spoof publication of *The Wit and Wisdom of Mrs Thatcher* that consisted of blank pages. In Len Shackleton's biography the chapter entitled 'What the Average Director Knows about Football' was likewise an empty sheet. It was Wilf Mannion who told the tale of travelling away with Middlesbrough before the Second World War and, at half time with the match goalless, the director accompanying this fine First Division team instructed them, 'what I want you to do this half is to get that ball between those goal posts', as though grasp of the game's purpose had collectively escaped them.

For all that, it must occasionally have occurred to United faithful in the intervening years between 1919 and 1939 that such motivational amnesia was epidemic in the Old Trafford dressing room. Manchester United's successes in the inter-war seasons could certainly be most effectively described by and on a blank sheet. Hence a re-coinage of Suzette Tarri's signature tune *Red Sails in the Sunset* is an apposite subhead for this chapter on a football team in such decline. Let us bite the bullet, swallow the medicine and grasp the nettle. Let us have done quickly with these twenty years of mediocre behaviour.

In summary, after three years loitering in the subways of the First Division, United were relegated to the Second Division for three seasons, before, having laboured for six uneasy years in the upper stretches, it was down again for five dismal winters. The yo-yoing continued. It was one year, 1936/37, up; one, 1937/38, down, and then one year up again for the ultimate pre-war season of 1938/39. It had been a narrow squeak, for United only pushed ahead of Sheffield United to accompany Aston Villa into the First Division in 1938. Manchester United were an unconvincing 14th at the end of that last full pre-war season, but it meant that, when post-war football recommenced, they were safely in the First Division. This was a stroke of luck, for it meant that Matt Busby was able to conjure his spells with a top-flight side; indeed, the question might be pondered as to whether he would have opted to manage a Second Division team.

Thus, between the wars, United had eleven years in the First and nine in the Second Division. No wonder my friend, Norman Garner, who was born in Moss Side and supported Manchester City, used still, when we watched a lot of football together in the 1960s, to regard United as interlopers in the First Division. Their best campaign led them to 9th place in 1925/26; their worst the bitter months of 1933/34. The last match of that dreadful season found them tottering in 21st position in the Second Division. It was at Millwall, who had a point in hand and only needed a draw for what the old-style *Punch* might have called 'collapse of stout party', that is, the relegation of the Reds into the Third Division and the rescue of the Lions. Come Arsenal, come Bayern Munich, come Real Madrid, this has to be judged as just about the most critical fixture in the club's history, for descent into the Third Division might have been catastrophically irrecoverable and altered the saga of European, let alone English, football. Johnny Cape and Tommy Manley scored to secure the 2-0 win and a last-gasp reprieve...maybe that should read St John and St Thomas.

The naive reader may be seated comfortably, awaiting news of Manchester United's valorous cup performances, for the modern years of league famine were often relieved by copious suppings from the FA Cup. Alas, there was, sorrowfully, just the one bare highlight. This was a 1925/26 semi-final at Bramall Lane, Sheffield, where Manchester City, on a high-scoring cup run, beat the Reds 3-0. They then halted this brisk goal-scoring at Wembley, losing 1-0 - a great goal from David Jack - to Bolton Wanderers, a dubious consolation prize for United fans, if ever there were one.

Through the clenched teeth of despondency, it must be confessed that Manchester City were much the more successful team of the two in those sobering times. They were in three Cup Finals, losing to Everton 3-0 in 1933, as well as to Bolton, before a handsome 2-1 win against Portsmouth in 1933. Tilson scored both goals after Portsmouth had taken the lead, leaving the young Frank Swift in a dead swoon at the end of the game, overcome by the nervous tension. This was the fleet-footed and artistic City of Eric Brook, Alec Herd and Matt Busby, with Sam Cowan an excellent captain at centre-half. City also had some lively league campaigns, winning the First Division Championship in 1936/37, but that is enough of tolerant and non-partisan admiration.

There seemed to be more of a mixed economy in the Football League in those days. Despite their bright successes, Manchester City suffered a drop into the Second Division and found themselves stranded therein - by, it must be confessed, the slimmest of margins - as the Second World War encroached, leaving them to begin the post-war struggle in that lower flight. Arsenal, managed in urbane style first by Herbert Chapman and then George Allison, were always a supreme power in cup and league, but the likes of Huddersfield Town, Newcastle United, Aston Villa, Sheffield Wednesday and Preston North End all enjoyed moments in the sun. The transfer system appeared to have evened-up affairs without distorting matters, so that the switches of success and failure were more equitably distributed.

Footballing methodology had changed. The ever-troublesome offside rule was altered in 1925 so that only two, rather than the more restrictive three, became the monitor, something of a release for attackers, although the inclusion of the 'stopper' centre-half did something to dispel overmuch gaiety among forwards. The sinuously delicate dribbling of the pre-1914 days was less fashionable, with accurate passing the norm, to the extent that some disgruntled watchers felt there was undue passing and insufficient shooting. Heading, with Dixie Dean of Everton in the van, became more of a science, as had the improved positional displays of defenders. The constructive wing-half and the ball carrying inside-forward came to the fore, alongside the famous 'W' formation of the five forwards. The sweep of pincer attack down the flanks, with the goal line seen as second priority to the goal itself, was all the rage.

Football continued to evolve as a social institution. From the 1890s, beginning in the engineering trades, the '12 o'clock Saturday' had been gradually introduced, a useful consolidation of the availability of working men, pies carefully chewed and pints faithfully imbibed, for the terraces. The Football League gates averaged some 20,000 a game in the inter-war years, with something like 700,000 in attendance at 40-odd matches each Saturday, giving a total of 30m or so spectators each season. This, of course, masks a differential between the high and the lowly divisions, but it does underline the popularity of football across the nation. With travel an expense and with time still limited, the idea of following one's team to away grounds was rarely canvassed, except for nearby 'derby' fixtures or special cheap 'oop for the coop' rail outings. Football was more of a fortnightly ritual, as habitual as chapel going on pre-1914 Sabbaths. Its incidence and place in the working class calendar was amply recognised by J.B. Priestley in the opening pages of his jovial novel, published in 1929, *The Good Companions*, the preface to Jess Oakroyd breaking free of his harsh workload and embittered home and heading for the glittering lights of the theatre:

'Something very queer is happening to that narrow thoroughfare to the west of the town. It is called Manchester Road because it actually leads you to that city, though in order to get there you will have to climb the windy roof of England and spend an hour or so with the curlews. What is so queer about it now is that the road itself cannot be seen at all. A grey-green tide flows sluggishly along its length. It is a tide of cloth caps.

These caps have just left the ground of Bruddersford United Association Football Club. 35,000 men and boys have just seen what most of them call 't'United' play Bolton Wanderers. Many of them should not have been there at all. It would not be difficult to prove by statistics and those mournful little budgets (How a Man May Live - or rather, avoid death - on 35 shillings a week) that seem to attract some minds, that those fellows could not afford the entrance fee. When some mills are only working half the week and others not at all, a shilling is a respectable sum of money. It would puzzle an economist to discover where all those shillings came from. But if he lived in Bruddersford, though he might still wonder where they came from, he would certainly understand why they were produced. To say that these men paid their shillings to watch twenty-two hirelings kick a ball is merely to say that a violin is wood and catgut, that *Hamlet* is so much paper and ink. For a shilling the Bruddersford United AFC offered you Conflict and Art; it turned you into a critic, happy in your judgement of fine points, ready in a second to estimate the worth of a well-judged pass, a run down the touch line, a lightning shot, a clearance kick by back or goalkeeper; it turned you into a partisan, holding your breath when the ball came sailing into your goalmouth, ecstatic when your forwards raced away towards the opposite goal, elated, downcast, bitter, triumphant by turns at the fortunes of your side, watching a ball shape Iliads and Odysseys for you; and, what is more, it turned you into a member of a new community, all brothers together for an hour and a half, for not only had you escaped from the clanking machinery of this lesser life, from work, wages, rent, doles, sick pay, insurance cards, nagging wives, ailing children, bad bosses, idle workmen, but you had escaped with most of your mates and neighbours, with half the town, and there you were, cheering together,

Red Shirts and Roses

thumping one another on the shoulders, swopping judgements like the lords of the earth, having pushed your way through a turnstile into another and altogether more splendid kind of life, hurtling with Conflict and yet passionate and beautiful in its Art. Moreover, it offered you more than a shilling's worth of material for talk during the rest of the week. A man who had missed the last home match of 't'United' had to enter social life on tiptoe in Bruddersford.'

In that evocative account, its lengthy set of subordinating clauses rolling like the 'grey-green tide' down Manchester Road, J.B. Priestley captures the mood of the between-wars football crowd, predominantly male and artisan, in search of it two-weekly sporting solace, anonymous yet bound together in collective fidelity to the cause. Although Old Trafford was more an arena of Conflict that a theatre for Art in these days, the crowds assembled - the male gender heavily in the ascendant - dourly fascinated by the twists and turns, the snakes and ladders, of United's erratic performances, arriving from the engineering works and the docks and the other factories and mills of the vicinity. They were grimly, even despondently, loyal to Manchester United, as they were to their families, their neighbours, their work-places, their holiday resorts, could they afford a break, as they had been to the Manchester Regiment or the Lancashire Fusiliers.

There were a few Jess Oakroyds who tore themselves away but it was not so commonplace that Jess Oakroyd does not make an uncommon literary figure. There was less switching of jobs, less movement of house, less choice of leisure pursuits, less change of holiday resorts and less divorce than nowadays. Old Trafford was familiar territory and that is where, every other Saturday, thousands wound their way - and plenty turned up on the alternative Saturday to watch the Reserves play in the Central League. It was stoical enough. Feelings were roused and there was noisy anger and despair, interspersed with regretfully infrequent rejoicing, but the emotional levels were in keeping with men who had survived the trenches and were now expected, for many years, to survive on a miserly dole. The degree of expectation was not ambitious. One perhaps expected one's team to win some and lose some. When things went haywire, it had been anticipated by canny souls; when things went well, those same prudent hearts were looking over shoulders, awaiting nemesis. 'There's bad news', as Noel Coward would burble, 'just around the corner'.

The management of Manchester United responded by preserving a hard core of players, with whom the crowd developed an affectionate and lasting relationship. The fans at least were not often subjected in this sphere of their existence to the anguish of divorce any more than in their private domesticity. In fact, it is likely that the tirades of abuse were more common in the riven homesteads of Salford and Manchester than on the terraces of Old Trafford. Naturally enough, the payer of the shilling reserved the God-given right to be disrespectfully critical of the professionals hired to impress him but there was a greater likelihood of the sceptical rejoinder than the obscene curse, with, for instance, as another Red hopeful made another hash of it, some such gruff stage-whisper as, 'they should have charged him to come in'.

88

Red Shirts in the Sunset

It all began, properly enough, in defence. Jackie Mew, the Sunderland goalkeeper, played 199 times for United in the Football League and FA Cup. Indeed, including wartime games and all competitions, he played well over 500 times for United teams and earned two benefits, although it is salutary to relate that his first award of £1,000 was reduced by edict of the authorities to £650, for it was not thought wise to overdo the largesse. He won one England cap in 1923 and enjoyed other representative honours, and, for a spell, he went into business with the Lancashire cricketer, Cec Parkin.

Not of tall stature, Jackie Mew had exceptionally safe hands and he, in turn, benefited from the stalwart full-back pairing of Charlie Moore and Jack Silcock. This triumvirate shared the defensive duties together, in an era, when, almost new-rugby style, they were definitively the back three, on scores of occasions. A Staffordshire boy, Charlie Moore, with a tangle of dark hair surmounting his cheery face, was both dependable and gentlemanly, his record in 328 games for United all but unblemished. His partner, an ex-miner from Wigan, was tough Jack Silcock, who topped this with 449 games for United, an amazing sum of approaching 800 games for this obdurate duo. For all his bulldog countenance, Silcock was not lacking in style to combine with his evident power. He won three England caps, both backs suffering, in respect of international recognition, from playing in an inferior team. Both became, in the tradition of the time, publicans; Moore at Brooke's Bar and Silcock in Stretford.

Both backs made their debut in the first post-war game, as did Lal Hilditch, the lightweight but clever half-back. He played 322 times for United, was player-manager for a few months over the 1926/27 season, and ended his football days with a season training the Old Trafford colts. He won a few representative honours but, by and large, he was content to devote himself to the daunting task in hand at Old Trafford. With his glossy hair and luminously dark eyes, there was something of Rudolph Valentino about the looks of this child of Cheshire, but, unlike the present day, there was little or no feminine following to swoon and weep. He certainly had the politesse to go with that Sheik-like role: it is said of him that he never once committed a foul.

Joe Spence was another debutant on that 1919 day at Derby and he was another long stayer, probably United's most popular player of the two inter-war decades. Spence was a Northumberland lad who, on demobilisation from the army, joined United and scored four times against Bury in one of the last of the wartime 'Lancashire Section' fixtures. His record of 481 League appearances (510, including Cup games) endured until the time of Billy Foulkes in the 1950s and 1960s. Including some yeoman service with Bradford City and Chesterfield, he played 613 League matches and in nineteen of the twenty mid-wars seasons. It is an astonishing tale of hardy commitment on the part of this stocky north-easterner, with his homely features and distinctive fairish quiff.

He was regularly United's top scorer and few have bettered his 168 goals for the club. Above all, he was an entertainer, at centre-forward or, more frequently, on the wing, popping up with an electrifying finish or a beguiling piece of fancy footwork. He left United, aged 35, in 1933, just after I was born, but one of the first sporting cries I learned as a babe was 'Give it to Joe', the motto that had so repeatedly been chorused in unison from the terraces.

Red Shirts and Roses

Just after the Second World War I was with my father at damage-strewn Old Trafford, watching a reserve match. In the opening minutes a barrel-chested, fair-headed forward bustled through and struck a hard shot just over the bar. 'Bloody hell', exclaimed Ack, 'it's Joe Spence'. Those close by of a certain age chuckled and agreed. The lookalike was Ronnie Burke. Brought to Old Trafford by Jimmy Murphy, he soon became frustrated by the lack of first-team chances, such was the consistency of Jack Rowley, but he did well elsewhere, particularly with Rotherham. But the Joe Spence memory lingered long in the minds of United's fans.

In vast toto, this dedicated quintet - Mew, Moore, Silcock, Hilditch and Spence - made some 1,800 appearances for Manchester United. There were other stars, and, as in old-fashioned melodrama, the audience loved the villain they hissed as well as the hero they cheered. If Joe Spence fulfilled the latter function, then Frank Barson obliged in the former configuration. A Grimethorpe blacksmith, he demonstrated all the ferocity associated with that strenuous trade in legends such as A.G. Macdonell's irate fast bowling blacksmith of *England, Their England* notoriety. An enthusiastic and heartening captain, Frank Barson was what modern broadsheets would have labelled controversial. He compensated in rough play for Clarence Hilditch's smooth approach. His muscular assaults led him to be sent off twelve times in this rumbustious contest with the footballing forces of law and order. He was suspended once for two months while with United and later at Watford he was sidelined for six months. Rugged of countenance, swarthy of physique and heavy of boot, he was a stopper centre-half who took with the utmost seriousness the stoppage part of that contract. Had he later been a student of the Spanish Civil War of this period, he might have appreciated the legendary declaration of 'La Pasionaria', Dolores Ibarruri, 'They Shall Not Pass'.

Anecdotes abound. One tells of his being promised and given a pub - in Ardwick Green - if United were promoted to the First Division, but he chucked aside the keys after but a quarter of an hour, unable to bear the sycophantic adoration of the customers. Another story, probably apocryphal, as it has been related of others, is of a visit to Old Trafford by the glittering Arsenal of Eddie Hapgood, Cliff Bastin, Bryn Jones and the mercurial Alex James. Like many apocryphal stories, it speaks to the character of the person at its core. The manager came in the dressing room before the game and asked, 'right lads, who's going to watch Alex James today?' Replied Frank Barson, 'let Alex James watch us for a change.'

The managers seemed more ephemeral than the players. John Robson yielded authority to John Chapman, who was suspended by the FA in 1926 for unpublished reasons, whereon, after that brief interregnum of player-management featuring Lal Hilditch, Herbert Bamlett had an uneventful presidency, and then, in the mid-1930s, there was the rather debonair figure of Scott Duncan, who later enjoyed success in the rising fortunes of Ipswich Town. Throughout this period the key official to note and register is Walter Crickmer. Just after the 1914-1918 War he joined the Old Trafford administrative staff as a young clerk. He rose to become Secretary and twice - before and after the incumbency of Scott Duncan - he acted as Secretary-Manager. He ran the club virtually single-handedly during the Second World War. He was United's highly esteemed Secretary until the end of his days. Having luckily survived considerable injuries in World War II from German bombing while serving as a special constable, he died, in the service of Manchester United, on German soil and at a German airport, a victim of the Munich disaster of 1958.

There was, of course, a good deal of buying and selling in these years, as successive managers strove to find a winning combine. During the 1930s the likes of George Vose, the blonde-haired and very consistent centre-half; Tommy Bamford, a high-scoring Welsh forward and George Mutch, a native of Aberdeen, and another regular scorer of goals who found later fame with Preston North End - they paid £5,000 for him in 1937, quite a sum for the day and he won the cup for them in 1938. Permit a mention too of Ray Bennion, a Wrexham-born right-half, who played for nearly twelve years and made 301 highly consistent and lively appearances for United, as well as winning ten Welsh caps, before moving on to playing and coaching duties at Burnley. Permit a mention of him because he dated my mum a couple of times, before, a dutiful son hastens to add, Ack had set his jaunty cap in her appealing direction. They all went out in a gang dancing together as young people did; Ray Bennion told my father that the first Football League match he ever saw, he was playing in it - for United versus Everton.

Then there was the usual crop of oddities. One Saturday in 1925 Albert Pape arrived with Clapham Orient at Old Trafford; just an hour or so before kick off, he was transferred to the home side and played against Orient - but he was on his way again very shortly to Fulham. Walter Winterbottom, born in Oldham and a schoolteacher by profession, enjoyed a valued spell as a composed and efficient centre-half in the 1930s before a back injury halted his playing career. A Wing Commander in the wartime RAF, he was England's somewhat cerebral manager from 1946 to 1962, taking the team to four consecutive World Cups. In 1978 he became United's first ex-player to be knighted, pre-empting Bobby Charlton by sixteen years.

Walter Winterbottom's professional status marks him out from the usual run of ex-smiths and one-time miners in the Old Trafford dressing room. One of the links between player and spectator at this time continued to be forged by similarities of class and income. Most footballers were not earning much more than Jess Oakroyd's 35s (£1.75p) each week. Eddie Hapgood, the esteemed Arsenal and England captain claimed, in an interview towards the end of his life, that he had never earned more than £5 for a match. Dixie Dean's Evertonian face was utilised to advertise cigarettes before World War II - but he knew nothing about it and it was the board of directors that grabbed the perquisites of free fags. The shilling entrance money - in proportion to the average wage today worth about £10 - was handed over that one might spend an hour and a half in the company of one's peers. It was, of course, still regarded as a softer and pleasanter option than routine hours spent over loom and lathe or worse, hanging about on street corners on the dole, but, at bottom, there was little call for envy. Having your face on a cigarette card was a nice vanity but it did not mean riches.

Thus, for twenty years, the crowds came and watched and swayed on the terraces, in goodly numbers, in spite of their team's mixed results, mildly entertained by a brilliant burst from Joe Spence or an example of Frank Barson's skill as enforcer. There were a couple of big matches, but they did not involve United. In 1926 Scotland beat England 1-0, with an Alex Jackson goal, in the first full international match at Old Trafford, while, in 1939, there was Old Trafford's record attendance of almost 77,000 for the Wolverhampton Wanderers and Grimsby Town semi-final, which Wolves easily won 5-1. My father was one of the 76,962 of the official roster, but, like thousands of others, his best view was of those hanging from the framework of the stands. However, elsewhere, and not just at Highbury or at Wembley, football was gathering in cogency, with Britons to the fore in its advance.

Consider this exemplary story. Just prior to the Christmas of 1899 half a dozen expatriate Englishmen were consoling their homesickness with a glass or two of Tuscan wine in a Milan tavern, and, pining for the games they had played in the old country, they decided to form the Milan Cricket and Football Club. They were lace-makers, working for Nottingham companies with Italian outlets and they were shrewd enough to persuade Albert 'Papa' Edwards, a wealthy businessman with the successful Pirelli company to sponsor the venture and become President. In March 1900 six Britons and five Italians took the field, where now stands Milan's massive Central Station, emblem of Mussolini's boast to make Italian trains run on time. They beat another Milan team, Mediolanum. One of the Englishmen, Herbert Kilpin, earned the sobriquet 'il Diavolo Rosso', a nickname that, in homelier translation, would later find favour back at Old Trafford. Legend asserts that Kilpin, the all-star centre-forward, designed the historic red (for the devil) and black (to instil fear) kit. AC Milan won the first of many league championships in 1901 but perhaps because of anxiety, not for the last time, about too many foreign players, the British representation had vanished before the outbreak of the First World War

Before 1914 foreign workers had helped to start Internazionale Milano, AC Milan's abiding rivals, while Genoa - whose first goalkeeper was James Spensley, GP to the English community in the city - was also in part a cricket club and won six of the first seven Italian championships. Over in Spain, English sailors assisted in the birth of Bilbao, while British electricians were chiefly instrumental in the establishment of Dynamo Moscow.

One could repeat such yarns for Denmark, Hungary and other countries, including those, such as Vienna, where a joint cricket and football club was one of the originators of the spread of sport in Austria. Even further afield, Penarol in Montevideo, began life as the Central Uruguay Cricket Club, with English railway workers very much involved, whilst Britons working on and around the docklands of Buenos Aires started the famous River Plate club in Argentina.

Whereas cricket had been conveyed to most parts of the then British Empire, often by middle-class professionals, such as Army officers, colonial administrators, missionaries and traders, football, rather later, was more in the gift of artisans and craftsmen, who were finding lucrative openings overseas in the global spread of industrialisation. On the whole, this appears to have occurred more in non-imperial regions than in imperial possessions. In generalised summary, the Empire got the cricket and the world got the football. Apart from England in 1966, no country in the British Commonwealth has won football's World Cup and no country outside it has won the World Cricket Cup.

Red Shirts in the Sunset

This dichotomy was to have crucial ramifications involving English football and cricket, involving Manchester United and Lancashire, for, critically, United would soon be drawn into European and even worldwide competition, whereas Lancashire would remain, with the other county clubs, largely domesticated in habit.

10.

Red Rose Refulgent

THE ONLY sobering shadow to dull Lancashire's impressively sunny record of five Championship successes between 1919 and 1939 was Yorkshire's uncanny capacity to win even more times. Yorkshire were the cricketing Arsenal of the period. They won twelve titles; in fact, only four of the between-wars County Championships were not taken by either Yorkshire or Lancashire, and two of those went to Derbyshire and Nottinghamshire, with Middlesex picking off the remaining two soon after the 1914-1918 War.

It was a lengthy phase of dominance by the Northern counties, a time when the watchful virtues of professional craftsmanship, buoyed by the competitive edge of - and keen support for - league cricket, outpaced the cavalier abandon and panache of the old-style amateur cricketer. As in the English Civil War, the disciplined New Model Army of the Roundhead Ironsides gradually crushed the heady élan of the Royalist cavalry. For the most part, the Prince Ruperts - the Archie MacLarens and the Reggie Spooners - had departed the field and it was staunchly held by the Oliver Cromwells, by the Harry Makepeaces and the Frank Watsons.

Despite the seeming change of tempo in the cricket and the doubling of the entrance money, the post-war crowds held up strongly. For example, the 1920 Roses match at Old Trafford attracted 67,000 over the three days, a record attendance for a County Championship fixture. On the August Bank Holiday Monday of that game the gates close on a vast congregation of 32,000. Saturday crowds of 20,000 for the more promising fixtures were not uncommon and adult hearts were gladdened by the number of schoolboys passing through the half-price turnstiles. Membership, now at a cost of two guineas, was just over 2,000, but it rose to nearly 4,000 within a few years, although it remained lower than it is today. In the equivalent Roses game in 1926, there were 46,000, 39,000 paying, present on the Bank Holiday Monday, with 78,000 in attendance over three cloudless days. 46,000 remains the highest daily attendance record and 78,000 the highest three day record at Old Trafford. However, it is true that, as the Depression bit and as, perhaps, other pursuits began to distract people from the cricket, the crowds fell during the 1930s.

Although the anecdotal evidence suggests that the cricket support was more middle-class than the football fraternity, it was the workers' shillings that basically kept both clubs in business after 1918. Just as there were a few hundreds who paid an annual subscription to Lancashire, there was a relatively small following of business and professional men who sat in the grandstand for United's home matches. By and large, the amount of support for Manchester United and Lancashire, especially during the 1920s, was not all that different in numbers or class.

94

Red Rose Refulgent

Plainly, the shilling payers received rather better value, in terms of successful performance, at the more easterly of the pair of Old Traffords. Apart from an unconvincing 11th place in 1936, Lancashire were never out of the top six between the wars, a proud record of professional constancy.

Lancashire's first spell of major success was a hat-trick of wins in 1926, 1927 and 1928 under the strict leadership of Major Leonard Green. Not a dynamic cricketer himself, he has the sound sense to listen to the cricketing advice of his non-commissioned officers and impose a social discipline of his own fashioning. After a sluggish start in the drizzling spring of 1926, Lancashire picked up a few victories, only to be thrashed by the frail Leicestershire team at Ashby-de-la-Zouch, rather as if, at one of those medieval tournaments celebrated by Sir Walter Scott and others at that famed venue, some honest Saxon squire had toppled the champion Norman knight. Stung into retributive action, Lancashire never lost again that summer and ended with five straight wins and nine of their last twelve. They narrowly pipped an undefeated and miffed Yorkshire XI.

1927 started differently, with Lancashire rushing off at express speed, with seven victories in the first ten fixtures, but this time unfriendly rain fell in the later months and Lancashire also lost some momentum. Nonetheless, another moment for the minnow awaited. Combative Nottinghamshire visited Swansea for their last match, fully expecting to roll over Glamorgan, without a win to their name that year. Glamorgan won by an innings and Lancashire scraped home by the thinnest of margins.

The summer of 1928 was baked by exacting sun throughout, and Charlie Hallows foreshadowed the prodigious run-making of that warm summer with 1,000 runs in May. This was Lancashire's most clear-cut title. They won fifteen matches and were undefeated in the Championship, although, as in 1926, they were heavily beaten by 'the Rest' in the traditional end-of-season game with the Champions at the Oval.

It had been a fabulous few years. Nor was it quite done. Creaking a little in its ageing joints, and after sharing second place in 1929 and now led by the enthusiastic amateur, Peter Eckersley, they grafted astutely through the damp season of 1930, defeating the weaker brethren, drawing with the stronger and yielding not a loss to anyone. They cleverly banked wins and points in the dryer late spring and then ducked and dived through the wetter months, emerging as slightly sodden Champions, just in front of Gloucestershire.

Finally, in 1934, with Yorkshire robbed of many stars because of Australian Test calls and with Lancashire batting first in 24 out of 30 games and declaring 18 times, the Red Rose county proceeded cautiously to a fifth inter-war title. They secured thirteen victories, leaving Sussex in the runners-up spot. There was melodrama that summer at Trent Bridge, where Harold Larwood and Bill Voce, in the high-speed pomp of their Bodyline days, controversially had Lancashire six wickets down for one run, watched in dismay as five slip catches were dropped and then groaned inwardly as Ernest Tyldesley scored what many regarded as his finest century in the second innings. A strangled lbw appeal from Jack Iddon was answered in the affirmative in the last over of the last day, and Lancashire won an epic and injury-strewn contest by the unlikely margin of 101 runs.

Red Shirts and Roses

That series of five titles in nine years is, of course, easily Lancashire's best run of success, comparable only with Manchester United's domination of the Premiership in the 1990s. All in all, Lancashire had won one outright title and three shared titles by the reckoning of at least some pundits in the pre-official seasons before 1890 and just two - in 1897 and 1904 - before the watershed of 1914. A shared Championship with Surrey in 1950 has been their nearest brush with cricketing paradise on earth during the 70 years since that 1934 success. Thus, with five out of Lancashire's seven official and unshared titles, crushed into that tiny passage of cricketing history, it is difficult to dispute the fact that this was Lancashire's finest hour. Maybe the more poetically inclined of Red Rose supporters paused and recalled the lines of Thomas Osbert Mordaunt, written during the Seven Years War, 1756-1763:

> *Sound, sound the clarion; fill the fife.*
> *Throughout the sensual world proclaim,*
> *One crowded hour of glorious life*
> *Is worth an age without a name.*

Certainly, in terms of Championship successes, despite some valiant near misses and a host of brilliant cup victories since the 1960s, Lancashire's fortunes since 1934 have been something of 'an age without a name'. We should, therefore, linger admiringly over the heroes of that marvellous if short-lived era. Although many of these able cricketers played for England, not many of them were regularly committed in the national cause, nor, of course, was the national commitment as onerous as now it is.

It did mean that, especially during the successes of the late 1920s, the Lancashire team was a strongly built and rarely disturbed unit.

Curiously enough, Cecil Parkin, already buffeted by arguments over a ghosted newspaper article during the South African tour of 1924 (in which he was purported to be critical of his England captain, Arthur Gilligan) had returned to the less strenuous and better-paid reaches of league cricket before the county side reached its full potential. But, along with Billy Meredith and George Formby Senior, Cec Parkin made up the trinity of household gods worshipped in my household, at least when my grandmother, a staunch, unbending low Anglican in her father's wake, was not present.

These were my father's deities. Billy Meredith we have already met. George Formby only became 'Senior' after his untimely death, when his son, George Hoy, adopted his father's stage-name and became, deservedly, so famous as a film star that, in a poll in the USSR during the horrors of World War II, he emerged as the most well-known person in Russia apart from Joseph Stalin. The elder Formby was one of only two music hall artists - Gus Elen being the other - whom the ultra-critical Marie Lloyd would deign to watch. He created the character of one who, although naturally shy and diffident, believed himself to be forward and bold; only Tony Hancock, with cocksureness masking insecurity, has come close in British light entertainment to emulating that amazing piece of theatrical bifurcation.

Cecil Parkin was also a comedian, a term that only came into its modern usage as comic entertainer about the time of the First World War; hitherto it had simply been the opposite of a tragedian, a comic rather than a tragic actor. Indeed, Cecil Parkin has some claim to be assessed as the only original droll produced by first-class cricket. Others have caused laughter, some of them not always purposefully. One must also allow for the fact that, if a well-known cricketer does or says something slightly facetious, the crowd will howl with mirth, where, had it been some ordinary cove, they would have reacted mutely. The level of humour in a crowd at a sports event is not much higher than that of the modern House of Commons, where clumsy banality so frequently passes for elegant wit.

Cecil Parkin was the Joe Grimaldi of cricketers, a clown of effortless ease, and, without doubt, one of the most versatile right-hand bowlers the game has produced, mixing quickish off-spin with all manner of supportive tricks and practically unplayable on a sticky pitch. Local lore suggests that crowds began to drift a little when he retired. At home the tales of his antics were told and retold. His skill as a conjuror helped, not least at a cricket debate where he had been invited to put an opposing viewpoint, but where, assuming agreement with the previous speaker, he entertained a delighted audience to an evening of magic. This delicious sleight of hand enabled him sometimes both to take a catch when he hadn't and appear to have dropped a catch when he had caught it; or to field the ball and return an orange to a surprised wicket-keeper. He was the consummate master of the rolling ball arriving in the hand via the instep, while, from a purely cricketing stance, his facility for disrupting fields with misleading calls and sudden dashes, with overthrows often the consequence, was a beneficial attribute. Rotund Richard Tyldesley, toiling and protesting, would sometimes find Cecil Parkin, dark, tall and dextrous, trotting alongside him, as yet another fielding side found itself in disarray. Cecil Parkin was the Groucho Marx of runners between the wickets.

He accompanied himself musically. He would mark overthrows with a march back to the crease, bat shoulder armed, whistling 'The British Grenadiers', whilst he would run up to bowl in time to the whispered croon of 'the sky is blue and I love you', with the ball delivered on the final syllable. No wonder Leonard Green found him difficult to subject to military discipline and it was these maverick displays, rather than his form, that led to his removal from the Lancashire team. After all, in little more than four seasons he took 901 wickets for the county, at an average of 16 and a strike rate of 6 wickets a game. When one thinks of the mindless and unpleasant sledging of the modern game, it is salutary to reminisce about Cecil Parkin and his unmalicious humour. On one occasion a batsman made a number of un-Christian heaves at his bowling, the ball missing the stumps by whisker after whisker. 'And they're sending missionaries to China', he observed gently.

Cecil Parkin instinctively understood what so many never learn, let alone forget. Professional cricket is an entertainment as well as a sport - and he never succumbed to the temptation to take it all too solemnly. In a fine moment of satire, he had even persuaded Yorkshire to select him once as a stringy youth, although he was actually born over the border in Egglescliffe, County Durham, a horrifying offence against the Tyke blood-cult. The nearest I came to seeing him in the flesh was in 1944, when his ashes were spread in the heightening breeze of that dullish Saturday morning at Old Trafford.

In counterfactual fashion, Harry Makepeace and Charlie Hallows, the opening pair, probably created a form of humour out of their very prudence. The sheer sluggishness with which the scoreboard rotated gave a ghoulish pleasure, as heavily ironic cheering welcomed a ponderously taken leg-bye. However, having absorbed the lesson implicit in the fable of the hare and the tortoise, Makepeace had found a strategy in slowness. The fielding side, borne down by attrition, exhaustion and tedium, were, by teatime, easy meat, and Lancashire would frequently rattle up scores of over 400 in the day, the withering assault coming after the demoralising preliminary barrage.

The dogged Makepeace, with 25,000 runs, and the rather more lissom Hallows, with 20,000 runs, were team players, with Harry Makepeace in particular studying the niceties of the new ball, the approach of an interval, and the problems of different bowlers. Unlike some slow batsmen, there was not a hint of selfishness about them, and such was the case with the obdurate Frank Watson, with 22,000 runs, another cautious opener in the Makepeacean mould of that same era. Indeed, answering the needs of the side, Charlie Hallows subdued his natural flair for handsome shots - and if he occasionally erred on the sumptuous, the more innately watchful Makepeace would stroll down the pitch and chide him. It was if Savonarola had arrived from late medieval Florence and lit a cricketing 'bonfire of the vanities'.

Their nicknames - 'Shake' for Makepeace and 'Flight' for Hallows - convey an incomprehensible degree of velocity for this Puritanical alliance, for, if the Thomas Cranmer of Charlie Hallows (tall, good-looking, black hair sleekly brushed) was occasionally tempted by the incense of the perilous late cut or the risky hook, the John Knox of pugnaciously featured Harry Makepeace would remind him of the eternal verities. Makepeace also played right-half for Everton and was a double international. Middlesbrough-born, his loyalty to Lancashire, as player and coach, could never be faulted. Charlie Hallows was a native of Little Lever, a nephew of Jimmy Hallows - who had done the double of 1,000 runs and 100 wickets for Lancashire in 1904 - while Frank Watson, who scored 300, not out, against Surrey at Old Trafford in 1928, was born in Nottingham. One would have been hard pressed to spot those differing birthrights in terms of the devout service they offered Lancashire.

Ernest Tyldesley was John Ford's 'the Quiet Man' of Lancashire cricket. In pursuit of one or another pairing of these obdurate tradesmen, he was the unobtrusive technician, noiselessly adding the gleaming steel and mechanics of the innings to the sturdy framework they had carpentered. At the same time, he was the complete expert, attractive to observers in the very charm of his classic training, so assured in his grasp of the essential principles that runs accumulated freely and without any semblance of drudgery or strife. There was, it is true, little of the grandeur of a MacLaren or the dramatics of his older brother, John Thomas. Ernest Tyldesley's was a business-like approach, eschewing frills and searching for profits. In this he was eminently successful, for his county total of 34,222 runs (at an average of over 45) is Lancashire's best aggregate, and he is the only Lancastrian numbered among the 24 batsmen who have made a hundred centuries. Such was his efficiency, coupled with so politely mannered a demeanour, that he was canvassed for the Lancashire captaincy in the 1930s when such a blast against the amateur convention was unheard of, and he later became the first former professional to become a vice-president of the county. He played in only fourteen Tests, for reasons that, at this distance, are hard to fathom, not least because his Test average is 55.

Given that runs and often time were in such high credit, it remained for the bowlers to attack in strength. For the hat-trick of titles in the late 1920s the county relied heavily on Ted McDonald, the Tasmanian who, with J.M. Gregory, had terrorised English batting just after World War I. Having qualified residentially and played as Nelson's professional in the Lancashire League, he took the County Championship by storm, taking over 1,000 wickets for Lancashire in a relatively brief spell of nine years.

Dark and slim, there was an Italianate stealth in his velvety skills. His athletic effortlessness and downy rhythm generated a surprising pace and accuracy, something akin to the stiletto in the ribs of the Florentine assassin in Renaissance Italy. Groundsmen stared unbelievingly at the turf over which he had run up to the wicket, for, uncannily, he barely left a mark, so ghostly was his light-footed approach. He was the crucial match-winner for Lancashire in these their most expansive years. In 1937, having been involved in a car accident on the Blackrod bypass, near Bolton, he was killed by another car as he stood by the roadside, talking over the incident with a policeman and others involved in the first crash. For those who wish to emulate such graceful and lethal deeds and seek the secret of Ted McDonald's flair, it is reported that his luncheon always consisted of a fish sandwich and a glass of whisky.

As the Australian maestro wheeled away at high and deadly velocity, there stood in the slips the talkative, ever-complaining and corpulent figure of Richard Tyldesley, who had probably found the journey from Westhoughton as filled with problems as Ted McDonald's rather longer trip from Tasmania. In between the protestations and the anguished moans, he safely pouched over 300 catches, many of them off the startling pace of the Australian. He also took 1,449 wickets for the county at an average of 16 and stands fourth in Lancashire's bowling roster. There could have been no greater contrast than with the silently murderous quality of Ted McDonald.

Wheezing, perspiring, whinging, he weightily exerted himself in the massive undertaking of those few halting steps to the wicket, whence, with much jerkiness and exaggerated wafting of arms, he would release the ball. Sometimes its gently harmless curve would sufficiently tempt the batsman to destruction, rather as the wrecker's welcoming lantern on the perilous rocks decoys the trusting sailor. Sometimes, confused by the ergs of work output devoted to each delivery, the batsman would look wildly for serious deviation, but serious deviation came there none. The pads would be struck and, hoarsely, croakily, the umpire would be requested to further the departure of another baffled customer. Dick Tyldesley would grimly mutter, as his nearest flirtation with satisfaction but with scant regard for the normal usage of simile, 'it was as straight as a whistle'.

What a strange partnership this was, especially for cricket-lovers, who fondly expect their bowling duos to share characteristics, as in two fast merchants, like Ray Lindwall and Keith Miller, or two slow bowlers, like Jim Laker and Tony Lock. In Lancashire's all-conquering era it was topsy-turvy, as if, borrowing from the stars of that day, Webster Booth had teamed up with Robb Wilton rather than Anne Ziegler.

Red Shirts and Roses

There were, of course, other bowlers in talented support, none more so than Frank Sibbles, the Oldham-born medium-paced bowler of exactitude and intelligence, and that eye-catching all-rounder of the handsome shots and the telling left-hand spin, Jack Iddon. Many hoped Iddon, who came from Mawdesley, near Ormskirk, might have captained Lancashire just after the Second World War, but he too was killed in a road accident just a week or so before the start of the first post-war season in 1946.

Compared with their predecessors of the MacLaren generation, this Lancashire XI was a trifle leaden-footed in the field, but the bowlers were treated to the very agreeable compensation of having Warrington's George Duckworth as stumper. His record of 922 victims for Lancashire far outstrips the efforts of any other of the county's wicket-keepers. Quick, chubby, active, with the face of a man weaned on Lancashire hotpot, he, more than anyone, personified the enduring myth of the rough-hewn regional doughtiness of that pre-war Red Rose side. Not for him the courteous referral to a higher authority of some wicket-keepers. His vaunting cry was shouted more in divine judgement than in mortal doubt, one arm raised above him in decisive gesture. He was a fair man - but he also, after the manner of Cec Parkin, understood the responsibilities of the paid entertainer. Thus, unlike the scandalously promiscuous shrieks of many wicket-keepers and close fielders nowadays, he only appealed when sure the batsman was out - and, shrewdly, he comprehended that his trademark appeal would soon lose its lustre if he over-exposed it. So the crowd would wait...and wait...and wait...and then came that stentorian bellow and, in the best traditions of pantomime, there was audience participation, as everyone yelled 'quack, quack'. A simple pleasure, but somewhat more acceptable than on-field obscenity and off-field cacophony.

Having George Duckworth keeping wicket behind you must have been like fighting a war in an occupied country, when not only was the official enemy causing anxiety from the front but you also had constantly to fret about the guerrilla forces hidden to the rear. Nor did George Duckworth content himself with the civilised flick of the bail when it came to a stumping chance; it was a complete demolition job, with bails flying and stumps smashed awry. It was the resistance movement blowing up the armaments train, not some such subtlety as infiltrating a few grains of sand into the engine.

George Duckworth was readily literate and well-informed about cricket and cricketers, and a raconteur of immense gusto. It was he I heard recall the cricket match on a Pacific island where the international date-line ran through the middle of the pitch, so that one batted on Monday and bowled on Tuesday. It is gratifying to recollect that I saw him, even if only in war-time charity matches, wherein, just twice or thrice, he would raise his accusatory arm and sound forth his cocksure, trumpeting appeal - and, on cue, we all responded with a wavering 'quack, quack' and thought maybe the world, despite the war, was not such a bad place after all.

Another figure who shone in those wartime games but who played no part after the war was Eddie Paynter, the diminutive maestro from Oswaldtwistle. Several Lancashire players played on from the 1920s to be senior statesmen in the 1930s; a few, like Cyril Washbrook, suffered a delayed start to good careers in the late 1930s. Only one or two - Len Hopwood, a genuinely effective all-rounder; Len Wilkinson, a gangling leg-spinner and Buddy Oldfield, small of stature but handsome in attack - compressed most of their mainstream Lancastrian careers into the 1930s.

100

Red Rose Refulgent

The fleet-footed Paynter was as popular for his mastery of that Lancashire speciality, cover point fielding, as for his nimble assaults on enemy bowling. He crammed 20,000 runs into a truncated career, whirling away feverishly, as if aware that war would curtail his efforts, just as the consistency of his predecessors had kept him from any early regular place in the team. For so compulsively aggressive a bat, he played many a major innings, including 322 in 1937 against Sussex at Hove, then and until 1990 Lancashire's second highest individual total after Archie MacLaren's 424. He stands second, with just over 59, to Herbert Sutcliffe in the English Test averages and his 83 at Brisbane during the strife of the Bodyline series of 1932-33, when he tottered from a hospital bed to save England, is verily the stuff of legends and the making of screenplays.

Not excessively orthodox in fashion, he drove with a ferocity that belied his tiny stature, he hooked extravagantly, sometimes with both feet off the ground, he swept so urgently that the knee roll of his pad was soon besmirched, and he indulged himself in what he called his 'fancy cuts'. The key to his mighty success was undoubtedly his visual acuity and his eyes stared from his triangle of a face with an avian intensity. His eyesight enabled him to play late to the point of gross unpunctuality - and then he played with unleashed vigour. Eddie Paynter...fore and sur-names adhered closely together in the public imagining. One glanced and did not recognise the *Wisden* profile headed 'Edward Paynter'; one might have similarly bypassed the anonymous sound of 'Paynter', where 'Hutton' or 'Hammond' might have made one leap to attention; it is said he was known among his team-mates as 'Ted' - but 'Ted Paynter' sounds like a dance band leader or the secretary of a trades union of the 1930s. No, it had to be Eddie Paynter, as replete with character as he was bursting with talent.

Of course, George Duckworth, Eddie Paynter and their colleagues were as fortunate in their spin-doctor as was Tony Blair with Alistair Campbell or Samuel Johnson with James Boswell. Perhaps Neville Cardus, the literary portrait painter, was lucky, for his part, to come across so three-dimensional and characterful a bunch of working cricketers. There is no doubt that his interpretations were affectionately motivated by the calls of aesthetic rather than legal truth. The dourly consistent Yorkshire batsman, Wilf Barber, is said to have accused him of being 'flowery', at which Maurice Leyland intervened with the comment, 'that's more than can be said for thy batting, Wilfred' - or is that too an example of the Cardusian insistence on artistic verity, of recording what Maurice Leyland would have said had he remained true to his quintessential personality?

There is, whatever the veracity of the detail, some authenticity in the overall picture of these hard-working, accomplished craftsmen, treading the streets of their mill or colliery town homelands in decent boots and wearing tidy suits, earning not vast riches, but, with something less than £400 maximum for a full summer's graft in all matches (plus reasonable bonuses) showing an improvement on life at pit-face or loom. Complacently, without affectation but perhaps with a hint of understandable smugness, they enjoyed the quiet respect of their fellows, the spinners, weavers, miners and engineers of their previous employ and what, but for their cricketing gifts, would have been their destiny. Another abiding trait is the constancy of their service, almost like engine drivers, shunting in and out of Manchester Exchange Station, or electrical engineers in Trafford Park, soldiering on with the same company for years, until the time came for the gold medal or the clock to put on the mantelpiece in retirement. Ernest Tyldesley, Jack Sharp, J.T. Tyldesley, Harry Makepeace, Jack Iddon and Frank Watson form six of the first septet of Lancastrians in respect of first-class appearances for the county; the other one is Cyril Washbrook, strictly bred in the mould of these pre-war professionals and, save for those six missed war-time seasons, he would have topped the list.

Of all Neville Cardus' eloquent if, apropos judges' rules of evidence, flawed pen-pictures, the one that possibly summarises the character of this great Lancashire team most persuasively is his questioning of Richard Tyldesley, when an umpire had given out a batsman caught by that rotund soul at first slip. Dick Tyldesley had insisted on the batsman returning to the crease, for he knew he had marginally grounded the ball in attempting the catch. Neville Cardus wished to know why he had not let sleeping dogs lie and left it, according to the laws, to the umpire's decision. Dick Tyldesley answered (or, in terms of aesthetic integrity, should have answered), 'Westhoughton Sunday School, Mr Cardus, Westhoughton Sunday School.'

In the late 1950s I suddenly found I had an indirect connection with this Arthurian surfeit of myth and legend. Read all about it in a brief article I wrote in *The Journal of the Cricket Society in 2001*, the wordage granted leave to be repeated here by the journal's editor, that most urbane and fluent of cricket litterateurs, Clive Porter.

The Wedding of Neville Cardus

'Is this where I register my Auntie Edna's death?' It was a chill February Monday morning, and Auntie Edna had doubtless succumbed to the freezing damp over the previous bitterly cold weekend. The enquiring nephew had stuck his head around the door of the seminar room, just as I was in full swing on the topic of Louis XIV. His interruption brought us abruptly back from Versailles to All Saints, Manchester, a substantive switch in locations at the best of times, but never more so than on a wintry Monday morning about forty years ago. The boarder having been repelled, his aunt's death unregistered, and the Sun King's character having been summarily discussed, it was time to discover why anyone should think Auntie Edna's death could be registered within our precincts. The Old Chorlton Town Hall was an annexe to the college next door, and its long-serving caretaker was the fount of much information. Had he not supervised the comings and goings of an entire battery of potential African presidents, several of whom had been imprisoned for political offences, and all of whom, he claimed, had attended a pan-African conference within this very building, when independence had been but a dream?

For many years, it transpired, the building had housed the Chorlton Registry Office. For many years it hadn't, but cultural habits are slow to change. This particular tutorial base had apparently been the centre for operations and this gave rise to furious thought. Were we debating the causes of the War of the Spanish Succession on the very spot where Neville Cardus had been married? His own account of his nuptials is well-known: leaving Old Trafford soon after start of play, Harry Makepeace and Charlie Hallows prudently at the crease, going to Chorlton Registry

Office where he 'committed the most respectable and irrevocable act in a mortal man's life'; returning to Old Trafford to find the score had moved sonorously on to 17 for 0.

It was 17th June 1921. The bride was a schoolteacher, Edith Honorine Watten King, of nearby Albany Road, Victoria Park, and the registrar was C.H. Ramsbottom. It was that indefatigable researcher, Geoffrey Copinger, who was able to cry, after Jack Point and Wilfred Shadbolt in *The Yeomen of the Guard*, 'what a tale of cock and bull', pointing out that Makepeace and Hallows only opened once for Lancashire in June, and in a different match. It would also appear from the excellent *Association of Cricket Statisticians and Historians Complete First-class Match List, Volume 2*, that Lancashire were actually playing Middlesex at Lord's on his wedding day. Neville Cardus would have called to his defence the superior quality of aesthetic truth; Makepeace and Hallows should have been making un-merry during his marriage ceremony.

In any event, lecturing on that spot thereafter became a more highly charged emotional experience, for we could consider it a brush with greatness. Similarly with Louis XIV. Almost every time we finished classes and walked into the sombre streets of All Saints, it was tippling down: something about *après moi le déluge*.

11.

The Way it Was

A SPRAWLING and multifaceted city like Manchester was less vulnerable to the chill winds of the worldwide economic slump between the two great wars than, for instance, its neighbouring mill or colliery townships, with their over-dependence on a single staple.

The 1920s and 1930s constituted a peculiar social mix. The Great Depression certainly dominated economic life in those between years. It dived to its nadir in the years 1929 to 1933, when as many as 4m were unemployed. This meant that, with families, some 7m (a sixth of the nation) existed on a dole that began, for a male worker, at weekly 15s (75p). It was then means tested after fifteen weeks but, in any event, the less well-paid unskilled labourers, who were not included in the National Insurance scheme at that time, had to resort to the Poor Law for assistance. But, after the hike in prices consequent on the First World War, it subsided into a low price depression, so that, in relative terms, the gap between being in work on perhaps two pounds a week and being on the dole was, for example, much less socially daunting than the chasm between being the employed and the out-of-work in the Thatcherite slump of the dire 1980s.

Nevertheless, in spite of the genuine poverty consequent upon the depression, industrial output actually rose by a third between 1924 and 1937, one of the biggest increases ever recorded. What was noticeable was the modish growth in consumer goods, such as light bulbs, safety razors, cosmetics, toothpaste, artificial textiles, fountain pens and bicycles. The production of vacuum cleaners shot up from 18,000 in 1930 to 410,000 in 1935. Manchester's commercial spread was versatile and lively, from the electrical equipment of Ferranti's to the aircraft construction of A.V. Roe's, with all kinds of foodstuffs, domestic goods and the like being produced besides.

The styling of the high streets altered. Accompanying my mother on one of her daily shopping expeditions (no refrigerators nor freezers, so most foodstuffs had to be purchased on the day of use) we would not only stroll past the co-op but also past by now familiar multiple and chain-stores, such as Boots, the chemists; Thomas Lipton's, the grocers and, ineluctably, Woolworth's threepenny and sixpenny store. Manchester itself, of course, boasted department stores as well, like Paulden's or John Lewis or, at the posh end of the market, Kendal Milne.

Heavily branded products - 'Force' Wheatflakes, advertised by Sunny Jim, or the canned goods of Crosse & Blackwell and Heinz - were now all the rage, so that, while plenty of single-shop owners remained, few cured their own bacon or blended their own tea any longer. It was the first era of 'table-readiness', with convenience and reconstituted foods at the beck and call of the housewife. I shall not be alone in recalling the kind of 1930s Sunday tea that consisted of tinned salmon, followed by tinned pineapple chunks or peaches, smothered in custard made from a packet. Nor will anyone of that generation easily forget the blandishments of advertising, from Sunny Jim and his breakfast cereals to the Ovaltinies. Even the stolid potato, that ever-present in three-quarters of all British meals then, received the treatment: by 1938 a million packets of Smith's Crisps, complete with that elusive blue paper twist of salt, were being sold annually.

The National Grid was established during this time - and both the supply of electricity and the sale of electrical goods doubled during the 1930s. I remember the excitement of the family homestead being 'electrified' not many years before the Second World War. My grandmother preferred gas for reading; a 'softer' light, she reckoned. The wires and plugs and bulbs that brought instant brightness to every room at the flick of a switch enraptured all the rest of us.

Tinned salmon and electrical bulbs were signals of a countervailing movement to the drab misery of the depression. There was a definitive move towards a suburban culture. Between the wars 3m private and 1m council houses were built - there had only been 24,000 council houses in the whole of the country in 1914. This meant that, by 1939, two-fifths of British housing units had been constructed since the previous war. In 1914 90 per cent of houses had been privately rented; the 1920s and 1930s marked the switch to a mixed economy of owner-occupation and municipal letting. The aspiring lower-middle-class clerks and other professionals were ambitious to buy a little semi-detached house; the respectable tradesmen or artisans were ambitious to rent a new council house. The costs were similar: a weekly mortgage repayment might have been as low as 8s (40p), while the average council house rental was 7s (35p), when 60 per cent of those working earned between £2 and £5 a week.

The Englishman's home was certainly his castle - but it was also his sanctuary. He was more inclined to stay at home indoors. One interesting result was less drunkenness, at least in public. Convictions for intoxication declined from roughly 200,000 a year before 1914 to approximately 50,000 in the 1930s. The social historian, G.M. Trevelyan, believed that the first decades of the 20th century witnessed the exchange from drinking to gambling - with, of course, the allure of Littlewoods Football Pools to add to horse and dog racing wagers - as the premier working-class vice. He would have been fascinated by the case study of my grandfather, Ada's husband, Harry. Born 1870 and died 1940, he perched on the cusp of this transformation and distinguished himself by representing both addictions with conspicuous vigour.

Hire purchase - the 'never never' - was much utilised by way of furnishings for this widespread rash of new homes, with a typical bedroom suite priced at £28 and a pair of blankets at £1.3s. Feeling more secure about one's tenancy, either privately owned or council rented, many were converted to 'the religion of home improvements', so that there was an outburst of decorating and gardening, even if there was virtually no central heating and 'chilblains remained a unique English malady'.

Thus the fringes of Manchester became the scenes for considerable house building, some of it scattered and sporadic, examples of what came to be called ribbon development. On sabbatarian family walks we would stroll around some of these sites, in districts like Woodheys or Timperley, with my father growling 'bloody jerry-built' the while. However, it was the creation of the satellite town of Wythenshawe, the largest enterprise undertaken by the Manchester Corporation to that date, which was the more remarkable. The manor of Norwardine had been part of the tract of land between Mersey and Ribble donated by William the Conqueror to Roger of Poitou for services rendered during the Norman invasion. From being a knightly sub-fiefdom, it had passed through the hands of St Werburgh's Abbey, Chester and, after Henry VIII's dissolution of the monasteries, to the Tatton and then the Simon families. Now 5,000 acres of Cheshire plain were, from 1930, added to the bailiwick of Manchester, and housing for 100,000 people, then the largest such estate in Europe, was built.

The migrants included branches of my family from the Quay Street area of Deansgate, the old canal company house, for example, yielded up, with Great Uncle Sam ensconced in the Benchill sector of Wythenshawe, not too keen on the bus travel to work but rather enjoying the little garden. We would bus out to visit our relatives there. All was uniformly neat and clean, with the regular patterns of acceptable housing, with the stocky little garden gates and the glistening green front doors. Wythenshawe, like many another estate, might later take a social dip, but then and for a generation, it was comfortable, reassuring and thriving.

Those red corporation buses that took Uncle Sam to work or his relations to visit him were vital ingredients in the mix. Out-of-town estate development and the straggling filaments of suburban housing would scarcely have been feasible without the bus. They carried people not only to work but also to shops and cinemas and to football and cricket grounds, like the two Old Traffords. It was the halcyon period of the bus. More flexible than the train and tram, it could obviously manoeuvre more or less everywhere and, by the early 1930s, the buses carried more passengers than the trains.

Buses had been practically non-existent outside the big cities prior to 1914. Now they turned up everywhere. At home in Sale we had the 47 and 48 buses that carried on down through the main Chester road to Altrincham; then, in strict numerical sequence, the 49 bus that worked through the centre of the town and terminated in Sale Moor; and the 50 bus that wended across from Washway Road, part of the main Manchester/Chester thoroughfare, through Brooklands and Sale Moor and out the back way, so to speak, via Northenden and Didsbury, into Manchester, and very useful it was for getting to Maine Road, when United were domiciled there. The flexibility of the bus was of paramount value. As housing estates were built, they shifted or extended their routes and sometimes changed their numbers. There was a also a single-decker North Western company bus linking Sale Station with Ashton-on-Mersey and later a corporation 99 bus that somehow managed to negotiate a torturous path from the north-east of the borough, through Brooklands, Baguley and Wythenshawe and into the centre of Manchester. In addition, there were the fleets of 71 buses, transporting workers in their hundreds to and from Trafford Park.

Everyone had their own favoured bus route-ways, rather like the natural tracks of animals, conveying them hither and thither on a regular basis. A familiar sight in the outreaches of Manchester was the 53 bus, which seemed to be ubiquitous, perhaps because it followed a crossways direction, whereas most buses drove into and out of

The Way it Was

the city centre, usually via the bus terminus of Piccadilly Gardens. The 53 bus reminded one of the Flying Dutchman, as if it were an accursed vehicle, destined ceaselessly to roam.

These twenty or so years were hinge years. The variety theatre remained hugely popular. My father, in the 1920s, would study, with his mates, Monday's *Manchester Evening News*, in order to plan their nightly excursions to the twenty or so Hippodromes and Empires in the area. There were also 5,000 cinemas in Britain and, especially after the advent of the 'talkies' in 1927, two-fifths of the population visited their cinema at least once a week. Yet the more private pursuits of the 'wireless' and records were also at hand. In 1926 the British Broadcasting Corporation was founded as a public body by royal charter, and nine out of ten homes had a radio set by 1939. Manchester accommodated the North Region headquarters in Piccadilly. After 1926, when electrical replaced acoustic recording, the gramophone became very popular and the weighty black 78rpm discs sold in thousands. Gracie Fields sold 4m records between 1928 and 1933. These forms of leisure looked ahead to the post-war years when leisure became much more fixed on the home.

The rise in usage of the private car alongside the potent success of the public bus is another instance of this hinge-like quality of the age. At first the car had been viewed as the automotive substitute for the rich man's personal coach - that is, a very rare, costly piece of apparatus. Initially, Rolls Royce fashion, the plutocratic emphasis was on the luxury motor car. It took the genius of Henry Ford to envision the car as the vehicular tool of the common man. Between the wars the number of motor vehicles in Britain jumped from 1m to 4m; of these private cars numbered 200,000 in 1921 and 2m in 1939. There was carnage on the roads as a consequence. In 1934 7,342 were slain, compared with 3,598 deaths in 1996 when there were 38m vehicles, a dozen times as many, on the roads. It was this slaughter of the automobile innocents that led to the battery of driving tests, speed limits and Belisha Beacons. At the same time - another example of the 'pushmepullyou' style of the era - there were still 3m horses busy, in more ways than one, on the streets of Great Britain, pulling cartloads of coal and other goods for delivery. The covert dash into the street, bucket in hand, to recover the steaming manure for one's rhubarb patch, courtesy of the coal, milk, greengrocery or railway horse, was a frequent scene in the residential drama.

One commentator said 'the garage has replaced the nursery', for the widespread yearning for a car was one explanation of the collapse in the birth-rate and the conscious fashion, evolving since the 1880s, to have much smaller families and maybe purchase, complete with psychologically meaningful title, a 'Baby' Austin. Yet contraception was something of an iffy lottery. Although people became a little more knowing during and after the 1914-1918 War, only about one in ten couples used sheaths and about seven in ten couples employed the withdrawal method, while there were just a few diaphragms deployed by well-to-do progressive women. Many illegal abortions were performed in the working-class areas; one estimate claims 100,000 annually. Thus one is left with a blanket layer of abstinence to explain the comparatively abrupt switch to small families. Indeed, the famous historian, A.J.P. Taylor, warned fellow tillers in the historical field that, when studying Britain from 1880 to 1940, they 'had on their hands a frustrated people'.

Red Shirts and Roses

A.J.P. Taylor was wont to use this deliberate restraint as an explanation of why the British people between the two world wars were similarly lacking in enterprise and élan in the political and economic fields, although some psychiatrists might have expected that such sublimated energies might have been channelled into other ventures. Certainly it was an inward-looking, static age, what David Thompson, another fine historian of the period, described as being one of 'incorrigible immobilisme'. Ostrich-like, the English buried their heads in the sands of their island home, trying to forget the trauma of a First World War and trying to pretend that the Fascist posturings on the Continent were not the ugly omens of a Second World War. Even the architecture, such as the Manchester Central Library, opened in 1934, or the New Town Hall extension, built in 1938, was heavy, for all its gracefulness, of peering back to the classical assurance of the past, lacking any exciting imagining of the future.

It was a nervy and frenetic time, with lots of restless, superficial activity, from jazzy dances and fashions, to umpteen changes in the formulae of determining points in the County Cricket Championship, yet without any of the root problems ever being addressed. Alan Bennett shrewdly created the boarding school, Albion House, for his 1968 stage play of inter-war literary manners, *Forty Years On*. The claustrophobic, pre-occupied nature of such an institution was a clever metaphor for Britain between the wars. It suggests the conception of George V as some kind of bluff but aloof chairman of governors, and Stanley Baldwin, with his 'safety first' policy, as an avuncular headmaster and Neville Chamberlain, the forlorn if well-meaning appeaser, a deputy head somewhat out of his depth.

It has been suggested that the Russian Bolshevik government used the 1926 General Strike as a cue as to whether to back Leon Trotsky's vision of instant world revolution, or Joseph Stalin's opinion that 'single state socialism' should first be consolidated in the USSR. Joe Stalin proved the cannier assessor of events. The General Strike, compared with the political shenanigans on the European mainland, was something of a quickly extinguished damp squib, desperately although the miners fought for improved standards. Working with reminiscence groups of older people in the 1980s and 1990s, one found that the General Strike scarcely registered on the retina of the collective memory. The Abdication Crisis, a little later and decidedly more gossipy, was just about the only domestic political event that really scored on the account sheet of recall for that age.

It was a time of quiet despondency, relieved by mundane pleasures, not of colourful unrest and manic rebelliousness. The likes of Gracie Fields and George Formby cheered up everybody, helping them to resign themselves to 'the night of doubt and sorrow', rather than subverting them with ideological wiles and lampoons. Flanagan and Allen warbling *Underneath the Arches*, not some harsh intonation of *The Red Flag*, was the melodic emblem of the British Depression.

It was, as the hymn book also sings, 'the common round, the daily task' that adults remembered from that closeted, restrictive era - not much different from what children remembered. For me, it was a cosy, secure, cheerful home, then the harsher ordeal of school, tricked out with a couple of holidays in North Wales; a ride or two in a 'Baby' Austin (belonging to two spinster great aunts, who were district nurses in

The Way it Was

Collyhurst and Ancoats; they called it Bunty, which rather bore out A.J.P. Taylor's 'nursery' hypothesis); *Toytown*, with Larry the Lamb, Mr Growser and Ernest the Policeman, Romany and L. du Garde Peach's *Castles of England* on *Children's Hour*; Shirley Temple and *Snow White and the Seven Dwarfs* at the local cinemas; my first pantomime - to the Princes' Theatre on Oxford Street, soon to be bombed, to be enthralled by *Mother Goose*, starring Albert Modley ('Lancashire's Favourite Yorkshireman' - 'Me eyes are going funny; I keep running into pubs'); a Saturday afternoon stroll to watch Sale play rugby, with the strongly built England winger, Hal Sever, scoring a try; hearing every day the sonorous moan of the Metro's buzzer in Trafford Park a mile or so away, calling the faithful to work like so many religious adherents, or informing them toil had ended for the day; aware of the rattle of electric trains at the end of the road (from whence I derived 'Lectric Me' as a substitute for the unpronounceable 'Eric'); clambering up on the nearby bridge wall to watch the long coal barges being towed along the canal by one of those lonely 3m horses; listening to the 1939 Cup Final on the 'wireless', with Portsmouth beating Wolves 4-1 and running out into the street to replay those excitements with a shredded tennis ball...

Somehow the doings of Manchester United and Lancashire County Cricket Club caught the temperate mood of those inter-war years. The honest, homely, faintly uninspiring efforts of United in these seasons, as well as the brisk success, honed out of calculating, technical grasp and craftsmanship, of the Lancashire XI, was of a piece with an era of cultural domesticity and political introversion.

Then there was the fright, the alarm, of Munich in 1938 and, inevitably, the fatal Sunday morning, clear-lit and shining, of 3rd September 1939. There was talk of evacuation, of children being shipped to Canada; there was the musty, suffocating texture of the gas mask; there was the sudden launch of barrage balloons into the bright Mancunian skies; there was a flurry of ensuring the air raid shelter was in passable shape; there was the frisson of nervousness, and, it must be confessed, some infantile clinging, as father donned his black serge fire service uniform and marched off purposefully up the 'brew' to the fire station. All those memory banks that had saved little or nothing of political remembrance from the 1920s and 1930s were about to be sharply refocused on the unforgettable minutiae of total war.

PART THREE:

MODERN TIMES

12.

Emerging from the Red Shadow

HAVING SPENT one's junior years as a war child, the peace of 1945 arrived with the sporting promise of matters talked about, but barely remembered with any consciousness, suddenly adopting the mantle of reality. The time of parental recollection and anecdote, and of reading what records were available in the rather scanty football and cricket annuals available during the war, was finished. The historical period was ended. Now I would be able, as avid watcher and peruser of newspapers, to be a tiny part of, just a small cog in, the process itself. And, unlike the traditional course of Anglocentric history, the modern era swamps the preceding ancient and medieval phases. 60 years on - and it is a terrifying thought that I have been wedded, for better or worse, even unto a diamond jubilee, to a cricket team for over half its legal history and to a football team for nearly three quarters of its modern manifestation.

Thus the years 1945 and 1946 brought, in bewildering kaleidoscope, a series of spectating 'firsts'. In August 1945 I saw my first first-class match. Unlike the huge majority of first-class matches I thereafter witnessed, I more or less saw every ball bowled, whereas, for the future, a combine of working, playing and other duties made such total immersion often unfeasible. It was the Fifth Victory Test against Australia, effectively the pick of Australian servicemen available in Britain. A sort of Tolstoyan mood of 'war and peace' had prevailed, for the first four Tests had been played while at peace with Germany but still at war with Japan.

Diplomatic clarity prevailed by 20th August, when this three-day match began. 'VJ Day', which marked the end of the Japanese war, was 15th August, following the German surrender and the celebration of 'VE Day' on 8th May. The shattering detonation of two atom bombs had precipitately brought the Japanese authorities to the negotiating table. One fell on Hiroshima on 6th August and the other on Nagasaki on 9th August, with 110,000 killed in all. It is a sobering thought that, on the day that first bomb was used, it was August Bank Holiday in the UK, and Keith Miller was scoring 118 in the Fourth Victory Test at Lord's, in the presence of a record 34,000 people.

Emerging from the Red Shadow

A military air attended proceedings at Old Trafford. German prisoners of war were paid three farthings an hour for painting the scarred fabric of the ground and repairing sundry damage, while the heavy roller was still on active service in the Western Desert, whence it had been directed to assist with the preparation of airstrips. Perhaps in consequence, the wicket had a natural quality that brought the lively best out of bowlers and batsmen alike. Lancashire's Dick Pollard, who took more wickets than anyone in this rubber, soon got among the Australians, for whom Keith Miller's handsome 77, not out, was easily the choice innings. They were dismissed for 173. The impregnable defence of Len Hutton and the easy mastery of Wally Hammond distinguished a sound English reply, although rain halved the second day's ration of play. Late on the second day and early on the third day inroads were quickly made into the Australian batting, with Eddie Phillipson, Pollard's sparring partner, taking six wickets.

Then Bob Christofani, having bewildered with his leg breaks to some tune, scored a thrilling century that brought the crowd exultantly to its feet. Driving and hooking magically, it was an innings of which it was said 'even Victor Trumper could have taken pride' - and, famously, this was the event that Jim Swanton heard broadcast on a cackling radio in a Thai café when he emerged from a Japanese prisoner of war camp. Nor would Bob Christofani, who was to play little or no cricket afterwards, have managed this enterprise without the patient attendance of R.G. Williams, keeping up a doughty end at number ten and himself - again to the reward of much applause, the survivor of a four-year sojourn in enemy hands. This left England a target of 141 but with only something over two hours of play remaining. However, Bill Edrich and Jack Robertson led a sprightly assault and England squared the series, winning by six wickets.

Over 72,000 watched enthralled as a game of taut adventure unfolded. So much of the game is easily recoverable from the bunkers of memory - a catch by Hammond; a run-out courtesy of Hutton; Laurie Fishlock athletically patrolling the boundary, as well as a host of falling wickets and sterling boundaries. Some curios were to be garnered later: it always gives egalitarian pleasure to remember that Lindsay Hassett, a steadfast refusenik when it came to commissions, was basically an Army Warrant Officer, captaining a team of Air Force Officers. It remains a point of deep satisfaction that my 'debut' first-class match was close to a classic.

The moist summer of 1946 heralded two more 'firsts'. The County Championship recommenced in that summer after what Jim Swanton called 'the long hiatus' of six moribund seasons. The exigencies of school cricket meant it was impossible to gaze on Lancashire as they played Glamorgan in the opening home game of the post-war county programme. However, it was possible to undertake the six-minute electric train journey to Old Trafford a week later to attend my first day of Championship cricket. It was the darling buds of May and it was the terrible twins of Middlesex. One of the twins was in crackling form. Denis Compton more or less took on Lancashire single-handed, scoring a century in each innings. Thankfully, Cyril Washbrook, our hero, replied with a typically buccaneering 182, at that point the highest post-war English first-class score, while the persevering toil of Dick Pollard earned him the excellent reward of 14 wickets. Although Jim Sims

111

took six wickets in Lancashire's first innings, Eric Price, at number ten, made 54, not only his highest first-class score but also about a tenth of all his first-class runs. In the second innings an undefeated fourth wicket stand between Jack Ikin and Bill's brother, Geoff Edrich (both of them making good fifties) led Lancashire to a seven wicket win.

So this was another pleasing introductory memory, particularly in cricketing terms. It accorded with the Cardus schoolboy prayer for a genius in opposition (for Ranji read Compton) to perform miracles and for Lancashire to win. As a memorial to that remembrance, the Lancashire XI for those days was Cyril Washbrook, Winston Place, Jack Ikin, Nigel Howard, Geoff Edrich, Alan Wharton, Tom Brierley, who kept wicket, Jack Fallows, who captained the side, Dick Pollard, Eric Price and Bill Roberts.

Then there was the first official Test match. This was England and India. About a dozen of us waited an hour or so in the queues and ranged ourselves on the terraced seating opposite the pavilion, huddled together under a makeshift marquee of bicycle capes and gaberdine raincoats as the rain spattered down. It was late July. We joked and chatted and ruefully ate our sandwiches, about which it is no idle cliché to deploy the adjective 'soggy'. Bred in the Manchester area, one soon learned that as, allegedly, with the Inuit and snow, there are a dozen or so words to describe rain. This was 'fine', as in thinnish, but not excessively 'wetting' rain, so much so that, when it petered out around lunch-time, play was able to begin soon after 2pm.

There followed a minor feast of batting, redolent of all that was exceptional about English cricket just before and just after World War II. In less than four hours there were over 200 runs registered in a well-organised assault upon the Indian bowling, which included the skills of Lala Amarnath - who somehow contrived to bowl off the wrong foot - and the wiles of Vinoo Mankad. The opening foursome each scored characteristic fifties, their individual traits melded together as harmoniously as any string or wind quartet; the delicately etched technique of Len Hutton; the defiantly robust method of Cyril Washbrook; the cavalier extravagance of Denis Compton; the imperious ripeness of Walter Hammond. I had been lucky again in this induction as in those others, and maybe that mix of rain-affected morning and resplendent afternoon was, in its fashion, the portent and arbiter of cricket watching forever.

Dick Pollard made his full England debut and took 5 for 24 in the Indian first innings in a match that the tourists barely scraped through to a draw, their last pair surviving the last thirteen minutes. One glanced with some child-like awe on the Nawab of Pataudi, Senior, the Indian captain, but my chief recollection of this the first touring side of my cricketing experience was of V.M. Merchant. A fortnight before the Test match I saw him score 242 against Lancashire - the first 200 I had ever witnessed - and I was charmed by his lithe shot-making, yet with his resolute defence always the pragmatic base for a career in which his average of 71 is second only to Don Bradman's in the world listings. His stylishness was sublime: against the orthodox and well-regulated left-arm spin of Bill Roberts, for instance, he late-cut him with such dextrous finesse that the ball beat the sole and floundering slip and skimmed zestfully to the boundary as if the bowling had been of high velocity. I was entranced.

Emerging from the Red Shadow

The arrival of successive tourists to play against county and country was something of an enjoyable bonus. In the vintage summer of 1947 it was, memorably, the South Africans. Ken Cranston, the Lancashire captain, made his Test debut at Old Trafford. He did passing well, although he amazed the cricketing world a fortnight later when he ended the South African second innings with 4 wickets in 6 balls. As much else in that magical and - after the Arctic bite of the preceding winter and the flooding of the early spring - hot season, the stage was dominated by Denis Compton and Bill Edrich. At Old Trafford they added 228 in just less than 200 minutes for the third wicket, each of then scoring a century.

In 1948 it was the all-conquering Australians. They played three times in Manchester, twice against the county. From our usual spot opposite the pavilion we watched, open-mouthed, as, trotting down the pavilion steps in May, came Don Bradman, followed by a host of baggy green caps. That sight of Bradman leading out the Australians is one of the clearest of all memories. In the county match in August Bill Roberts, that naggingly precise left-hand spinner, took six wickets, including that of Bradman, in the Australian first innings, and many thought he had bowled himself into the Test team. It was not to be - and, as England were bowled out for 52 at the Oval in the relevant Test, he may not have despaired too long.

In the Test match itself, England made their best fist of the rubber, leading in the first innings and declaring in the second in a drawn match. This was the game in which Denis Compton, having retired hurt for 4, returned with five wickets down, and supported by the lower order, made a dashing 145, not out, scorning the weaponry of Ray Lindwall, Keith Miller and the rest of that strong attacking force. White plaster adhering to his forehead, over which the not-so-Brylcreemed locks of hair occasionally strayed, Denis Compton on-drove Lindwall over mid-on's head for four to complete a brave century. The ball rolled among us where we sat cheering on the grass and we - well, one of us - threw it up to a smiling Bradman as he cantered down to retrieve it. Also in that innings Dick Pollard hospitalised the sardonically talkative Sid Barnes from his post at mid-on, silly to the point of idiocy, with a blow to his kidneys. Sid Barnes would have been called a sledger today.

In the dry months of 1949 it was the turn of New Zealand, deliberately playing out four three-day Tests to four draws to make a diplomatic appeal for five-day duration fixtures. Led by Walter Hadlee - whom I encountered, with much pleasure, nearly 50 years later - and starring Martin Donnelly and Bert Sutcliffe, they faced England's youngest debutant, Brian Close, at Old Trafford. Seeking quick runs, he was caught on the mid-wicket boundary, opposite the pavilion, off Tom Burtt for a duck. Then it was the West Indies in the calypso summer of 1950, except that, in the first Test at Old Trafford, they were well and truly swamped. Although Alf Valentine took the first eight wickets to fall in his initial Test match, and although Sonny Ramadhin grabbed four wickets in his, it was, on this occasion, the turn of, to misquote the Caribbean lyrics, 'those two little pals that led to follies, Bob Berry of Lancs and Brum's Eric Hollies'. The two short-statured spinners took seventeen wickets between them as England won by 202 runs.

Thus, in five years, we witnessed the complete nap hand of the Test playing countries. It was an interesting introduction to international cricket.

113

Red Shirts and Roses

The international football scene was very different, with chiefly 'home' internationals on the menu and the dish served at Wembley. There were compensations in the forceful approach Manchester United took to the post-war challenge. Not long after that 1946 Test match against the Indians, we biked to Maine Road and watched our first ever First Division match.

Manchester United had had some good war years, finishing first in the 1941/42 League Championship and being runners up to Bolton Wanderers in the 1944/45 League Cup Final. A particular memory is one's first sight of Stan Matthews, akin to that initial sighting of Don Bradman. Stan Matthews was less authentically garbed than the green-capped Australian. It was a wartime cup-tie against Stoke City and Stan Matthews had a fitness test before the kick-off of a primitive nature that would strike dismay to the hearts of the sophisticated medical practitioners sixty years on. He was wearing his Air Force blues, tunic-less, with his grey service braces hoisting up his trousers over which he had pulled his football socks and then laced his boots for a desultory kickabout. He played but Stoke were defeated 6-1, for all the efforts of the Mountford brothers and Frank Soo. Stan Matthews was lively enough but there was a cheery moment when the tiny winger, Billy Wrigglesworth, tip-toed back as Matthews faced up to George Roughton, and back-heeled the ball from between the wizard's feet.

Stan Matthews grinned as much as anybody, but now in peacetime, it was, rather paradoxically, time for sterner stuff. One might have recalled the story told about Stan Matthews' father, Jack Matthews, boxer and barber. When, as a teenager, his son began his illustrious and epic career, Jack Matthews never asked him, on his return to the family homestead, how he had fared. 'He never asks me', explained the fighting hairdresser, by way of explanation, 'how many hair-cuts I've done'. There lay the essence of professionalism: get the job done without fuss and palaver; make your living the best way you can and cut out the frills. There also lay the grudging affection felt by many of the older generation for that drab era.

The abrupt end of the war against Japan took everyone by surprise, not least the impoverished British Government, for American aid ended on VJ Day, whereas fifteen months had been the cautious estimate of the war's extra length after VE Day. The August date caught the football authorities slightly napping. It was too late to reorder the 1945/46 season, so there was another round of wartime competitions, a decent chance for clubs to regroup and recuperate. There were, therefore, seven years of regional football, without the promise of promotion or the hazard of relegation, although in this final year guest players were rarely utilised. The only exception was the resumption of the FA Cup, which Derby County, stimulated by the fizzing talents of Raich Carter and Peter Doherty, won. United went out in the fourth round to Preston North End, but the third round enabled us to watch our first-ever FA Cup match. The home and away principle was used until the semi-finals and United, having drawn 2-2 with Accrington Stanley, gave them a lordly 5-1 caning, to our delight, in the home leg. It was a Wednesday afternoon and Jack Rowley scored a hat-trick.

After this lengthy preparatory phase, Manchester United's first post-war genuine First Division match was against Grimsby Town. The crowd was enormous and friendly; the buzz of conversation seemed to waver on the edge of laughter, so delighted were people to be standing, at 1s6d (9d for we juveniles) a time, on the terraces. Many of them, of course, had been in situations where they must have wondered whether indeed they would again enjoy that privilege. Unlike the dampening effect of Blackburn Rovers' defeat of United to mark my first-ever viewing, my heroes obliged with a 2-1 victory over a team that was not, in truth, long to grace the elite. There was Tommy Blenkinsopp up front for the Mariners, in their traditional black and white stripes; there was Harry Betmead and there was George Tweedy in goal, but they faded into the shadows as Matt Busby's first First Division selection settled into what proved to be a consistent stride.

From the onset, amid wild cheering, United stormed around the Grimsby goalmouth, but it was almost half-time before the pressure told and Charlie Mitten slid one home. Against the run of play, and with, defensively, United looking pretty solid, McGowan equalised. Ten minutes from full-time Jimmy Delaney scurried down the right wing for the umpteenth time and floated over a cross. Jack Rowley headed it briskly goalwards and it was diverted in by Grimsby's full-back, Vincent. United went on to win their first five games and peacetime appeared not to have been overrated. Their names, like Henry V's 'household words', ring down the decades. Jack Crompton in goal; Joe Walton and Billy McGlen, Jack Warner, Allenby Chilton and Henry Cockburn in defence, and Jimmy Delaney, John Carey, Jack Rowley, Stan Pearson and Charlie Mitten the original forward line.

One of the major changes, of course, was that the visitors now were more cosmopolitan, with aristocratic Arsenal and, then a powerful combine, Portsmouth among them. Wartime rations had provided but a regional diet. Except for the odd cup-ties, we would be unlikely ever to see again the likes of Halifax Town, Chester, Crewe Alexandra and Stockport County on a regular basis.

How different was the experience of going to the football then, compared with ultra-modern times, even allowing for the generational aspect of our being youngsters and not adults. The bicycle is, for instance, not the preferred mode of transportation in the automotive age. There are now few Premiership grounds that encompass within their precincts the backyards of terraced houses where one might leave one's bike in safe keeping for twopence in exchange for a cloakroom ticket. We swept merrily through the lanes and meadows, across the Mersey at Jackson's Boat, hopeful of dodging the lady who would demand of us a penny toll for crossing the bridge; after all, that extra twopence was two-thirds of the way to buying a programme - and that was three times as much as we paid for the penny scrap we were sold at wartime matches. Then through Chorlton-cum-Hardy and out along the highways, with but a few buses and trolleybuses and only the odd solitary car to hinder us.

When Winnie Wharton, our wartime guest and Lancaster bomber-maker, was married, they had to persuade the bus inspectors to shift two trolleybuses from outside her husband's home in Upper Lloyd Street to make way for the wedding cars. Manchester United were at home playing Wolverhampton Wanderers. We all went to the wedding and the 3-1 victory was as triumphantly announced during the ceremonial meal as was the toast proposed glowingly to the blushing bride: 'United Tame Wolves' squealed the headline in the Pink 'un. Both the *Manchester Evening*

News and *Chronicle* had - the Green 'un; the Pink 'un respectively - special football editions. If you missed the scores on the wireless, you had to run up to the station to buy one or both, just to check the scores and to read the staccato, piece-by-piece commentary of the game. Miss out on the evening papers and then it was a matter, following our visit to the cinema, of buying a copy of the *Sunday Empire News*, maybe with a cartoon by Tom Webster, outside one of the pubs, late on a Sunday evening.

With the bikes in intensive care, there was the rush through the back entries to the ground and the joining of a queue. It was the same for the big matches at Old Trafford cricket ground. One queued. At Old Trafford the queues spiralled and snaked around the waste ground on the Warwick Road side where I had watched the barrage balloon tumble and jerk in the breeze. At Maine Road we joined one of the junior queues amid a series of many tails of people, stretching back across the broad paved area outside the official entrance and chief stands. One queued. We were habituated to queuing and progressed patiently. The discipline was strict. There was scarcely a queue-jumping attempt to ripple the even accord. With all-ticket matches, the method seems to be to arrive ten minutes before the kick-off, usually having taken liberally of refreshment, and then mount an assault on the turnstiles that would have done credit to Richard Lionheart besieging a Saracen fortress.

The first ticketed affair I attended was the semi-final at Maine Road in the 1946/47 season. Of course, a ticket merely allowed you to enter the ground and then seek a reasonable stance. My schoolboy and longstanding friend, John Hough, something of an adept in these matters, had somehow laid hands on these two tickets and, our cycles safely in backyard repose, we were waiting well before the noon opening of the gates for a 3pm kick-off. We obtained places by the wall to the right of the Kippax End goal and had a clear view of Burnley, with their strong centre-half, Brown, and their busy inside-forwards, Morris and Potts, just have the better of Liverpool by the single goal of the match. Burnley then lost to Charlton Athletic, with Sam Bartram in goal, in the Final.

On this as on most other occasions the massive concourse of people was affable enough. For all the jostling and tidal waves up and down, as play altered the sightlines, there was never a moment of unease. Our parents did not hesitate to send us cycling off into the big city to add ourselves to the huge congress of spectators. They might have been alarmed to learn that we sometimes perched on the high walls on either side of the cavernous openings on to the terraces at Maine Road, but there was no trouble and there was hardly a policeman in attendance. It is shameful to think that one felt safer before, during and after a great football match as a child, even alone, than one does sometimes as an adult now.

Beswick Silver Prize Band or Besses O'th' Barn Brass Band would play a martial selection before the kick-off and march solemnly around the ground at half-time. Like awaiting the trapeze artiste missing his grip, the crowd roared as the drum major flung his mace in the air - but he always deftly caught it, so the crowd roared again. There was no public address system. A blackboard would be carried around the ground with the changes, telling us that Ted Buckle or Johnny Hanlon would be playing in this or that numbered shirt. For the half-time scores of other matches, including United

Reserves in the Central League, there was a board marked A, B, C and so on; in one's programme there was the code - 'A' would be, say, Arsenal versus Everton, and they would post up the interval score accordingly. There were pies to eat and Bovril to sup and unsalubrious urinals for relief. It was not the high life but it was thoroughly pleasurable.

There were opportunities to mimic our champions. We were lucky, in particular, that within a couple of minutes' walk from home, awaited a traditional park. We were lucky, in general, that the anxious Victorians had opted for the traditional park as a response to the demands of the public health movement. Backed by some dubious and later discredited pseudo-scientific evidence about the carbon cycle and 'public walks' supplying 'the lungs of the city', parks emerged as, in the words of Jacques Carré, an historian of parks and their culture, 'a spectacular manifestation of Victorian civic art'. They provided an outlet for that 'rational recreation' so beloved of a society that was both cramped and youthful. When the Regent's Park was thrown open to the public in 1841, *The Times*, in suitably Augustan tones, opined that the working classes should enjoy 'the liberty of taking a walk in the more plebeian portions of the park, provided they had a decent coat on'.

Parks came to be used widely for official sports - in 1908 the London County Council reserved 442 pitches for 10,000 players and 30,000 cricket matches - and some - Stanley Park, Blackpool, for example - became venues for first-class fixtures. Ours was not so ambitious, but it did slavishly copy the landscaping pattern borrowed from the work of Capability Brown and Humphrey Repton in the 18th century. A rural enclave was imported into the town, often by the adoption of a small estate, with a screen of dense foliage, interrupted only by grandiose entrance gates, which effectively shielded the park-user from intrusive urban nastiness. Just inside this perimeter of trees and shrubs was a circular macadamised pathway, described as 'Brownian'. This surrounded an expanse of turf. There were bowling greens, a sandpit and a children's playground on the edges.

It represented what, in the British cultural lexicon, was meant by 'park' - but it could have been so different. There were two other options. There was the Italian baroque fashion that saw the park, not as an escape from urban squalor but as a dramatic civic focus. The local equivalents of Beswick Prize Band, namely Ashton-on-Mersey Silver Band and Egerton Street Mission Temperance Band, playing in the park bandstand, offered a tootling tribute to this classic formula, but it would be fair to admit that the Boboli Gardens, Florence provided a more elevated statement. There was also the oriental convention, with the park a cipher for paradise, 'an oasis of beauty blooming in an earthly desert'. The colourful flowerbeds, the aviary and the occasional statuary in our park paid some obeisance to this genre, although many would regard the Taj Mahal, dating from the 17th century, as a more comprehensive example.

In everyday effect, the flowerbeds got in the way of the cricket, even if those strict authoritarian figures, the park keepers or 'parkies' - their repute rather like that of traffic wardens in the current era - adhered to the reverse view. Otherwise the triumph of Capability Brown was complete. On one side the 'Brownian' path delineated the boundary or touchline, as with scruffed 'corkie' for cricket or shabby leather ball for soccer, we pursued endless games, sometimes as few as three of us, sometimes enough to pick up sides, as the gentlemen at the original Old Trafford or the railwaymen at Newton Heath had done in the 19th century. The scores, especially in the football matches, were gargantuan, with goals galore. Had we kept copious records of those 32-27 kind of encounters, there would have been individual tallies likely to render Thierry Henry green with envy.

Even the surrounding bushes had their role. As a substitute for wickets, we had a mantelshelf that was no longer needed, at least that was our boyish presumption. At dinner time or when the park bell tolled the closure in the evening, we hid it in this undergrowth, to save carrying it home, where its degree of domestic necessity might have been subject to a more rigorous jurisdiction.

What was most peculiar, and what served to underpin the faith in our youthful souls, was the refusal of anyone to adopt the part of the foe, were it Manchester City or Yorkshire or, for our horizons were gratifyingly global, Australia. This was a culture where most boys actively preferred to be the 'baddies' - the Germans or, in another flight of geopolitical imagination, the 'Indians' - opposed respectively to the honest Tommies or the hard-riding, trigger-happy cowboys. Yet no one would risk the shame of being designated Bert Sproston, Maurice Leyland or even Ray Lindwall. Thus the games took on another aspect of those inter-club 'sides' matches at Newton Heath or the original Old Trafford. It was as if we were running perpetual trial and practice matches, with, in our 'three-and-in' kickabouts, Jack Rowley forever shooting against Jack Crompton and, in cricket, Dick Pollard everlastingly bowling to Cyril Washbrook.

Two other flirtations might be mentioned in connection with Old Trafford cricket ground. During the war and just after the local Sale club was connected with Major Rupert Howard, who lived in Brooklands and some time later had his Christmas post delivered by the author in the guise of a student postman, but, rather more germanely, was Secretary of Lancashire. His two sons played a little for Sale. I can recall them opening the batting together, wearing Rossall caps, aged about 15 and 16, in a wartime game against an RAF eleven. They both scored undefeated hundreds, with a teatime declaration made at over 220 runs, and then the airmen were summarily dismissed for 13. Nigel Howard, of course, went on to captain Lancashire and England, dying sadly, aged only 54, in 1979. The stylish Barry, who played over 30 times himself for Lancashire and scored a century at Blackpool in 1947 against Warwickshire (after having, incidentally, played for one of the Manchester United junior teams) is happily still among us, enjoying the amiable delights of spectating.

My scorer-father's favourite extract of autobiography was of the one time when Sale, with a player injured at the last minute, persuaded him to exchange pencil for willow. Batting at eleven against Didsbury or Cheadle Hulme in a Manchester Association fixture, he 'propped and copped', as he termed it, for a period that, in some bizarre aberration of Einsteinian physics, increased the more often the yarn was related, and partnering his skipper, Nigel Howard, earned an unlikely draw. 'How I saved the side with the assistance of an England captain' was the subtitle of this epic, told and retold at the fireside like a Nordic saga.

Emerging from the Red Shadow

Rupert Howard was more intrigued by Ack's scoring in the book than at the crease. Years afterwards I did some work with Michael, later Lord, Winstanley, medico, Liberal politician and well-known club cricketer, and the energetic presenter of Granada's social advice show, *This is Your Right*. I had first met him when, with me still spinning the rollers on the scoreboard, he had been playing for Urmston. It was in Granada studio, on the very site of the ancestral domicile, that he declared my father had been the first of the modern scorers, with his flurry of coloured pencils, his run-charts for batsmen, his tracking of 'how outs' and other sophistications. Major Howard, on the strength of this artistry and having examined the Sale scorebook to appreciative satisfaction, offered my father a job as the Lancashire number two scorer, with the unspoken promise of promotion to the top spot.

What excitement in the household! We firmly believed that such a prestigious appointment would mean instant entrée to Old Trafford for family members, complete with direct access to the inner sanctum of players. Enter wise old granny, stage right. My grandmother was far from being an adherent of the Marxist school of economic determinism, but she knew a thing or two about domestic budgets. Most scorers of the time were retired cricketers or chaps who found winter work, clerking in offices. It was pointed out that the fire brigade was reluctant to release its employees for four summer months and then re-enlist them for the winter. The question was the one posed by Blackpool landladies when accused of over-charging: 'how do you think we'll manage in the winter when you've gone?'

Dialetical materialism won the day; father stayed in the fire brigade and our hearts were broken, except that, for the Gods are forgiving, he finished his stint with the fire service by becoming fireman at the Manchester Palace, where he was able to secrete me periodically and for gratis in the gallery. The Palace had been built in 1891 at the height of music hall's popularity and accomodated 3000 customers. Our other common interest was variety, especially comedians, so another important cause was well served.

A year or so after this brush with destiny I found myself playing at Old Trafford cricket ground. It was Lancashire's farsighted practice to host school fixtures in the hope, vain in our case, of spotting future stars. It was 1948. Although we played on the practice ground at the Stretford End, since that time much curtailed in area by building, we were the first to occupy the visitors' dressing room after the departure of the Australians on the completion of their May fixture with the county. With our use of the same hooks, the resemblance ended. We were playing Stretford Grammar School and we were, importantly, served a very good tea.

When we batted they opened with a sharpish left-hander. Our number one cocked up the first ball to short leg. Our number three cocked up the second ball to short leg. I was our number four and I had half pulled my sweater over my head when I realised he had dropped it. No sooner had I restored my sweater to its proper creases when our number three cocked up the third ball to short leg and this time he made no mistake. Off came the sweater and I scrambled down the steps. The Lancashire coach, Harry Makepeace, with his melancholy Robb Wilton countenance, was standing at the foot of the stairs, observing the mayhem with the resigned fortitude of the captain of the Titanic watching the ship submerge. He trenchantly offered me the only technical counsel ever given me by a first-class cricketer. 'For Christ's sake, lad', he muttered tersely, 'put a bit of wood to it.'

Red Shirts and Roses

I instantaneously adopted this stringent dogma. I advanced down the wicket, making the fourth ball of the over a full toss, and banged it into the covers. Wildly we ran two. Adrenalin flowed in cascades. Harry Makepeace had not had the chance to introduce me to the niceties of running between the wickets. The fifth ball I breathlessly repeated the stratagem, driving the ball straight to cover point and galloping off again. Our captain and number two, Billy Hughes, had witnessed the carnage, if not with the same stoicism as Harry Makepeace, from the other end. Without having faced a ball, he was run out by about six yards; in fact, we had barely crossed. Our number five survived the sixth ball, but it had been an eventful over and we were 2 for 3.

Another place and another time must be found to chronicle the beguiling story of my match-winning 15 - perhaps I had omitted to mention that our opponents had been previously dismissed for 43 - and we won by five wickets, leaving my personal success rate at Old Trafford on a comfortable 100 per cent.

Those self-indulgences aside, that series of post-war 'firsts' are simply glued in the sticker book of memory. On reflection, it is difficult to believe that any subsequent sporting experience measures up to those initial sightings. As we shall explore, both Lancashire and Manchester United did their level best, in those post-war years, to test that hypothesis.

13.

Mancunian Victories

A SOCIAL CURIO of World War II was that expenditure on recreation more than doubled, and this trend continued after hostilities ceased. Apart from an understandable wartime mood of making merry 'ere worse befall, there was more money available, what with full employment and with Ernie Bevin, as Minister of Labour, organising the wartime work-force with undeniable command and ensuring that working conditions were improved as much as was reasonably possible. It must be said that there was much less to spend the money on; food was, of course, rationed and its costs subsidised, while, because of the shortages, the sales of clothing and household goods fell dramatically.

In the main, this increased investment in leisure pursuits involved 'going out'. Max Miller, the jaunty 'Cheeky Chappie' and premier stand-up comic of the age, used to record the raunchy activities of the bow-legged dairymaid (who couldn't, he reminded us, 'keep her calves together'). She was, he asserted, always 'out on pleasure bent'. She was joined by countless millions of her fellow-countrymen. Although the radio came of age during the 1939-45 War, when the BBC staff trebled to 12,000 and its weekly output trebled to 150 hours, it was almost alone, with the exception of records, as a purveyor of entertainment directly into the home. People went out.

This continued after the war, to the delight of football clubs like Manchester United and cricket clubs like Lancashire. Indeed, the continuum of the 1940s into the early 1950s is, in a domestic vein, very marked. Nothing could deny the relief felt at the end of the war but, in many social ways, there were telling continuities.

The diversion of American aid to war-torn Europe, in part in response to the perceived menace of Soviet imperialism, ensured that rationing and shortages remained until the 1950s, with, for instance, even bread rationed as a temporary measure in the immediate aftermath of war. Those same fears of the Iron Curtain and the very real peril of the 1950-53 Korean War prompted the perpetuation of the American military presence and the furtherance of National Service for many years, so that uniformed personnel were a constant in the streets and thoroughfares of Britain. It also took time to switch to a peacetime economy and, a major problem, resolve the dire quest for housing, first with the highly useful 'pre-fab' dwellings and then the rash of new council estates and the planned series of new towns. The country had been rocked, financially and in terms of the destruction of its essential fabric, by the heavy demands of a war sustained bravely, and for some time alone, for six long years. It is not surprising that the maxims of 'austerity' and of 'we work or want' were post-1945 coinages.

Despite the economic difficulties, the Government elected in 1945 was a Labour Government (led by the laconic Clement Attlee) which kept its promises and pulled its weight. It consolidated the Welfare State, with its centrepiece the National Health

Red Shirts and Roses

Service. Within a year of its inception in 1948, 8.5m people had had much-needed free dental treatment and 5m people had obtained spectacles that they had not hitherto been able to afford. There was a wholehearted welcome for this 'silent revolution' in social care, while the public ownership of industrial utilities, like the coal mines, the railways, gas, electricity and water, was also accepted with little demur.

A chief reason for this was the strong belief in high levels of public service and rational planning. These virtues had contributed to the winning of the war; it was widely felt they would contribute to the winning of the peace. What came to be known as 'War Socialism' - the state control of food, railways, hospitals and most other important national assets - eased the way for the Labour Government's policies of state and municipal ownership.

The mood was quiescent. Crime, or the paucity of it, is a good indicator. Family and street codes prevailed, so that community discipline was strong, even to the point of being repressive. The immediate post-war years brought a 5 per cent reduction in crime figures. There were less than 5,000 annual offences of violence in the 1940s and early 1950s; by 1968 this had risen to 21,000; now it is over 100,000 a year. One must not paint too facile a picture of chirpy innocence; there was a black market and there was, during the war, some looting. These are comparative reflections, which on the whole speak of a patient, well-humoured, if also weary people.

The queue was the dominant social symbol. It was not only for football and cricket that one queued. One waited in lengthy coils for the cinema and the theatre, for entry to the dance hall, at the shops, for the buses and trains - just as soldiers had queued for boats to lift them from the beaches of Dunkirk in 1940. Queuing is an ambivalent social symbol. It was said in those days that if three Germans assembled together they formed an army; three Frenchmen, a political party - and three Englishmen, a queue. It has an aspect of forlorn, tired dreariness but it also has a more positive feature of people more willing to cooperate and share.

A.J.P. Taylor, an historian not overly sentimental, wrote that 'the British people came of age' at this point and stayed unyieldingly 'tolerant, patient and generous'. There was 'a sense of crusading idealism' that brought 'virtually to all a feeling of involvement in national affairs'. Stolidly grumbling perhaps, they mustered the will to join together in common cause both in war and peace. This collective spirit was well to the fore in the pursuit of leisure over this period. We shared our leisure with thousands of anonymous others, yet bonded with them in the selfsame focus of entertainment. With petrol rationed and a war economy concentrated on the manufacture of tanks, army lorries and jeeps, there were still only 2m cars on the roads in 1948, exactly the same as in 1939. So our conveyance was mainly collective, courtesy of trams, buses, trolleybuses and trains, as we wended to varied places of recreational pleasure.

Blackpool and the North Wales resorts of Rhyl and Llandudno remained the summer holiday venues of prime choice for Mancunians, especially during the Manchester Engineering Wakes, traditionally the last week of July and the first week of August. Trafford Park fell deserted, and the charabancs and special trains carried thousands of families to a seaside still often littered with the wartime impedimenta of pillboxes and tank traps, a reminder of the recent threat of invasion.

122

Mancunian Victories

Back home the cinema was the principal centre for communal leisure. By the 1940s 30m cinema tickets - 'one and nines on the right; two and threes round the corner', cried the commissionaire - were sold each week, that is over 1.5bn a year. There was, in Lancashire, a cinema seat for every nine people in the population and a third of people went to the 'flicks' at least twice a week. Often they would roll up during the show and sit around until, as the saying became common, 'this is where I came in'. One did not have to travel far for such cinematic delights. In our town of about 30,000 souls there were four cinemas, apart from several others within easy reach in outlying areas. One or two would change their main feature film in midweek and, as well as children's matinées, there were from midway through the war (and with a percentage cut to local charity as a sop for the sabbatarian conscience) Sunday programmes.

With up to 60 showings of some twelve or fourteen movies, the discerning and persevering cinema buff could easily have watched a different film every day without travelling a mile from home. After playing football or cricket on Saturday, a crowd of us reassembled at, in pecking order of prestige, the fourth of this quartet of cinemas and queued in draughty conditions, marshalled by a disgruntled commissionaire, for the second house. Such was the demand that we knew by the time we could collect together, it was our only chance of seeing even *Nanook of the North* or an early Freddie Bartholemew film. With all those seats thrice available on a Saturday for a matinée and two evening performances, and with every seat taken, a huge fraction of the township's inhabitants must have been engaged in Saturday cinema-going.

For the lads of the town, we were at that intermediate stage of pretending to be boys on the buses and adults at the cinema, the former to preserve our half-price rights, the latter to dodge into films classified as 'A', for adults only. As it was, the cashiers turned a blind eye to our beseeching pleas of 'will you take us in, mister?', as we begged some kindly stranger to act as our sponsor and impromptu legal guardian.

There was never any need to go to 'town', that is, Manchester, for the cinema, so flush were we with such parochial temptations. The first film I saw in Manchester was not until 1945, when John Hough's mother took the pair of us to the Gaumont to see Margaret Lockwood and James Mason in that rumbustious historical drama, *The Wicked Lady*, highwaymen, hangings, heaving bosoms and all. It was rather to Manchester we went to the theatre, to catch the latest variety bill or, seasonally, the pantomime.

There was a profusion of theatres. As well as the Manchester Palace, there was the Opera House, on Quay Street, almost opposite where my great-grandfather and then my great-uncle Sam had lived, and where, for example, the D'Oyly Carte company annually toured with several weeks of Gilbert and Sullivan's Savoyard comic operas. There was the Manchester Hippodrome, where, soon after the war and for its Golden Jubilee programme, I saw G.H. Elliott, with what would be now his non-politically correct bill matter of 'the chocolate coloured coon'. He was top of the bill, while Morecambe and Wise were at the bottom, in the 'wines and spirits', as they used to say, doing ten minutes at the start of each half. There was the Hulme Hippodrome, the

Queen's Park Hippodrome and a couple of variety houses in Salford. One could pick and choose, watching out for special favourites, like Jimmy James, with his Lowry-like brand of contemplative insanity, just about my all-time preferred comic, or the tinkling bells and shifting sandals of Wilson, Keppel and Betty, the essence of the music hall, with their immaculately timed spoof of the sand-dance.

Occasionally, the cinemas would turn to variety. The Longford, Stretford, offered a live show almost once a month throughout these years. I saw Frank Randle there on several occasions, plus the hullabaloo of the Billy Cotton Band-show and, a genuinely classic treat, an appearance by the lugubrious Robb Wilton. One week Ted and Barbara Andrews performed their piano and ballads act. When they took a bow, they were joined on stage by a smiling infant girl in a ballet dress. I enquired who she was, and my father growled, over his cigarette, 'they're blooding her for the stage'. He was right and they did so successfully: that is the only time I have seen Julie Andrews live, just down the road from Old Trafford.

With the exception of the pubs and the dance halls - and, apart from the big city 'Ritz', every town had its own 'Locarno' or local dance band, such as Percy Pease and his Orchestra in the town hall, and with the 'Lidos' or swimming baths often doubling up as dance halls - this whole assemblage of leisure activities was cross-generational. Sporting, theatrical, cinematic, vocational, whatever, children were in evidence, even where, at the sporting arenas, for instance, there was still something of a gender bar. In the main, the entire population, young and old, was up and about when it came to enjoying itself.

The hundred years of what might be called 'Collective Leisure' reached its apogee in the Festival of Britain in 1951, a celebration of the centenary of the Great Exhibition of 1851, itself the gateway to this concourse of congregated recreation. The Festival was, it was written, 'a testimony to a people still vital and vigorous in its culture, still at peace with itself and secure in itself'. Michael Frayn called it 'a rainbow - a brilliant sign riding the storm and promising fairer weather.' 17m visitors were attracted to the South Bank Exhibition (with the Skylon as 'the luminous exclamation mark') and to the Battersea Funfair.

The Festival mood was adopted nationwide in a final vast alfresco venture. Amid this wholesale extravaganza of outings, it seemed perfectly natural to go out on impulse, to make up one's mind to go to the pictures at 6pm or the football at 2pm. There was no need, it appeared, for the more careful weighing-up of the social odds, the preparatory considerations and the booking of tickets weeks and months before, proclivities that characterised the later age.

And Manchester boasted one of Britain's finest epitomes of 'collective leisure'. This was Belle Vue, billed as 'the Coney Island of the North'. Belle Vue Gardens had actually been laid out as early as 1836 with a zoological imprint, and they were described in 1902 as being 'where the democratic zest in natural history is pleasantly diversified with not too light but sometimes very fantastic indulgence in the pleasures of the dance.' Belle Vue, by the 1930s and 1940s, catered for every recreational taste. With the zoo salient, there was also boating on a lake with an island where, annually, there were nights of firework displays, based on historical events, like the Relief of Lucknow or the Capture by General Wolfe of the Heights of Abraham. There was a wondrous funfair, with a frightening 'Bobs' ride and a scary 'caterpillar' experience. There were lots of rides on elephants and lots of cafés for snacks. For the sports lover there was a host of allurements: rugby league and occasional rugby union, like the North-West versus the touring Australians; speedway; greyhound racing, as a complement to White City and Salford dog tracks; world championship boxing, wrestling... There was the Christmas circus, famed for ringmaster George Lockhart's performing elephants; there were visiting circuses, like the fabled Moscow State Circus, with the legendary clown, Oleg Popov. There were brass band championships; American stars on tour such as Louis Armstrong; regular dancing; political meetings, with great orators like Aneurin Bevan holding vividly forth... It would be difficult to exaggerate the range of diversion and entertainment available at this one single complex and our extended family gatherings there took on a ritualistic bent.

Thus it was that, amid this welter of outdoor public activity, we flocked as teenagers to watch Lancashire and Manchester United and were rewarded, in those early post-war seasons, with golden glories in either camp, even if, by comparison with the storming football grandeur, the cricketing finery was more muted.

The astounding saga of Manchester United's makeover might have done justice to the transformation scene in the pantomime, *Aladdin*, with Norman Evans as Widow Twankey, at the Manchester Palace. The 'Open Sesame' of Matt Busby's appointment as manager, and his shrewd Abanazar-like mixture of, so to say, new and old lamps has rightly become one of the legends of sporting chronicle. While Manchester City slumbered a little with an ageing team in the Second Division (although, with Frank Swift still as authoritative in goal as ever, they were soon promoted), United blazed away. The carthorses of the 1920s and 1930s were now the thoroughbreds of the late 1940s and early 1950s.

Lancashire were not quite the dominant side they had been in the inter-war years, but they contrived, nonetheless, to be leading players in the County Championship. The upheavals of war had left them short of key senior players, but the modern intake blended well with the ancient retainers and 'Lanky' were always among those in contention. Still, in terms of outright triumph, both teams gave rise to concern among their supporters. Manchester United and Lancashire kept winning well and in handsome style but it was some years before trophies came to the Old Traffords, in the shape of an FA Cup victory, a shared County title and a coveted League Championship.

United were drawn away at Aston Villa for the third round of the Cup in the January of 1948. We tuned into the wireless at 5pm for the results. This tie was the first result on the sheet: 'Aston Villa 4...'; in that brief second, we looked at one another and grinned ruefully - another Cup campaign had been terminated early - ' ... Manchester United 6'. It had been one of the greatest games of even this age-old competition, played before a gate of 59,000. Aston Villa scored after thirteen seconds but, calmly, methodically but speedily, United's famous forward line made it 5-1 by the interval. A strong Villa side swept back in the second half, reducing the United support to silence, and in a frantic session made it 5-4. Just before the end, with Aston Villa seeking the equaliser, Stan Pearson added United's sixth.

Red Shirts and Roses

It was a fair opening to a classic Cup crusade. Because of Cup clashes, United had to make shift with neutral venues, and they played only First Division clubs. Liverpool, with Billy Liddell, were thrashed 3-0 at Goodison Park, where 75,000 entered and 15,000 were locked out; Charlton Athletic were outplayed in the drizzle of Huddersfield Town's Leeds Road ground, with only the desperate agility of Sam Bartram keeping the tally as low as two; 74,000 watched absorbed at Maine Road as Preston North End, with Tom Finney and Bill Shankly among their company, went down 4-1; and there were 60,000 at Hillsborough as a Stan Pearson hat-trick destroyed Derby County, starring Billy Steel and Raich Carter, with a 3-1 score in a compelling semi-final.

Blackpool, with Stan Matthews seeking his first Cup Winner's medal, were their opponents in the final. The United players, on £12 a week (£10 the week after the Final, when the close season started) were promised a derisory £20 for reaching Wembley. Even for that day and age, it was rather miserly: as that inveterate gambler Charlie Mitten commented, the band that played at half-time received £330, while his team-mates and himself shared £220. They may have drawn some solace from the fact that Don Bradman and 63-year-old Billy Meredith were numbered among those present.

Certainly had the game been valued for its artistry and drama, both sets of players would have walked off millionaires. Some still claim it was Wembley's supreme exhibition of Cup Final football. Incidentally, other games were in progress; 20,000 were at Maine Road, for instance, to see Manchester City and Arsenal battle out a goalless draw.

Manchester United, in royal blue shirts, felt a chilly Blackpool breeze at the onset and, within a quarter of an hour, the Seasiders took the lead with a disputed penalty. Allen Chilton tripped Stan Mortenson and he crumbled in the area, although there was a margin of doubt as to where the foul occurred. Eddie Shimwell struck the ball under a diving Jack Crompton. United seized the initiative and were rewarded with an equaliser, as Jack Rowley pounced on a long ball from Jimmy Delaney, lobbed it over the goalkeeper's head and poked the ball home. Stan Mortenson, however, was irrepressible. He darted through the defence and fired in a fierce shot to make it 2-1, and only a splendid save by Jack Crompton from a shot by the dangerous winger, Walter Rickett, kept United in the running.

Manchester United seemed distinctly disunited for another twenty or so minutes - then they re-found their fluency. Johnny Morris took a quick free kick and, assessing the weighting of the ball and the context of the defenders with aplomb, Jack Rowley cracked in United's second equaliser. Then, rapidly on the rebound from a combative Blackpool assault, Stan Pearson raced away and scored a brilliant third, with some Blackpool players still in the Reds' penalty area. It was in this closing phase of the match that, far from being on the defensive foot, United played exquisite attacking football, culminating in a speculative 35-yard goal from right-half John Anderson.

It was 24th April 1948. It was only United's second Cup win but it set in motion the post-war saga of their trophy-winning expertise. Over the season John Anderson, who rather anonymously had been on the Old Trafford books for years, had taken over from the loyal and long-serving Welshman, Jack Warner, while John Carey, that man

126

of a thousand faces, had slipped back to his ideal position of right-back, displacing the young Joe Walton. Thus there appeared at Wembley that day the eleven that Manchester United fans of some dotage are able to recite readily and at will: Jack Crompton; John Carey and John Aston; John Anderson, Allenby Chilton and Henry Cockburn; Jimmy Delaney, Johnny Morris, Jack Rowley, Stan Pearson and Charlie Mitten. What a sociologist would make of six Johns, and another as twelfth man, is anybody's guess.

24th April 1948 was also the first day of the school cricket season and, in those far-off days, the discipline was strict. If one was picked, one played or faced punitive consequences, something that, for the most part, we accepted as right and proper in that we enjoyed playing and esteemed the honour. Nevertheless, it was a trifle galling to be involved in a cricket match, even in the sunny weather that prevailed that day, when all this drama was being played out at Wembley. We were fielding. We suddenly realised that a tiny group of spectators picnicking on the boundary had, rarely for the time, a mobile radio. Those fielding nearby could catch crackly spurts of Raymond Glendenning's excitable commentary. Gradually, practically the whole of the team felt the urge to field at third man, so that it looked as if we had adopted the strategy of the umbrella field and then transferred it to the boundary. Faced with some sort of sportive mutiny, the two teacher-umpires yielded and good-naturedly allowed us to listen to those last absorbing twenty minutes. Maybe they were as fascinated as we were.

On Monday evening we took the train into 'town' and stood among the cheering crowds on Oxford Street, as an open bus carried John Carey, his companions and the Cup slowly towards the Manchester Town Hall. Jack Warner, although deprived late on of his place, appeared as enthusiastic as anyone, waving a streamer and grinning energetically. Then we went to the News Theatre near Oxford Road Station and watched the black and white highlights, courtesy of *British Gaumont News*. They don't have News Theatres any more, do they?

A couple of years later it was Lancashire's turn in the sun, when they shared the County Championship with Surrey. Like Manchester United, Lancashire had shone without outshining their rivals. They were third five times out of seven seasons, with a nasty lapse to eleventh in 1949, and they obtained their half-grasp on the pennant in 1950.

The Lancashire post-war batting was staunch and obdurate but the bowling had begun to look a bit elderly and lacking in penetration. In 1950 events conspired to turn around this imbalance. In 1949 the streetwise Australian, Ken Grieves, had arrived at Old Trafford, full of runs and wickets and catches, whilst Alan Wharton had matured into a useful all-rounder. Young Malcolm Hilton found a ripe seam of form in 1950, taking 127 wickets, while Brian Statham burst on to the stage of world cricket part-way through the season. It was, however, the conversion of Roy Tattersall that was the key. Just as Matt Busby's astute re-routeing of careers, as in the cases of John Aston or Roger Byrne, paid dividends, so did the missionary evangelicalism of Harry Makepeace. He changed Roy Tattersall's denomination from that of medium-pacer to that of off-spinner. In 1950 he took the amazing total of 193 wickets, 171 for the county, at a shade over 13 apiece. It was a conversion of Pauline dimensions.

Lancashire were out of the traps zestfully, winning three of their first five games, including what the Duke of Wellington would have called a 'close-run thing' at Sheffield. Then they won seven matches on the trot, six of them by an innings. One of them, against Sussex at Old Trafford, took only six and a half hours and 123 overs. Sussex were dismissed for 101, John Langridge carrying his bat for a gritty 48; Lancashire scored 239 with some dispatch; and then Sussex were ousted for only 51, leaving Lancashire victors by an innings and 87 runs. Yes, of course, the pitch favoured spin, but, then again, presumably Sussex had spin bowlers, too. Oddly enough, Roy Tattersall could only stand and stare, as Peter Greenwood and Malcolm Hilton shared the wickets, and the only other bowler used, with three overs in the first innings, was Bob Berry.

67,000 - 32,000 of them on August Bank Holiday Monday - paid to see the county nudge and nurdle their way to first innings points against Yorkshire. Then Lancashire won three games and only needed to beat Warwickshire at Old Trafford to assume the title unilaterally. With Lancashire well positioned, their old enemy, what was then the eighteenth player (and now the nineteenth) in the County Championship, the weather, took control. Irksome rain fell after a Washbrook century and after Tattersall's 7 for 29 had removed Warwickshire for a lowly 80. That was one of the days I had decided to go on a weekday whim to Old Trafford and I stared, transfixed, as the Warwickshire batsmen shuffled backwards and forwards, with Roy Tattersall unplayable.

However, Lancashire could only draw and went to the Oval for their last fixture needing first innings points to secure first place, against a Surrey side then embarked on a strong run. Lancashire never recovered their equilibrium when Cyril Washbrook and Winston Place were dismissed cheaply in three balls. Peter May, 92 in five hours, ensured that Surrey overtook Lancashire's 221. The match crawled along over-cautiously and was drawn. Surrey won against Leicestershire in their final game and drew level on points with the Red Rose county.

After the exhilaration of that summer of stunning victories, the final outcome was a wee bit disappointing, but, after all, it was a title, albeit shared; the membership had risen to 10,000 and a waiting list had to be established, while a quarter of a million had flocked through the turnstiles. Although there was some teasing over doctored (or rather undoctored - the heavy roller was not deployed and watering was kept to the minimum) wickets, Lancashire won nine of their sixteen victories away from home, six batsmen scored a thousand runs and Cyril Washbrook averaged a commanding 56. For the most part, the Lancashire squad over 1950 was normally: Cyril Washbrook, Winston Place, Geoff Edrich, Johnny Ikin, Ken Grieves, Nigel Howard, Alan Wharton, Alf Barlow keeping wicket, Roy Tattersall, Malcolm Hilton, Brian Statham, Bob Berry and Peter Greenwood.

Back across the main road at the other Old Trafford, Manchester United were gearing up for their first League title since before World War I. Manchester United were undoubtedly the shock team of the post-war era. Combining the dazzling brilliance and the consistent hardness of the choicest diamond, they were four times runners-up and once fourth in the first five post-war seasons. First prize strangely eluded them. Then in 1951/52 they were eventually crowned champions, their third such success after the two victories of 1908 and 1911, all of 44 and 41 years previously.

An artist's impression of the view from Old Trafford cricket ground
circa 1880 towards what would become the site of the
Old Trafford football ground. The scene emphasises
the still rural nature of the area.

The Lancashire county team in 1880 with A.N. "Monkey" Hornby seated third from the right and R.G. Barlow at the front.

The Newton Heath team in its first season in the Football League when it was increased in size in 1892.

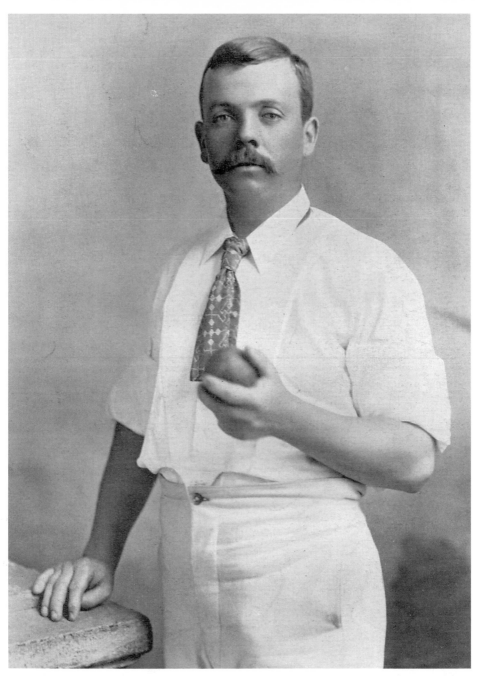

The tragicomic figure of Johnny Briggs. He was the most cheerful of cricketers, his chubby features twinkling with happiness and his plump frame full of bounce as he plied his left-hand spin for England and Lancashire, cavorted at cover point and struck handsome blows with the bat. Brian Statham is his only rival as the most popular player in Lancashire's saga. Beset by severe epilepsy, he also had mental problems and died in Cheadle Asylum in 1902.

The Players:

The "Welsh Wizard" Billy Meredith (left) joined United from
Manchester City after being embroiled in a scandal over illegal
payments, whilst his contemporary in cricket, Sidney "S.F." Barnes,
the best bowler in the world at the time, played just two full seasons for
Lancashire before deciding he could earn more money in the leagues.

The Gentleman and the Player:

Under the generalship of Archie MacLaren (left) Lancashire were one
of the leading counties of the pre-First World War era. John "J.T."
Tyldesley was a rare breed of player, a professional in an England pre-
War batting line-up. Both had lengthy careers at Old Trafford.

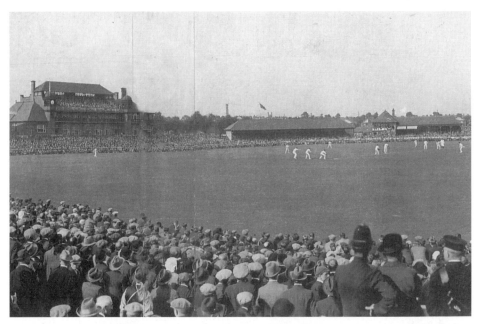

A packed house watches the 1934 Old Trafford test, above.
Whilst United spent much of the inter-war years in the doldrums, it
was the greatest period in the history of the cricket club, both on
and off the field. The successful 1920s team was followed by the
dominant force of the early 1930s. The club were the glamour side of
the era, even becoming the first sports team to fly to a fixture, below.

Despite losing what may have been their best years to the Second World War, Winston Place and Cyril Washbrook emerged together at the head of the Lancashire batting order after 1945 to become one of the most prolific and well-known county opening pairs of the immediate post-war years.

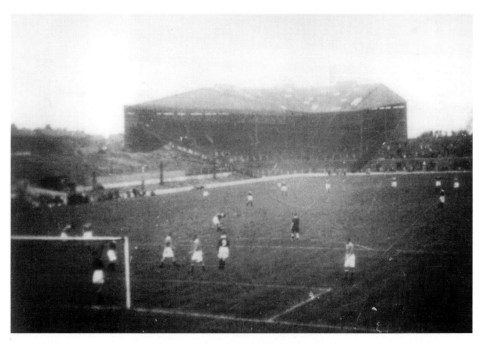

United were forced to play at Maine Road after the end of the war due to bomb damage. One of the first games played at the recovering Old Trafford was a Public Trial in 1948. Above, Jack Rowley (No.9) has just scored. Note that the only area that survived the bombing was the Stretford End Paddock. Below, a view of the construction of covering of the popular side (North Stand). Glover's Cables factory can be seen in the rear at the Stretford End.

The magnificent Johnny Carey, right, was the captain and driving force behind United's first great post-war team, which won the FA Cup in 1948.

With the end of hostilities in Europe and with normal service resuming at home, crowds flocked to sport in the late 1940s and early 1950s. But one thing remained constant: The Old Trafford cricket crowd protect themselves from the weather, above.

With Matt Busby's Babes making their mark on the world, Lancashire were in need of a hero. It came in the form of Brian "George" Statham, a bowling phenomenon who starred for the county and England for more than a decade.

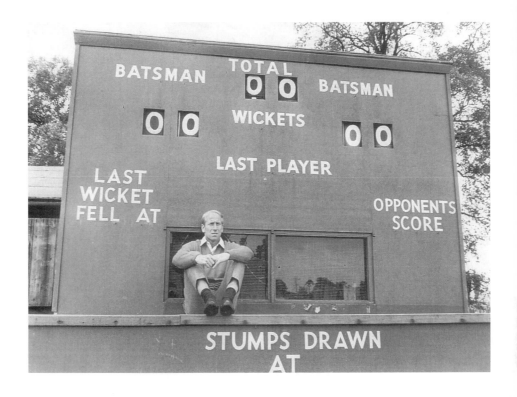

There is a tradition of an interest in each other's sports from the two Old Trafford clubs. Above, Bobby Charlton relaxes at a game before the 1966 World Cup Final and, right, Nobby Stiles plays a classic loft through mid-wicket.

The arrival of Clive Lloyd, above, was the catalyst for a change of fortune for the Lancashire club. Having been in the doldrums for almost 20 years the introduction of One Day Cricket seemed to suit the mentality of the Lancashire players.

The One Day game certainly brought in the spectators, leading to a new golden age at Old Trafford cricket ground. Above, a packed house watches their heroes play Kent in the 1972 Gillette Cup and, below, massive queues preceded the famous Gillette Cup encounter with Gloucestershire in 1971.

Freddie Goodwin, who was born in Heywood near Rochdale, was the only man to play for both Lancashire and Manchester United at the top level. He appeared in 11 matches for the county as a right arm fast bowler and produced his best display at Lord's in 1955, taking 5 for 35. He scored seven goals in 106 games for the Reds. He made his league debut in the 1954/55 season against Arsenal as a replacement for Duncan Edwards, but only became a regular after the Munich Air Disaster.

The Lancashire of 1981, above, still contained some of the great names of the club's One Day era, including Jack Simmons, David Hughes, David Lloyd, Clive Lloyd and Harry Pilling. Jackie Bond was still involved as first team coach (end left, middle row) and, below, shows his delight at Lord's three years later when the Benson and Hedges Cup is added to the Old Trafford cabinet.

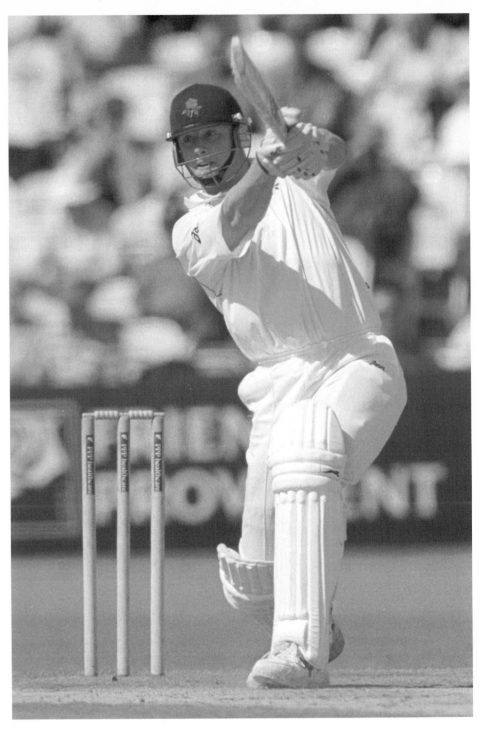

....a mighty man is he,
With large and sinewy hands;
And the muscles of his brawny arms
Are strong as iron bands.

Mancunian Victories

The season started brightly enough, with Jack Rowley gunning down the opposition with a flurry of goals, including two hat-tricks in four days against West Bromwich Albion and Middlesbrough. Christmas found them well placed among the front-runners. A surprise removal from the FA Cup by unfancied Hull City permitted them the platitudinous motive of concentrating on the League and, unhurried and constant, they continued to pick up points. Heavy defeats of Liverpool and Burnley over Easter hauled them clear at the top, but it was the penultimate weekend of the season that was crucial. On Saturday 19th April the two other contenders, Arsenal and Spurs, won and drew respectively, while United tied 2-2 with Blackpool. On Monday 21st April, with Spurs more or less out of the running, United, with the assistance of a marvellous left-footed goal by John Carey from outside the penalty box, beat Chelsea 3-0 at a relieved and noisy Old Trafford - Arsenal, meanwhile, crumbled to a 3-1 loss at West Bromwich.

There was just one match left and it was, in the theatrical nature of these affairs, Arsenal who were due to visit Old Trafford. Arsenal were required to win 7-0 to steal the Championship. They lost 6-1. A choir of 54,000 voices was lifted to the skies in praise. The team on this mould-breaking occasion was: Reg Allen, Tommy McNulty, John Aston, John Carey, Allenby Chilton, Henry Cockburn, Johnny Berry, John Downie, Jack Rowley, Stan Pearson, with Roger Byrne in his original if unusual position on the left wing. Jack Rowley scored three of the goals, with Stan Pearson adding two more and Roger Byrne the other.

The discerning will have noticed that Manchester United were back at Old Trafford. The wait for grants and building materials had been, in the aftermath of war and with a tortoise-like bureaucracy, slow. The Ministry of Works spoke of a ceiling figure of £6,000 by way of compensation for bomb damage, but estimates for a sensible refurbishment were put at £40,000. In 1949 - when United completed another spectacular Cup run with a 1-0 loss to Wolves in a replayed semi-final - the repairs to Old Trafford were finally sanctioned. A roofless stand with 3,000 people would be erected and all the terracing cleaned and, where necessary, concreted. Having entered the post-war era with a £15,000 overdraft, United were now financially sound: the 1947/48 season, for example, revealed a £22,000 profit on gross gate-money of £100,000. Now they would not have to pay Manchester City the rental of £5,000 for the use of Maine Road, where United had only lost seven matches in three league seasons.

On 24th August 1949, with a 3-0 beating of Bolton Wanderers, there was the grand homecoming, slightly marred by it being a Wednesday afternoon. The leaders of industry were much opposed to midweek football, as the nation's struggling economy - and their profits - suffered. 40,000, however, realised that they had a grandmother to inter or some such other alibi and there was no desperate run on the stock market.

Both Lancashire and Manchester United were back along Warwick Road and the world, at least technically, was at peace. Both teams, especially United, were playing well and attracting great crowds. It is time to scrutinise the players in more loving detail.

14.

Manchester Fighters
and Lancaster Bombers

THEY OFFERED Matt Busby a five-year contract at £750 a year. It was twice as much as he was earning in the Army or, for that matter, as a footballer but it turned out to be a profitable investment. Since 1937 Walter Crickmer had resolutely combined the secretarial and managerial roles, but in 1945, following an approach by that long-serving United chief scout, the eternal Louis Rocca, James Gibson, United's chairman, interviewed Matt Busby for what became a new type of post.

Throughout British football the club directors, with maybe a suited, collar and tied secretary-cum-manager administrator to advise them, had bought and signed players and picked the sides. Then there was a trainer - Tom Curry at Old Trafford - who supervised the training, perhaps talked over some rudimentary tactics and carried the bucket and sponge on match days. Matt Busby, not without a few brushes with the authoritarian Mr Gibson, heralded the era of the manager as director or chief executive of a club's playing capacity and productivity. A cultivated wing-half (complete with the obligatory 1930s central parting) for Manchester City, for Liverpool and - once for real and in eight wartime internationals - Scotland, Matt Busby was then only 35, having been born about the time Manchester United had settled into their Old Trafford haven. Indeed, Liverpool had offered him the post of player-coach, as assistant to their manager, George Kay, obviously believing his playing career had not ended. Very much a thinking footballer, he was full of modish ideas about the nature of the game and how it should be played, while he was replete with, behind the smiling eyes and pleasing beam of that plumply rounded countenance, a steely, occasionally ruthless confidence in his beliefs and personal aptitude.

It makes for an intriguing moment in social terms. The Crickmer figure was probably more at home in the boardroom or the main office; the Curry figure was certainly more at ease on the training pitch. The Busby figure had to find a balance between the two. He had to justify his executive actions to a board of businessmen, owners of a blitzed ground, with only a cinder car park for training, a £15,000 overdraft and the pressing need to scrounge clothing coupons to buy gear for United's four teams. He had to instil confidence into and earn respect from a bunch of working-class blokes, most of them returning from military service. A sporting analogue might be the veteran senior professional in the county team, who, in the differing format of cricket, actually ran affairs in the dressing room and on the field, although a bum-fluffed young amateur might notionally be in charge. Yorkshire's Wilfred Rhodes is the model, even unto, as coach at Harrow, invasively removing pupils from lessons for cricket practice, the masters helpless in the face of such dour and ancient authority.

The butler in the great house, lauding it over the servants' quarters and tolerating the solecisms of the family above stairs, yet, in general, ensuring the efficacious continuance of both, is another comparison.

However, the truest analogy is with what Matt Busby actually was. He was a Company Sergeant Major, inducted into that brand of non-commissioned officers that, strictly controlling the other ranks and carefully counselling the officers, had long provided the spine of the British Army. He may not have seen action or paraded outside Buckingham Palace, but the learned traits were the same. In organising physical training and sports for soldiers, Matt Busby had found in himself and honed the skills of that essential compromise. In those early years as manager, he would both persuade the board that his advice and ways were wisest and then, tracksuited and active, merit the confidence of the players and cajole them into outstanding feats.

In the cricket and football annuals and almanacs the single line - '1939-45(6) no competition' - looks dismissive and empty. In fact, plenty was happening. For many footballers and cricketers the war's duration marked a half or more of their working lives thus far. Thinking back to that sight of Stanley Matthews having a pre-match fitness test at Maine Road in his RAF blues, one is reminded that England's premier star had been subjected to the rigours of square-bashing, bulling boots to a resplendent sheen, queuing for fags, char and wads in the NAAFI and all the other seemingly mindless disciplines of service life. 'Beds will be made up as laid down in standing orders' was hardly a 'cod' notice; all these men and women were regulated by an endless stream of orders and demands. Amid the abject nastiness of the hostilities, there were many who were finding an experience of future value. Matt Busby was one of these. His success as a Sergeant Major was undoubtedly the platform for his success as a new-style football manager.

Of course there would be times when this delicate conciliation of the positions of board and playing staff was tilted. Much as players esteemed him, there would be the occasional one who strained at the authority imposed. Argumentative Johnny Morris, still the youngest member of the team, took his leave and went to Derby County for a record £24,000 as early as 1949; John Giles would be another notable antagonist, transferring to Leeds United in 1963 for £37,500. James Gibson and his fellows also took a little time to adjust to being more or less non-executive directors. Generally speaking, the harmony was shrewdly maintained, success, of course, the chief dispeller of woes.

It was February 1945 when Matt Busby was appointed, but it was October before, his war service over and his demob suit neatly pressed, he took up the appointment. In the meanwhile, he had met up again with Jimmy Murphy, another wing-half, of West Bromwich Albion and Wales, who was running sports for troops in Italy. He was to become assistant manager, with special responsibility for youth development. It was a portent of their joint ambition that, when United Reserves won the 1946/47 Central League competition, sometimes attracting crowds of 25,000, Jimmy Murphy bluntly told Matt Busby that none of those second stringers was good enough for the first eleven.

Busby and Murphy were to prove as successful an alliance as Marks and Spencer and, like all the best double acts, from Hornby and Barlow to Morecambe and Wise, they compounded opposing qualities to prosperous account. It was said of Louis XIV of France that 'he was a king but only in the externals of kingship'; Matt Busby's glorious reign found in his chief minister, his Richelieu, a man who provided the 'internals', the complementary pragmatic strengths to his own imaginative ideals. Choler and phlegm were the contributing humours. Jimmy Murphy was fierceness, brusque fidelity and instinctive commitment; Matt Busby was calmness, intelligence and visionary artistry. For a quarter of a century the two men worked wholeheartedly together to create a world-class football club.

Matt Busby, with his henchman, constructed three great and distinctive teams. The first set the standard, unfurling the ensign that proclaimed that Manchester United were no longer a run-of-the-mill outfit but one to be seriously reckoned with in the upper echelon of football. Because it was the first, and because it sprang from nowhere after the lean years of dearth, it was perhaps the most surprising; afterwards it was expected, even following the trauma of Munich, that Matt Busby, like some sort of footballing Merlin, would conjure up another Camelot.

In cultural parallel with the war, it was something of a 'make-do and mend' team. Where a modern Arsenal or Chelsea might draw together an assemblage of football's global aristocrats, the post-war Manchester United impatiently awaited the return of its native sons from across the planet, as the slow process of demobilisation ground on. Jack Crompton from, aptly enough, Newton Heath, was quiet, unshowy but bravely alert in goal, and had been Jack Breedon's wartime back-up. Invalided out of the RAF with a leg injury diagnosed as terminating his football career, he kept goal efficiently and later returned from a post with Luton Town at the time of the Munich air crash to become United's trainer.

Sturdy John Aston, honest in mien and face, was a Prestwich lad, his 18th birthday falling on the day war was declared. Miraculously converted from inside-right into an England left-back of some stature, he saw Army service as a Royal Marine commando in North Africa and Sicily and then was in Australia when the war ended. Never over-blessed with confidence, he wasted two or three weeks looking for a job before plucking up the courage to return to Old Trafford and discuss matters with Matt Busby. He never left. When he finished as a player in 1954 he was retained as junior coach and then chief scout.

Right-half John Anderson, from Salford, joined United in 1937. He was a stoker on a destroyer, the first ship into Tokyo harbour after the Japanese surrender, and it was to be the summer of 1946 before he arrived home just in time to play in the last reserve fixture of the season. He was abroad almost five years and found himself playing soccer for the Navy in places from West Africa to China and Fiji. The centre-half, the big, rugged Allenby Chilton, originally came from Durham and joined the Durham Light Infantry. After service in Iceland, he was wounded by mortar fire in Normandy soon after D-Day, and, awaiting demob, actually absented himself without leave to play for United in May 1945. He had made his debut for United versus Charlton Athletic on 2nd September 1939, about 20 hours before Neville Chamberlain's fateful broadcast.

Rarely suffering or admitting injury, his regularity and consistency were much admired by Matt Busby, who, for all his admiration of polish, always recognised the need for a defensive marshal of commanding vigour and gritty courage. Allenby Chilton eventually went into management, where he notched up some good achievements with Grimsby Town.

Henry Cockburn - and how we reverently acceded to the 'Co'burn' pronunciation - was the exception-proving exception, the one who was deferred from military service because he was on essential war-work in an Oldham textile mill and continued to work there, even after he had been picked for England, after only seven league games. With his slight build, his flapping lock of lank hair and his crinkle-toothed grin, this child of Ashton-under-Lyne was a distinctive figure at left-half on a football pitch, the more so as, contrary to the fashion dictates of the hour, he never rolled up his sleeves, but clutched the cuffs tightly in his palms, as he chased and harried. He evoked zoological simile. He tackled like a snapping crocodile and jumped like a kangaroo, surprising taller men with his heading dominion. There was an aesthetic glow in every pass, as, with the mathematical exactitude of a Joe Davis, he angled the ball into inviting spaces. In 1954 he moved on to Bury.

So, secured by the fortress to the rear, to the forward line, said by experts to be the finest club quintet ever, 'ere the 1960s revolution deconstructed the long-standing 'W' formation. They obeyed to the letter the triple Busby mantra of speed, position and accuracy, switching themselves as well as the ball with stunning velocity. It was mesmeric. Defences were left bewildered and leaden-footed. Like Frank Richards' 'Famous Five' at Greyfriars School, they existed as a cohesive gang yet each member had his specialist role and character.

The one import was Lanark-born Jimmy Delaney. He was brought down from Glasgow Celtic for £4,000 in 1946, to race helter-skelter down the right wing and whip in alluring crosses. Born just after the outbreak of the First World War, he was the oldest of the 1948 Cup-winning side, the only one in his 30s. Nor did his balding pate and spindly brittle legs do other than reflect such veteran status. The crowd howled with delighted astonishment as he shot past fumbling left-backs, like a granddad in a movie cartoon accelerating past a toddling grandson. Years later, on a professional visit to Coventry where my great friend, John Rennie, was doing wondrous things of an educational brand, I bumped into a niece of Jimmy Delaney's. She told me how he was confined to a wheelchair. The contrast of this with the mental image of him hurtling down the touchline was almost unbearable.

On the left wing, by advantageous divergence, Charlie Mitten was more inclined to linger on the ball and consider his options, including a lusty left-foot shot that brought him 61 goals for the Reds. His biography is not mundane. He was born in Rangoon, the son of a Sergeant Major; he served as a PT instructor with the RAF in the Azores; and he went to play for Santa Fe in Bogota in 1950, along with the Stoke City centre-half, the classy Neil Franklin and the doughty Roy Paul, a great future captain of Manchester City. Compared with his £12 a week with United, a detached house, plus maid and car, £2,500 signing on fee, £35 win bonuses and a £1,500 end-of-season bonus proved very tempting for one who had found his Cup Final earnings so beggarly. On his return he was fined £250 and banned for six months by outraged authority, before picking up the bones of his career with Fulham, with Mansfield

Town as player-manager and as manager of Newcastle United. The exotic life-story sits well with this harmonica-playing, greyhound-owning rascal, the 'card', the Denry Machin, of the post-war United eleven.

Johnny Morris from Radcliffe, at inside-right, was the youngest of the team, being 22 when post-war football resumed and when his busy spell with the Royal Armoured Corps, crossing the Rhine on the Western front, then embarking for India, was over. With his chubby face and dark curls there was something of the juvenile about him - and this 'Just William' sense was revealed in his self-assured facing up to authority. He was as likely to cock a snook at the high command as he was to show the ball to a perplexed defender before shimmying past him. His mind shone; his toes twinkled; his skills glittered.

Stan Pearson, at inside-left, was more meditative. A Salford lad, he saw service with the 2nd/4th Lancashire Regiment before returning to act as Manchester United's major strategist. Calm, lethal in the air as well as on the ground, as his 149 goals for United suggest, he was a quick mover of the ball, a forerunner of the one-touch football of the 1960s and, equally, a prototype of the attacking mid-fielder of the 1980s. To adopt a not inapposite Army metaphor, he was like the military policeman at the crucial cross-roads, quickly directing hectic traffic down the appropriate tracks without error.

When Walter Winterbottom was coaching physical education students, he used to show them two shots of an England versus Italy match, where two passes from the quick-thinking Stan Pearson would have produced two near-certain goals - had the centre-forward also had the wit to realise what was possible. Composed he may have been, but we all assembled outside the main entrance at Maine Road when he invited, courtesy of the *Manchester Evening News*, a man who had insulted his rather more outspoken wife to explain himself; a policeman persuaded him to return to the sanctity of the dressing room. He moved on to Bury and later Chester, as player-manager, turning out when he was 40. He loved football and had the humility not to consider retiring when at the top; he did not mind what other people thought as long as he could continue playing and tales circulated about him playing in older age for pub teams on Sunday mornings. He was a good-looking, brainy, artistic footballer, held rightly in huge esteem.

Jack Rowley moved into the penalty area and let fly. Pinned in the dense crowd behind the Kippax End goal at Maine Road, the weighty leather ball skimmed the cross bar, thumped me squarely on the forehead and bounced back briskly on to the playing area. For just a minute I wondered whether I had suddenly been infected with some terrifying brain disease, such was the agony. I file this as circumstantial evidence for the case that Jack Rowley had about the hardest shot in the business. In all, he scored 208 goals for Manchester United. Wolverhampton-born, 'the Gunner' came to Old Trafford via Wolves and Bournemouth and he afterwards enjoyed fifteen years of varied management. During World War II he served with the South Staffordshire Regiment but was at least stationed 'somewhere in England' at the close of the war. He benefited from a fine balance of brawn and pace, and, apart from the volcanic left boot and the deadly head, coated with black wavy hair, he was an uncommonly effective footballer.

134

Manchester Fighters and Lancaster Bombers

John Carey was my special hero. He was the generalissimo. Dry humoured, prudent with money, a singer, under pressure, of 'Paddy M'Ginty's Goat', this deep-thinking Irishman, knowledgeable enough to captain the Rest of Europe against Great Britain in 1947, must be the best right-back United have had. Corporal Jones' *Dad's Army* counsel, 'don't panic', was his text. His mind seemed refrigerated, so chilled was his unshakeable poise, as he quietly jockeyed wingers up and down the touchline until the ball appeared magically to drop at his feet. In an age when backs were still wellying the ball skywards and every-which-ways, John Carey, versatile enough to have played every position, even goal, had the composure and the skill to promote attack with a delicate prod forward or a flighted pass to a waiting companion. He never fell over. That may sound a rum assessment, but defenders, even in the modern age, are constantly throwing themselves under the flying legs of opponents, usually at the expense of a free kick against them, and, at best, removed temporarily from the action until they regain their footing. John Carey kept his feet as well as his cool and his gentle leadership, rooted in his tranquil style, made him possibly the most priceless gem in that case of precious jewels. He was elected Player of the Year for the 1948/49 season.

A Dubliner, and yet another spotted by Louis Rocca, he demonstrated genuine patriotism by opting to fight for the country where he was earning his living and he served with the Army in North Africa and Italy. After his playing days ended, he made his mark in top-level management with Everton, Blackburn Rovers, Nottingham Forest and Leyton Orient, running down towards eventual retirement with some scouting for Manchester United and a little job in my home town's borough treasurer's office in Sale. In 1971, when preparing a local radio programme, the producer asked me to interview a 'boyhood hero' and, unhesitatingly, I selected Johnny Carey. What was transparent about his memory of that post-war football was the United players' sheer delight in it all. I was charmed by his genial, lilting tones, in particular his admiration of Billy Liddell, the great Liverpool winger. Hearing that Billy Liddell had had a street named after him, he responded 'they should have named a town after him', proceeding to rhapsodise about the tourneys they had enjoyed together and with what pleasure he had anticipated them. It was evident that, just as Hedley Verity disdained cheap wickets and preferred to be testing his art against Don Bradman and Wally Hammond, so was John Carey the happier the more worthy the opponent. He gave the life-enhancing impression that Billy Liddell and he had played football together rather than against one another.

These were the eleven men who brought the FA Cup back to Manchester in 1948. Ten of them were on United's books when Matt Busby arrived, even if they were spread sporadically across the planet. It is fair to say that Manchester United were growing a trifle more enlightened about player development in the later 1930s, but, equally, Matt Busby was the alchemist who transformed the dross into gold, Meredith Willson's 'the Music Man', who, with the help of a few positional alterations and tweaks of tactics, persuaded nine ex-servicemen, an ageing Scot and a textile worker in a 'reserved occupation' that they were world-beaters - 'go out and enjoy yourselves' was the instruction; and, freed from the incubus of war, they did. And so did we who were lucky enough to watch.

A few missed out, such as Jack Warner, who moved on to Rochdale; the sleek-haired full-back, Joe Walton, who had always sensibly clung on to his day job as a plumber, but who had a good career at Preston North End; and, unlucky Johnny Hanlon, of whom much was expected, but who, after three years in a German Stalag - he was a Sergeant in the Durham Light Infantry and was captured in Crete - never quite recovered his speedy flair of the last pre-war season. John Carey won many honours, as did Jimmy Delaney, who ended with English, Scottish and Irish cup medals, while all but Jack Crompton, John Anderson and, surprisingly, Charlie Mitten of the Englishmen in the 1948 Cup-winning team played for England in a full international. Truth be told, they did not, in a period when international fixtures were sparse and when England's strength was unrivalled, earn many caps. John Aston's 17 and Henry Cockburn's 13 England appearances were the most; Stan Pearson, 8; Jack Rowley, 6; Johnny Morris, 3, and Allenby Chilton, 2, were the others.

Lancashire had rather more internationals in their immediate post-war ranks. By 1950, when they shared the county title with Surrey, ten or so of their number had played in a Test match. Nonetheless, Lancashire, like Manchester United, had scrambled together an eleven and then shaped it into a hard-working and accomplished team.

Peter Eckersley, a pre-war captain from 1929 to 1935, had been killed in the early stages of the war, dying in a flying accident in 1940 when serving with the fleet air arm. In fact, he was the only fatal war casualty from among the senior performers at either Old Trafford. Captains were in short supply. W.H.L. Lister, Peter Eckersley's successor, who was actually summoned to join his regiment as war threatened, while padded up waiting to bat against Northants, was not available; nor was Tommy Higson, his deputy, able to take up the appointment; poor Jack Iddon, ready to appear as an amateur, was dead. Jack Fallows, who had captained the Manchester Club and Ground side and who had been an army officer, was drafted. Leaning heavily on the advice of Cyril Washbrook and Dick Pollard, he coped well enough organisationally. Travel and accommodation were primitive and the justice he meted out at breakfast, when, in a riff on the Henry Fonda film, 'Twelve Hungry Men', there were only four eggs, bordered on the Solomonic. If Lancashire were fielding, the bowlers ate the eggs; if batting, the batsmen. The wicket keeper presumably had to make do with cornflakes. However, his county cricketing ability was nugatory and for the next two seasons Ken Cranston took up the reins. Nigel Howard then captained the eleven until 1953, including the half-title summer, and he also captained England in four Tests in India in 1951-52.

In the grey shades of the late 1940s the Ken Cranston story flashed with romance and transluscent colour. A dentist and noted cricketer, with service in the Royal Navy to boot, he swept in, scoring runs and taking wickets with an élan redolent of the Edwardian era, playing for England, touring the West Indies in the winter of 1947/48, apparently enjoying the social life as well as the on-field sparring, and captaining England in the West Indies when G.O. Allen was injured. Aged 88 in 2005, he has appeared until recently at Lord's and still appears at Old Trafford, urbane, mellow, courteous, the most gentlemanly of companions, and now England's senior captain. Like the Lone Ranger, he disappeared as suddenly as he had arrived, returning to his dental practice, having fired off the silver bullets of his cavalier shots and bracing off-pace. The movie reference is a conscious one. Groomed dark hair, Ronald Colman features, tall and debonair, often with the cravat carelessly knotted, he resembled the stills we stared at outside the local Pyramid and Savoy cinemas. It was as if James Mason and Stewart Granger had pooled assets, and then borrowed a schoolboy fiction on which to base a screenplay, 'now showing at Old Trafford'.

These skippers gathered about them patchwork elevens, with the likes of burly Phil King of Worcestershire, Tom Brierley, the Glamorgan wicket-keeper and the merry, balding Eric Edrich from Norfolk. The incomer who made most impact was Eric - and Bill's - brother, Geoff. Of all the footballers and cricketers at either end of Warwick Road, Geoff Edrich had just about the roughest wartime experience, weighing in at barely six stones after a gruelling three and a half years in Japanese hands. The resolution he had shown in surviving that merciless regime was represented in his indomitable batting; he scored close on 15,000 runs for Lancashire, and later proved an excellent captain, chiefly with the second eleven. Strongly principled, he was wrongly dismissed by a feudalistic committee over the disciplining of young players, but, after a calming spell as coach and groundsman at Cheltenham College, he was voted President of the Lancashire Players' Association, the sort of backstairs accolade of which any professional would be proud.

The years and siren calls meant that the likes of Eddie Paynter and George Duckworth were not required, whilst Buddy Oldfield and Albert Nutter preferred first the leagues and then Northamptonshire. Len Wilkinson, after his purple patch of 151 wickets in 1938, found himself, as an Army PT sergeant, removed abroad from much of the cricket that kept several of his colleagues in some sort of sporting connection. This was unhelpful for a leg-spinner who was injury prone and liable, if anything, to try too hard. He quickly vanished from the first-class game. Corporal Eddie Phillipson, that very useful all-rounder, saw the peak of his career sliced away by the war.

These were heavy debits. But there were counteracting credits. In the early 1960s, while I was running the history department in a teacher training college, one of the physical education staff beckoned me to join him at the threshold of a brand-new gymnasium. Laying the sprung floor was a brawny chap who, although on his knees and with his back to us, fired off vibrations of totally absorbed dedication. It was Dick Pollard, showing all the commitment to the gym floor that he had previously given to the boomeranging of his prodigious out-swingers in the cause of England and Lancashire. He was as difficult to drag out of the attack as it is to haul Ken Dodd of the stage. Eventually, with a thousand wickets under his ample belt, he modestly retired. Known as 'T'Owd Chain-horse', an affectionate reference to the doggedly persistent animals that towed barges on the neighbouring canals, he was popularly respected for both his craft and his diligence, qualities much esteemed by the bulk of his tradesmen's audience. The fact that ginger-topped 'Westhoughton Dick' was no mean pianist made him welcome on Lancashire's travels among a complement reared on Cec Parkin's comicality and Eddie Paynter's acrobatics. With Eddie Phillipson gone and Brian Statham yet to come, Dick Pollard too realistically resembled the lone horse, patiently bearing the towpath load, but, whole-hearted and strong, he was never deterred.

Red Shirts and Roses

One of the joys of the then county programme was its fullness. Although the modern cricketer would be horror-struck, the county elevens criss-crossed the nation on wheezing trains and resided in mediocre hostelries, in order to play six days a week - and, as the Sussex veteran, John Langridge, later said, when once asked the knotty query about playing too much, they were sorry there were not more games. It meant that, especially if one were within easy distance of a county ground, one could make a late decision to attend for a day or even part of a day.

Such a date was Thursday 29th May 1947, which fell during the Whit week break, then the most important of Manchester's holidays, when, apart from a Roses' match, there were major closures of shops and public offices. On the Monday and Friday, the Protestant and Roman Catholic churches of the area mounted lengthy and colourful processions bearing witness to their respective creeds. These trailed, with children in white finery and bands playing, through the main thoroughfares of Manchester. If the shone sun, the mothers murmured, 'God knows his own'; if, a more likely outcome, it poured with rain, they whispered, 'God waters his little flowers'.

Ack came home from a fire service shift to find John Hough and I messing about the house in desultory fashion. 'Let's go to Old Trafford', he said, and fifteen minutes later we were sitting opposite the pavilion and watching Dick Pollard skim the last two Sussex batsmen, with just five runs separating the teams on first innings. Ten minutes short of four hours play remained as Cyril Washbrook and Winston Place opened the Lancashire second attempt. John Nye bowled the first ball from the Stretford End and Cyril Washbrook lofted it into the stand close by us for a toweringly hooked six. It set the gorgeous pattern for a Pentecostal slaughter of memorable impact. At close of play, it was 350-0, Cyril Washbrook, 204; Winston Place, 134.

Scrutinise the Sussex analysis carefully, for, to their credit, and after the manner of the period, they crammed 80 overs into those four hours, with never a thought of being miserably negative. Thousands gathered on the Friday, for Lancashire needed only 19 runs to break the 44-year-old first wicket record held by Archie MacLaren and Reggie Spooner. Pragmatism prevailed. There was a declaration - and Lancashire just shifted the last of the Sussex batsmen before the promised rain fell. That 350 reigns as Lancashire's largest unbroken stand.

It was a high moment for teenage memory and a high moment in one of Lancashire's finest traditions, the moulding of opening bats and opening partnerships. Cyril Washbrook, back from being a Sergeant-instructor in the RAF, and Winston Place, released from essential work in engineering, formed an alliance that stood comparison with those of Hornby and Barlow, MacLaren and Spooner and Makepeace and Hallows. Cyril Washbrook was the John Carey of that Lancashire dressing room, an international star, with his 37 caps, and his conveyance to a new age of pre-war sporting tenets. He played exactly 500 times for Lancashire; he scored 28,000 runs for the county; he established a partnership with Len Hutton for England second only in durability and renown to that of Hobbs and Sutcliffe (and the Hutton/Washbrook unbroken 359 against South Africa in 1948/49 is still the England Test record) while his fabled 98 against Australia at Leeds in 1956, when he was recalled from veteran pasture, still has a *Boy's Own Paper* sheen about it. Winston Place made some 16,000 first-class runs and 36 centuries, playing the subordinate but necessary foil of Washbrook's adjutant, the

138

sensible Doctor Watson to the other's Sherlock Holmes, the concise wartime Clement Attlee to the other's vibrant Winston Churchill.

The buccaneering jauntiness of the war-like airman and the tidy precision of the civvy artisan somehow suited them. The authoritative and sometimes intractable character of the backroom Cyril Washbrook mediated itself through his cricket in a piratical vein. The idea that bowlers formed the 'attack' was to him laughable, did he allow himself so trivial an act as a smirk. It was the Matt Busby syndrome, transferred down the road. No batsman, chest thrusting, cap perkily donned, heel confidently raised, has so thoroughly understood the professional vocation both to entertain and to win. The Donner of his extravagant hook and the Blitzen of his swirling square-cut formed the logo of his storming marketability as a cricketer, while, honouring another great Lancashire convention, he was the premier cover point of his age, swooping and hurling with frightening velocity. Oddly, for so flamboyant a showman, the death of this cocksure, strutting fellow was a hush-hush affair; his private funeral was on the day after his death and only then was it announced.

If Cyril Washbrook was Gilbert's Pirate King, sandy-haired Winston Place was Samuel, his lieutenant, from *The Pirates of Penzance*. 'When I sally forth to seek my prey, I help myself in a royal way', sang the Pirate King of Old Trafford, while, phlegmatic, technically flawless, Rawtenstall's Samuel prudently occupied the crease and accumulated his runs with a decent humility. At the end of his first season they asked Winston Place where he was going for his holiday; 'mine's just finished', he diffidently replied.

Cyril Washbrook shrewdly took his benefit when the Australians visited Old Trafford in 1948; over 50,000 paid at the gates and his £14,000 bonanza was a record that endured until the inflated prices of the mid 1970s. During the luncheon interval, he expressed his appreciation over a somewhat tinny public address system. These were blessed days, when embarrassed sports personnel were not expected automatically to have the gift of the gab and were not endlessly dragged reluctantly in front of microphones and cameras to bleat out weasel words and spluttered banalities. We watched rather than listened to them, so that this new-fangled amplification was very modish.

As Cyril Washbrook began to speak, a buzz of whispered comment circled the ground. Although there was a modicum of broader Clitheroe vowels, his accents were modulated and decidedly middle-class, not at all like the Lancashire professional of the Cardus dispensation. He sounded like our headmaster, Mr Norrish, who, incidentally, had been Harold Wilson's history teacher and his was a name that, I discovered, Harold Wilson could recall when, for even dementia has its compensations, he could not bring that of Mrs Thatcher to mind. We impertinently nicknamed him, the headmaster that is, 'Knocker'. After this dignified school speech day address from Cyril Washbrook, calling him 'Washy' had that same connotation of a familiar impudence.

Sometimes, in the silent watches of dark, sleepless night, I parade across the drill square of memory the images I would like, if possible, to recollect on my death bed, when the bugler shrilly blows 'The Last Post'. Amid that rather macabre register is Thursday 29th May, 1947.

Red Shirts and Roses

Thomas Hardy described Giles Winterbourne in *The Woodlanders* as 'nature's very gentleman'. John Ikin had the same natural politesse, a charming quality that carried indiscernibly to the terracing. It was also noticed that his sartorial appearance was always as immaculate as his manners. Whether batting - left-handed, with some grace and much bravery - bowling his looping right-handed leg-breaks or, best of all, pouching impossible catches at short-leg, everyone knew he was, socially if not sociologically, a toff. Despite ill-luck with injury and illness, he completed for many summers what seemed like an eternal foursome, with the openers and Geoff Edrich, at the top of the order, scoring over 18,000 first-class runs and enjoying occasional Test honours. A 'desert rat' with Monty's 8th Army who saw service at Tobruk, his innate courtesy paid off, in so far as a Lancashire groupie of tedious leanings, from whom the other players sheered away, leaving the courteous Ikin to listen to his babblings for precious hours, left him a small fortune.

In that period no self-respecting school or village or works team would shame itself by taking the field without a left-hand spin bowler and, as if to accentuate the convention, Lancashire had four exponents in the post-war seasons and sometimes played two of them.

On Saturday 22nd May 1948 Sale played, as was their wont, Manchester Club and Ground (tantamount to the Lancashire second string) at Old Trafford. A freak rainstorm in Timperley had falsely persuaded the Sale opening bat that play would be impossible and he failed to show up. These were days when cars and telephones were minimally deployed. The second XI was already entrained for somewhere like Bolton or Wigan. A protesting third eleven player, who would have been better qualified, had there been one, for the fourth eleven, was press-ganged into service. His real name, printed here to protect the innocent, was Albert Roberts. His sole shot was a swing modelled on Bombadier Billy Wells striking the gong as the trademark for the J. Arthur Rank movies of the period, while, to further yet another cinematic analogy, his footwork was likened to that of an Al Capone protection racket victim with his legs embedded in concrete, as so many thrillers of the time demonstrated, prior to his being flung into the river.

Going in at number eleven to exhibit this conjoined filmic style, he hit the young Lancashire spinner for three fours in the only three balls he received before Sale declared.

The Manchester scorer turned to my father up high in the score box and said placidly, 'that will do him the world of good; it wouldn't do for him to get too big-headed'. The following Wednesday, 26th May, he was picked for Lancashire and bowled Don Bradman for 11 and then had him stumped for 43 in the second innings. It was, of course, the teenaged Malcolm Hilton, although Albert Robert's claim to be Bradman's superior on the strength of these few days was not seriously contemplated by competent judges.

Bill Roberts, cheerfully undemanding and exceedingly orthodox, to the point where old men grimly muttered 'he bowls 'em in'; the goose-stepping Eric Price with the high action; and cherubic Bob Berry, flighting deliveries like hand grenades, were the other three, but Malcolm Hilton, a native of Oldham, was overall the pick and, spinning away at zesty pace, ended with just on a thousand first-class wickets. His penchant for the

140

monologues composed by Marriott Edgar and associated with Stanley Holloway was an additional cultural bonus for his team-mates. Much later, and in a chivalric espousal, the widowered Bob Berry married Malcolm Hilton's widow.

However, the true cutting edge as regards bowling came with the maturity of Roy Tattersall as a legitimate and international standard off-spinner. Bolton-born, tall and willowy, he took 1,369 first-class wickets at an average of 18 and in 1950 was, as we have observed, the crucial element in Lancashire's title challenge. Pitches were, of course, fresher then and unprotected. Ken Cranston reckons that, on some shire out-grounds, they didn't know where the wicket was until the umpires erected the stumps. Nonetheless, his pensive loping arc of a run up, his angled off-spin and off-cut and well-disguised occasional leg-cutter were capable of deceiving the best.

Karl Jung, presenting the psychological opposites of the extravert and the introvert, could have done worse than to have fielded Cecil Parkin and Roy Tattersall at the lecture rostrum. Where the former's personality was jubilant and elated, the latter's temperament was thoughtful, mild-mannered and diffident, maybe too much so when his career was mysteriously fouled up in oddities of selection. When, in the present day, fielders mob a bowler who has at last managed to eke out a moderate victim, embracing him, hugging him and high-fiving him, as if he had done what Malcolm Hilton had done on that May mid-week day in 1948, one might valuably recall the demeanour of Roy Tattersall. The studious arithmetician, he calculated the geometric angles and estimated the mathematics of his science, and sought to remove his opponent with the rectitude and tranquillity of the accountant balancing the company's complicated books. He would have shuddered had, on completion of what he was paid and wished to do, he been subjected to pseudo-sexual assault. It is a tribute to him - and to Lancashire's followers - that, for all his monkish disposition, he is held in as fond affection as his more dazzling predecessor, Cecil Parkin.

Roy Tattersall, the consummate craftsman, would willingly acknowledge he would have been less of a bowler if he had not had cricket's closest equivalent to a cart-load of monkeys at slip and in the leg cordon. Elsewhere I have compared them to the Three Musketeers: the martial shrewdness of Aramis in pugnacious Ken Grieves, that good all-round servant to Lancashire, at first slip; Porthos' tough loyalty in Geoff Edrich and Athos' self-effacing composure in Jack Ikin in the leg trap - where they were joined, if Werneth may stand proxy for Gascony, by the young, agile d'Artagnan of Malcolm Hilton. This prehensile quartet took 1,391 catches for Lancashire, Ken Grieves' 555 catches making him top of the Lancastrian list by some distance. Possibly John Ikin, squatting restfully between balls, his eyes attuned so efficiently that he watched the ball out of the bowler's hand and off the bat, may have been what Israel Hands, fondly remembering Cap'n Flint in *Treasure Island*, called 'the flower of the flock'.

The good-humoured Malcolm Hilton used to spin a yarn that illustrated the wizardry of what may have been cricket's most lethal leg-side ambuscade. He fielded at backward short-leg and it was his duty to shout 'duck', should Roy Tattersall let a delivery fall short, an occurrence apostrophised by the narrator as happening about three times a season. One day, for a lark, he stayed mum and the batsman, scarce believing his good fortune, struck out boldly. 'Dear, oh dear.' Malcolm Hilton would continue, chuckling, 'wasn't Johnny Ikin cross with me? He hardly spoke to me for a month'. He would pause, knowing that some innocent would be bound to ask anxiously whether Ikin was badly injured. 'Oh, no', replied Malcolm Hilton blandly, 'he caught it.'

In the late August and early September of 1947 the family decided to visit our kindly great-aunt Sarah, who had somehow managed to get herself married to a Southerner and lived, now a widow, in a tiny cottage in a tiny hamlet near Tunbridge Wells. It was our first trip to London, shabby and begrimed after its wartime battering, but - Big Ben, the Thames, Downing Street, Westminster Abbey, Buckingham Palace, the Tower - of an imposing grandeur to awe our provincial sensibilities. Ack, with a strategic prescience that would have commended him to Clauswitz, had elected to take his annual holiday to coincide with the appearance of Lancashire at Lord's. We arrived there about 11 o'clock on the second day of the match, with Lancashire in some command against Middlesex, the champagne champions of that wondrous summer. 'We'll just give it an hour, Edna', said father to an unbelieving mother.

As we marched with the throng at 6.30pm towards St John's Wood tube station, it was a happy thought that my first visit to Lord's was a Lancashire occasion, with their defeat of Middlesex the following day - and in 1947 Middlesex lost about as many times as Roy Tattersall bowled loose deliveries in 1950 - a cherished dividend. Cameos included Jack Ikin bowling Denis Compton around his legs, the silence of the Middlesex lambs broken by, it seemed, just our two voices, high and low-pitched, a Flotsam and Jetsam cry of adulation; Bill Edrich battling to a competent 50 before holing out to the very able Alan Wharton in the covers, also off Ikin; and Washbrook's comprehensive running out of a startled young Ian Bedford. Denis Compton equalled Jack Hobbs' record of seasonal centuries in the second innings, but Lancashire won by 64 runs.

One might suppose that the deeply engaged sports fiend treasures three sorts of favourite teams or sets of players. First, there are the ancient gods that one hears of at a father's knee or reads about reverentially in the annals. Third, there are the more human troupes of performers, observed more objectively in adult life, sometimes even with a rueful acceptance that these mortals might be flawed. The middle group are the heroes of boyhood and youth, the first teams of which one is truly conscious. Nothing dulls their lustre in the mind. They are never forgotten and the recollection of them remains lucid and strong. These have been the great footballers and cricketers described lovingly in this chapter.

The ranks grow thinner. There is no one alive now who played regularly for Manchester United or Lancashire before World War II. Those who captured my youthful post-war imagination in United's Cup-winning and Lancashire's title-chasing eleven are much fewer in number. On some mornings over the years I have picked up the *Guardian* and been abruptly shocked to spot another death - Winston Place; Geoff Edrich; Jack Rowley; Henry Cockburn - in the obituary columns. Each reading is like a physical wrench.

15.

Watershed

ON THAT TRIP to Kent, during which we watched Lancashire at Lord's and visited Hastings and Eastbourne, we clocked up another first. Great-aunt Sarah's next door neighbour, in a series of cottages with the same great beam running through them all, and with dry closets, as opposed to fairies, at the bottom of the garden, had a telly. Television had not yet spread to the north and this was our introduction. We were ushered in respectfully as if into a private chapel; the curtains were drawn and we gazed in disbelief through the gloom at the flickering, spectral shadows twitching on the tiny, grey screen. We saw a bit of misty cricket from the Oval for which Francis Thompson's line 'a ghostly batsman plays to the bowling of a ghost' might have been inscribed, followed by an Agatha Christie mystery, during which hazily wobbling performance one of the corpses rose from the dead and walked off the set, a resurrection that gave rise to press remark the following day but had fooled us and rendered the plot unintelligible.

Times were changing. Some of it was, in the natural way of things, personal. The sudden transition from school to Army for National Service, prior to college, was a decisive shift, for many would agree that one learned more in three weeks in a barrack room than in three years at university. Luckily, I passed a course with a 50 per cent failure rate, some of the losers finding themselves on troop ships heading, with the Middlesex and Gloucester Regiments, for extremely active service in Korea, facing Chinese units on the Imjin River. Off I went to Germany, as part of the Army of Occupation, and, in my first summer there, I found myself playing cricket for four different teams - weekly for, first, the dispatch riders (I have never to this day had a driving licence or sat behind a steering wheel in anger) in a signals regiment inter-troop competition; second, for the regiment, including some two-day games; third, for the divisional eleven; and, fourth and less regularly, for the corps.

Once, while batting with the young subaltern who ran the regimental cricket, in an inter-troop match where those in khaki out-numbered those in whites, we ran a quick two. Delightedly, he pranced down the wicket and told me that this was his 10,000th run in all cricket: from being a sentient infant, he had kept a tally of runs, in the garden, on the beach, at prep school, everywhere, irrespective of the status of play. Even now he may, a sportive pensioner, be knocking up a single or two with his walking stick off his toddler grandson's tentative underarms and heading towards 100,000 runs. The regimental team, just to keep me in touch with real life, had a staff-sergeant, an ex-Lancashire league player, and also the gently left-hand spinning son of Frank Sibbles. A modest, upright yet incisive medium-paced bowler in Lancashire's inter-war championship teams, Frank Sibbles had, during the war, risen through the ranks to become a Major and had settled comfortably into a Manchester sports business with which Cyril Washbrook was also involved.

Red Shirts and Roses

We also had a tyro of a legendary family of Sussex cricketers in our midst. Not being quite up to the standard of his uncles and cousins, he was our twelfth man and frequent umpire. We played on Dutch wickets, matting stretched on rolled shale, so that the bounce was almost boringly predictable. While batting against a Civil Commission XI, the ball struck me somewhere around the waist and there was a desultory appeal from third man. To my horror, our Sussex-bred umpire unhesitatingly raised his finger and I was obliged to depart, attempting that Thespian demeanour that conveys to the watcher both a willingness to accede unprotestingly to the arbiter's decision and a certain propensity to hint that an injustice may have been perpetrated.

At tea he approached me diffidently, realising perhaps that I felt aggrieved, not forgetting, moreover, that I was a Sergeant and he a mere Lance-Corporal. 'You were out', he murmured, 'it would have hit your wickets.' I demurred, suggesting that the ball wouldn't have hit the sightscreen. 'No', he replied, 'it would have just nicked your leg bail.' Would all judges, in whatever walks of life, be so gifted with such sensitivity of insight! I recommended to our prolific captain that he be selected the following week, on the grounds that he would do less damage.

However, growing up and batting, if not fighting, for King and Country, in the face of the threat of gormless umpiring, was only one aspect of change as the 1950s dawned. It could be argued that only then did the war really come to an end, in the sense that the social conditions and climate underwent basic change. Of course, for those personally and perilously engaged in the war, it must appear offensive to speak of such a continuum, but, for several cultural and economic reasons, such was the case.

The true social watershed came in the 1950s. There was the end of rationing and of other controls; the 'New Look' presaged a return to femininity in fashion; the 'spiv' looked ahead to escalating crimes rates; divorce rates - three times higher in the late 1940s than in the 1930s - anticipated the so-called 'sexual revolution' and the widespread use of the pill in the 1960s; with India's independence realised in 1947, there began that comparatively orderly withdrawal from Empire, marred by the debacle of Suez in 1956, the touchstone of Britain's demise as a global power; in the 1950s 150,000 Jamaicans came to the United Kingdom, the beginnings of today's multicultural society.

Jumping wage and salary rises heralded the hedonism of the Macmillan era when we 'had never had it so good': the 2m vehicles on the roads in 1948 were suddenly the 6m vehicles of the late 1950s, bringing traffic jams and the beginning, in 1959, of the motorway matrix; where one in ten households had had a washing machine in the early1950s, it was seven in ten by the mid-1960s; by the 1950s 30m Britons were taking regular holidays and, by the 1960s, one in six of these were taken abroad, for flying, previously a chiefly military exercise, was at the behest of, so to speak, the man on the Clapham Omnibus.

The American rhythms of Glenn Miller and the acrobatics of jitter-bugging had altered the dance hall mood, certainly from the time when Bert Ambrose would instruct his band not to play so loudly that they could not hear the swish of the ladies' dresses - and, in the 1950s, Bill Haley and the Comets would proclaim the advent of

144

the rock'n'roll cult. Kingsley Amis' *Lucky Jim* (1954) and John Osborne's *Look Back in Anger* (1956) were messages in the higher culture that older values were being rejected. The swallowing of 'purple heart' pills, from as early as 1951, was, in retrospect, a mild omen of modern drug usage, while the Teddy Boys of the mid-1950s was the first evidence of a widespread detachment of the youth cohort from society at large, and one that would have a startling influence on football spectating.

For all that Stan Matthews had at last gained a Cup Final medal, that Gordon Richards, on Pinza, would ride home his only Derby winner and that, in whatever sequence, Sherpa Tensing and Edmund Hillary had conquered Everest, Coronation Day, 2nd June 1953, was a miserable one. The Queen may have had a good time but I didn't. Having, after Army service, taken up my place at Cambridge, it was to prove a day of impending starvation. My landlady had arisen before the lark and vanished songless, so there was no breakfast; the college served a buffet lunch, all of which had been scoffed before I had cognisance of this, and had cancelled dinner, so that the college servants could enjoy the Coronation; all the shops and cafes were closed, while the pubs - not that taverns sold food in those unenlightened times - were packed solid, mainly with American airmen who also seemed to have been given the day off from fronting up the Iron Curtain. It poured with rain and a friend and I ended up watching *The Life and Death of Colonel Blimp*, the 1943 film, starring Roger Livesey, which we scarcely absorbed at all, given the wet clothing and aching gripe of hunger.

Yet, putting aside this personal despondency, one came to understand that this was a salient day in British social history. This was not because, with a vivid flurry of mock-traditions and pseudo-medieval flummery more or less invented in the late 19th century by officials who would now be labelled spin doctors, a new monarch had been enthroned and there was fond hope of a New Elizabethan Age. It was more to do with the whereabouts of my landlady, who should have devoted herself to my egg and bacon, of the college servants, who should have scraped the potatoes and braised the meat for my lunch and dinner, and all those shop and café assistants, who should have been available to sell me comestibles.

My landlady was at her daughter's home watching the television and one might have gambled that many of the others had found a niche of a similar kind. It has been estimated that, on Coronation day, 20.5m people, close on half the population, watched this high-class piece of regal processing on 5m sets, clusters of relations and neighbours gathered in darkened living rooms, bearing witness to the muzzy pictures of the crowning of the dignified young queen.

This was the realistic beginning of the post-war world, one in which society came to find, in television and its attendant electronic devices, like the video, the computer, the mobile phone and varied brands of reproductive mechanisms, almost a monopolising art form. The manner in which the playing and watching of sport was radically changed by the social shift was to be colossal. It was the commencement of the 'miniaturisation' of society. Gradually, just as the ice storage units, to the temporary detriment of British ice-rinks, gave way to fridges and then freezers and the public washhouses and laundries had yielded to the washing machine, the cinema turned up in the corner of the living room and, courtesy of the music centre, the concert hall was located close by.

Red Shirts and Roses

By the 1960s over half of Britain's 4,709 cinemas had been closed and in 1980 audiences reached an all-time annual low of 101m. The numbers have risen a little since to 160m in 2004 but that is a tenth of the 1,635m of 1946. By the 1960s the power being utilised in the modern kitchen was equal to that used in a Manchester cotton mill a hundred years before. With the car increasingly becoming the chief mode of personal transport (12m vehicles in 1970) and with the Beeching slashes of the railway network a factor (a loss of a sixth of the network after 1963), the primarily collective nature of social life pre-1953 was slowly replaced by a much more private, a much more individualised, existence.

The home and the car began to take precedence over the street and the bus in the mind-sets of the many. Suburban values, with their accent on privacy, ruled, and with the nation mounted on a spending spree of enjoyable and large proportions, the admass and the American influences dominated. There was more money - earnings rose 130 per cent between 1956 and 1969 - and, very acceptably, a wider range of products and pursuits upon which to expend it. In 1953 there was one TV channel; in a generation, there would be hundreds. Whatever was lost in the jettisoning of some of the old-style communal tenets, it would be the height of folly to pretend that there were not real gains in the material well-being and comfort of ordinary people.

Take central heating. Prior to these times, most homesteads had a coal fire in one room, often used for cooking, and, on icy wintry nights, the family clustered around it, perhaps listening shivering to the wireless, a journey to another part of the homestead comparable with Captain Scott embarking on a race to the South Pole. We heated firebricks in the oven and carried them, clad in old woollies, upstairs to heat our chilly beds. You may have nastily grazed your toes on them or awakened the neighbourhood when, in restless slumber, you kicked it out of the bed, but they were thankfully cosseted. By 1971 a third of housing units had central heating. One now takes for granted the casual stroll over one's abode, a stable temperature throughout. For those old enough to make the comparison, it is the stuff of miracles.

Manchester and its suburbs, for example, grew awash with coffee bars of pseudo-Italianate designation, with harlequin pigmented crockery, percolators like model steam engines and startling concoctions, like the jet-black espresso and the chocolate-spotted cappuccino. With ultra-long student scarves and duffel coats in vogue, the problems of the world were incessantly solved over and again in such Latinate establishments, during eternal conversations about the failure of Soviet-style state capitalism, the moral threat of commercial television, the mythic existence of God, the strident message of anti-Americanism, the grasshopper action of leg-break bowler, Tommy Greenhough, and the befuddling shimmy of tiny right-half, Eddie Colman.

The post-war cultural settlement had its effect on the quantity and the quality of the crowds at the two Old Traffords. At its simplest, they went down at the cricketing one and changed character at the other, the footballing one. The cricket crowd - like much of cricket's construction - was a bequest from Victorian England. The concept of the 'integrated culture' had still held sway. That concourse of respectable middle and aspiring working-class people, who had watched and sung along with the Gilbert and Sullivan comic operas, avidly awaited the arrival of the next Dickens serialised

146

episode or attended, in, respectively, let and free pews, at church and chapel, had, in the next generation, adopted the Reithian 'wireless', library books and decorously censored cinema. Now this formula began to crumble and, with it, the cross-class solidity of cricket spectatordom.

In the often attractive diversity of post-1953 experience, with the private car on the driveway and the TV set in the living room the main props, this disintegrated rapidly. If only one word were allowed to explain this change, it might be 'acceleration'. The pace of inflationary onrush, of personal mobility, of everyday life - they all contributed to this fell decline of first-class cricket as a spectator sport. It is true that the immediate post-war crowds had invited a phoney optimism, for they had sometimes been greater than those of the 1920 and 1930s. Nonetheless, by the end of the decade they had lunged below a million, something of a 70 per cent decrease from the heights of 1947. There would never again be first-class county matches when children and agile adults were allowed on the grass, so full was the seating. I recall in 1946, when Lancashire looked probable winners, seeing the burly Maurice Leyland stride with impressive purpose down the pavilion steps; sitting opposite on the grass, even my juvenile psyche could read the runes of his no-nonsense body language. With his skipper, Brian Sellers, in tow, he soon put a dismal stop to childlike hope.

Test receipts now contributed about 15 per cent to county coffers and television began to throw something into the begging bowl, but gate-money dribbled away and the counties were scared of raising member subscriptions - MCC charged new members £4 from 1946 and Yorkshire only raised its annual fee to £3 in 1958. The innocently expressed 1940s notion that one could run a first-class county for £10,000 a year was rudely demonstrated as imprecise: by the late 1950s, £60,000 was a more realistic figure. Over the decade the average national wage doubled from £400 to £800 a year, just keeping tidily ahead of fast rising costs. The job of being a cricket 'pro', or, it must be said, a budding shamateur, looked much less welcoming and the average professional income of £300 of the pre-war seasons looked and was pitiful. What is more, those salvagers of cricketing debts, the wealthy patrons, were much thinner on the ground, especially with a much more egalitarian tax regime than hitherto.

There were complaints that cricket itself had become utilitarian in the era of 'utility' when, as the arch-romantic Neville Cardus, intimated, 'life in this country is rationed'. Certainly there were some 'safety first' tactics, some rigidified coaching and some major loss of input from more carefree amateurs, while half the first-class games in the 1950s were drawn, as opposed to a quarter of those in the 1930s and 1940s. It was said of dour Harry Makepeace, the Lancashire coach, that he taught the bowlers to bowl off the wicket and the batsmen to leave them alone. This was something of a calumny. We were watching one day when there was a stir on the players' balcony; Harry Makepeace appeared holding aloft a set of stumps, which he waved angrily at a tyro Lancastrian quick bowler. The message - bowl at the stumps - was evident enough.

In fact, the 1950s was a fine decade for English cricket, with the experienced professional batting of Len Hutton and company refreshed by the last vestiges of the amateur dispensation, with Peter May and Colin Cowdrey supreme, plus the emergence of the high and deadly pace of Frank Tyson, Brian Statham and Fred Trueman and the cunning spin of Jim Laker and Tony Lock. Surrey fielded a team of well-nigh international status throughout these years and scooped the county crown with the same aplomb and regularity as Yorkshire in decades gone by. If anything, it was a more impoverished spell for English football, idiotically beaten by the USA 1-0 in the 1950 World Cup in Brazil and outwitted and outgunned by the Hungarians in 1953 - the year England regained the Ashes. It was more to do with the social canvas than the intrinsic cricket or football played.

Football crowds fell drastically, too. However, it was more graded than in the total collapse of the cricketing following. Where, in the inter-war years, many clubs with a half-decent populace around them would pull in many thousands irrespective of results or league standing, football started to take on the mantle of the big city sport. Manchester United, with a dense catchment area and with the spring of victory in its collective heels, had no problems, while London and the large industrial cities usually provided a handful of other leading clubs with reasonable support.

Where football suffered was in losing some of its cross-generational focus. Against a background in which the youth culture was increasingly dominant and in which a wealthier economy was paying agreeable rewards to young people, football became something of a token of the detachment of boy-men from the old communal constrictions. One element was the increase in Sunday league football. This allowed those who wished to play the chance to do so without losing the opportunity to watch Football League matches. As fewer older men participated in the rite of support and as the scenes grew noisier and more abusive, fewer younger children were to be found on the terraces. It had its compensations. Rather as the West Indian Test victories of 1950, celebrated with joyful calypso and dance, woke up tired cricket, the banners, slogans and chants of the youthful fans added a zest to what had sometimes been a dismal, colourless assemblage.

Nonetheless, there was also some violent misbehaviour and needlessly abusive comment, the ceaseless hubbub drowning out the sharp-witted waggery of yesteryear.

Old Trafford's Stretford End gained some notoriety as such a ghetto of mindless partisanship. Paying some of his last visits to Old Trafford, my father leaned to the opinion, as the 1950s drew by, that the Stretford End should be bricked up. I understood this to be a solution derived from the medieval punishment of errant monks and nuns, sealed up by stonework in their penitential cells; that is, Ack thought the Stretford End should be bricked up with the inmates inside.

A further development, arising from the changing tenor of life, was the phenomenon of travelling 'away'. More money, special trains weekly rather than just for big games, more cars and coaches and, gradually, a complex of motorways all conspired to encourage this. The habit of, on the alternate Saturday, cheering along the reserves and waiting to hear the first eleven result announced after the final whistle, was dying. With often large groups of visiting fans in attendance, the prospect of conflict between opposing factions conveyed a dread threat of something like the Nika Riots in Justinian's Constantinople in the year 532AD. The supporters (with distinctive hair-styles, showy costumes and favours) of the 'Blues' and 'Greens' chariot racing teams reduced parts of the city to ashes.

Watershed

There arose one of the most unpleasant developments in modern sport. Supporters were forcibly segregated by police action and under stewards' control. Standing together and engaging in good-natured raillery was abandoned. It might be expected, especially at Cup Finals and the like, that fans might wish to gather together to cheer on their favourites, but enforced separation, because of the very real hazard of public disorder, has sullied football from that time onwards. It reaches the point where, in cases of major tragedy, like the Heysel Stadium disaster, the police are blamed for weak control, as if it might be accepted as normal that, without the reins of policing, fans should attack one another.

It is always correct to acknowledge that hooliganism was not an entirely new element. In 1909 6,000 spectators danced around a bonfire of the goalposts, fences and ticket kiosks of Hampden Park, Glasgow, during a disturbance in which every street-lamp in the vicinity was destroyed and 50 policemen were injured. Things are rarely cut and dried in social history. Nevertheless, the misconduct that arose in the 1950s did seem to be more systemic. It was a brutal manifestation of the disaffection of youth and it would grow worse.

The 'discovery of children' in the 19th century, the realisation that there was a discrete condition of child-likeness, had been a force almost wholly for good. A useful date for the dawning acceptance that children were not simply little men or, ominous title, 'little women', was 1865, with the publication of Lewis Carroll's *Alice's Adventures in Wonderland*, with its hidden agenda that children might enjoy a separate lifestyle, inclusive of appropriate literature, clothing and activities. All-children's parties were, for example, practically unknown before the 1860s and the commercial launch of Happy Families (with designs by John Tenniel, Lewis Carroll's illustrator) in 1860 and Snakes and Ladders in 1870 was no coincidence.

The economic cause among the others behind this development - the technical advances that rendered child labour redundant and removed them from the work-place - slowly worked up through the age groups. Then there was the discovery of 'youth' and 'adolescence'. As the school-leaving age rose, it absent-mindedly passed the advent of puberty, something that would have a devastating effect on a schools system that tried, with despairing results, to deal with young adults in a format designed for children. Youth found itself literally in no man's or no woman's land.

Apart from the education service, among the first responses to the teenage challenge were disciplined youth organisations. The first of these, established in 1883 by William Alexander Smith in a north-west Glasgow mission hall, was the Boys' Brigade, the world's first voluntary, uniformed agency for boys. There would be others, many of them, like the Boys' Brigade and many of the mufti-clad youth clubs of the 1930s and 1940s, church-centred. There was, for instance, the CLB, or Church Lads' Brigade', or, in Ack's acronym, Cheeky Little Buggers. In 1908 Robert Baden-Powell, the hero of Mafeking in the Boer War, published the ambivalently titled *Scouting for Boys*. One of his biographers describes him as 'a perennially singing schoolboy'; he called his best friend, an Army officer, 'the boy', and he named his son after Peter Pan, created in 1904, by J.M. Barrie, like Baden-Powell an arch devotee of the idea that children should not grow up.

Red Shirts and Roses

The scout movement was a global triumph. My father was an early member, joining the 1st Brooklands Scouts before World War I and thinking nothing of pushing a handcart of camping gear twenty miles into Cheshire. Although I persevered at youth club, finding it a good outlet for football and theatricals, I am afraid that the illogicality of scouting left me cold. Its pseudo-sylphan absurdities, the consequence of Robert Baden-Powell's oddball view of reality, were too much, although one could not but gape in astonishment at scouting's worldwide appeal. We were assigned to patrols, each named after a creature local to the area, so that, when communicating with our fellows, its call would not seem unusual and a passer-by would think, 'ah, that is merely one of the pee-wits prevalent in this area'. My 11-year- old anxiety that my call might be similarly viewed by a fellow patrol member and ignored was eased by my assignment to the tiger patrol, its call a fiercesome 'grrrr'. The thought that, when we attempted to commune with colleagues, that same passer-by might dismiss this beastly noise as one of the tigers prevalent in the suburbs of Manchester, was preposterous.

For all my incipient lampooning, there were some sixteen scout troops in the borough, together with wolf cubs and rover scouts and with a parallel set-up for girls, as well as several youth clubs and church-based agencies, and, with the onset of war, a rash of army, air and sea cadet groups.

This formula, like the attendant communal disciplines of work and family that it essentially copied, now came under some pressure and disaffected youth turned more and more to less formal, less starchy devices of their own shaping. Where, in an earlier and less widespread manifestation, the dancehall had, in the 1930s, been the scene of such activity, now the football ground became the stage for young people disaffiliated from the body of the community. In this respect Manchester United had a particular focus. Not only was it a newly successful and fashionably well-patronised club in a big city, its motif was youthful - and youth attracted youth.

The football and cricket cigarette cards of the era show grown men, often clean shaven - England captain George Hardwick's moustache was an exception and just a few cricket amateurs sported some clipped fuzz below the nose - and often with what were known as 'blow lamp' haircuts, leaving a reddened neck and throat. They looked like men who, like all other tradesmen, had served their apprenticeship diligently and assumed man's estate. It was, of course, a proclivity that was accentuated by the war. Those first successful United and Lancashire sides of the post-war seasons were composed of men who had served a different and compelling kind of apprenticeship.

Matt Busby, from the first, rightly and innovatively insisted on a productive youth policy; indeed, one might suspect that some preliminary efforts by Manchester United in that direction might have helped to persuade him to take the job. He seemed able, perhaps with the help of financial inducements, to persuade parents that Old Trafford was the most advantageous base for a promising youngster. It was an eminently lucrative approach, in both financial and artistic terms. The exciting allure of youngsters vying for top honours and providing exhilarating pleasures was undeniable. The downside was that it too closely mimicked the emerging self-worship of youth. Inadvertently, it may have fuelled the self-obsession of Mancunian youth and, through this, furnished a national model that produced some havoc in the country's social life. Needless to say, neither Matt Busby nor his exceedingly well-behaved young players could be found culpable. It was one of those extraordinary conjunctions of a socially engendered cult finding a ready outlet.

Jimmy Murphy, who played such a leading part in the recruitment and instruction of the 'Busby Babes', always rejected and disliked 'Babes' as an epithet, preferring his own coinage of 'Golden Apples'. Perhaps, unconsciously, he sensed that overplaying the youth imagery had its negative connotations. All that said and there is no doubting that, as the 1950s progressed, all the glamour and drama was to be found at United's Old Trafford, while, at Lancashire's Old Trafford, it all looked a trifle grey and moribund. It was as if the football looked forward eagerly to the flamboyant years of the last half of the century, while the cricket club looked back to the solid and composed years of the first half of the century.

16.

Those Whom The Gods Love...

IN MYTHIC legend and real history alike, from the tales of Troy to the World War I poets, the premature passing of heroes, the youthful sacrifice of those adored by the immortals, is a constant refrain. The tragic story of the Busby Babes is as moving and as short-lived as many of these. From just after the 1951/52 Championship, when the dismantling of Matt Busby's first great team began, to the carnage on a cold, slushy German airport in 1958, was but a brief span. It was less than 20 years after the last fatal time that, with the vain attempt of Neville Chamberlain to negotiate with Adolf Hitler, Munich had entered the British historical consciousness.

Abraham Gosling, a Newton Heath fruiterer, had organised the famous Goslings, from which had sprung the likes of Jack Crompton and Henry Cockburn, justly rewarded with onions and apples for their youthful application, while, pre-war, the MUJACs, United's colts team, had nurtured such as Johnny Morris and John Aston. Matt Busby and Jimmy Murphy, with an astute and committed squad of assistants - Bert Whalley, Tom Curry, Bill Inglis, Joe Armstrong - built spectacularly on this interest in youth, with the British Isles relentlessly scoured for talent. Unlike most of that previous galaxy of stars, these were not all Manchester-born - Duncan Edwards from Dudley; Mark Jones from Barnsley; David Pegg from Doncaster and Jackie Blanchflower from Belfast are examples - but they were drafted in early.

Our first sense of this unique developmental process was gleaned from United's year-on-year dominion of the English Youth Cup. Thousands would roll up to Old Trafford on a Saturday morning to watch yet another rather one-sided exhibition, with a boyish Dennis Viollet and Bobby Charlton, with a full head of hair, firing home the goals. What inevitably caught the eye was the stature of Duncan Edwards. At first glance, it looked like a schoolboys match in which the gifted sports master had deigned to join his 21 pupils for a friendly training session.

Not that Matt Busby was, or could afford to be, unduly sentimental about his exceptional nursery brood, although even the incomers tended to be on the youthful side. After Jack Crompton, Manchester United seemed to find it difficult to nurse into ripeness an apprentice goalkeeper. After the slightly manic displays of Reg Allen, purchased from Queens Park Rangers, came Ray Wood, then only eighteen, from Darlington, and, later, Harry Gregg from Doncaster Rovers. The smiling face and impressively all-round calibre of Tommy Taylor, signed from Barnsley for a psychologically comforting £29,999 as a 21-year-old, soon saw that quick, high-scoring centre-forward established in the England eleven, while Johnny Berry, the clever winger, was bought from Birmingham City as Jimmy Delaney's successor. Moreover, it was the success of the previous incumbents under Busby's ministrations that motivated players, young or not so young, to opt for Old Trafford.

152

Those Whom The Gods Love...

It took a year or so for the newcomers and the juniors to bond - and then there was a volcanic explosion of football, of a lava-flowing pace and tempest. The two Championships of 1954/55 and 1955/56, the first won by a margin of eleven glittering points and the second by eight points, were the superb and, alas, sole trophies won by this troupe of juvenile entertainers, bristling with a fearless confidence. The average age of the team was 22. The culture shock was immense. Cliff Bastin, the pre-war Arsenal star, had been nicknamed 'Boy' because of the rarity of youth. Football fans had been bred in the industrial convention of the long apprenticeship and the emergent adult craftsman, while, for my own generation, the added protracted intervention of the war had, if anything, reinforced that image. To watch breathlessly as this bunch of young lads scuttled and skipped over the Old Trafford turf, leaving the older hands of famous First Division opponents gasping in their wake, was, psychologically, a quickening adrenalin injection.

There was the disappointment of the 1957 Cup Final. Ray Wood was badly injured by Aston Villa's Peter McPartland after only six minutes and, in those substitute-less days, Jackie Blanchflower went in goal, and bravely although the ten youngsters battled, United lost 2-1, the villain of the piece, McPartland, such are the ways of destiny, scoring both. There was the exciting compensation of Europe. The European club tournament had only been running one year and the ultra-conservative Football League were not keen on such alien interludes intruding on the even stillness of the domestic scene. Matt Busby was more imaginative, understanding that, for players, spectators and revenue, this was part of the future of good-class club football.

Manchester United thereby became the first British side to compete in the European Cup. It was the 1956/57 season - and they began with the annihilation of Anderlecht. Soon the quarter-finals brought them up against Athletico Bilbao. Torrential gales, which flooded the pitch and afflicted the in-flying voyagers with airsickness, tempestuously environed a 5-3 defeat, leaving United with quite a task on the return leg. This was at Maine Road, where there were floodlights, the canny Busby hanging on to judge, after due consideration, what consumers would call the 'best buy' for Old Trafford.

It was the first floodlit and European match I ever attended and, again, I was fortunate with another 'first', enjoying a game one journalist described, with commendable hyperbole, as 'the greatest victory in soccer history'. The searchlight effect of the players caught in the glare, whilst darkness enshrouded the fans, enhanced the theatricality of the evening. Roared on by a capacity crowd, half-crazed with anxiety, John Berry, Tommy Taylor and Dennis Viollet eroded the Spanish lead and took the Reds into the European semi-finals at that initial attempt.

It was the sort of game from which one carried many epic moments, but, oddly, two less directly sporting memories also adhered to memory's uncertain flypaper. Many of the crowd, packed on the somewhat narrowly ridged Maine Road terraces, found their sightlines obscured. At one point the ball was bouncing up and around with a series of indecisive headers in progress. 'Get t'ball on t' ground, United' bellowed an apprehensive supporter. 'For Christ's sake, don't tell 'em that', whispered a middle-aged man of short stature nearby, 'I can only see it when they kick it in the air.' Then, at the end of the match, I was taken aback by the circles of males urinating against the interior walls of the ground. This automatically made me assume that the gentlemen's (if that is not too satirical a term) must be overcrowded; yet, when I ventured therein, I found myself almost alone. Was, I asked myself severely, alfresco micturition another sign of the times?

Real Madrid, the smooth-running frontrunners of European competition and global recruitment, with Puskas and Di Stefano and other silky white-shirted 'galacticos' - as they later would be called - were the next opponents. Although United lost 5-3 on aggregate, this was another marvellous evening, the first night of European floodlit football at Old Trafford, the lamps having finally been installed. My father, in a different part of the ground to me, found himself what he thought was a viable perch, but, soon after the kick-off, there was one of those regular precipitous crowd sways that rendered him, like Samson, 'eyeless in Gaza'. He rushed home at half-time and watched the second half on the telly from the comfort of his favoured armchair, another portent of things to come. Nonetheless, the opportunity to watch dazzling Continental footballers at club level was very appetising. With relative suddenness, a completely novel dimension was bolted on to the English, the very English, game.

It was, of course, the pursuit of the 1958 European title that found Manchester United marooned at Munich airport. The quarter-final match at home against Red Star Belgrade, with Hungarian stars like Kostic and Tasic, was a colourful encounter that United won 2-1. In between whiles they beat Bolton Wanderers 7-2, inclusive of a Bobby Charlton hat-trick, and then, en route for Belgrade, there was the Greek drama of Highbury, when, in a much written of and well-recollected epic, the Busby Babes beat Arsenal 5-4 in their last ever bravura performance on British soil. The players practically collapsed exhausted in each other's arms as the final whistle blew and the final curtain fell.

Back at Old Trafford we were among some 15 or 20,000 fans watching the Reserves who, not to be out-shone, were having a ding-dong high-scoring struggle with a strong Wolves combine. One or two players, like Billy Whelan and Geoff Bent, the reserve full-back, then left for London to join their comrades for the fatal Belgrade trip. As usual, we awaited what was the startling news from Highbury and everyone went home in high glee.

I was returning late on 6th February 1958 from an adult education class in international affairs I was teaching in Macclesfield. Travelling on the top deck of a lightly peopled corporation bus about 11.30pm through the centre of the city, I noted a peculiar sight. In Manchester Piccadilly there were long queues of people patiently waiting to buy what was obviously an extra late edition of the *Manchester Evening News*, while others who had preceded them were huddled in knots, perusing their purchased journal. It was a Lowry-like scene.

On arriving home, Ack was standing in the kitchen, a little ashen-faced, listening to the radio. In his hand was an old envelope on which he was pencilling the names of the slain, as their identities were released. It was one of those rare Jack Kennedy or Princess Diana moments that, gruesomely, are so frequently associated with celebrity death. I was in my first main job, teaching history in a Wythenshawe school, which did at least mean, when the school dinner was not up to scratch, I had a choice of relations to tap for extraneous grub. The mood was abnormal. It quivered between silent gloom and a near hysterical unease. Not a lot of learning took place. The preoccupation of Manchester with the scope and sadness of the air disaster was close to total. The Lord Mayor launched an appeal and practically all the pupils gave, where, had it been lifeboatmen or guide dogs, they would have been much more reluctant. We were close to what we still called Ringway Airport and, each time one of the dead players' coffins was flown in, the children rushed to the main road to observe and weep over the cortège as it made its slow, solemn journey to the centre of Manchester. There were the usual rumours that cling like limpets to sudden, famous death, like coffins with bricks in because the corpses were too shattered to be boxed.

As with the mourning over the deaths of Jack Kennedy and Princess Diana, to which gruesome tittle-tattle also attached, it was difficult to distinguish what was ghoulish and what was genuine. As with that similar mourning, it is likely that we, the participants, could not ourselves have drawn a line between the conflicting emotions.

It is unnecessary to dilate unduly over the causes and effects of the crash and the culture of blame that attaches to modern tragedy. All the technical debate apart, there may have been fear of missing the next Football League match at a time when European competition was suspect to the authorities, while, at its simplest, there was no coward courageous enough, in so macho a collection of football and press representatives, to refuse to board that threatened plane and lead a passenger revolt. Harry Gregg, an undemonstrative hero, re-entered the wreckage of the plane, after it crashed and exploded, and this time it was lives that he saved. 21 died, comprised of eight players, eight well-known journalists, among them that immense presence as a goalkeeper, Frank Swift, and the *Manchester Guardian*'s 'Old International', Don Davies, surely the most lyrical of football correspondents; and as well as two other unfortunates, three United staff members, the long-serving and influential Walter Crickmer, the trainer Bert Curry and first-team coach and chief scout, Bert Whalley, whom we had watched as a player in many wartime games.

Football, like life, had to continue. Each home match was like a memorial service. Deaths were mourned; then survivors began to play again, sometimes for the reserves; there was a taped message in the feeble tones of Matt Busby, just beginning to recuperate from near-fatal injuries, and working men in overalls wept openly; the surgeons and nurses of the hospital that had done so much for the injured were fêted at Old Trafford, where they were greeted with the sort of ovation usually reserved for a crack cup-winning team. Worst of all, perhaps, was the dreadful, agonising wait, as Duncan Edwards fought his last, long battle. His was the last death to be announced.

Jimmy Murphy made emergency signings, like Stan Crowther from Aston Villa, registered about an hour before his first game, and Ernie Taylor from Blackpool, who, vociferously and paternalistically, guided the scratch team. For its first game - a third round cup-tie with Sheffield Wednesday - the programme was blank where United's team should have been listed, but there began a fervent mission on the back of growing regional and then national support that conveyed United to Wembley for a successive Cup Final. It was almost as if each set of opponents felt too guilty to be the black-hearted fellers of the gutted Manchester United. Reality kicked back on Cup Final day; Bolton Wanderers won 2-0, led by a storming performance from Nat Lofthouse, 'the Lion of Vienna'.

Red Shirts and Roses

(In parenthesis, just a year or so back I found myself in delightful converse with Nat Lofthouse at a Old Trafford cricket ground. He recounted being asked to report to Burnden Park, having left school as a teenager, on 4th September 1939, the day after the outbreak of war. He was given a £10 signing-on fee and told to go home to his collier father's terraced house and await developments. Developments were all too immediate. His father was minded to thrash him, refusing to believe that any sane citizen would give a youngster £10 and assuming he had stolen it.)

Manchester United, having been blisteringly on track for a third Championship, slumped to 8th and lost a predictably flat European semi-final to Fiorentina. Their Wembley side in 1958 was Harry Gregg, Billy Foulkes and Ian Greaves; Freddie Goodwin, also a sensible medium-pacer for Lancashire, Ronnie Cope and Stan Crowther; Alec Dawson, Ernie Taylor, Bobby Charlton, Dennis Viollet and Colin Webster; four Munich survivors, two signings and five, basically, reserve players.

One is forced to compare that with the team that played in both that last Arsenal game and then went on to cede a three-goal start against Red Star Belgrade, the draw being enough to see them through to the semi-final. This was Harry Gregg, Billy Foulkes and Roger Byrne; Eddie Colman, Mark Jones and Duncan Edwards; Ken Morgans, Bobby Charlton, Tommy Taylor, Dennis Viollet and Albert Scanlon.

Although it may even be distasteful to make the comment, tragic disasters make harsh selectors. United emerged from the Munich calamity with two goalkeepers intact - Harry Gregg and Ray Wood - but with its talented half-back line, certainly its finest since the ancient years of Duckworth, Roberts and Bell, wiped out, together with the loss of Jackie Blanchflower, who fought out a tough rivalry for the centre-half spot with Mark Jones, and who never recovered from his injuries sufficiently to resume playing. As well as the stylish captain, Roger Byrne, his deputy, Geoff Bent was killed, as were Tommy Taylor, the thoughtful schemer, Billy Whelan, and the speedy outside-left, David Pegg. John Berry's career was also ended by injury, while Ken Morgans never recovered his confidence and moved to offer sterling aid to Swansea City and then Newport County. Albert Scanlon took some while to recuperate from his injuries but then resumed service as a thrustful left winger, while the wan, waif-like figure of Manchester's Dennis Viollet also returned to drift through defences in spectral fashion, his 32 goals in the 1959/60 being a club record.

Arguably, England took longer to recover from the air catastrophe than United. When one has calculated how many Championships and cups United would have won if this team, still only on the brink of rich maturity, had survived and prospered, one must also recall that Duncan Edwards would surely have played in the World Cups of 1958, 1962, 1966 and even, aged 33, 1970. I watched Roger Byrne's international debut - the first of 33 consecutive appearances - at Hampden Park; in the opening minutes he deftly lobbed the ball over his opponent's head, in his own penalty area, before threading a shrewd pass forward. The story that this son of Gorton was being groomed for the England captaincy could well be authentic. People used to marvel at the space he would allow Stan Matthews or Tom Finney, but he had the sheer pace and the shining intelligence to organise his defensive duties with aplomb. Having been a reluctant outside-left, he did transfer to his full-back role some left-wing gifts; he was an overlapping wing-back before such a blasphemy had been uttered by

Those Whom The Gods Love...

human voice. A Prince Rupert of a young leader, charismatic and clear-headed, he had a football brain like Alan Turing, down the road at Manchester University after his Bletchley Park decrypting exploits, had a mathematical brain.

Tommy Taylor, with his dash, his sharp-shooting and his jack-in-a-box headers, was already first-choice as England's centre-forward, while Mark Jones, Eddie Colman and David Pegg, who had already obtained one cap, were knocking on the international door. With the dancing Colman to his right and the awesome Edwards to his left, big Mark Jones concentrated, coolly, impassively, on being the chief of security and protection. Journalists searching for a helpful metaphor could scarcely believe their luck when they learned he was a bricklayer by trade and that they could employ lots of literary devices about stonewall defences and cornerstones.

They would, therefore, have become the greatest club side the world has ever known...the alternative argument might be that they were what they were: their youthful insouciance and flair the key to their immediate success, not the sign of a later life luxurious prosperity. One outcome was that, at the horrible price of their young lives, Manchester United assumed a national mantle. There were some signs of this before Munich, as the ease of coach travel improved and expatriate Mancunians and assorted groupies rushed to follow the banner of fresh, invigorating, bright excellence. The Munich disaster identified Manchester United as a national institution. Much as it was to irk more parochial minds, this characteristic became more and more consolidated over the years.

In turning to look at the Busby Babes individually, one regret among many more sombre ones is that not all of them had the interval of time to develop as three-dimensional performers. One remembers them largely as footballers, as brilliant footballers, assuredly, but not so much as 'characters', in that connotation beloved of sports watchers. They remain a crèche of 'babes' in the memory, somehow not fully formulated. The rounded emergence, after merciful and fortunate survival from the Munich wreckage, of Bobby Charlton exemplifies the opposite case.

Naturally, there are exceptions to that generalisation. The swivel-hipped rumba chassé of diminutive Eddie Colman made the crowds shout with mirth, but the sheer impudence of his cheeky tackles and sly passes spoke not so much of Cuba but of the streets and back-alleys of his Salford home. He took over at right-half from another young prodigy, Jeff Whitefoot, a neat, clever footballer, who offered Nottingham Forest yeoman service and is sometimes remembered as 'the babe that got away'. Rather as Harry Pilling was about to earn the amused sympathies of the other Old Trafford fraternity through the impertinence of his Jimmy Clitheroe configuration, Eddie Colman, 5ft 7inches and 9 stones - he could barely reach the goal from the penalty spot when the Cliff training ground at Broughton was marshy - was the sort of Mudlark character that, from Robin Goodfellow to Just William, has entranced audiences. The local gossip that, at leisure, he paraded in miniature Teddy Boy gear and was a minuscule, frenetic jiver had the healthy ring of veracity.

Sage judges vowed that Billy Whelan was, Duncan Edwards apart, by far the greatest footballing loss in terms of profound potential. Unlike his colleagues, he lacked a trifle in self-belief; only that remediable glitch of personality then marred his essential genius. An unruffled mind, a paranormal ball mastery at close quarters and a crisp finish - these were his virtues. Like Stan Pearson of old, he seemed more deliberate than his allies, with time always on his side, but also as with Stan Pearson, it was all an illusion created by composed speed of judgement and motion. Dark and quiet, he came from Dublin, a discovery of the prescient scout, Billy Behan, and, not unusually for Old Trafford, he was a very devout Roman Catholic. As he worked the ball around the pitch, one could imagine him, cowled and serene, treading the bogs of medieval Ireland, the itinerant friar bringing solace to the peasantry.

Now is not the time for mincing words or for indulging in persiflage. Now is the moment for the plain, unequivocal pronouncement. Duncan Edwards was the best footballer ever to tread grass.

His desperate struggle for life ending in Munich's Rechts Der Isar hospital, he did not survive long enough to be an icon, domestically like Stanley Matthews, culturally like George Best or globally like Pelé, but they, like almost all the cited idols, were assailants and swordsmen, the final deliverers of the *coups de grâce*. Duncan Edwards had the lot. If one set out with the idea of finding a Carey-like personage to play every outfield position (never forgetting that John Carey played in goal against Sunderland in 1953), it would have to be Duncan Edwards. He could decisively head away the searching cross in defence, no less than he could startle the opposing goalkeeper with a stinging header; he could mix the raking long ball with the mild finesse of the short, clever pass; he could tackle with the ferocity of the gin-trap, yet dribble with the tenderness of a ballet dancer; he could shoot like a pom-pom gun with either foot; he had an incisive football sensibility as mature as his body, tough, pacy, sturdy and brave as a young bullock. One recalls him in all these positions, with the choicest memory being perhaps of his picking up the ball somewhere around the halfway line and beginning one of his cavalry charges, antagonists drooping as he bypassed them, before unleashing a deadly artillery blast.

The fable of Matt Busby arriving at his Dudley home, to the annoyance and then delight of his parents, Gladstone and Sarah Edwards, in the early hours of 2nd June 1952 to ensure his signing is one of the nicest of football tales. Off he went to Birch Avenue, near to the cricket ground and just a stroll to 'work', where, along with Jackie Blanchflower, David Pegg and Mark Jones, he was mothered by Mrs Watson, one of the carefully selected landladies of the Busby era. A basically decent and honest young man, of the Titanic build and affable disposition of a John Charles, I saw him make his teenage debut against Cardiff City on 4th April 1953. 37,000 spectators looked on and admired what turned out to be the only ray of sunshine, for every silver lining portends a dark cloud and United went down unbelievably 4-1 to the Welsh visitors, recording their only away victory en route to relegation.

Real Madrid's Di Stefano had no hesitation in including Duncan Edwards in his world best-ever team, but the most impelling tribute came from Bobby Charlton, who played with and against the greats and, without doubt, was meritoriously numbered among them. Explaining how, as youngsters at Old Trafford, they were intently taught the quintessential asset of confidence, that major advantage in every walk of life, he went on to say that Duncan Edwards was 'the only player that ever made me feel inferior'.

158

Those Whom The Gods Love...

Exactly 300 years before, in 1653, during the dominion of Oliver Cromwell, another all-rounder with Duncanesque qualities, there was published the first edition of Izaak Walton's *The Compleat Angler*. Duncan Edwards, who would have been 70 in 2006, was 'the Compleat Footballer'.

17.

Wilting Red Rose...

THE WANE in the popularity of spectator sports was relative in the case of soccer and near absolute in that of cricket. For all that, just a few yards measured the geographic gap between the two Old Traffords, the social chasm was broadening. The brilliance of the new United, Europe-bound and with a national following, over against the comparative decline of Lancashire cricket, even by the drifting standards of the hour, served to accentuate the difference.

The 1950s were workmanlike enough and Lancashire were runners-up in 1956 and 1960. It was the 1960s that spelt out bitter results. The county that, since 1890, had known its lowest ebb in being eleventh trice, found itself languishing at double-figure standings every summer, apart from a sixth placement in 1968. The captaincy was unsettled. Whether it was Bob Barber, bright and athletic, a naive amateur forced into feudal practices in an avant-garde era, or Cyril Washbrook, the veteran warrior finding communion difficult and incomprehensible with novitiates of post-war stamp, it was problematic. Players seemed to vanish inexplicably: the reliable Alan Wharton; the ginger-mopped Peter Marner, a strong and hard clouter of a cricket ball who, mimicking the Busby Babes, became in 1952, aged 16, Lancashire's youngest first-class debutant; the wicket-keeper, Geoff Clayton, and several others. There were, conversely, players who slipped through what must have been a hole-strewn net, among them Frank Tyson, Keith Andrew and Basil D'Oliveira. Sometimes, in both directions, the reasons were political and disciplinary rather than economic and sporting.

£416 was the 1945 guarantee for capped players. During the 1950s a complex pattern of basic retainer, match fees (£12.10s), talent money and expenses (£10 for away games) was introduced, which, in effect, offered a £463 minimum and a £650 maximum. Footballers were then pushing towards a £20 weekly maximum, which, with a reasonable summer retainer, gave top players something in the region of £1,000 annual income. With full employment, improved job prospects and higher wages one had entered an era in which even a coal miner would think twice before being whistled up from the pit to bowl fast for Notts or play inside-right for Newcastle United. Relations with and recruitment from the leagues was not as straightforward as once it had been. Unlike some of the smaller shire venues, where a few thousand sustained an air of what Ken Dodd might call 'plumptuousness', Old Trafford felt and looked cavernous, with disappointed and sometimes censorious members huddled in the pavilion and with isolated paying spectators dotted around the terracing and stands. A club that had been prosperous in 1951 slumped into financial crisis by the 1960s, the victim of upward costs and downward support. Where, in the immediate post-war seasons, over 250,000 had paid to watch Lancashire's home matches, the 1966 figure was a pathetic 24,669.

160

Wilting Red Rose...

Nonetheless, a few players burgeoned in this arid and forlorn habitat. Ken Higgs, inheriting the mantle of Dick Pollard, bowled with dour but bounding stamina, ramrod of back and inflexible of spirit. Tommy Greenhough was that Lancashire rarity, a leg-spin bowler. From the mystic and exotic climes of Rochdale, he marched everywhere with sprightly gait and then, when bowling, treated watchers to a series of marsupial hops after the manner of Kent's Doug Wright, on his way to taking just over 700 wickets. Geoff Pullar, nicknamed Noddy because of a narcoleptic placidity that enabled him to sleep at the drop of a cricket cap, was in the foremost tradition of Lancastrian opening batsmanship. Obdurate and rational in style, with a first-class average of 35 and a Test average of 44, his statistical profile tells a fuller story than his undemonstrative mien. He abhorred fielding and, when posted to the boundary edge, he would ask spectators for, hopefully inclement, weather forecasts or anxiously search the skies for errantly sable clouds.

They were unlucky to play in generally mediocre sides. The Lancashire Centenary of 1964 fell at an awkward moment in the county's saga. At the end of the summer MCC played Lancashire to celebrate the occasion and it was good to watch Cyril Washbrook and Jack Ikin open the batting and complete a big stand in the company of Denis Compton, Frank Worrell and other notables and to note, with approval, impressive bowling from Tommy Greenhough. The real centenary dramatics were performed off the field. Cedric Rhoades, a Manchester textile merchant, was Old Trafford's answer to Che Guevara. A vote of censure and the sweeping aside of the aldermanic bench of vice-presidents inaugurated a more modernistic administration, one that first turned to the two tasks of restoring financial stability by investment in the real estate of Old Trafford, and also of reinstating business viability by a refurbishment of the ground. In profit and with an enhanced venue, the county was on a footing that could expect and afford some improved cricket.

These hard-headed changes came at an apposite time, for first-class cricket itself was at last being forced to face up to the omissions and errors of its past and stare down the abyss of possible extinction. It was said of Mussolini that he was an autodidact with a poor teacher. The question was: had cricket self-taught itself sufficiently well to guarantee more prosperous days?

Lancashire played a small role in the impending renaissance. In May 1963, after a trial run in the Midlands in 1962, Lancashire played Leicestershire in the first official limited-overs encounter. It was the bye round of the Gillette Cup, for which the company had donated a lavish £6,500 in sponsorship funding. A century from, and the first 'Man of the Match' award to, Peter Marner enabled Lancashire to emerge victorious from a cold and rainy meeting, which, ironically, took two days to negotiate. The dreary explanation for Lanky's presence in that elimination round was that, in 1962, they had been second from the bottom of the table, the lowest to which they had ever plunged - the two worst placed sides played to reduce the teams to sixteen for a more straightforward knock-out tourney.

In 1970/71, at Melbourne, there was a one-day international between Australia and England. Theatre historians claim that there is never an hour when Gilbert and Sullivan's *The Mikado* is not in production somewhere in the world. The limited-overs international is cricket's Mikado. It may not be an apt metaphor for either the

161

Red Shirts and Roses

summer game or that mock-Japanese lampoon of Victorian courtship, but, if ever anyone rolled a small snowball down a snowy slope, this was it: what's the betting that, as you read these words, somebody somewhere is playing a one-day international cricket match?

Sponsorship, at shire and national levels, was suddenly on the agenda. Baccy - the John Player Sunday League from 1969 and the Benson and Hedges competition from 1972 - and booze - Schweppes for the County Championship from 1977 - contributed, with the soothing balm of insurance - Prudential on the international scene - not far behind. Today neither a village team nor a parochial league exists without being plastered with company logos. Where the lords of the manor or the Schlottjunkertum, the 'chimney aristocracy' of Manchester mill-owners, had forked out to keep cricket going, from henceforward it would be chiefly corporate cheques that sufficed. In 1968 the limited registration of overseas players was permitted, an exciting development that brought legendary names into county action.

Earlier, in 1963, the distinction between Players and Gentlemen was at long last obliterated. All were now Cricketers. All were now, sociologically, if not in the sense that Anthony Trollope would have comprehended, Gentlemen. In 1968 the Cricketers' Association agreed a minimum professional salary of £4,850 and soon free equipment, travel and accommodation was permitted. This constituted an income comparable with professionals working in local government or teaching. Its typology, as salary rather than wage, with the likely corollary of owner-occupation and car ownership, had the social effect of transforming professional cricketers from proletariat to bourgeoisie. The insistence of men, like Herbert Sutcliffe and Wally Hammond, that the amateurs should be out-Heroded and that 'pros' should, after the same fashion of Henry Cotton in the field of golf, elevate their status from working-class tradesmen to middle-class professionals, had finally been realised.

For all this, there was something gaudy and shallow about the heroic surgery that sought sponsorship for limited-overs cricket for which overseas stars were recruited and paid for by sponsorship. Along with incessant tinkering with the rules governing the County Championship, it was something of an administrative bag of beans. Although limited-overs crickets had a marked benefit on fielding and on running between the wickets, it made, according to some experts, for slovenly batting and defensive bowling. More pertinently, it did not act, as advertised, as an avenue to first-class cricket. Close on a million watched first-class cricket each year in the late 1950s; this dropped to below half a million quite rapidly. Where in other sports the shortened version - five-a-side soccer; seven-a-side rugger - is the cheerful carnival taster, cricket's abridged edition became the tail that wagged the dog.

Perhaps a more active effort to retain the construct of the game without so many artificialities would have been preferable. Bowlers and fielders are patently restricted; wides are differently assessed; declarations are extinct, and the Duckworth-Lewis method rules; the winning or losing of a cricket match on the basis of some abstruse formula that no spectator finds intelligible is like some insane excursion into medieval theology. Cricket's trouble is that, because in ancient times, four innings were normally easily completed on one fine day, it never chose, as previously observed, one of the two regulators - stated time or given target - for which almost every other

162

sport opted. Only cricket rejoices in the inconclusiveness of the so-called draw, so much so that it has to call a genuine football-style draw a 'tie'. Could not bold steps have been taken - larger stumps, more natural wickets, the godsend of a comprehensible lbw law, as in if your body stops the ball hitting the wickets you're on your way - to preserve the fundamentals of cricket while reducing, for knock-out purposes, the time required?

Be that as it may, the authorities shied away from another poser, one discussed towards the end of the war but never acted upon, and that was the sanctity of the county structure. The conurbations had continued to make the pastoral image of the shire appear rather foolish, with the 1972 local government reforms underlining the city-bound nature of first-class cricket. Apart from the virtual disappearance of counties like Glamorgan, Middlesex and Yorkshire as administrative entities, the number of county headquarters that were not actually in the relevant county - Edgbaston, the Oval, to say nothing of Old Trafford, for example - was high.

What this did was to emphasis the old-fashioned nature of the county set-up. Its degree of impervious cementation was substantial. The County Championship was the Garrick Club of cricket when it came to entering, and the Alcatraz when it came to exiting. Just two in since 1914; and none out: gone was the audacious experimentation of the Victorians as the first-class edifice refused to crumble. The notion that other counties, let alone other sorts of institutions or agencies, might aspire to first-class standards was simply not encouraged, while the concept of a smaller, tighter, regional. more effective first-class realm, akin to the practice of other Test-playing countries, was not contemplated.

The nervy, giddy round of revisions undertaken was in kilter with the national mood, as what cricket groundsmen call the top-show of the 1960s was celebrated. The benchmarks of this febrile, feverish era need only to be listed. The 'Lady Chatterley' trial of 1959; the 1963 Great Train Robbery; the Government-rocking Profumo Affair, involving Christine Keeler and Stephen Ward, in 1963; the abolition of theatre censorship in 1968, and, of particular anguish in the Manchester area, the Moors Murders trial in 1968, with its sordid background of urban isolation and anomie. There were vivid cultural gestures, like Premium Bonds and the unshackling of gambling; Beatlemania; flower-power and the 'permissive society'. The chief social reforms of the period were either libertarian, worthily freeing up for the individual repressive laws on homosexuality, capital punishment, divorce and abortion, or busy creating such enduring symbols, of what is sometime scoffingly called 'sixties socialism', as the Open University.

Less meaningful were any collectivist endeavours, as in the 1940s, to build a more equal and wholesome community. After the relative blossoming of the post-war new town movement, the high rise accommodation that succeeded this was largely catastrophic. The explosion at the Ronan Point system-built tower block in East London in 1968 was the critical terminus of a policy of social spoliation, commercial exploitation of systems construction and negligent and, in too many cases, fraudulent infrastructural supports. The case of T. Dan Smith in Newcastle-upon-Tyne and the general impact of the Poulson scandal illustrated the depths of criminal behaviour in the redevelopment industry.

Red Shirts and Roses

It was usually poorer people who were marooned on high in lonely tower blocks or out of sight in estates cast away on the moors, all sense of communal cohesion and amenity abandoned. They became paradigms of social ills and dereliction. From, in Mancunian terms, the horrors of the new Hulme to the bleakness of Hattersley Heights, dropped it seemed by dreadful accident on the Pennine wastes, these architectural travesties were the extreme sample of the quick-fix, fizzy, thoughtless solution. As Les Dawson mordantly intoned, 'I'm not saying our council house is a long way out of Manchester, but our rent man's a Norwegian.'

The satire, say, of television's seminal *That Was the Week That Was* now seems soft-centred and self-indulgent. From the Cavern to Carnaby Street, there was colour and excitement, but there was precious little challenging of the basic propositions of society. Maybe the cricketing establishment, chastened by the apparent defects of first-class cricket, was caught up in this hectic frenzy and, rather than subject its charge to deliberate and solid analysis, settled for the thrills and spills of sterile alteration, breaking faith with the organic growth of well-nigh three centuries.

Yet there sailed sublimely through the tumultuous seas of sporting, regional and national upheaval one of Manchester's greatest sons. Brian Statham played 430 times for Lancashire from 1950 to 1968, by a street the feeblest period in the county's story, although, in tandem with either Fred Trueman or Frank Tyson, he enjoyed a much more lucrative time winning his 70 Test caps. Lucrative, that is, in the sporting connotation…at one point, when Yorkshire and Lancashire were paying match fees of £50 and the England Test fee was £75, Fred Trueman and he, forced to miss two county matches, were £25 out of pocket. His 1,816 wickets for Lancashire is the highest personal tally in the county colours, while his all-round first-class haul of 2,260 wickets was culled at an average of 16.

His nagging accuracy was, for a bowler of high velocity, breathtaking. Almost a quarter of his overs were maidens and his economy rate was not much above two an over. Frank Tyson paid him the lovely modest compliment that, bowling at the other end, 'it felt like having Menuhin playing second fiddle to my lead'. A supple athlete in the chase, he fielded with alacrity and a predictably accurate throw, he nonchalantly took 231 catches and is said to have dropped only one chance - and that off a forgiving Freddie Trueman - in his long Test career. Flexible, wiry, loose-limbed and rhythmic, he must have been the most exact fast bowler the game has known, as is betokened not only by the paucity of runs scored off him, but by the fact that over half his victims were either bowled or lbw. Where fast bowlers notoriously fuel themselves on snorting aggressiveness, Brian Statham, warm-heated and polite, depended entirely upon his technical control and whole-hearted stamina for his success, a courteous enquiry of the umpire his nearest to an intervention. He had thoroughly mastered his craft and plied it daily, without recourse to the psychobabble of the coming generation.

He was born in Gorton in 1930 and played football with Roger Byrne for Ryder Brow youth club. He slipped into cricket quietly, and almost fortuitously, but soon made the welkin ring and buzz from his debut in 1950 against Kent. I joined 26,000 others for the Roses battle in the August of that year, when Brian Statham tumbled on damp grass a time or two in his opening over, before, racing through the sawdust like a skittish circus pony, he took 5 for 32, with even the lordly Hutton looking a bit hurried. Then I saw him bowl his last over, also against Yorkshire, in 1968. Yorkshire had been demolished - Statham 6-34 - for only 61, but hung on painfully for a draw. Brian Statham bowled the last over of the day. It was his 12,699th over for Lancashire and, typically, it was also his 3,381st maiden for the county, Brian Close unsentimentally blocking each of six precisely delivered balls. The picture of Brian Statham leaving the field, head lowered, shoulder ducked, protected by a policeman and embarrassed by clapping adults and children, is very revealing. Off he slipped into the silent shadows.

I came to know Brian Statham personally in the few years before his death in 2000. Sports lovers are faced with a conundrum in this regard. The temptation to consort with one's idols has allure but, like the song of the Sirens, it may lead to destruction, that is, of carefully nurtured illusion. We do expect our heroes to be able to talk, as well as play, fluently or to demonstrate socially the elegance they evince in performance. One is doomed to manifold disappointments. There have been some much-admired sportsmen that it has been a vaguely unsatisfactory experience to encounter. To some degree, I have cultivated the theatre approach, where the concept of the 'fourth wall' is sustained. It is about the suspension of belief. That is Hamlet on the stage, not Bert Snooks pretending to be, so that bumping into Bert Snooks, in his dressing gown and still in his make-up, in the stalls bar is too much of a shock for the cultural system. It is sometimes equally worth keeping footballers and cricketers at an aesthetic arm's length, admiring them for their weaving dribble or silken cover drive, not expecting them to be saintly beings and humane conversationalists.

I once had the opportunity, in the Liverpool FC hospitality room when United were the visitors, of speaking to Matt Busby. I avoided the privilege. Even 40 years on, I am still undecided whether it was because he might have disappointed me or I might have irritated him. Perhaps Moses had the same concerns when faced with the countenance of Jehovah. Mortals and immortals make for tricky mixes.

Brian Statham did not and could not fall into this categorisation. The most extraordinary aspect of his personality was its ordinariness. One can only marvel that a human being could undergo so dazzling a course of supreme accomplishment at world-class level without being in any way touched or tainted. It might be added that, because he in no way sought to build on his fame, simply because he genuinely had no intrinsic awareness of it, he never thought of being a gimcrack pundit or whatever. Though it meant he never groaned under the weight of luxury, he thereby remained a hallowed emblem of all that is best about the human condition, about its honesty of thought and purpose and its natural tendency to embrace companionability. There are not many people, let alone sportspeople, that one may say, as one can of 'George' Statham, that he had not one enemy.

The boundlessly energetic and affable Keith Hayhurst, doyen of the Lancashire committee, organiser of the old player's association and single-handed builder of the Old Trafford museum, after Lord's the finest cricket memorabilia gallery in the country, tells the following tale. He was sitting in Brian Statham's house when someone rang the former fast bowler, inquiring whether he would donate, for charity or museum purposes, one or other of the balls with which he had been presented after sterling performances. Brian Statham's first response was that he had allowed his children to play with them and did not think he had such memorabilia. Then he glanced across the living room and broke off the conversation. 'Hang on a minute', he said to his caller; 'Keith, is that an old cricket ball on the floor near the fireplace?' Keith Hayhurst took a look; 'No, Brian, it's a ball of wool'. That little conversation encompasses the antithesis of bumptious self-inflation.

When he once told me about the capture of his first first-class wicket, I recognised that I was hearing a cameo that not only epitomised the quintessential Stathamite nature, but also captured an item of cricketing social history. It was June 1950 and Brian Statham, who had barely ever been on a cricket ground and had had no induction into the mysteries of the Red Rose dressing room, was picked for the Kent match at Old Trafford. Before beginning to bowl his opening overs, he was warned by Cyril Washbrook not to bowl short to Arthur Fagg, apostrophised rightly as one of the nation's most efficient hookers. In his second over, Arthur Fagg, who made 2,000 runs that summer, but maybe surprised by unusual pace, mistimed a hook and was caught at forward short-leg.

The fall of any wicket these present days is the object of a gala of Romanesque grandeur. This was the fall of the dangerous Arthur Fagg and the young man's first first-class wicket. Yet joy was not unconfined. Cyril Washbrook stormed over in a rage. 'Statham', he shouted - and the Senior Professional's curt deployment of the surname may have reminded Brian Statham of an aloof prefect when he was at Manchester Central Grammar School on Whitworth Street or of a snarling NCO when he was doing national service at RAF Stafford - 'Statham, I thought I told you not to bowl short at Fagg.' So much, in the reserved dourness of existence in 1950, for hearty congratulations.

Part of Brian Statham's ordinariness was an ordinary, but always unruffled, refusal not to be cowed by self-opinionated authority. 'So you did', he responded calmly, 'the trouble is you didn't tell me which one was Fagg - and, while we're on the subject, I don't know half the names of the bloody Lancashire team.'

One might say of Brian Statham, after Horace, if in a different context, 'you have made an ordinary one seem original'.

18.

Soaring Red Comet...

WHILE LANCASHIRE, like Albert Ramsbottom's lion, 'lay in a somnolent posture', amid the often empty reaches of Old Trafford, at the other end of the road the broken-backed football club was undergoing urgent rehabilitation. Courageously, Matt Busby embarked on the creation of his third great team.

The footballing climate had changed. The BBC's *Match of the Day* was first broadcast in 1964, the beginning of a more comprehensive media coverage of the game; under militant pressure the £20 minimum wage was scrapped in 1961, which, with the weakening of contractual restraint with the George Eastham case, loosened the feudal hold of clubs on players; equipment was more efficiently designed, with the plasticated, waterproofed ball a major boon. One could long conjecture on the effect of this inventive design. The demise of the dumpling ball, which one headed at the peril of concussion and kicked at the risk of lameness, enabled footwear to be less clog-like and more in keeping with a flexible, mobile sport. In the imagination, one may crow wondrously over the sort of beguiling displays we would have seen from past wizards of the dribble - Tom Finney, Stan Matthews, Len Shackleton, Wilf Mannion - had they been gifted a spheroid of this malleability.

The European and, in some degree, the South American influence began to dictate tactical changes. The 2-3-5 system, which, since the adoption of the centre-back role, had served well enough for many years, was now deemed too rigid and too imprudent. More adaptable and defensive formations were envisaged. I recall watching the start of the USSR versus West Germany World Cup semi-final at Goodison Park in 1966. The Germans prepared to kick off and a puzzled, amused buzz went around the crowd: the Russians appeared to be just hanging about in an amorphous grouping, with only the goalkeeper standing where we expected him to be. Soon we would become habituated to the stratagems of 4-4-2 and of variations as enigmatic as any of Elgar's.

It is part of the Busby heritage that he was able both to adapt and contribute to these developments, as Old Trafford, its new cantilevered stand erected in 1965, funded by the FA in readiness for the 1966 World Cup, continued to alter architecturally in tune with these new moods. The Football League, somewhat spitefully, denied United access to the European Cup the season after Munich, a sympathetic invitation having been issued by the European authorities, but a series of friendlies with the sparkling Real Madrid kept the Old Trafford aficionados in some contact with exotic Continental flavours.

Football, being the Johnny-come-lately of sport compared with cricket, and with lots of football having originated in cricket clubs looking for exercise in cold, wet weather, had always been kidded that winter was their season. Thus the muddied oafs had yielded the pleasant warmth of late spring and summer to the flannelled fools and

167

shivered in the snow and fog of winter. With the incursion of European football, at club and national levels, there was a growing realisation that this was something of a cultural confidence trick. It was actually preferable, for players and spectators, for soccer to be played in placid sunshine rather than in a severe blizzard.

As the edges of the respective seasons began to overlap at both ends, one of the attractive side effects was the perfect day out. On several occasions I found myself watching Lancashire on Saturday and then, about 2.30pm, strolling down the street to watch United, then sauntering back to watch the closing hour or so of cricket, a further bonus being the avoidance, fore and aft, of cattle wagon travel. It was occasionally a diverse experience. On 25th August I observed, dismayed, the dismantling of Lancashire, all out against Somerset for 70, Ken Palmer doing the damage. Having beheld the completion of a full first-class innings, I wandered down the road to hail the debut of Denis Law, signed from Torino for a record £115,000. United were two goals up after seven minutes, the second a delicately flicked Law header. It was one of those days when you just knew West Brom would be slaughtered about 10-0. It ended 2-2: back to the cricket ground, where Somerset were comfortably building an unassailable lead.

The 1960s were initially a struggle for Manchester United. Their league positions were unconvincing and they sank to 19th in 1962/63. There was some coming and going of players, such as Albert Quixall and Maurice Setters and also of John Giles, who seems not to have plugged into the Busby allure. However, such stuttering was replaced by an articulate discourse in the Cup Final against Leicester City in the May of 1963. Pat Crerand and Denis Law revelled on the metropolitan stage. Denis Law steadied the ball on one foot, swivelled horizontally and beat Gordon Banks with a low shot from the other foot. Although Leicester rallied briefly late on and pulled back a goal, David Herd's brace was enough to send Noel Cantwell, that spick and span full-back and skipper, up the Wembley steps for the Cup. An emotional congregation of 300,000 welcomed United back along the Mancunian roadways for this first post-Munich celebration.

This seemed to settle the club. After being runners-up to Liverpool in 1963/64, United ran out champions in 1964/65, a season in which Denis Law scored 39 goals. With average crowds approaching 50,000 and yearly profits of between £50,000 and £100,000, Manchester United were the best-supported and wealthiest club in the country, although some of the crowd behaviour patterns remained troublesome. Their national following was consolidated. The makeshift coach park on the then derelict land across the way from Old Trafford cricket ground was an automotive geography lesson: Bridgewater (Somerset); Ayr - these were normally the first two in line - and there were regular trips from every part of the British Isles. It was suggested that the London branch of the supporters association had more members than the Manchester one...and there were pert remarks from the envious about this national network of backing.

Manchester United thus returned to mainstream European competition (they had played in the Fairs Cup the previous year) and readily processed to the semi-finals, where the tough Partizan side awaited them in Belgrade, a mentally sapping destination, last visited, of course, prior to the Munich tragedy. Over two contests charitably described as physical by polite journalists, United narrowly lost the opportunity to play Real Madrid in the final. Nevertheless, the quarter-finals produced a display that Matt Busby believed to be his team's 'finest hour'. They had beaten their Portuguese opponents, the regally talented Benfica, boasting the bewitching gifts of Eusebio, at Old Trafford in an enterprising, free-running encounter. Taking a one-goal advantage to the Stadium of Light in Lisbon, everyone expected a Puritanical caution. George Best scored two early goals, the second after brushing aside three defenders as if they were crumbs on his lap, while Bobby Charlton, John Connelly and Pat Crerand made it 5-1. Listening in disbelief to this gorgeous concoction on a transistor radio, shuddering with interference, created a curious haze of delirium.

The heady 1960s were replete with attacking football and Manchester United swept ahead in the 1966/67 season to another title, as they gained another chance to win the European Cup. If the superstitious were looking for portents, England had won the World Cup in 1966, Nobby Stiles and Bobby Charlton offering starkly contrasting but equally valuable inputs (Old Trafford had hosted three games and received development grants accordingly, the Stretford railway bridge being one consequence, while the new North Stand was also constructed). Glasgow Celtic had stunned the continent with a gutsy 2-1 victory over Internazionale Milan in 1967, the first British, indeed, the first North European team to win the European Cup.

Sarejevo in Yugoslavia and Gornik Zabrze in wintry Poland were the first two tenacious obstacles to be vigorously overcome before the magnetic quality of a semi-final with Real Madrid, who had dominated the European Cup from the outset. The Old Trafford leg was a thrilling affair, although it was graced with but a sole goal, George Best's left-footed shot giving the Reds a slender thread for the return game before 125,000 people in the Bernabeu Stadium. Real dazzled in the first half and were 3-1 in front at the interval. Manchester United responded nobly. In the last fifteen minutes, first the deftness of David Herd and then the unlikely marksmanship of Billy Foulkes drew them level on the night and ahead on aggregate.

Football fans are not the pick of ambassadors. A friend of mine who was at the game spent the coach journey back to the hotel cowering under his seat, as the windows were broken by Spanish stones. He did not know whether to cheer or weep over the ancient Mancunian who, oblivious to the risks, leaned out through the smashed glass at the rear of the coach, gesticulating obscenely and bawling 'but you'll never get your hands on Gibraltar, you bastards'.

Wembley, on 29th May 1968, was less of a war zone. Fortuitously, and after four European semi-finals, Manchester United were on home soil for the biggest night in their history. Apart from a visiting Portuguese contingent, there was generally solid backing for United. It was not 100 per cent. John Rennie, then playing for the Manchester Education Committee football team, had won two final tickets in his club's raffle at the beginning of the year and had hoarded them, possibly anticipating some such mouth-watering contest as Real Madrid and Inter Milan. He always claims that, along with another Manchester City mate, he was the only one supporting Benfica that evening, apart from the 4000 Portuguese fans in attendance.

Red Shirts and Roses

In all-blue for the occasion, United found it a tense and rather fractious time, but, not long after the interval, David Sadler's curling centre was nudged in by Bobby Charlton's balding pate. John Aston had the game of his life on the left wing and George Best and David Herd almost made it 2-0, but the clever Benfica side struck back. Jaime Graca scored a delicious individualist goal and then Eusebio had three good chances - one went wide and Alec Stepney made two important saves. Manchester United, having survived that assault, now superbly dominated extra time. A Brian Kidd header found George Best not far into the Benfica half. He left the defender as if he were sucked down into quicksands and then had the impudent nerve to wrong-foot Henrique, the goalkeeper, pulling the ball backwards and then around him before scoring. Brian Kidd, 19 that day, headed a third after a Charlton corner and then delivered a cross that Bobby Charlton, classic exponent of the darting positional run, met at pace but with instant control for the fourth.

The framed blow-up of the Papas cartoon that illustrated the *Guardian*'s commemoration of that royally splendid night honoured the walls of the house. It could not be better than this - there was even a part of me that wondered whether it might be best if Manchester United closed altogether for business at that peak moment. Matt Busby was knighted in the summer of 1968, it not being in the gift of the British Government to bestow sainthoods.

In the meanwhile, on the last day of the season before this Trojan battle, United had lost 2-1 at home to Sunderland, while Manchester City, by dint of a thrilling 4-3 win at Newcastle, had temporarily reversed the natural order and pinched the First Division title from their neighbours by a couple of points. There followed the unappetising and grisly spectacle of a World Clubs Cup meeting, with Estudiantes of Argentina. It ended in a 2-1 loss on aggregate, but the matches, especially the away leg, were unseemly in the extreme. United went off the boil in the 1968/69 season, although they were unlucky to lose another European semi-final, this time to Milan.

But, on 14th January 1969, Sir Matt Busby announced his retirement and the world stood still.

The last team he had fashioned had brought him the just and ultimate reward, so it was an appropriate time to finish. Moving with the times and into a cross-national market of rising process, this side had cost more than its predecessors. It was an adroit compound of mainly home-grown youngsters nurtured into maturity and clever purchases. The eleven who brought joy and glory to Manchester were: Alex Stepney; Shay Brennan and Tony Dunne; Pat Crerand, Billy Foulkes and Nobby Stiles; George Best, Brian Kidd, Bobby Charlton, David Sadler and John Aston.

Matt Busby paid a record £35,000 for Alex Stepney to fetch him north from Chelsea in 1966 and, not least in that European Cup Final, he gave value for money over many years. He positioned himself well and did not panic, cutting out flamboyant mannerisms and concentrating on security. He was a bank manager of a goalkeeper.

The full-backs were Shay Brennan, who ten years ago had made a precipitate debut for the first team and scored twice in the immediate ante-Munich cup-tie against Sheffield Wednesday, and Tony Dunne, another Dubliner defender, who also served United loyally for a dozen or so years. Shay Brennan, Manchester-born of Irish parents, was a composed back who, after some disappointments early on, found himself preferred to the less experienced Scot, Francis Burns, for the crucial final. Tony Dunne, sharp of wit and foot in the Roger Byrne tradition, was highly thought of on the world stage. In front of them Billy Foulkes, native of St Helens, ex-collier, survivor of Munich, was a rugged centre-half in the solid convention of the mining industry, the analogue of strenuously hewing coal and rigorously kicking lawful lumps out of attackers being almost too close to boys' fiction. He made 679 appearances for the Reds; that is the equivalent of 42 days or six weeks continuous football - and he was never less than totally dedicated to the cause throughout every minute.

Where Billy Foulkes looked like the miner in red, Pat Crerand was the Scottish shipyard worker with a vengeance. Purchased from Glasgow Celtic in 1963, this craggy, unyielding man brought to United the orchestrational arts of the Clydeside shop steward, in addition to an exceptional eye for spotting trouble, a rapid response system for dealing with said trouble, and - for it was part of the innate character he represented - a certain genius for starting trouble. Accused of being a one-paced footballer, he nonetheless contrived, with stern defence and shrewd prompting, to bring a significant dimension to United's European and other campaigns.

Up front were three younger men. There was Brian Kidd, from Collyhurst, tall and mobile and with a raking shot, enjoying a first season that must have passed for him like a strange dream, and much later becoming Alex Ferguson's assistant; there was John Aston, son of the 1948 full-back, lustily direct on the left wing, in the purple patch of his young career; there was David Sadler, Kentish-born, who was soon to develop a versatile part for himself as a bright and thoughtful defender.

The missing star, for whom David Sadler ably deputised, was, of course, the injured Denis Law, a mourned absentee from the greatest, thus far, of Red nights. Denis Law, the man who became King, ascended to the monarchy of Old Trafford from constitutional nonentity. It was as if Ethelred the Unready had been transformed into Henry V. Weedy and bespectacled, he was suddenly, like the man in the Charles Atlas advert having sand kicked in his face or Clark Kent's Superman other, modified into the whirling, twisting, avid, insolent stylist, extraordinarily quick to anticipate opportunities and extraordinarily dextrous, with fair-locked head or rapid foot, to capitalise upon them. He scored 236 goals for Manchester United, each of them, not unlike the lethal stab-wounds of Lancashire's fast bowler Ted McDonald, a cameo in Borgia-style assassination, as he lurked on the fringes of goalmouth incident, preying on the hapless unfortunates vainly endeavouring to shield the path.

Just to grab one at random, from a routine cup-tie demolition of Bristol Rovers, with Denis Law flicking the ball from the centre circle into the full flight of Bobby Charlton, careering down the right-hand side, to hit a booming cross that was met first time by the Puck - 'I'll put a girdle around about the earth in 40 minutes' - of footballers, who had sped expeditiously to crash the ball into the Stretford End net.

With his flopping tresses, his shirt hanging loose outside his shorts, his grinning, beaky face and his tightly held cuffs, there have been few sportsmen more easily identifiable. He raised his arm and clenched fist in salute to the cheering ranks of his Stretford End subjects. He had triumphed once more in the breach. It was like Agincourt every other Saturday.

Red Shirts and Roses

Everyone has had infantile fancies of playing for their favourite club, kicking in with Jack Rowley or opening the batting with Winston Place. The artistry of Denis Law or George Best, their necromantic skills bringing football as close to high-class circus as is feasible, were enough to make even the most callow dreamer choke on his pillow. Nobby Stiles was popular for the opposite reason. They were somebody; he was anybody. Like Brian Kidd, he was bred and schooled in Collyhurst and, at 5ft 6inches, arrived in the half-back lineage of Henry Cockburn and Eddie Colman. Awkward, bandy, gawky, gap-toothed, complaining to referees after a mistimed tackle that the floodlight glare had affected his contact lenses, he could have been - indeed, he had been - one of the unhealthy thousands, chomping on meat pies and hiccupping on pints of ale, wheezily tramping to watch him. One could imagine that only ten had turned up and they had dragged someone off the terraces to make up the numbers.

An overtly crunching tackler, it took some time to realise that he read the game like a Kremlinologist of the period perusing the latest text from Moscow. 'Watch him; watch him', Norman Garner muttered to me, as we watched United playing Everton at Goodison Park. The ball seemed to be hung up inconclusively in the Everton half, when Nobby Stiles, over on our side of the ground by the centre line, suddenly struck out on a diagonal run towards the other corner flag. There was a sudden flurry of Evertonian action - and there was Nobby Stiles in the left-back position, damping down a minor conflagration, just as one might snuff out a candle. As for the overtly crunching tackle, Nobby Stiles was only sent off twice, once in a friendly and once against the infamous Estudiantes, that is, never in what one might define as a real match.

Just before the World Cup semi-final against Portugal in 1966, the commentators were engaged in pre-match analysis. Billy Wright, whom you might have thought would have known better, was bemoaning Stiles' lack of class at international level. A colleague simply said, 'nobody likes playing against him'. That, as events proved, included Eusebio, and, bow-legged jig and, oddly, being the first United footballer represented in Madame Tussauds to boot, he collected a World Cup medal. It is an intriguing thought. No one sat in a dressing room relishing the concept of being marked for ninety minutes by Nobby Stiles. With that psychological trump card, the game is partly won. No leg-spinner reclined in a pavilion, rejoicing in the thought that he would spend the afternoon bowling to J.T. Tyldesley. No reluctant witness ever anticipated with glee the idea of being cross-examined at the Old Bailey by the Thespian razor-sharp mind of the larger than life advocate, Mr Marshal Hall.

Nobby Stiles' World Cup colleague, Bobby Charlton, was spoken to by the referee at Old Trafford. It was late in his career and it was believed to be the first such occasion within it. A crackle of outrage ran through the host, the sort of irascible sound that greets an arbitration granting the away team an unmerited penalty. Then, before it had risen to anything like a crescendo of irritation, there was a collective sighting of the funny side of it, and the whole ground burst into laughter at the sheer folly of such an absurdity. 'El Melone', as Latin European fans fondly called England's leading goal-scorer, applauding him when he went across to take a corner, could no more act unsportingly than the Archbishop could steal from the poor-box. Utilising cricketing terms that were now redundant, he combined the best qualities of the Gentleman and the Player and then ensured that the whole was greater than the sum of the parts.

Soaring Red Comet...

Jettisoned willy-nilly from the doomed aircraft at Munich, he recovered and went on to make over 750 appearances for Manchester United. Born in Ashington, and a deeply emotional and committed man, he is still, smiling and quietly avuncular, closely involved with United's activities. In 1974 I made a special journey to Deepdale to watch him for a final time, during his brief, rather unsatisfactory spell as Preston North End's player-manager. One was immediately reminded that, apart from the surging runs and the booming shots for which he was so famous, it was his awareness of space that helped to lift him into a world-class in which there are just a handful of students. He studied and had an instinct for space that Galileo and Copernicus would have admired. The surging runs and booming shots paid dividends in that his adoption of position was unparalleled. But above all, he was a gentleman as well as a player.

He was knighted in 1994, the first player since Stan Matthews so to be rewarded and, like Geoffrey Chaucer's Knight in *The Canterbury Tales*, he was:

> *....a most distinguished man,*
> *who from the day on which he first began*
> *To ride abroad and followed chivalry,*
> *Truth, honour, generous thought and courtesy,*
> *He has done nobly in his sovereign's war*
> *And ridden into battle, no man more,*
> *As well in Christian as in heathen places,*
> *And ever honoured for his noble graces.*

'Who's this Best?' members of the United fraternity asked each other, as, in the 1963/64 home match against West Bromwich Albion, several changes were announced. No one had heard of this dark, elfin creature from Belfast, aged 17 and more leprechaun than footballer. It was not long before the world and his wife, most particularly his wife, had heard of Georgie Best. A week or so afterwards I clocked him, waiting unnoticed with friends at the player's entrance, wearing a collar and tie with the discomfort adolescents usually demonstrate when saddled with such accoutrements. A year or so later, I was leaving Anfield, when he walked from the main entrance towards the team coach. He was besieged by screeching girls, clutching and clawing at him. One perhaps clutched and clawed too privily and she staggered out of the tight circle, as he cracked her with a stunning right jab. In the new world of boutiques and discos, he was a celebrity, forerunner of the mad media-strewn torments of Paul Gascoigne, David Beckham and others.

A rainforest of timber has been devoted to the paper chase of his biography. He was the first British footballer forced to have a split personality, his off-field antics assuming as much meaning as his on-field virtuosity. Everyone knows all of that, but, as Matt Busby exclaimed, using a rare if mild expletive, 'he was the bloody best'. Sinewy, brave, slithering snake-like in the dribble, balanced like a ballerina, he approached perfection in that other dichotomy - the exquisite harmony of professional athlete and professional entertainer. Some might do excellent work with a dreary face; others might delight with juggling tricks that led nowhere. George Best killed-off teams with a consummate artistry that left the fans entranced. Think Don Bradman and Denis Compton in unlikely single harness, or perhaps Laurence Olivier, enveloped into the character in which he was cast but never forgetful of the audience he was keen to woo.

George Best used to get some frightful kickings and, unlike Bobby Charlton, he was not forgiving. Once at Old Trafford he had been subject to grievous bodily harm by a Neanderthal full-back and, believing the referee to be neglectful in his protective responsibilities, he determined to resolve matters personally. The referee took his name for these retaliatory measures. A young man near me was on the verge of apoplexy. 'He was provoked', he screamed, 'he was provoked'. Among our number was an ancient Salfordian, old as Methuselah, edentate as Nobby Stiles, grimy of feature and flat of cap, an ankle-length raincoat clinging to his scraggy bones, a moist fag end clinging to his lip. Had it been allowed, he would probably have had his whippet on the end of a string beside him. He would have none of this spurious defence. 'For a hundred pound a week', he mumbled, 'they could bloody well kick me round Stretford Town Hall'.

I have often cited that comment as a text for right-thinking professionalism.

The social aspects mingle with the performances. For all this was an era of liberation and uninhibited gaiety, one of my firmest memories is of Tony Dunne. He lived in a Manchester United house, a 'club' house, as it was called, although it had obviously shared some of the legal and other features of the farm labourer's tied cottage. Billy Foulkes had resided there before him. Half a mile away there was another, inhabited in turn by Jack Rowley, Jeff Whitefoot and Harry Gregg. Certainly, years ago, it must have been a considerable boon in a let and rent housing economy, but it seemed a trifle passé in the 1960s and early 1970s. I used occasionally to catch the 112 bus into Manchester close to this house and, once or twice, Tony Dunne would come racing round the corner and leap aboard, on his way to the Warwick Road bus-stop and presumably a training session. Brilliant Irish full-back and European Cup medallist, he was still leaving behind an unassuming semi-detached home, to jump on a bus to go to work. It is little more than thirty years ago. Nowadays he would be ushered out of a garrisoned mansion, his only doubt which of several monstrous cars, with, as Michael Flanders said, 'teeth at both ends', he might choose to transport him to the Carrington training establishment. *O Tempores; O Mores*.

19.

Domestic Interlude

TEACHING HISTORY to a bright bunch of Wythenshawe first-formers, one attempted, if in somewhat callow fashion, to intertwine a thread of relevance, at once local and up-to-date, so we were doing th e Romans and trying to link it to Manchester. Either encastled near where Knott Mill now lay or in summer camp where the Cathedral majestically stood, Roman soldiers kept watch over the fringes of their massive imperial domains. It was the 1950s. Many of the youngsters had brothers, cousins and uncles doing National Service, some of them overseas, manning distant outposts of the British Empire, performing the same duties as those Roman legionaries nearly 2,000 years before.

I asked for examples and they flowed readily ...Malaya...Cyprus...Kenya... Southport...this from a little boy to the right on the front row of desks. Everyone chortled and he hid his face in his arms, embarrassed by his error and grimacing in anguish... 'Sorry, sir', he corrected himself, 'Stockport'.

It was once said that God made Stockport in a fit of temper and, during these years, I had cause to muse over the possibility that it might be regarded as a far-flung base of the British Raj. A minor fluttering with the Iron Curtain over and back on the English sod, a total abhorrence of practice (that only saviour of meagre ability) had led me to abandon any hopes of real club cricket, to Ack's chagrin, and play social or 'rough' cricket with my Old Boy mates, like Peter Day, Brian Eldred and John Hough, with a mixture of equally social or 'rough' soccer and rugger to wile away the winter months.

Ours being an itinerant eleven, Sundays meant often convivial times spent in Cheshire villages like Toft and Weaverham, but Saturdays engaged us in the North Cheshire League, with a week by week immersion in the soggier environs of Stockport. The umpires were old age pensioners, each paid half a crown (12.5p) for their troubles, but, of course, no play meant no pay. They would have us slithering about in what my mother would have called slutch, in the middle of some rain-sodden Stockportian meadow, with the precipitation stair-rodding down, for a few overs. Then they would call it off; trouser their two and six, and splash contentedly off through the puddles.

One, however, was as Shylock described Portia, 'a Daniel come to judgement'. Standing at mid-off, I overheard our bowler, Brian, complain about the incoming batsman. He was 50 years ahead of his time, in that he exemplified the 21st century penchant for obesity. When it came to value for money, his pennyworth on a weighing machine was a sound investment. Brian could not see the wicket, or, for that matter, the wicket-keeper, when this rotund character plumped himself on the crease. The ancient umpire peered dimly down the pitch. 'Here, you', he called sternly, 'if he hits you on the leg, you're out lbw'. Brian smiled with some satisfaction. The umpire slowly turned to him. 'And you', he growled, 'if you hit him on the arse, it's a wide'.

Up at University, horizons expanded. While the Cantabrigean dream of some is of gliding gently in a punt along the Backs, mine are more along the lines of going to Fenners to watch Lancashire. Among the oddities of memory are of a chilled May morning, with Winston Place and Malcolm Hilton, raincoats belted and collars raised against the fenland gusts, strolling round the perimeter of the ground, as their sweatered pals batted placidly in the face of the student attack.

Vocational calls took me further afield. There was a brief sojourn in the North-East, where, it was muttered with dejected resignation, they have nine months' winter and three months' bad weather and where a cardigan-free human on Whitley Bay beach, battered by North Sea gales, is an uncommon sight. That meant trips to St James' Park and Roker Park to watch United and sometimes United Reserves or, if watching other varieties, patiently to await the announcement of half-times scores to see how United were doing. There was some desultory cricket in the same league as Rohan Kanhai and Lance Gibbs, although the historian's thirst for rectitude insists that the corollary should be appended that they performed about seven grades up from our little lot, with our pleasant trips to places like Blyth, Beddington and Ashington, birthplace of Bobby Charlton.

A second and longer spell on Merseyside followed, with regular outings, accompanying Norman Garner, to Anfield and Goodison Park, still with an ear cocked for those half-time scores. There were occasional visits to watch Southport, too. One could take children to Haig Avenue and they could play unimpeded by a vast pack of fans. Except for one Easter Monday…Southport had already been relegated to the then Fourth Division. Their opponents, Oldham Athletic, had just about gained promotion, assisted by a very heavy defeat of Southport in the back-to-back Good Friday fixture. When we arrived at Southport Station there was unexpected tumult and confusion. Half of Oldham had decided to have a daytrip to the seaside resort to celebrate the team's success. A bus inspector struggled to contain this busy scene of cheery disorder. A bus appeared and he cried 'anyone for the hospital?' A thickly Oldhamite accent answered, 'no, but your goalie were lookin' a bit peaky a'Friday.'

There was also the opportunity to spend many days on Lancashire's out-grounds, at Aigburth, Southport and Blackpool's Stanley Park, where, in the company of a one-year-old son, we witnessed Jack Simmons' debut in 1968 against Northants. In Harold Brighouse's comedy, *Hobson's Choice*, the eponymous and autocratic shoemaker is faced with ruin, so much so that he is told by his former hand, Willie Mossop, that details of his shame will be published in the *Salford Reporter*. '*Salford Reporter*!' roared Hobson, emoting outrage, pointing out that, when men of his repute are hounded by the press, the news is to be found 'in t'*Manchester Guardian*, for all t'world to see.' The neat, compact setting of the Southport ground in Birkdale was the stage for a similar cameo.

Lancashire's merry-go-round of success in limited-overs cricket was very attractive to holiday crowds and, for a Sunday League match against Essex, the arena was packed tightly and the gate closed. We perched wherever we could, some on broken chairs, in serried ranks, seven and eight deep, and with precious little elevation, so that watching was not easy. Just as the game started, the groundsman appeared with two chairs and placed them on the grass between the ropes and the white boundary line. A man and his two children, who were conducted to the chairs, accompanied him. Immediately about a couple of thousand spectators could no longer see. 'Shift those bloody kids', went up the cry. The groundsman turned to the crowd and, by way of diffident explanation, indicated the father, saying 'He's from the *Daily Telegraph.*' 'Shift those bloody kids', repeated the same stentorian, Hobsonian voice, 'it would have been alright had it been the *Manchester Guardian.*'

The children vanished and the humiliated reporter fled the scene. One suspects the *Guardian* had already emasculated itself of its Mancunian vitality, but, like thousands of us, the man in the crowd persevered with it, hoping fancifully that it might some day forego its effete, facetious Southern practices (although its crossword remains peerless and Polly Toynbee diligently maintains the argument for social equality) and return to its sturdy roots as the *Manchester Guardian.*

Every other home match we bought stand tickets and journeyed over to watch Manchester United. Amid the sorrows and disasters of the 1972/73 season, I took my four-year-old son, Matthew, to watch for the first time. Yes, yes, Matt is named after HIM, although, had Busby been christened Algernon or Cuthbert, the distaff side might have been disputatious. I agonised over which fixture to choose, wondering whether classy opponents and likely defeat outweighed the converse. Recalling my own salutary inductive experience with Blackburn Rovers, I opted for Norwich City, thinking that a victory, however predictable and low-key, was a victory. Off we went and, in another fit of sentiment, the traditional Mars bar was purchased. Norwich City hung on for 80 minutes, but honest to goodness Mick Martin headed in for a 1-0 win, to family satisfaction all around. It was a good beginning. Apart from the football and the Mars bar, there was also the excitement of being lifted by exultant youths on to the luggage rack of the packed train to avoid the crush, although this only applied to 50 per cent of the kinship group.

In the spring of 1974 there was the horror of relegation for Manchester United for the first and only time since World War II. Watching a team of United's recent calibre flounder was like seeing Calvin's Geneva yield to the Counter-Reformation; you could not believe that such a cultural stronghold could be so undermined. The following year I watched Manchester United as often as possible, determined to keep the faith. At the first home game of that Second Division season, in which United became champions at a canter, the atmosphere was hysterically feverish, so much so that the Millwall manager said afterwards that he had trouble persuading his charges to take the field. As the United players ran out, the usual roar of welcome was touched with another tone, passionate, forgiving, pleading, intimately supportive.

Suddenly, as if from nowhere, I heard this voice shouting, 'we'll always be with you, United'. With something of a shock, I realised it was my voice, the voice of one I had complacently thought to be rational, well-educated and logical. It was a moment of emotional self-revelation.

There was a winding-down of cricket by way of a local club's Sunday team, with all the games at home, a pleasant saunter down to a tidy little ground, an old-fashioned cricket tea, a pint after the game and no administrative cares; a jeweller, a bookmaker and myself were the three who topped the team-list every week, as we had elected to play only on the Sabbath, in entire reversal of my grandmother's strict

177

tenets. I also, in and around those years, ran an occasional eleven of academics, whose talents ran the gamut from heavy-duty northern leaguers to fugitives from *Watership Down*. These games were mainly 20 overs a side, with ten bowling two overs each and with a strenuous effort made to ensure most had a bat as well. Among our opponents was Langworthy's Drunks, a Sale-based and jovial outfit. We played them on the Wednesday before the first day of the Australian Test at Old Trafford in 1964 and then stayed over and attended the match on the first day.

The cricket has been forgotten but the après-ski conviviality lives on in the memory, and, along with a chicken luncheon at Old Trafford the next morning, there were hairs of the dog in hirsute and canine profusion. Part way through the afternoon I glanced along the row. I was the only one of my faithful team awake. Open-mouthed, heads askew and tenderly snoring, they more resembled a line of Rip Van Winkles than a super-fit sporting combine. Bobby Simpson, on the way to 311, and Bill Lawry, 106, proved to be the perfect sleeping draught. Ever the conformist, I took a nap as well.

Later professional duties led to the leaving of the north-west, asked, like so many Greater Mancunians, to undertake missionary work in London. Now it was a matter of trailing round to all the grounds where Manchester United were the visitors, even unto Watford, Luton Town, Queen's Park Rangers and Fulham. The move coincided with a mood-swing in favour of cricket and, Manchester United apart, football became a lesser interest. For instance, I only watched *Match of the Day* if the Reds were involved. A major reason for this was a rising involvement in the field of cricket writing and buffery. I began to write cricket history, including - and the publisher's commission made me wonder if it was Christmas Day - a history of Lancashire. As well as several books, there were reviews and articles for *The Cricketer*, when the amiable Peter Perchard was executive editor, and a lengthy and rewarding stint for *Cricket Lore*, founded and magnificently sustained by the enthusiastic Richard Hill. There was some mercenary involvement with Surrey, under the direction of Paul Sheldon, soon to become one of the shrewdest as well as the most courteous of cricket administrators. There followed a pleasing engagement with MCC, editing the club's yearbook or annual.

Cricket buffs include a fair, even an unfair, share of curmudgeons, spluttering litigiously about the number of pads worn by C.B. Fry in 1902 and wearing their scholarship like a QC's silk. Nevertheless, the majority are a civilised and merry bunch. One thinks of such generous spirits as Dave Allsop, for years chairman of the Cricket Society; Clive Porter, editor, brave and humane, of the Cricket Society's journal; Peter Wynne-Thomas, holed up in his Trent Bridge library and long-time, long-suffering secretary of the Association of Cricket Statisticians and Historians, of which I served as President, despite my daughter's cruel jibe that there could not be enough of us to warrant having a president. There is Rev Malcolm Lorimer, Lancashire's statistician and chaplain in ordinary, who so happens to have his Methodist's Superintendent's abode on the land where a Thatcherite vandalistic council demolished my old school; I have claimed, falsely and in public, that his home is bang on our old school cricket square and that, moreover, his fridge freezer is on a length.

Domestic Interlude

'Wider still and wider', as *Land of Hope and Glory* sang...and, full of the former and replete with the latter, the London base enabled us to transverse the land in search of Lancashire away fixtures. I had now made the acquaintance of Charles Oliver, former Lancashire statistician and by now a county vice-president. Until his much-mourned death in 2004 we travelled together - we lived quite close to one another and were both non-drivers - not only on innumerable occasions to Lord's and sometimes the Oval, but also to wherever Lancashire were appearing within train timetable radius. Chelmsford, Canterbury, Southampton, Hove, Leicester, the hospitable inner sanctum of Trent Bridge, chattering non-stop about cricket, politics, musical films and a dozen other issues. Charles Oliver, the original walking *Wisden*, had encyclopaedic recall of cricketers, but he was also so well-known on the county circuit that he was one of those people who not only knew all the players but most of the audience. In rainy moments we constructed the selfish division one of the county championship, comprised of the teams whose grounds we could easily reach by train to watch Lancashire, the preferred octet being Middlesex, Surrey, Kent, Sussex, Essex, Leicestershire, Northants and Notts.

Another long-term co-watcher of 40-odd years standing was and is Brian Walsh, Blackpool-born, and changeless, in that, amazingly, his moderate temperature of sociable personality has apparently suffered no ups and downs over that period. We met as academic colleagues and became close in a friendship that, in practice, revolves around a series of ritualistic cricket occasions, often beginning with the first day of the season at Fenners, with lunch in the Hobbs' Pavilion wine bar on Parker's Piece and continuing with odd Lancashire games, plus the Lord's finals, where two fellow-members of the London Savage Club, the amicable Philip Talbot and the estimable Jeremy Hardie, may also be found in this goodly company. There we often meet the effervescent Eric Hughes, a cheerful sporting enthusiast of myriad memories.

It was Charles Oliver, along with that unrepentant enthusiast, Keith Hayhurst, and Derek Peaker, someone I had known as a youngster when he was scoring 10,000 runs for Sale in the Manchester Association before he had gravitated to being Lancashire's treasurer and then President, who introduced me to the annual enchantment of the Lancashire committee room and balcony. Apart from it being about the most hospitable on the county circuit, with the largesse of tea, complete with hot Eccles cakes (a lip-licking experience) the welcome is friendly indeed. On the first of many visits to that eyrie of joy, I excused myself for a few minutes and strolled round the ground to the position at square-leg, opposite the pavilion, the spot where I had sat in 1944 when I first visited the ground. I looked up and across at the committee balcony. Harold Wilson was famously photographed as a child on the doorstep of 10 Downing Street and that was endlessly touted in the press when he became Prime Minister in 1964. He probably had feelings of having made it - so did I.

The shift southwards was about the time when the national character changed. Once one erases the fallacy of birth-place and genetic endowment as the key to ethnic, regional or any other form of group character, analysis is much more plain sailing. Thus national character, the result of nurture not nature, is subject to alterations in the cultural context. In 1985 the scholar, Benedict Arnold, spoke evocatively of the nation being 'an imagined community'. A nation-state is keen to preserve and delineate its identity through a colourful composite of emblems, like flags, anthems, monarchs and other leaders, heroes and heroines, language and lore, sport, stamps and other ingredients. The citizenry adopt these tokens eagerly and seek to exhibit the corresponding traits, coming often to believe they embody not just the persona of a community but arise organically through being born within the frontiers of the state. The same applies, of course, to regional traits. People play out the roles for which they believe they had been cast by nature's school of drama.

It is cultural, not eugenic. The Victorian version of Englishness (for other faces of Britishness were being cosmetically made up elsewhere on these islands) differed from the Hanoverian/Regency strain. The incisive social historian, Harold Perkin, was unequivocal on the subject, writing in 1969 that 'between 1760 and 1850 the English ceased to be one of the most aggressive, brutal, rowdy, outspoken, riotous, cruel and bloodthirsty people in the world and became one of the most inhibited, polite, orderly, tender-minded, prudish and hypocritical'. For example, in a less combative and belligerent society executions fell from over 500 in the years 1816-20 to just 51 in 1836-40. Public executions were banned from 1868, not because it was easier for the victim, for the state hanging behind closed gates could be more frightful, but because it was felt to be debasing of those watching and a threat to public order. That period, from about 1850, encompasses the mainstream tale of the rise of Lancashire and then Manchester United.

Why, if it were not an abrupt transfusion of genes, did this happen? The eloquent cultural historian, Jeffrey Richards, argues that two complementary tides flowed to create the sea change. 'Evangelicalism' introduced earnestness of motive, while 'chivalry' cultivated the 18th century notion of 'decency', interpreting it as a restrained courtesy. The 'low' Anglican and non-conformist creeds pressed the buttons of conscience and strict conduct, and these were virtues that became the watchwords of Pooterish providence among the ambitious middle classes and the aspiring artisan classes. The chivalric tendency, dosed with Evangelical primness, became the standard of the English gentleman, stoical and well-mannered after the style of Baroness Orczy's Scarlet Pimpernel or Jules Verne's Phileas Fogg. Later we would go the pictures and gaze at Ronald Colman, Leslie Howard and Manchester's own Robert Donat representing these acknowledged stereotypes. Playing a straight bat reminds that, as an earlier chapter suggested, these formulations were significant in the development of modern sport.

However, the influence of this variation of national character on spectator sport was immense. Crucially, the crowd was no longer feared so much. It was accepted that great gatherings would assemble to watch football and cricket and that, by and large, these would be peaceful occasions, calling for the deployment of just one or two policemen.

Then, put briefly, the self-restraint of the 1850-1950/60 era yielded place to the self-gratification of the succeeding period. In Jeffrey Richards' concise terms, the 'rough' element in society, for so long subdued by the 'respectable' element, became preponderant. In a sense, national character reverted to the pre-industrial free-for-all Hogarthian spirit of devil-take-the-hindmost. It must be stressed that this is an adjustment of emphasis, not an absolute modification; 'the 'rough' and 'respectable' components are ever present, perhaps in individuals as well as groups, with one or other the temporary victor, from period to period, as dictated by changing combines of circumstances and ideas. Now the crowd would be feared again.

The next question to address is the way in which society changed to bring about so swift and basic an effect. The answer has been touched upon in passing, with references to the switch to a more individualistic mind-set after about 1953, exacerbated by the mood-swing of the 1960s. The 'integrated culture' of the late 19th and early 20th centuries, illustrated by the cross-class nature of cricket spectatordom, gave way to a more multifaceted culture. The creative desire to be both 'classical' and 'popular' declined, as abysses opened generationally - with child and youth cults - as well as artistically. The word 'highbrow' was first used in 1908 and, in the arts, the divisions predominated, where beforehand there had been a stabilising middlebrow ballast. Truth to tell, one aspect was a welcome end to prurient censorship and the technologies that, with, for example, hundreds of satellite TV channels, bring multitudinous choice. It has to be said that, such were the rigid controls and primitive techniques of the past, the public often had Hobson's choice of book, film, radio or television broadcasts. The 'integrated culture' had been a closet culture, ruled by a Mrs Grundy elite.

Some commentators blamed the confusion about national roles consequent on the loss of Empire, coupled with the compelling model of 'Coca-Cola-isation' from the freedom-loving, materially-minded United States. J.B. Priestley spoke bitterly of the 'Admass' in 1973, while, around the turn of the century, Christopher Lasch wrote feelingly of 'the culture of Narcissism', with civic virtue derided and moral relativism lauded. The 'gentleness', the law-abiding spirit, that George Orwell had noticed among the English in the 1930s or the mature patriotism that, for all there was an undertow of petty crime, of World War II, was replaced by a more xenophobic tinge, visible in the hooliganism at international football fixtures in the last 20 years of the last century.

The oil crisis of 1973/74 was a key juncture. The fourfold increase in oil prices precipitated something of economic chaos on a global scale and some of the old certainties were lost. There was inflation - the 1962 Retail Price Index of 100 jumped to 500 by 1981 and 1,000 by 1992; the worldwide termination on the control of the movement of capital; a decline in growth from a post-war average of 3 per cent to 1 per cent; and 3m unemployed. The Welfare State, predicated on full employment to pay the taxes for its upkeep, was imperilled, while Keynsian economics - budget deficits to stimulate demand in recession; budget surpluses to quieten demand in boom - were jettisoned in favour of the simplistic horrors of synthetically balanced budgets, tight money control, low taxes and market freedoms. There was wholesale privatisation of public amenities, together with a plethora of internal marketeering devices.

Manufacturing industry, already under the cosh, disintegrated. Manchester and its environs had already witnessed the death of its great textile concerns and, in some part, had weathered that storm; the next to go was its engineering base, principally Trafford Park, for so long the human source for Old Trafford's football crowd. When

181

my brother, Bryan, began work at Metrovicks in 1942, 24,000 were employed; when he left in 1992, there were less than 3,000 and now it is no more. It was he, by the way, who, helpful as always, sought out for me most of the detail of Trafford Park's history. Although some enterprises continue there, the Trafford Centre, a vast conglomeration of retail outlets, symbolically as well as commercially, dominates the estate.

Salford Docks has transmuted into Salford Quays, an attractive complex of housing, restaurants, hotels and leisure facilities, including the Lowry Centre and the northern edition of the Imperial War Museum. Over the way the giant scarlet letters of Manchester United gleam above the totally refurbished stadium, with its scores of private boxes and its supermarket for the sale of accessories and souvenirs, a stadium that Bill Shankly, described simply, enviously and admiringly as 'a palace'. Across the busy main road lies Old Trafford Cricket ground, served now, as is Salford Quays, by the light transit vehicles of Metrolink. Sauntering around, staying on, Salford Quays is a surprising experience. As a child and young man, I passed close to this area very regularly, but never visited it, simply because one does not visit work-places unless one is in employment there. Now the cars queue to shop at the Trafford Centre and there is canoeing in and around the configuration of waterways at the eastern end of the Manchester Ship Canal.

That switch of Trafford Park and Salford Docks from production to service is the national economy in microcosm. Less than 10 per cent of the labour force is now employed in manufacture, compared with 28 per cent (48 per cent counting distribution and transport) in 1911. There are as many - one in five - in financial and business services as there are in manufacturing. Agriculture in 1911 was the second biggest employment type, with nearly 2m workers. Now there are as many workers - about 500,000 - in telephone centres as there are on the land. There are now more members in the associations for chiropodists, airline pilots and magistrates' clerks than in the miners' union, for that once great industry, which employed 250,000 as recently as 1980, fields less than 5,000 today.

Although between 1979 and 1991 average income rose by 36 per cent, that of the bottom tenth of the population dropped by 14 per cent. Those officially in poverty, using the yardstick of living on less than half the average income, rose from 5m to 13.5m. The top 10 per cent of the population enjoyed a rise in income of 50 per cent; there was no change for the bottom 10 per cent, and a quarter of Britain's 20m households existed on less than the slewed average income. There were many social side effects. For instance, in a typical day in 2002, eleven crimes were committed and four people were arrested every minute in the United Kingdom, a total of 16,500 crimes in 24 hours.

A free market in economic matters gave rise to a free market in cultural affairs and to the elevation of the individual above the collective entity. It was said that 'Thatcherism was the political expression of this mind-set', although many historians would agree that Mrs Thatcher, during her long premiership after 1979, rode rather than created this mood. Liberal-minded opponents of Thatcherism, with its contempt for do-gooders, forever 'drooling and drivelling' over social distress, are quick to forget that part of its appeal was the reaction against the frustration resultant from the

182

anonymous bureaucracies that administered the collectivist state. The mantra of personal choice was very convincing, given the abrasively drab services on offer. Nevertheless, Mrs Thatcher's ministries were the first to scorn the concept of public service and exalt self-indulgence in its stead. Even the most right-wing of Victorian administrations had normally tempered their instincts with a modicum of civil concern. Intellectually, this scoffing at the ethic of civic responsibility was as damaging as the legislation that released selfish genii from the communal bottle.

The pursuit of private happiness is not of itself a malign idea. The previous age was stained with deferential and intolerant censoriousness and those attitudes were to be found everywhere, from the home and the street to school, church and work, and, through varied kinds of control, in books, films and plays. It is perhaps a pity we cannot find some harmony between the tolerant expression of liberties today and the calm serenity and community discipline of yesterday. Aneurin Bevan, one of the architects of the Welfare State and the founder of the NHS, believed that, aside from all the historical interpretations, societies did puzzlingly swing from a more social to a more individualist focus. He compared this with cats and dogs, the feline world one of outright selfishness and aloof suspicion, the canine world one of cheerful if sometimes obtrusive sociality. Increasingly from the 1950s, with high concentration from the 1970s, it has been life in the cat-basket rather than in the dog-kennel.

The feared crowd of the late 20th century was more of a football than a cricket phenomenon. The chief cricketing worry continued to be the loss of the crowd. Even so, and especially with the instant dramatics of limited-overs cricket, some of the same garish, outgoing habits of the football crowd infected the cricket fraternity. It was never as menacing. Rarely was it the cause of what criminologists call 'incivilities', that miasma of unease with which a gang of football fans, without committing any offence, but shouting, racing, brandishing beer cans, may bring to a town centre. Cricket's 'Barmy Army' may not be as belligerent as the ferocious element of English football support abroad, but it is noisy, unduly partisan and highly coloured. The banners and fancy dress at the alcohol-fuelled assemblies of cricket and football's big occasions are similar. One emphasises here the difference in atmosphere from yesteryear. It is not a question of better or worse. These occasions are often a good deal jollier than they used to be.

The dispersal and decline of crowds did affect football as well. One aspect has been a concentration of spectators on fewer prestigious events. Team England, as the English cricket squad is egregiously known, and the top-line one-day cricket matches draw good crowds, as do the main Premiership football clubs, including Manchester United, and the England football side. There is a nugatory paucity of support for lower-grade football clubs, as well as for the run-of-the-mill county cricket matches. Outside the football grounds of the chief conurbations, J.B. Priestley's tide of spectators has dwindled to a trickle, and the grey-green caps have yielded to replica shirts. This compares with other examples of 'collective leisure'. The blockbuster West End musical will pack in sell-out audiences for months, whereas a township like Sale, where once there were three or four cinemas and, for periods, a repertory theatre, now has no such amenity. People currently have so many leisure choices, inside and, car-driven, outside the home.

Red Shirts and Roses

Manchester, like other great cities, constantly reconstitutes itself. It is now the service capital of the region, offering the new-style economy the financial and allied supports it once offered the manufacturing heart of the area. It updates its cultural attributes, as 'Madchester', with a key role on the pop, gay and club scene. More traditionally, the Bridgewater Hall replaced the Free Trade Hall as the locus for classical music. In 2002 the Commonwealth Games were organised with efficiency, even panache, in East Manchester. Less salubriously, Moss Side, where my mother was born in rather more mild-mannered times, became for a disturbing while a byword for drug trafficking and gunplay.

Along with other regional capitals, the cottonopolis had given a bold lead in Victorian times, pioneering advances in architecture, education and public amenities, with 'the gas and water' Municipal Socialism of the day. Come the brutalism of the 1970s and 1980s, both the architectural fabric and the constitutional core of these provincial centres had been ripped out. One of the paradoxes of unrestrained private enterprise is that, as in Pinochet's Chile, it relies heavily on strong central control to preserve its excesses. One of the several victims was local government, so much so that, by the end of the last century, a city like Manchester had direct governance over only a quarter of its income and expenditure.

But cities are tough and they fight back. Manchester is still 'the city of iron with the heart of gold' and the two Old Traffords are still its most prominent sporting embassies. Having sketched in the personal picture and set the national stage, it is time to direct attention on the substantial affairs of Manchester United and Lancashire County Cricket Club over the last 30 or so years.

20.

Rollercoaster Years

MANCHESTER UNITED, in the Busby aftermath, appeared to undertake a psychological experiment, dabbling with varying personality types to see which one would fit the management bill. There was the greenhorn tyro; the disillusioned, shrinking violet; the cheeky monkey; the modish technocrat and the outgoing celeb. With Matt Busby still around in the early years, five coaches or managers - Wilf McGuinness; Frank O'Farrell; Tommy Docherty; Dave Sexton and Ron Atkinson - could only scramble about sixteen seasons together between them, where their predecessor, inexorably casting a deep shadow, had continued for something like a quarter of a century.

During United's season in the Second Division, I was, accompanied by my son, loitering outside the players' entrance, waiting to cheer the arrival of United's coach and ready to give our opponents the once-over. It was York City. First off the coach was what, from the rear, seemed to be an oldish man, practically bald, save for greying fringes, not unlike Doc, the leader of the Seven Dwarfs. I commented aloud on his apparent antiquity and was corrected by one more knowledgeable. It was Wilf McGuinness, now the York City manager, aged 37 and the victim of the nervous stress of failure.

The reflection of each of these contrasting images on team selection was never quite right. Jumbles of bought stars, inexperienced incomers, Soviet-like toilers and disdainful glamour-boys could offer no consistency. A second place in 1979/80 was the closest to a Championship title over what became a drought of 26 years, equal to the period Matt Busby had been in charge. The busy workers were not quite smart enough and the fancy-dan drones were not quite energetic enough. This was the time when the Liverpool hegemony was at its peak and, although United's football was often glamorous, it was rarely successful, even if they scarcely lost my support, while average first division gates plunged by over 30%.

Cup Finals were the oases in the Sahara of First Division aridity. Even these were not entirely satisfactory. In 1976 a goal pleading for an offside flag to be raised allowed Second Division Southampton the pleasure of a major upset, but United did, like General MacArthur, return. In one of their best performances of this uneven era, they outplayed a strong Liverpool side, winning 2-1, with excellent goals from Stuart Pearson, an industrious striker, and that gifted footballer, Jimmy Greenhoff. Having been two goals down to Arsenal in the 1979 Cup Final, Gordon McQueen and Sammy McIlroy scored late on for United to draw level, only for Arsenal to snatch the winner, whilst the Old Trafford players still seemed to be celebrating their good fortune. In 1983 Liverpool revenged themselves with a 2-1 win in the Football League Cup, but United were back at Wembley a couple of months later for the FA Cup. Goals from Frank Stapleton and a rare stunner from Ray Wilkins salvaged United in the heavy weather of a game with lowly Brighton & Hove Albion. Two goals from Bryan Robson and one each from Arnold Muhren and Norman Whiteside routed Brighton in the replay.

Red Shirts and Roses

In 1985 Manchester United returned again to Wembley to play a fancied Everton side in the Cup Final. It was a taut and evenly matched affair, but Kevin Moran was sent off by a referee who was maybe seeking to be the first such arbiter to send someone off in an FA Cup Final. This rather ordinary game went to extra time and was saved by an extraordinary goal. Despite the loss of a player, the energetic coupling of Gordon Strachan and Jesper Olsen scurried tirelessly over Wembley's broad acres and, suddenly, there was a breakthrough. I happened to be observing as if over Norman Whiteside's left shoulder, as he pulled the ball inside on to his left foot, just on the right-hand edge of the penalty area. With an in-swerving low shot, he found the precise corner to the right of a sprawling Neville Southall. It was a brilliant match-winning Cup Final goal, scored by a young player who compounded skill and purpose in equal measures.

And that was that...three FA Cup titles in the interregnum between Matt Busby and Alex Ferguson. Odd appearances in European tournament had been disappointing and strife-torn, while there was a chaotic crowd invasion at the last match of the relegation season. Yet when one recaps on the roster of players that served United during this fallow period, one is surprised at how such talent had not led to higher achievements than that. The mysterious alchemy of producing the pure gold of a great football team is profound indeed.

Among those unlucky to be associated with these years of erratic under-achievement were the jet-heeled Lou Macari, nicknamed 'the electric dwarf' in grudging admiration by the inveterate City-head, John Rennie; Sammy McIlroy, another diminutive forward of brisk flair; the sharp-eyed old-fashioned winger, Steve Coppell; big Joe Jordan leading the attack with military power, and the tall, fair-haired Gary Bailey in goal.

Bryan Robson is remembered for his frontal leadership. An heroic box-to-box player, he was the very model of the modern midfield general, of whom, like the ideal cricket all-rounder, it was hard to assess whether attack or defence was his major expertise. Unfortunately, he rivalled Action Man not only in the martial arts but also by way of falling apart, his dislocations and other injuries reducing his effectiveness for club and country. Manchester United have always had a fondness for pugnacious centre-backs, and Ian Ure, Jim Holton and Gordon McQueen brought a Caledonian flavour of *Braveheart* to the role during these years; later Paul McGrath, perhaps employing a little more stealth, provided the Hibernian equivalent. However, it was the Scot, Martin Buchan, who, calm and resourceful in defence, anticipated the silkier arts of the modern defender with delectable competence. A thoughtful leader (although that did not stop him once cuffing the ears of the bushy-tailed wingman, Gordon Hill, when he positioned himself maladroitly) and thinking performer, after the pattern of John Carey, I would certainly select him as my man of that inconstant and distressing quarter-century.

Lancashire caught the cup bug, too. One could try a literary flourish, along the lines of this being a glamorous, exciting time of short-term gratifications and highly pigmented pop-art displays - except that, somewhere, someone was winning the First Division and County championships, demonstrating the tough virtues of mental stamina and physical consistency. It was as if Lancashire had turned their back on the

Championship - or maybe the Championship had turned its back on Lancashire. John Rennie, when not bustling among the country's most radical educational reformers, is as ardent in his passion for the red rose of Lancashire as for the pale blue of Manchester City. Each year, without a flicker of irony, he calculates that Lancashire would have won the County Championship, had it not been for this or that untoward event and, moreover, he asserts they are bound to win it next year. Granted that, when they were second from the bottom in 1962, his creative accountancy took on some of the panto taste of Baron Hardup explaining to Buttons why he had no wages; 'though this be madness', as with Hamlet, 'yet there is method in't'.

Doleful weather is the chief culprit. As Keith Hayhurst is wont to comment, the County Championship is not so much a league table as a meteorological report. One must be plainly honest. There were some genuinely disastrous seasons in the Championship, but there were some near-run things. These were notably in 1987, under David Hughes' spirited stewardship, when bare loss of batting points yielded the title to Nottinghamshire; in three consecutive runners-up years, 1998, 1999 and 2000; and then, most horrendously, in 2003, when stormy weather interfered on some five occasions when Lancashire were in unassailable positions, with a consequent accumulative loss of 684 overs. What an eccentric competition this is, where a defeat may bring eight bonus points but an abandoned match or one heavily marred by weather may leave a team with only four points! The Lancashire aria might well have been delivered by the old music hall star, Bessie Bellwood: 'why am I always the bridesmaid and never the blushing bride?' 'One fine day', as that moving lament ends, 'pray, let it be soon, I shall wake up on the morning of my own honeymoon.'

With no outright championship since 1934, and just the shared 1950 one with Surrey as half a comfort, Lancashire have processed to no less than seventeen limited-overs titles since such systems were introduced in 1963. This golden collection comprised four Gillette Cups in the 1970s, including a hat-trick, 1970, 1971 and 1972, with Sussex, Kent and Warwickshire the respective victims, and then the fourth in 1975, when Middlesex were easily beaten; a further three NatWest Trophies in the 1990s, with Northants (1990), Essex (1996) and Derbyshire (1998) offering but puny resistance; four Benson & Hedges titles in 1984 against Warwickshire, in 1990 against Worcestershire, making it a double year, in 1995 against Kent and in 1996, another glorious double, against Northamptonshire; together with an express start to life in the fast lane of the one-day leagues in varied guises, with Lancashire taking the first two titles in 1969 and 1970 and then later ones in 1989, 1998 and 1999, plus the one and only Refuge Assurance Cup in 1988.

No other county comes near to that record in limited-overs tourney, any more than many football teams approach Manchester United's achievements in the FA Cup. Folklore unfolded, among the tales David Hughes' 24 in an over in the 1971 semi-final against Gloucestershire at Old Trafford (with the clock standing at ten to nine, for those who could see it in the pitch blackness) or Jack Bond's dolphin-like catching out of Asif Iqbal in the subsequent Lord's final versus Kent, being among the most Homeric. Year on year, John Rennie, Brian Walsh and I, accompanied by assortments of Lancastrian mates, strolled with proprietorial complacency through St John's Wood. The long drawn warble echoed down the streets and round the stands: 'Lanky-sheer; ra-ra-ra; Lanky-sheer; ra-ra-ra'; Lord's became one of Lancashire's out-grounds. It was a breath-taking attainment. The swelling series of victories merges in the mind into a Bayeux Tapestry of picturesque cameos. Two samples from that host of delicious memories must suffice.

In 1972 at Lord's Warwickshire, including the four fine West Indians, A.I. Kalicharan, Lance Gibbs, Rohan Kanhai and D.L. Murray, as well as the English talents of D.L. Amiss, M.J.K. Smith and R.G.D. Willis, and despite brilliant Lancashire fielding, amassed the formidable sum of 234. The response was faltering. Lancashire were 26 for 2 and Clive Lloyd fiddled about disconsolately for six runs in eight overs. John Rennie, constitutionally unable to observe these heart-rending events, left us and tramped around the back of the stands, sucking moodily on a cigarette.

Two huge shouts suggested to his morbid sensibilities that further inroads had been made by the Warwickshire attack. In fact, it was two huge blows from Clive Lloyd, emerging brightly from his dull cocoon and beginning an assault that Denis Compton was to describe, perhaps with a becoming modesty, as the best innings ever played at Lord's. With his hefty bat and his lengthy reach, he struck blow after blow on the front foot, the ball soaring into the stratosphere or ricocheting yards back off the fencing. It was as if a benign Goliath had been ordained by Heaven to tame a troupe of wayward Davids. Like Duncan Edwards in Manchester United's youth team or Gulliver towering above the inhabitants of Lilliput, he seized the game and carried it way out of reach of the wilting opposition. Of the many world-class performances the great West Indian contributed, not least with his fielding exploits, redolent of the hunting leopard, to the Lancashire cause, this was his finest moment. Rather like J.T. Tyldesley, Clive Lloyd in gangling repose, peering through his Jodrell Bank glasses, was a temperate man, but in action he was rapacious. Apart from his one-day record of 8,456 runs at an average of 41, he scored nearly 13,000 first-class runs for Lancashire, his average of just under 45 being very similar to that of Ernest Tyldesley.

Talking of Lilliput, one of his companions in that chase against Warwickshire was Harry Pilling, the Clitheroe Kid of Lancashire cricket, the Tiny Tim of Ashton-under-Lyne. He shared many one-day partnerships with Clive Lloyd, bringing to mind the bill-matter of variety's 'cockney kids', Revnell and West; 'the Long and Short of It'. A wheedler and nurdler of prodigious application, he became the first batsman, as other biffed and smote aimlessly round him, to reach a thousand runs in Sunday League cricket. The Eddie Colman of the cricketing Old Trafford, this popular number three batsman made nearly 15,000 first-class runs for the county, as well as coaxing the ball into empty areas for another 4,000 or so limited-overs runs, for he was one of the pioneers of one-day improvisation.

Another who profitably joined Clive Lloyd on that fresh September evening was Frank Hayes from Preston, a Lancelot figure, good-looking, fair-haired and brimming with knightly gifts, possibly never quite fulfilling his promise, but maybe his promise was too Arthurian for mundane compass. As it was, the young Paladin scored nearly 11,000 handsome runs for Lancashire, with an average - 37.45 - better than either Archie MacLaren or Harry Makepeace, and over 4,000 sumptuous runs in one-day competitions. Whether off-driving with Edwardian opulence or racing athletically in the field, he might have been the hero of an old-fashioned schoolboy story by Frank Richards or Talbot Baines Reed.

As the Lloydian onslaught continued at Lord's, John Rennie returned to his seat, sunny and optimistic, laughing gaily as if the bad times had never been. In a quieter moment, as they were trying to recover the ball from a tangle of drying equipment where Clive Lloyd had deposited it, John Rennie crowed loudly in the direction of an ashen-faced group of Warwickshire fans - and, to their credit, spotting the joke was on the Manchester as well as the Birmingham-born contingents, they chuckled as much as we did - 'our West Indian's better than your West Indians.'

Now for a gentler remembrance; it was 1985 and Lancashire were playing Suffolk in a preliminary round of what had become the NatWest Trophy - apparently Gillette had become too familiar a logo and market researchers had found that some people thought the cup was named after a veteran cricketer, W.G. Gillette, presumably. The game was at Bury St Edmunds and, by accident and design, a group of family and friends were assembled for a quiet encounter in quiet surroundings. It was one of those lovely days that, out of nothing and into nothing, suddenly become singular.

In front of us on the grass sat a bevy of prep schoolboys, garishly capped and blazered, and not creating undue mayhem, but, when Jack Simmons removed his rather more faded cap and stuffed it into his back pocket, I solemnly alerted these juniors to the prospect of a display of spin bowling not often seen in remote rural parts. Their teacher took up and reinforced my instruction and silence reigned. Jack Simmons' rotund frame, constructed on the anti-anorexia principle, was at odds with the stingy attrition of his bowling, as if the soul of the unredeemed Silas Marner inhabited the carcass of Billy Bunter. He took over 400 one-day wickets and made over 3,000 one-day runs. Moreover, he took 1,000 first-class wickets and notched close on 10,000 first-class runs for Lancashire.

It was, however, the calorific value of his intake of comestibles that read like the astronomic figures of Tendulkar or Brian Lara. Graeme Fowler has told of how he and Jack Simmons stopped on the way home from the cricket to buy something like fish and chips or even perhaps the infamous 'Simmo Special', available at the take-away close to his Great Harwood residence, a dish so replete with carbohydrates and cholesterol that worried legislators might have considered insisting it was retailed with a Government health warning. As it was drizzling, Fowler offered to run the all-rounder home, but Simmons, so the after-dinner yarn ran, refused - he would walk and eat in the rain, for, if he arrived home with a bag of fried goodies, his wife might not give him supper.

On that balmy late spring day at Bury St Edmunds, he once more made the case for the subtle mind in the satisfied body. He proceeded to dip the ball into the dust around the batsmen's legs, tucking them up like kippers. Delivery followed virginal delivery. The very negativism of the cricket fascinated the boys, just as the eyes of the old-time crowds watching Makepeace and Hallows were glued to the sheer nothingness of the process. Jack Simmons only took one wicket but, three clumsily swished singles apart, it was a spell of 69 runless balls out of 72, his 1 for 3 a record for economy in a twelve-over stint. The schoolmaster and his young charges were respectfully impressed by my remarkable gift of prophecy, and everyone had a good day out.

Red Shirts and Roses

With David Lloyd and Barry Wood the durable openers of international credentials and with quick bowlers of the fierce quality of Ken Shuttleworth, Peter Lee and Peter Lever, the team that surpassed all others in limited-overs play in the 1970s - and led with such guile and warmth by Jack Bond - was one of Lancashire's most gleaming combines. There was no weakness. It shone, too, in the dimension that had first interested A.N. Hornby and had later inspired those of the Washbrook and Ikin era. Clive Lloyd, Harry Pilling, David Hughes, David Lloyd, Barry Wood and Frank Hayes were superb fielders, so much so that hapless batsmen found themselves stranded, as the hymn has it, 'midst encircling gloom'.

The standard-bearer for this array of smart and disciplined fielding was Farokh Engineer, Lancashire's leading wicket-keeper-batsman. A man of chivalry and jollity, he brought gracious poise both to his venturesome hitting and to his zesty wicket-keeping. With his mane of black hair and his quick smile, he was instantly popular among Lancashire fans and he obliged with approaching 6,000 runs in the first-class game and 3,000 speedy runs in the limited version, together with 464 first-class and 183 limited-overs dismissals.

He exemplifies a significant point, already referred to, about the response of supporters to the player who, although born far away, dedicates himself sincerely to the local need. Neville Cardus once asked Peter Lever from which side he hailed of the frontier that runs through Todmorden like an invisible Berlin Wall and he reluctantly confessed he was from the Yorkshire side. Farokh Engineer, overhearing this admission, whispered blithely, 'bloody foreigner'. Even more telling as a short, simple lesson in multicultural living is the anecdote related of when disquieting civil unrest occurred in India. Cedric Rhodes asked whether these bloodthirsty disturbances might affect Farokh Engineer's family. 'Only if the fighting reaches my family's village,' he gravely replied. 'Which village is that?' asked the chairman. 'Altrincham', announced the Indian wicket-keeper.

Lancashire's limited-overs triumphs fell into two main bundles, with Jack Bond's extremely imposing team of the 1970s, and then the squad that evolved in the late 1980s and early 1990s. Straight in his batting and throwing, no less so in his human dealings, David Hughes reinvigorated the second of these exercises in enjoying and working at cricket at one and the same time. Gehan Mendis and the irrepressible Graeme Fowler, yet another entry in the gallery of scintillating Lancashire out-fielders, opened the batting and Warren Hegg began his long and valuable part (as wicket-keeper and later captain) in Lancashire's affairs. John Abrahams supplied genuinely good service to the county, while Paul Allott ('nearly a good name', murmured John Arlott on television, when the tall bowler first appeared) and Mike Watkinson, later to be the highly regarded coach at Old Trafford, came on the scene.

As the century wore down, some very big names prospered, as Lancashire continued to hunt down the one-day prizes. There was Michael Atherton, destined to play a hundred times for England, well-organised technically and well-sustained mentally, fluently illustrating the long Lancashire heritage of indomitable opening batsmanship. He scored just short of 10,000 runs for the county at an average of 44, while his strategic planning of and contribution to several crucial Lancashire one-day innings was invaluable. I watched, with Keith Hayhurst, as the young student, lately captain of Manchester Grammar School, scored his first century for the 2nd XI at Old Trafford against Surrey, a persuasive exercise in control and style, the inordinately mature head on the fine young shoulders. In spite of bearing the almost Shakespearean onus of expectation, having been, it seems, destined for greatness almost from the cradle, like some infant prince, he brought enormous private intellectual and emotional resolve to govern an orthodox technique that his opening Lancashire forebears would have admired and cherished.

John Crawley was another England bat and former Manchester Grammar School skipper, who captained Lancashire before, amid controversy, leaving for Hampshire, and who, with patience and fluid skills, could build lucrative and attractive innings. This is evidenced by his tally of just over 10,000 runs, but more so by his average, which, at 51, is the highest of any regular Lancastrian batsman ever.

There was Neil Fairbrother, who, especially in limited-overs cricket, where, as well as fielding with panache, he expressed himself with palatable relish, a jazz instrumentalist of a batsman, improvising with delectable flair. Nonetheless, his first-class record is exceptional; his 19,603 county runs make him the most productive Red Rose bat of the modern era; indeed Ken Grieves is the only player whose career was entirely post-war to exceed that total. From Pakistan came the gifted all-rounder, Wasim Akram, another who adopted the county and allowed the county to adopt him, surging through his relatively moderate run-up to generate indescribable zip into his left-arm pace and always threatening to slam the opposing attack into faltering submission. He took 374 wickets for Lancashire at a cost of 21 runs each. Like the best overseas players, and like Clive Lloyd and Farokh Engineer before him, his presence was a positive and conscious boost for the whole team.

Another for whom that is equally true is the Sri Lankan sorcerer, Muralithran, who in only 14 matches for Lancashire around the turn of the century baffled his beguiling way to 116 wickets at a cost of just 15, and an average of eight bewitched victims a game. It was said that one grizzled ancient member, dozing in a pavilion that had held out too long against the arrival of women, was startled by the announcement of the spin bowler's advent, assuming it was Muriel Atherton, Michael's sister. Muralithran was another healthy overseas presence, a merry companion on the team coach, a committed student of Lancashire's current fortunes and, perhaps to the shame of one or two, a knowledgeable scholar of cricket history. He played 1999-2001. Exactly a hundred years before, 1899-1903, the nonpareil S.F. Barnes had played 46 games for Lancashire, taking 225 wickets at just less than 20. It would have been intriguing to observe them in tandem, both as bowlers and as personalities.

Old Trafford itself had undergone the necessary and typical refurbishments of all sports arenas that wish to avoid the sad fate of shabby dilapidation. The old nursery ground beyond the Stretford End had gradually been reduced in acreage over the decades with office blocks and commercial premises, while stands were rebuilt or modernised. A press gallery at the Warwick Road End, recently renamed the Brian Statham End (although that was regularly the receiving rather than the delivery end for his potent assaults); the largest cricket school in the country was built in 1997; and an on-site hotel, the Trafford Lodge, opened for business at the end of the century. With 12,500, the Lancashire membership outstripped the other counties and although, one-day cricket apart, the turnstiles still failed to rotate briskly for County Championship games, the pavilion, still preserved in its ancient grandeur, and members' areas were decently full on most match days.

However synthetic and ephemeral the rites of limited-overs cricket may be, the knockout version certainly has a dramatic appeal. As with its football cup equivalent, it brings together the faithful and concentrates its collective mind on a single aim. A Lord's final is a fatiguing experience, emotionally draining, as one counts off the balls and the overs and the bowlers' allotments of overs and the run-rate and sundry other bits of arithmetic. One would have swapped three or four cups for one Championship pennant, but, failing that, these were joyous days by way of compensation.

Lancashire was, apropos bonny cup-fighting, the Manchester United of the county scene - and vice versa. Then all was changed. While one Old Trafford steadfastly managed to eschew the main league title, the other Old Trafford was hardly able to avoid the crown.

21.

Ferguson

ONLY A.N. HORNBY in the formative days of Lancashire cricket and Matt Busby in the post-WWII years stand comparison with Alex Ferguson at the two Old Traffords as an individual team-builder and maker of champions. Both in the cricketing and footballing arenas there had been other good times and good teams, but in those alternative cases the organisation had been more collective and anonymous. All three men built support casts around them - Alex Ferguson, for example, benefited hugely from highly effective second-in-commands, like Brian Kidd, Steve McClaren and Carlos Quieroz, just as Jimmy Murphy had been leader of the orchestra that Matt Busby conducted. However, the reigns were plainly monarchical.

On what would have been my mother's birthday, 8th November, 1986, Alex Ferguson, having moved from his high-profile attainments at Aberdeen, watched with probably growing horror as his new charges collapsed to a 2-0 defeat away at Oxford United. He may gloomily have taken the cold comfort that upwards was now the only possible route-way and, inevitably, it took rather longer than weary supporters wished, before, in Panglossian mode, 'all is for the best in the best of all possible worlds'. It was worth the wait.

Where Matt Busby's background was in the Lanark coalfields, Alex Ferguson came from the shipyards of the Clyde. Along with Bill Shankly and Jock Stein, they represented a fascinating group of Scots from tough working-class areas, who, after careers of distinction rather than worldly glamour, excelled as managers, in a craft littered with the bones of better-known playing performers. Superficially, Matt Busby, affably courteous and religiously devout, and Alex Ferguson, abrasively vinegary and witheringly spiky, seemed as different as Davie Balfour and Alan Breck in R.L. Stevenson's classic tale, *Kidnapped*. Below the surface similar traits ruled the managerial metabolism. The hunger for success that shades into a ruthless appetite; the innate clarity of football intelligence; the stomach for unremitting labour and the expectation of the same stamina in others - these key qualities were shared by both men.

Like Bill Shankly, they recognised that the creation of a top team is not an inclusive, self-contained job, after the fashion of finishing a painting masterpiece before moving on to the next canvas. As coaches of a football club rather than any one team, they had to have an eye turned toward continuity, to something close to perpetual renaissance. Both Matt Busby and Alex Ferguson successfully adopted the joint strategy of pertinent, often expensive, purchases, alongside intensive youth development. It is probably the case, even today, that Manchester United have more first-team players from the club's own cradles than any British club of equal stature. For the most part, players found in both managers the motivating and educative forces they could respect and to which they could whole-heartedly respond. It would be idiotic to suppose that this would be a fireproofed hero-worship; with both managers, there were, occasionally, star players for whom the magic did not work or the relationship soured. These would be soon on their way, for both men put a great store on loyalty and, far from suffering fools gladly, neither came close to suffering fools at all.

Peter Tinniswood, an old schoolmate and a foremost comedy writer, created the character of Uncle Mort, who was played on television in the series, *I Didn't Know You Cared*, by Robin Bailey, who doubled as the orotund narrator of Peter Tinniswood's *Tales from the Long Room*, in which, *inter alia*, our shared favourite of youth, Winston Place, played a prominent part and in which, in one yarn, 'an extremely sunburned' Harry Pilling and 'a dusky Wee Georgie Wood' are likened to the opening pair of a pygmy XI. Uncle Mort once envisioned an Elysian dawn in which Manchester United held the FA Cup 'in perpetuity'. In the 1990s Manchester United approximated to this nirvana by monopolising the newly founded Premiership.

Uncle Mort would have relished the eight Championships in 1992/93, 1993/94, 1995/96, 1996/97, 1998/99, 1999/00, 2000/01 and 2002/03. Having won seven previous titles, this silver collection more than doubled the total to a rich fifteen. As well as a League Cup win in 1992, when a Brian McClair goal was sufficient to outwit Nottingham Forest (as well, it should be quickly added and dealt with, two losses, to Sheffield Wednesday in 1991 and Aston Villa in 1994) there were five more FA Cup wins that would have gladdened even Uncle Mort's acidulous heart. This almost doubled the tally, making it eleven cup wins in all, another record. This included a 4-0 thrashing of Chelsea in 1994 and a highly creditable 1-0 defeat of Liverpool, in both of which games Eric Cantona assumed elegant authority. In 1995 there was a loss by a single goal, to Everton in the final, but, in the meanwhile, Manchester United had completed two cup and league doubles in 1993/94 and 1995/96.

Throw in a European Cup Winners' Cup and a European Champion Clubs' Cup and the catalogue of success mounts to seventeen major trophies in the age of Ferguson. There were some global exploits, among them the Roy Keane goal in 1999 that won the Inter-continental Cup in Tokyo against SE Palmeiras, a goal that officially confirmed what many had known for a lifetime, that Manchester United were the best team on the face of the planet.

Second and third places in every other Premiership season and a consistent place in the closing rounds of every European Championship competition confirmed and polished the aura of invincible splendour. In season 2003/04 Manchester United were third in the league, advanced to the quarter-finals of the European Cup and won the FA Cup. The curtains were sombrely drawn and raiment was tearfully rent, such was the desolation felt by supporters at such a miserable outcome. Heaven knows how they would have coped with the 1930s.

It was not all plain sailing. There were the doldrums of Alex Ferguson's early seasons, with moderate league positions, discomforting cup runs and even mutinous landlubbers on the terraces, before the breezes freshened and, or so it is said, the manager's exploration was salvaged by the FA Cup win in 1990. Steve Coppell's Crystal Palace were on the way to causing a major upset. They were leading 3-2, Ian

Wright having scored twice late on, Bryan Robson and Mark Hughes being the Reds' scorers, but the Welsh striker saved United's bacon a few minutes from the end of extra time. Les Sealey, who acted out mock-palpitations but performed steadily, replaced Jim Leighton in goal for the replay and a Lee Martin goal brought Alex Ferguson the respite he sought.

Thereafter the good ship 'Manchester United' sliced through the high seas like the *Golden Hind*, as successive crews plundered their way to buccaneering glory and filled the coffers with silverware to overflowing. As part of this voyage, akin to that of Sir Francis Drake's semi-official piracy on the Spanish Main, there was the rediscovery of the new world of Europe. In 1991, over two decades after that initial success, there was a second night of Continental achievement, when Manchester United beat Barcelona 2-1 in Rotterdam, thereby capturing the European Cup Winners' Cup, with Mark Hughes again being the corsair finisher, with a delicate terminating touch and a shot from a virtually impossible angle.

14th April 1999 is a date that may stand as an emblem of this period of golden accomplishment. Manchester United, en route to a seemingly unlikely treble, were drawn in the semi-final against their great rivals, Arsenal. After 120 minutes of football, the teams were still locked together, and thus there was a replay at Villa Park. David Beckham gave United an early lead with a trademark shot but Dennis Bergkamp's deflected reply, deep in the second half, and the sending off of Roy Keane were unpropitious events. In the closing seconds of full time, Arsenal won a penalty, which Dennis Bergkamp struck smartly - only for Peter Schmeichel to bring off an extraordinary save. Extra time was required. The ten men struggled on. Then, in the 109th minute, Ryan Giggs picked up a wayward - and untypical - pass from Patrick Vieira. He advanced rapidly, with United colleagues acting cleverly as decoys, dribbling past defenders in some kind of fleet-footed frenzy, before lashing a shot of such ferocity that the top of the Arsenal net bulged like sails in a gale.

The newspapers strove over the superlatives as desperately as the Arsenal defence had tried to halt that mazy, unstoppable gallop. The only doubt in the combined media mind was whether it could be both the greatest match that had ever been played as well as providing a referential frame for the greatest goal ever scored. Whatever else, it was one of the high spots of an era in which Manchester United produced a dazzling series of the equivalent of West End hit musicals, where once the club had laboured to present the occasional out-of-town, provincial play.

'Ferguson's Fledglings' were airborne. Victory followed victory. My son, Matt, offered a paradigm of United fanhood in 1999 between 16th and 26th May. It was a rewriting of John Reed's stormy revolutionary classic, *Ten Days that Shook the World*. He watched Manchester United beat Tottenham Hotspur 2-1 at Old Trafford - goals from David Beckham and Andy Cole, after United had first fallen behind - to clinch another Premiership title; he travelled to Wembley to watch a somewhat routine taming of Newcastle United, with Teddy Sheringham, in superb form, and Paul Scholes, from a Sheringham assist, the scorers; he flew to Barcelona to watch entranced at the Nou Camp Stadium, as United completed the treble with a melodramatic capture of the European Cup.

Red Shirts and Roses

The truth of this victory was stranger than any fiction that might have been conceived for the delectation of the schoolboy reader in the *Hotspur* and *Wizard* of long ago. This was after visiting the Stadio delle Alpi, home of Juventus, for the second leg of the semi-final, after a 1-1 draw at Old Trafford, and coming away with an aggregate win of 4-3, Roy Keane, Dwight Yorke and Andy Cole being the scorers. Frankly, Bayern Munich had the better of a United side missing the talents of the suspended Roy Keane and Paul Scholes. A Mario Basler free kick gave Bayern the lead and only Peter Schmeichel and provident woodwork kept United in the game.

UEFA officials attached the Bayern Munich colours to the trophy, as the tie entered stoppage time. Metaphorically speaking, the proverbial fat female songstress was clearing her throat, prior to that final rendition. Peter Schmeichel rushed into the Bayern Munich penalty area, as United won a late corner, and created confused diversion. David Beckham's corner swung into and through an area packed with twenty-one players, the corner taker being the only absentee from that crowded Piccadilly Circus. Ryan Giggs mis-hit a shot and Teddy Sheringham, a late substitute, pushed the ball into the net. A dazed Munich team kicked off and promptly lost the ball and conceded another corner. This time the in-swinging Beckham cross was touched on by Teddy Sheringham and his fellow-substitute, the faithful and nippy Ole Gunnar Solskjaer hooked the ball into the German net.

There was a hurried readjustment of the ribbons on the trophy. None of the players looked as if they quite believed it, but it was easy to detect the unbelieving ecstasy from the unbelieving misery. The Bayern Munich players looked as if they had emerged from fox holes, having suffered a six-week artillery barrage. Manchester United fans, who had slipped away just before the final whistle, thought their team had lost and found it difficult to catch up with the news. In suitable acknowledgement of Manchester United's quest for the elusive treble having a national resonance, Alex Ferguson received a knighthood.

It did seem a far cry from those ancient wartime days, when young Matt's father and friends were cycling to the match, parking rusty bikes in a back yard and watching Crewe Alexandra or Halifax Town.

So how is one to deal conscientiously with this supersonic journey into footballing space, as the proportionate part of a saga stretching back into the 19th century, way back to the mire of Newton Heath?

First, it is a familiar tale. Everyone knows how brilliant United are and have been throughout this short, frantic, concerted period. The only difference is in the popular reaction. P.G. Wodehouse once wrote that the world could be divided up between those who are prepared to black up their faces and take part in a minstrel show, and those who are not. It is the same with Manchester United, loved to distraction and loathed beyond redemption by millions, with just a modicum of neutrals.

Murray and Mooney, the crosstalk comedians of orthodox character, consolidated the formula of the monologue with the interposition of the 'I say, I say, I say' interjection and the corny riddle. ('What's got one leg, a yellow belly and crushes stones?' - 'I don't know; what has etc...?' - 'a one-legged, yellow-bellied, stone-crusher.' - 'I don't wish to know that; kindly leave the stage.') One of Harry Murray's recitations began, 'It's a funny old world we live in, but the world's not entirely to blame; it's the people we meet as we walk down the street...' and he was lucky if he proceeded that far, before being interrupted by Harry Mooney. It serves, however, as a comment on the ambivalence about United. It is indeed a funny old world, with funny old people dwelling therein, when there can be such cultural antagonisms. It is funnier still to recall that few hated United in the 1930s when they were in the second division. The power and the glory of sport are frighteningly potent stimulants, brewing philtres of mutual antagonism.

For all that, and because of that, the recent story of Manchester United is a well-known one.

Second, it has all been such a whirligig of success. One has revelled in it as one enjoys a merry-go-round, as a careering orbit of pleasure, the scenery swirling hectically past, a twirling flurry of flashing colours. Even the most scholarly or obsessive supporter, reeling under the intoxication of these delights, finds it difficult to distinguish one Championship title from another. Maybe the 1990s is best remembered as an orgasmic blur.

Third, with reference to this text as, in part, a memoir, one must recognise the well-observed phenomenon of time accelerating exponentially as one ages. This is more than a 'slipper'd pantaloon's' fad. There does seem to be some scientific explanation of sorts, involving the position one has reached in the lifespan. As a child, pretending to be Cyril Washbrook or John Carey in the local park, the days seemed long and life loomed large and endlessly. As an old man, there is more of retrospect, with but a little to anticipate, hence the quickening of the temporal pulse. Thus, from a narrative viewpoint, where the winters of Jimmy Delaney and Jack Rowley or the summers of Winston Place and Roy Tattersall were deliciously prolonged, the last decade has flown by abruptly. The one is like watching a slow, deliberate sunset; the other is like the eye being startled by a strike of incandescent lightning.

Amidst a filmy spray of goals and matches and silver pots, it is, in fact, the players that stand out as signal memories. One such was Peter Schmeichel. Manchester United had tended to haemorrhage goals, ever dependent on their strike force to cause even higher blood loss at the opposing end. Here was a tourniquet for the 1990s. Here was a huge Viking of a Danish giant, his slightly porcine features capped with Scandinavian flaxen locks, his gigantic frame capable of quickly adopting the star-burst configuration that was his hallmark blocking save. Clean sheets had been as rare at Old Trafford as in a Victorian lodging house in Hulme. Now United's defence took on something of the waterproof quality of one of Charles Macintosh's Manchester-produced covers.

Manchester United had never had a world-class goalkeeper. They had had good quality national custodians, mixed, truth to tell, with some genuine Mary Ellens. Indeed, Peter Schmeichel's Gallic replacement, Fabien Barthez, contrived, in his entrancing if alarming insouciance, to display the gamut of United goalkeeping down the ages, miraculous to disastrous, in 45 minutes. Lancashire have had similar problems with the analogous vocation of wicket-keeping. Granted they have had three outstanding keepers in Richard Pilling, George Duckworth and Farokh Engineer, while one or two others, such as Bill Farrimond and the current long-serving incumbent, Warren Hegg, have obliged with creditable steadiness. However, compared with the score or more top-rank opening bats - or, in United's case, strikers - there has often been a question mark over that crucial role at both Old Traffords.

Peter Schmeichel is, in that sense, a man alone. Were one to choose a Manchester United team of shades and spectres, as well as mortal flesh, he simply has no rival for the post of goalkeeper. Manchester United fans sometimes peered enviously across the urban landscape to Maine Road, where, especially in the peerless examples of Frank Swift and Bert Trautmann, Manchester City seemed fortunate with goalkeepers. The less polite Red supporters would hint that, given City's wobbling frailties, their goalkeepers might have excessive opportunities to hone their gifts, but, at the last, Peter Schmeichel brought world-class security to the United fortress. He also emulated that other legendary last line of defence - the cackling geese of Rome who gave the alarm as Barbarian invaders sought the cover of night - in an incessant earwigging of his colleagues. The chatty goalie is now as fashionable as the garrulous stumper.

In front of him there was usually a set of industrious tradesmen, efficient, unruffled and, above all, consistent. Denis Irwin, Cork-born and transferred from Oldham Athletic, was, at left-back, a model of this kind of faultless and undemonstrative defending. At right-back, from nearby Bury, the tall, brusque Gary Neville grafted away, season on season, another exemplar of professional rectitude and reliance. Daring to prophesy, using the background of successful British management as a research base, one might predict that Gary Neville, the Sergeant Major of English football, could become a highly competent club manager. The Northumbrian, Steve Bruce, a commanding centre-back and doughty captain, joined with the former Middlesbrough player, that tower of aerial defence, the forceful Gary Pallister, to prowl in protection of the United interest. In his turn came another Horatius to keep the bridge free from invasive Tuscans. It was Jaap Stam, with the pallor of a ghost and the strength of an ox, an authoritative presence from Holland, marking as closely as a lover's embrace. He was one of those unmissable players, like a lighthouse looming on a rocky coast.

The midfield buzzed with energy and élan. Scribes exhausted their Franglais lexicon as they tried to capture the quintessence of Eric Cantona, justifiably regarded as the key to United's domination of English football in this period. What a twist of good fortune it was when Alex Ferguson, thwarted in a £3.5m bid for Sheffield Wednesday's David Hirst, compromised by spending a third of that for the Parisian's signature from Leeds United in 1992. Eric Cantona proceeded to write a lyrical chapter or two above that signature of a kind that made that £1.2m about the best footballing bargain of modern times. It is said that the man from Ashton-under-Lyne who wrote the song, 'Tipperary', sold it for five bob: as Florrie Forde and the British tommy made it famous, he must have suffered the same emotional pain as the Leeds United board did, as Eric Cantona detonated the Manchester United explosive mix.

An artist and cult-hero who zoomed from being one of Plato's Philosopher-kings to being one of those disruptive Frenchmen tracked down by Simenon's Maigret in the back streets of Paris, he was much travelled, the cynosure of Pickfords' heart, and something of a loose, if blazing, cannon. It was typical of his strutting flamboyance that, faced with racial taunt, he did not flail an angry fist, but hurled himself in Bruce Lee mimicry over the barrier at his vile-mouthed abuser. Even in wrongdoing, he was not humdrum. In right doing, he was serious and committed. Not the least of his influence on his younger brethren was his workmanlike attitude to training. One thinks how the sorcery of Ranji, conjuring magical cricket in the spacious days of Edwardian cricket, was the result of arduous practice. The coupling of genius and resolution is underestimated, for the benchmark of the unduly gifted is the appearance they give of facile ease.

Eric Cantona, collar high on his neck, darkened brow furrowed, eagle-beaked, rode the Premiership grounds like an emperor on imperial progress. Subtle in footwork and visionary of eye, he disdained any comparison with republican France and recalled the opulent years of Bourbon monarchy and the palatial richness of Versailles. As Cardinal de Richelieu inspired the Musketeers, so did the majestically self-confident Eric Cantona breathe something of the same motivation into those around him.

Roy Keane, too, has had his on and off-stage moments of angst, but few would deny him the honour of being elected United's player of the 1990s. In fiscal and cultural retrospect, his record fee of £3.5m from Brian Clough's Nottingham Forest in 1993 was another clever investment. For ten and more years he has ploughed his battling way from the trenches of defence to the heights of assault, the ultimate soldier-footballer, as dedicated to the grime and punishment of repulsing the foe as to the accolades and finery of overwhelming them. Cork-born, and with some of Michael Collins' focus on the cause, his darkly saturnine good looks turn fierce, should United wilt or his companions cede ground or be guilty of foolhardy lapse. Psychologists may argue whether one might best conquer addiction by satiation or by starvation. Neither works for Roy Keane. His hunger for success is stimulated by the one and enlivened by the other. Were his appetites gastronomic, he would be obese. Moreover, he clearly grasps what fans vaguely understand: 'this club is an institution', he has said, 'it will be around a lot longer than any of the players'. Patrick Pearse said something similar about Irish nationalism in Dublin Post Office during the Easter Rising of 1916.

Some judges have gone so far as to say that his display against Juventus in the European Cup semi-final of 1999, when the Reds fought back to victory having been two behind, was the equal of any personal performance in the long story of the club. He has shunned the popular limelight as comprehensively as he has stamped his dedicated, skilled personality on the field of play. Occasionally tales trickle through of his humane kindnesses, particularly towards children. Perhaps were these to be too widely broadcast, he might feel his ferocious persona would be embarrassingly undermined; Geronimo was not celebrated for helping old squaws across the reservation. More likely, an intrinsic decency forbids him from accepting such deeds as properly in the public domain.

The variety of entertainers has been sumptuous. Eric Cantona and Roy Keane have been different in style and emphasis. What, then, about the impact of Paul Scholes? Firstly, he was one of the local boys making good, like that compact sentinel of the midfield Nicky Butt, or the Neville brothers. Secondly, his sparse gamin build and startling coppernob shriek of ordinariness; the crowds identify readily with both his provenance and his appearance. Thirdly, where he captures the souls of the supporters, he seizes the minds of the players. They used to call Jimmy James 'the comedians' comedians'. Dozens of other comics, from Peter Sellers to Tony Hancock, would avidly watch him time without number, as if seeking the counsel of the Oracle. Paul Scholes is 'the footballer's footballer', much admired by players for his parcel of skills. Although his tackling, like Eric Cantona's, has a bovine trait, his offensive arts are exceptional. Rarely dispossessed and rarely failing to communicate with his comrades, he jinks about the turf, linking and distributing with nonpareil mental imagery, his unexpected arrival in the penalty box for a lethal shot or header the final piece in the mosaic of his proficiency.

Where Peter Schmeichel, when it came to florid oratory, was a Lloyd George (after all, that great liberal statesman was born in Ancoats) among footballers, Paul Scholes has taken a Trappist vow of silence and keeps his thoughts entirely to himself, slipping quietly away, a contented family man, from the international scene in the summer of 2004. Would that some of his contemporaries could emulate his feats, both of footballing dexterity and of vocal austerity.

Strikers came and went, sharpshooting like gunslingers in the Old West, for brief, vivid spells and then departing to the Boot Hill of deposed centre-forwards. Mark Hughes, a Wrexham lad, reigned for two longish spells, beginning as long ago as 1983, well before the Ferguson era. To mix the metaphors crazily, he was a Jesse James among strikers, in that he was as effective at hold-ups as at pot shots; he cosseted and shielded the ball like a nursing mother with a newborn infant, and then, bristling with will-power and strength, he 'volleyed and thundered' like the Russian artillery at Balaclava in the Crimean War. Airdrie-born and with plenty of experience at Glasgow Celtic, Brian McClair, shrewd and perceptive, was another from that earlier epoch to bring an intelligent element to United's forward play.

In what may be termed Alex Ferguson's middle period, the goal-scoring mantle descended on Andy Cole and Dwight Yorke, who, despite ups and downs of form and fortune, pranced and probed at the opposition, as if attempting to rival a couple of West Indian pace bowlers causing discomfort amid the England middle-order batting. Ole Gunnar Solskjaer, a Norwegian version of Bugsy Malone, rifled home critical goals with the icy dispassion of the Chicago hit-man; Teddy Sheringham, as wily a fox as ever misled a red-garbed hunt and ravening pack of hounds, brought, in the aftermath of Eric Cantona's retirement and in spite of a pact of unholy non-communion with Andy Cole, a dimension of animal slyness to the United cause.

Sandy Turnbull - Joe Spence - Jack Rowley - Tommy Taylor - Denis Law - Mark Hughes: Ruud van Nistelrooy comes at the end of a long line of distinguished spear carriers for Manchester United and, in his distinctive way, compares favourably with them all. His executive task carries a tough responsibility. It is not ice-skating or synchronised swimming and there are no points for glamorous style. As my old *Rover* comic story subhead ran, 'It's goals that count'. His longish black tresses and slightly doughy features give Ruud van Nistelrooy a not unpleasant canine aspect, and he runs hard and works unselfishly in that same vein. Predatory and aware like all great strikers, he also manages attacks with dispatch, with hints then, perhaps, of both Denis Law and

Mark Hughes about these double contributions. Again, like many of his ilk, he may be anonymous for stretches of time, the Dutchman placidly waiting in his clogs among the tulips under the windmill, only for the critical millisecond to reveal him as the cruel executioner.

There is a phlegmatic element. He is a thinking rather than an instinctive goal scorer, with intellect not intuition the ruler. A sea-lawyer among strikers, with a scholarly grasp of the niceties of the offside statutes, he outwits defences with intelligence, including a pretty line in the geometry of angles, linked with a robust mobility. This is the Bertrand Russell, as opposed to the George Armstrong Custer, approach to being a centre forward - and the evidence is persuasive that brains prevail over bluster.

The flanks of Alex Ferguson's era at Old Trafford have been patrolled by Ryan Giggs and, until his departure in 2003 to Real Madrid, David Beckham. The first point to make about this pair of diamonds is that they are both industrial diamonds. There have been one or two indolent stage door Johnnies at Old Trafford over the years who have given the impression that they were doing the club and the supporters a favour by arriving in time for the kick-off. Not Ryan Giggs and David Beckham. Both have toiled strenuously in and for the cause, tearing up and down the wings, facing up to the opposing full-back, offering cover to their own full-back. Both, Ryan Giggs early on his career, David Beckham more potently as his career has unfolded, have been subjected to global media pressure and have, as a major part of their work-programme, been obliged to enter the marketplace as advertising icons. Both have studiously tried to ensure that, while in pursuit of unfathomable wealth and stardom, the little matter of ninety minutes of football and three more points in the bag for Manchester United has never been forgotten. Ryan Giggs, in particular, appears to have found a decent compromise of private quietude and public stardom.

Giggs, born in Cardiff, signed the dotted line in 1990, and Beckham, born in Leytonstone, in 1992, both after assiduous nursing. Both made teenage debuts, being among the 'kids' whom, according to pundits, could not possibly carry off a Premiership title. It was, of course, the cunning mix of bright kids with mature masters, Tom Browns and Thomas Arnolds, that did the trick, but there was no denying the precociousness of the pupils. Ryan Giggs published his autobiography when aged 20, rather like Winston Churchill's *My Early Life*, and became at 27 the youngest-ever United player to be awarded a testimonial. On the opening day of the 1996/97 season, David Beckham scored a goal against Wimbledon from inside his own half, the equivalent of Nick Faldo holing out in one from a par four St Andrews' tee.

Commentators speak of elegant footballers having an 'educated' right or left foot. David Beckham's right foot must have a curriculum vitae of Oxbridge calibre, with a doctorate from Harvard or Yale for good measure. Concentrating just on the precision and control exerted by that single extremity, it is hard to believe any other footballer has attained the same degree of accuracy and finesse. Occasionally, he appeared to find himself isolated, a Robinson Crusoe figure, but over most games there would be opportunities for the finely fashioned cross or the punishing free kick. One must needs turn to snooker, and the careful accuracy of a Steve Davis or a Stephen Hendry, to draw sporting comparisons with that precious right boot.

Red Shirts and Roses

Ryan Giggs provided an alternative means of offence. Concisely balanced and speedy, he has been the Galloping Major, sucking in defenders and then outstretching them, making and scoring goals amid the chaos he had himself provoked. His straightforward Celtic dark appearance in stark contrast to the blond and shifting hair-dos of his compatriot, he gave Alex Ferguson a stable and long-term option on the left-hand side where, for example, England and several Premiership teams have been found wanting. Sven-Goran Eriksson has ruefully said that, were he able to naturalise anybody, it would be Ryan Giggs. It is barely credible that Giggs has supplied this service now for fourteen years, that is, for almost half his existence.

These, then, were chief among the stars that brought unprecedented success to Manchester United during the 1990s and into the 21st century. The choice has been an invidious one for two reasons. First, there were others who might have easily earned a paragraph in a lesser era and who supplied talent and energy to the ceaseless fray. Second, this glorious history of achievement was not so much about the dominion of a few individuals; it was about the cohesion of a team.

The chemistry of team building is an elusive science. It is more than the tossing into the cauldron of dissimilar ingredients and hoping for the best. In the chemistry lab at school we did experiments to demonstrate that one can blend some elements into a settled compound, and not others. Were there a Nobel Prize for that branch of chemistry, Sir Alex Ferguson, the ultimate alchemist of football management, would be the initial winner.

22.

Now

'For present joys are more to flesh and blood
Than a dark prospect of a distant good...'

SO WROTE John Dryden, some 300 years ago, in his poem *The Hindu and the Panther*. We must seize the moment and gaze steadily at the present. The culmination of a parallel text such as this should ideally be the description of a situation where both Lancashire and Manchester United are cock of their respective middens. Failing that, the next best option would be for one or other of them to be in the box-seat; 1930, say, with Lancashire reeling off County Championships or 1968 with Manchester United's first European Cup triumph. But impoverished penny-a-liners are frowned upon by the sporting gods and humbled before their capricious donation of such gifts. The worst possible time to complete a study like this is with both teams staggering somewhat - and thus it has proved in the year 2004.

Where there was similarity was on the hospital cot and the clinical couch. Both Manchester United and Lancashire fans must, during 2004, have wondered whether their favourites had opted for a sporting edition of one of television's medical series such as *Casualty* or *Holby City*. One was reminded of the scene in *Gone with the Wind*, where the band near Atlanta forlornly and bravely struck up with Dixie, while the ancient band master and the women folk wept over the ever lengthening casualty lists of Confederate dead and wounded. Every day seemed to bring another United striker or Lancashire quick bowler to the surgery. Lancashire at one moment had something like six bowlers out of action, while there were injuries to almost all the mainline batsmen, as well as to Warren Hegg, the skipper and wicket keeper. Manchester United began the 2004/05 season with a motley collection of damaged, suspended and otherwise unavailable players, amounting to almost a full team. No one could recall a time when both teams simultaneously had been in the throes of such heavy losses.

Lancastrian hearts sank when the sages declared that the county, with its heavyweight batting and vigorous bowling, would win the 2004 County Championship title and have a pertinent statement to make in the three limited overs tournaments. Stridently confident prophecy is frequently the unconscious foreteller of doom. Lancashire began strongly but June, rather than April, proved a cruel month. Defeat followed defeat in all competitions and, a second place in the one day league tournament apart, we grew resigned to a further prolonged wait for success.

In the fallout from Michael Atherton, Neil Fairbrother and John Crawley departing, Lancashire, with the astute Mike Watkinson as cricket manager, had sought to bolster the batting with the importation, inter alia, of the rugged, high-scoring Queenslander, Stuart Law, who was destined to be naturalised and an English citizen for the 2005 season (a summer thankfully heralding the third coming of Muralitharan)

Red Shirts and Roses

Iain Sutcliffe from Leicestershire; and Mal Loye, an especially profitable move, from Northants. Mark Chilton, correct and estimable, represented the home interest, and, in the aftermath of the debacle of 2004, was made captain for 2005, whilst the West Indian all-rounder, Carl Hooper, amply filled the other overseas place. As well as Peter Martin, in his last of many hard-working seasons, and Glen Chapple, now approaching the veteran stage, and the registration from Derbyshire of the competitive Dominic Cork, there was a wholesome string of budding quick bowlers. These included James Anderson, who stormed unceremoniously, if perhaps not enduringly, into international cricket on the back of scant first-class experience; Sajid Mahmood, from Bolton, a player of handsome promise; and Birmingham-born Kyle Hogg, son of the Lancashire and Warwickshire bowler, Willie Hogg, and grandson of Sonny Ramadhin, who played a little for Lancashire in the twilight of his mystifying career. Chris Schofield, brimming with assurance, but, like other leg-spinners, somehow not measuring up to the more exacting standards, was not to be a world-beater, but Gary Keedy, from Wakefield, had shown, not least in 2003, that he could wheel away his left hand spin to some tune.

However, our new grand champion was strapping Andrew Flintoff, the affable giant from Preston, England's premier all-rounder, forceful bat, urgently combative bowler and athletically secure slip field. Could he, in time, vie with Johnny Briggs, Lancashire's best England-born all-rounder, almost always picked for that reason in Red Rose all-time elevens? Moreover, he has something of the same merry disposition that made 'Boy' Briggs so popular a champion and bids fair to becoming the national hero of the hour, saving the country's honour like that previous bowler and buoyant assailant, Sir Francis Drake.

I have been lucky enough to witness half a dozen of his more epic innings, when a hundred runs are accumulated before you can finish your sandwiches or drink your cup of coffee. His is a burly frame, surmounted with an open, honest, ruddy face and, unlike John Tyldesley or Clive Lloyd whose quiet personalities belied the tempest of their batting, what you get is what you see in that frank countenance. What you get, if you are a bowler, is a plain, unvarnished, straightforward belting, the ball soaring to unprecedented heights and lengths off the shortest of back-lifts and the most modest of follows-through. To deploy an apt television analogy, Andrew Flintoff prefers the satellite to the terrestrial route.

Borne up the sheer exuberance of it all, one might do worse than seek poetic succour in Longfellow's *The Village Blacksmith*:

> *....a mighty man is he,*
> *With large and sinewy hands;*
> *And the muscles of his brawny arms*
> *Are strong as iron bands.*

> *...His face is wet with honest sweat,*
> *He earns whate'er he can,*
> *And looks the whole world in the face,*
> *or he owes not any man...*

204

Now

Thanks, thanks to thee, my worthy friend,
For the lesson thou hast taught!
Thus at the flaming forge of life
Our fortunes must be wrought;
Thus on its sounding anvil shaped
Each burning deed and thought!

Unfortunately, Andy Flintoff - and James Anderson - played precious few first-class games for Lancashire in 2004.

A couple of years back Charles Oliver and I were watching the first game of the county first-class competition, with Lancashire fast out of the traps and pulverising the opposition, so much so that, by mid-afternoon, they had collected two bonus points. Scanning the other scores as they were announced, we realised that, what with poor weather, two or three teams without a fixture and some dilatory approaches in the remaining matches, no one else had gained a point. We speculated on the possibility of a climate-warming monsoon of four months duration or, on scriptural precedent, rain falling for 40 days and 40 nights, beginning at that very second and leading to the abandonment of the entire programme. This would presumably have yielded every county 64 points for the forsaken games, with Lancashire on 66 points and thus champions. It does get that desperate sometimes.

Never did it get more desperate than during the forlorn summer of 2004. Lancashire were relegated to the second division of the County Championship for the first time, amid yelps of anguish and accusations of listlessness from a distraught membership. It will be the summer of 2006 at least before there will be another opportunity of a Lancashire Championship title, a goal proving as elusive as the Scarlet Pimpernel, and with Lancashire adherents sympathising with Citizen Chauvelin in his hopeless attempts to come to grips with the slippery Sir Percy Blakeney.

Manchester United, too, had cause for some despondency in the 2003-2004 season, although that was about avarice rather than, in Lancashire's case, malnourishment. One of the differences now is that, compared with earlier times, there is a fluidity about playing staffs, in part because the players, both cricketers and footballers, rightly have a little more control over their professional careers, but mainly because of the pressures on clubs and managers to succeed in situations where the prizes, unlike their unbounded availability in Alice's other Wonderland, are necessarily restricted.

There is something of the character of the repertory company about the make-up of top cricket and football teams. Particularly in the theatre of football, there is intense activity in the minute chink between seasons, as well as during the later mid-season 'window', to renew and reassemble, just as, for instance, the old style seaside resorts recruited a drama group afresh each summer to perform Agatha Christie mysteries and Ben Travers' farces for the amusement of holiday-makers.

Red Shirts and Roses

Manchester United, true to its long-established practices, have adhered to a yearning for youth. The first Ferguson neap tide, which washed up the best part of a team, including six or more internationals, was unlikely to be repeated. Indeed, the next two waves were tremulous and weak; a group of good players learned good habits and then moved to lesser clubs to enjoy good, but not outstanding careers. The fourth little ebb flow has been kinder, with the Irish full back, John O'Shea, showing stylish aptitude, and the young Scot, Darren Fletcher, displaying classy virtuosity. In spite of persistent and galling injuries, Wes Brown has shown an instinctive flair in defence, an organic rather than a genetically modified plant. Other recruits have joined the fray from further afield. Tim Howard, the American goal keeper, brought no little agility and Roy Carroll, the Irish goal keeper, no little resolve to that continually fraught position; Mikael Silvestre, the quick-footed, young French centre back, has performed very impressively and now the combatively energetic South American, Gabriel Heinze has arrived from Paris St-Germain to strengthen what in 2003-04 was sometimes a fragile fortification. Celtic's Liam Miller promises youthful strength in the mid field, while, rescued from the meltdown of Leeds United, the still youngish Alan Smith, full of tenacity and thrust, has also joined the ranks.

Rio Ferdinand, an expensive import from Leeds United, demonstrated immense, if undemonstrative, influence at the centre of United back-line. It was of a character revealed by Manchester United's tumble from leading place when he was banished for a long spell on the charge of missing a drug test. That is very properly regarded as a sin calling for condign chastisement. However, the sentence was severe enough to raise the faint suspicion that an example was being made of the aristocracy, with the FA playing the role of the Jacobins and Old Trafford regarded as an aristo's chateau. The FA had possibly forgotten the appeal of the peerage in *Iolanthe*: 'spurn not the nobly born with love affected, nor treat with virtuous scorn the well-connected.'

In any event, eight months for a missed drug test and being banned for three games for a vicious, red-carded, career-threatening tackle does seem to reflect those patent and absurd anomalies of jurisprudence where property is respected more than persons.

Ironically, as Rio Ferdinand approached the end of his term of exile, the Toytown town hall smallmindedness of the FA, among whose officers Alex Ferguson had presciently said there were those with overweening ambition, was itself shattered by the foolish and strictly unnecessary Faria Alam scandal and other problems, including its inability to cope with the Montague/Capulet feud of the Arsenal and United managers.

It is possible to pursue a youth policy abroad as well as at home. Matt Busby went seeking his young maestros in British regions beyond the northwest, Duncan Edwards among them. Alex Ferguson brought from Portugal the captivatingly diverting Cristiano Ronaldo. Once recovered from the shock that he was baptised with his first name after Jesus and his second after President Reagan, it is mainly joy. The diamond studs in his juvenile ears flash no more glitteringly than his twinkling toes, as he high-steps past and around bemused opponents like an exquisitely trained horse in a soft-centred Gene Autry western movie of long ago. Gradually, the young winger grew more effective and topped the bill in Cardiff in 2004, when United beat the underdogs

Millwall in the cup final, 3-0, a satisfactory score-line, for less would have look fortunate and more gluttonous. As for Ronaldo, show pony metamorphosed into Shergar, although youthful misjudgement continues occasionally to plague the thoroughbred's contribution.

With the first flush of Ferguson's fledglings now beaky older birds, one anticipates that the continuum of veteran maturity and youthful vigour will soon restore the Premiership trophy to the Old Trafford boardroom sideboard. Moreover, what might be termed the global goslings now include the nippy French striker, Louis Saha, the Spanish teenager, sturdy Gerard Pique, for defensive duties and the junior US-born Italian forward, Guiseppe Rossi. Further to that, another clutch of local nestlings, several of whom showed confident promise in the pre-season of 2004/2005, have been hatched. A glance over the staff register is enough to convince that, true to the Old Trafford doctrine established by Matt Busby, Alex Ferguson, who, like Helen of Troy and her ships, has launched a thousand United teams, is pinning his faith in the creation of another young team, albeit one drawn, as befits the footballing culture of the times, from all corners of the world.

Suddenly, too, there came to complete the pattern, Wayne Rooney, astonishing the footballing world with an eclectic hat trick on debut - left foot smash hit, right foot low glide, carefully placed free kick - in the European Championship in the September of 2004. Immediately the comparisons were traced back through the annals, with all agreed that this bullet-headed, bull-necked teenager had somehow contrived to compound together the complementary traits of mental buoyancy and coolness and of physical resolution and aptitude. His slightly unprepossessing, rough-hewn features might remind ageing perusers of *The Dandy* or *The Beano* of one of those mischievous rogues, like Dennis the Menace, who prowled through those cartooned pages, albeit with a physique more reminiscent of Desperate Dan. His cavalier adventures carry recollections of more youthfully oriented heroes, like Roy of the Rovers, while, such is his footballing intelligence, one might finally have to turn to the *Spectator* or the *New Statesman* to complete the journalistic metaphor. Heat and cold remain in dangerous imbalance as yet, but there was the yearning thought that, injected with a very necessary fix of the essence of composed maturity, he could become the field-marshal of a grand army.

One might have to be patient. Soon after Lancashire fell from first divisional grace, Manchester United opened the 2004/05 season with stumbling gait, looking a little faltering and ungelled. It may take months, maybe a year, for the mould to reform and for United to rise again to victorious heights.

We were watching Lancashire bludgeon Middlesex at Lord's in the summer of 2003, when a home supporter disdainfully glanced at his scorecard and exclaimed, 'why, there are no real Lancashire players in the first half of the team.' It did not take long for Charles Oliver, unofficial registrar-general of cricketers' births and deaths, to leave this upstart Middlesexual squirming, as he ticked off the origins of the Middlesex eleven, half a dozen of whom had contrived to be born in Africa, including Len's grandson, Ben Hutton, a native of Johannesburg, leaving Paul Weekes from Hackney the closest to a local. We gently added that, in any event, Middlesex had faded somewhat geographically to the postage stamp of a postal district, having been reduced, using a shire-like parallel, to the equivalent of the Cheshire Cat's grin.

This underpins the previous argument that birthright is an arbitrary and narrow-minded touchstone in sporting as in other matters. Even Yorkshire cricket club have been forced by the logic of events to forsake their bizarre obsession with soil-based parturition. Upbringing, for preference, and, failing that, personal commitment to the area must be the keys. A.N. Hornby and J.H. Davies were foresighted enough to give both Lancashire and Manchester United a cosmopolitan impetus in this refreshing direction, insisting that the primary task of a sports club reliant on public support is to offer maximal value, irrespective of often negative, even offensive, yardsticks, such as racial or ethnic considerations. In turn, that would seem to approximate to all that is best about humanity bonding and overcoming divisiveness.

One of the chief similarities between mainline football and cricket at the top club level is the willingness to recruit overseas players, many of whom are taken to the hearts of spectators, as have been Eric Cantona, Peter Schmeichel, Clive Lloyd and Wasim Akram, alongside their undoubted affection for those - Michael Atherton, Neil Fairbrother, Paul Scholes, Gary Neville - from more homely surrounds. Footballers arrive from all four corners. Manchester City employed a Chinese full back. How that would have delighted my father, who never tired of his cod media report that City had signed two Chinese full backs, Wee Wun Wonn and How Long Sin.

The introduction, almost to the point of fetish, of continental football managers and, of course, commonwealth cricket coaches, adds to the festive multiculture. It gives rise to a rouble-rousing Chelski, luxuriating in the opulence, whatever its provenance, of Russian wealth and international stars, and a marvellously victorious foreign legion at Highbury, where, it has been suggested, *La Marseillaise* might be preferred to *God Save the Queen* as the pre-match anthem. It gives rise to piquant rivalries, like those between such totally disparate personalities as Alex Ferguson, now the fiery old-timer from an old-fashioned working class background, and Arsene Wenger, modern, sophisticated, urbane. Despite, as my daughter, Kate, another United enthusiast, is keen to point out, his disconcerting resemblance to Mr Burns, Homer's employer in the wonderful *Simpsons'* TV cartoon, Arsene Wenger has obviously graduated from good football coach to good man-manager, presumably persuading, at least for some of the time, what was a rather ill-tempered bunch of great players to concentrate on not losing any matches. After a decade of relatively easy pickings, Manchester United now must look to their laurels in the face of this two-track competition from London, all in a context of multinational grandeur.

The potency of the two great London clubs is a reminder of the shift in economic power back to the southeast. In medieval times the region south of a line from the Wash to Bristol was all-important, with political as well as commercial trading across the Channel pressing the levers of authority. After all, it was easier, in that water-driven economy, to get from London to Calais than from London to York. With the collapse of manufacturing industry, with the prominence of the European Community and with such devices as the Channel Tunnel, the current picture takes on some of the same shape and colouring. The hundred years or so from the battle of Waterloo in 1815 to the Battle of the Somme in 1916, the years in which Manchester United and Lancashire were born and matured, were the prime years of northern, and other provincial, heavy industrialism, a phenomenon stimulated by accidents of physical geography.

Now

On the long graph of British economic history, the Industrial Revolution now begins to look like an eminent blip, a supreme moment when the great industrial cities heaved themselves into articulate and lively status. Now, like the city republics of ancient Greece or Renaissance Italy, they have lost some of that drive and impact. It is perhaps significant that, as of 2004, six of the 20 Premiership clubs are based in the London region and that all four of the northern counties are among the nine second division county cricket clubs, with the four home counties teams residing in the first division. Nonetheless, Manchester continues to impose its ready wits and resource on the kingdom in the post-industrial, London-dominated epoch, with the two Old Traffords among its treasures. The city is a financial and commercial centre of enormous prestige, but it is also the site of nightlife and daily living.

There is a determination to make the city orderly once more. Manchester is the chief arena for the calming balm of the palliative ASBOS. Of the 2455 Antisocial Behaviour Orders issued in the UK between 1999 and the beginning of 2004, 474 had been visited upon neighbourhood miscreants in Manchester, many, many more than in any other comparable conurbation. They appear to be having beneficial effects to the point where some of the tough estates around Manchester may have a chance of some respite from excessive noise, vandalism, affray and all the other instruments of social torture that, unreasonably and mindlessly, neighbour visits upon neighbour in an atmosphere lacking in community discipline.

120,000 pleasure-seekers descend on the city every weekend to test out its 550 licensed premises, while, after the dereliction caused by the IRA bomb of June 1996, there is a modish feel about the newly developed central complex of work, leisure and retail outlets. The old Exchange area has the bustle of a late medieval trading town in the Low Countries. In turn, there is a marked willingness for residents to rediscover the buoyant joys of city centre nightlife. Indeed, there might be some tension between the clubbers and the incomers. Old customers of the Hacienda, the club of choice of the 1990s, might, according to one report, react apoplectically to the Crosby Homes marketing slogan, 'The Party's Over, You Can Come Home.'

Both cricket and football have a dependency on television. In these days when I watch more and more live cricket and less and less live football, it is, in fact, possible to see Manchester United three or four times a month on television, especially with the extensive coverage of the European club championship. If one reads the statistics aright, this is mainly because, when United are involved, over 3m subscribers tune in, whereas it is only 750,000 should lesser brethren be screened and that is apart from the hundreds of thousands watching in pubs and clubs. Even better, there is a special channel devoted entirely to Manchester United, promising all sorts of goodies. It makes for a cosy way of watching Manchester United - and Manchester United Reserves, always an intriguing prospect - more often than at any time since my late childhood. It only needs Lancashire to promote a similar programme and a televisual Eden would be available here on earth.

On occasion, my son, for greater love hath no man, allows me to use his Manchester United season ticket for the theatre of dreams. It is a stimulating and theatrical experience, carefully orchestrated like a military tattoo, evoking the maximum involvement. One consequent peculiarity of the almost ubiquitous season ticket process is that, as they are faithfully renewed year after year, your neighbours are bespoke for a generation. Behind the equivalent of our family pew sits, or rather shifts nervously, a highly emoting character. United were 4-0 up and ran out comfortable 6-1 victors, but this panicky male could find no solace for his anxiety complex. Should the enemy venture over the half way line or seek to capitalise on the danger implicit in a throw in near their own corner flag, he was thrown into paroxysms of fretful apprehension. A breakthrough on the right and one wondered whether it might be necessary to seek medical attention for him, as a heart attack seemed imminent. Not that he is without judgement: commenting on one young United incomer from abroad, he remarked of his rather clumsy ball control, 'he traps it further than I can kick it'.

The season ticket, averaging £450 a year for nineteen league matches and the chance of buying in for extraneous games, is not a bad bargain, at roughly £24 a match, comparable with a medium priced West End theatre ticket. It means that Manchester United, inclusive of their scores of hospitality boxes - the most expensive costing £40,000 a year - and their corporate seating, are taking, with constant capacity crowds of close on 70000 and a regular programme of European and English cup matches, roughly £65m annually at the box-office alone, regardless of all other marketing, at home and overseas, where it is said they have a shop in every country bar Afghanistan, plus receipts such as television rights.

With, in the financial year 2002/03, TV income of £31m, group turnover of £146m, group profit of £34m, kit sponsorship of £34m, a market value of over £825m and a global fan base of 10m, the wealth of Manchester United is well rehearsed. The club exists in a context of ruthless private enterprise and is sometimes castigated by less successful concerns, just as the large supermarkets are censured by small shopkeepers, who, knowing the rules of the game, or the lack of them, had still decided to enter the competition and then wished the rules to be altered when things start going personally awry.

In 1792 Walton Henry Smith, with his wife, Anna, started his newsvendor business in London; in 1849 Jesse Boot opened the British and American Botanic Establishment at 8 Goose Gate, Nottingham; in 1869 London's Drury Lane witnessed the opening of a dairy owned by John James and Mary Ann Sainsbury; and in 1884 Michael Marks, a Russian-born Polish refugee, first stood, initially, Spencer-less, behind his stall in Leeds' Kirkgate market. Their stars soared. So with Manchester United: they, too, have risen and risen from lowly origins, just as many others would wish and aim to do. If mighty oaks from tiny acorns grow, they destroy many weaker saplings and plants in so doing, for that appears to be the essence of nature as it is of capitalism.

However, it is in this huge wealth of some football clubs that one finds the major difference between the two Old Traffords, between, in fact, the Premiership and the County Championship.

In 2003 Lancashire hosted eight County Championship games in a season in which they were frustratingly close to ultimate success. 6619 people paid at the turnstiles for, notionally, 32 days cricket, an average of not much more than 200. Lancashire, with its strong membership of 12,500, the highest count in the nation, fills the pavilion and much of the members' enclosures, so that there was a further 36,000, giving a total average of about 1400 a day. There were 25000 customers for the thirteen one day games, also attended by about 66,000 members, a daily average of approximately 7000. All told, the daily average attendance was less than 3000, members and paying spectators. It is frightening to recall that nearly 15000 (12000 paying at the gates) watched the first day of the University match in 1947. By the time the Oxbridge first-class fixture was banished from Lord's, that multitude had been reduced to a scattering of petite sweethearts and antique curates.

The upshot is that members' subscription and gate-money contribute less than £1m to Lancashire's expenditure of almost £9m, whereas United earn the equivalent of over £2m at the turnstiles every time they play. Lancashire is not alone; in fact, it is, by cricket standards, not in an unhealthy financial state. It is customary for all counties to make a disproportionate amount, in many cases, less than 10%, through the devices of subscriptions and gate-receipts. It is not remarkable that the inflation in ticket prices has not accelerated at the one Old Trafford as much as at the other, although it is fair to say that United's prices are not exorbitant when compared with one or two London-based clubs. Nonetheless, one may watch a day's county cricket at a much cheaper price than 90 minutes' club football - if one is able to find a football ticket. With relatively few tickets for sale, given the massive uptake of and waiting list for season tickets, Manchester United's accountants must inwardly groan at the fortnightly arrival of applications in infinite proportion to what is available, and wish that the ground were twice the size. In any event, the true historical comparison is with the time, 60 and 70 years ago when the 'workman's shilling' would have enabled you to affect an entry at either ground.

The county cricket clubs have grown increasingly reliant on other sources of income, including sponsorship, the non-cricket usage of real estate - given United's proximity, Lancashire's car parks, hospitality suites and hotel are tailor-made for football purposes - and, most meaningful of all, income from the central authority of the ECB, based on international cricket and allied media and other commercial proceeds. If one looks closely at the accounts of a county whose ground is deployed for international fixtures, one might draw the business conclusion that disbanding the cricket team and just hiring out the premises for Test and international one day cricket would make the best commercial sense, rather like race courses being used just for a meeting or two a year.

In recent seasons, less than 150,000 people have, on average, paid at the gate to watch some 150 County Championship matches, a matter of about 250 a scheduled day. It was 500,000 in the 1960s when the alarm bells were rung. Even with higher county memberships - counting in MCC, the national total is about 150,000 - it is not a high rate of commitment. The old-time theatricals used to say of a mediocre house that 'you could have shot a stag in the gallery'. On many county grounds during a championship match you could organise a safari. It was while once, years ago, at Trent Bridge watching the enthralling drama of Richard Hadlee bowling to David Gower in a well-nigh empty stadium that I coined the phrase 'Much Bowling in the Morgue'.

Red Shirts and Roses

It is true that football crowds have fallen from the halcyon winters of the 1930s and 1940s, when there were 40m spectators, with an average of 30,000 for gates in the four divisions. However, the Premiership and the three Football League divisions still attract 16m customers a season, of whom half attend Premiership matches, that is, at an average of some 20,000 a game, the three or four larger clubs, such as Manchester United, obviously tipping the scales of that average considerably. Football League finances have become, like cricket's, over reliant on outside funding, and the sudden collapse of the ITV Digital venture seriously incommoded many clubs. As a consequence, the number of professionals employed in its three divisions fell by 20%, from 2091 in May 2003 to 1673 in May 2004. However, the Premiership, in spite of the non-sterling efforts of now relegated Leeds United, remains fairly robust in terms of spectatordom and club marketing. Such is the strength of club football that the top Premiership clubs, such as Arsenal, Chelsea or Manchester United, would probably beat the England team nine times out of ten, whereas it is unlikely any current county would be quite so dominant against the England eleven. Therein lies a critical distinction with cricket, where the central authority holds the financial hand, the trump cards that matter.

The chief outcome of this huge difference is in players' income. A touching cameo was presented at the two Old Traffords some years ago. The back pages of the newspapers shouted of wage demands. Andy Flintoff wanted £50,000 a year and Roy Keane wanted £50,000 a week. Andy Flintoff ended up with £32,000 and Roy Keane on £52,000 and the latter is said to now earn over £90,000 a week. Debate will rage over whether this has good or bad results. At a dinner recently, for the benefit of Surrey's Adam Hollioake, the Chelsea footballer, Damien Duff, paid out £4500, close to the annual old age pension, for the number plate CFC11. At least, it was a goodish cause and much more hair-raising tales could be told about young footballers with obscene amounts of money to burn into gigantic conflagrations. It has been suggested that David Beckham buys a new motor car every time he is depressed.

At 7.30 one morning, in cold, rainy, muddy conditions, I was told by a cheerfully unenvious Jimmy Greaves (we regularly crossed paths on dog-walking exercises for some eighteen months: he reckoned he would earn £50,000 a week if he could run as fast as my lurcher, Holly) that young footballers running amok on astronomic salaries should not be judged too harshly, as the good times arrive too suddenly, before one has assembled the experience to cope with such riches. There is, however, rather shallow talk about the pressure created by these huge sums of money. A deeper analysis might suggest that too little money also creates plenty of pressure. Imagine the stress on Herbert Strudwick, the brilliant England and Surrey wicket keeper of days of long ago, doing his job with flimsy protection against fast bowling, forced so to do, by the 'no play; no pay' ruling, with broken fingers, knowing that, without that pound or two, there would be little or no food for his wife and family. As Keith Miller, a little contemptuous of sportsmen who blamed 'pressure' for their errors, remarked in the voice of experience, 'pressure is flying at 2000 feet with a Messerschmitt up your arse.'

However that might be, the modern footballer had, in fairly brisk time, surged economically ahead of the modern cricketer. John Arlott, writing in 1977, waxed, as ever, sagely on the subject. With Wally Hammond as his main witness, but speaking

212

broadly of the 1930s cricket 'pro', he wrote, 'This was a fruitful period for the cricket professional...Socially and financially, too, his position was better than that of his generally comparable competitor, the professional footballer. Several leading cricket players of the period had a choice. Walter Hammond, for instance, preferred to concentrate solely on cricket...By the accepted criteria of the time, the established cricket professional in the thirties could afford to run a motor car; the average football professional could not'.

As we have noted, that state of affairs, with the footballer on capped wages and maybe living, like a farm labourer, in a tied cottage, continued for years after World War II. Herein lies the main reason why cricket sometimes seems to struggle to reveal top-line performers. One hears a lot of foolish tommyrot about this failure to produce sufficient talent, schools being among the first to be blamed in many a saloon bar discussion. In effect, apart from a brief period from the 1950s to the 1970s, when playing fields began to be sold off and other priorities prevailed, the majority of schoolboys over the last 150 years never had much of a chance to play cricket at school. Hobbs and Sutcliffe could open the batting for the non-school cricket World XI. In any event, it can scarcely be the motive for the educational system to produce eleven England cricketers or, while on the subject of relative failure, a Wimbledon tennis champion or an Open Golf contender.

The fact is that recreational cricket is in good heart, with some 14000 clubs and the regular commitment of some 500,000 players, about a quarter more than in the inter-wars years, and with most clubs arranging graded cricket for children and youth. The Lancashire County handbook, edited by the judicious Malcolm Lorimer, which neutral observers judge the best on the circuit, boasts over a half century of pages on the leagues in the county's ambit. There are 23 leagues logged, involving some 350 teams, many of them with subsidiary elevens in subsidiary divisions and appropriate junior sections, the whole an amazing conglomeration of cricketing action, hardly evidence of a major reduction in cricketing interest. By way of comparison, the FA has 40,000 football clubs registered, with some 2m active players at all ages, and a national team that does not quite hit the high notes, while UK has 3500 golf courses, 2m regular golfers and sparse sightings of the next Nick Faldo. Perhaps the schools should simply practise football, tennis, golf and cricket all day long.

Discussion of sport in Britain has for too long been dogged by the confusion between the health and leisure needs of the many and the global competitive edge of the few. The resources needed for each are widely different. It is the Olympic-sized swimming pool for the few hardy, single-minded protagonists versus, according to the research, the circular baths with lots of gently sloping inclines and maybe a palm tree or two, which is the demand of the masses. There is no automatic connection between giving children and adults the chance to keep fit or find recreational pleasure in sports and the combative drive of high professional competition. Australia, for example, has a very low numerical base of cricketers, with just a very few top places, hard to get and hard to keep, for the genuine, out-and-out activist.

If English cricket is sometimes below par compared with football (an intriguing motion for debate in itself, given the exploits in 2004 of both national teams) the single and all-encompassing reason must be that, given the choice, anyone hoping for

213

a professional sports career would elect for football - and perhaps, golf, tennis, even athletics or one of the rugby codes - ahead of cricket, where the pickings are relatively impoverished. We have all experienced the schoolboy sporting prodigy who has the physical attributes and mental stamina to master many sports. Gary Sobers might well have been a baseball ace, had be been born in a different habitat. Transfer the conditions of the last ten years to the 1930s and 1940s. Although his perceptive biographer, Gerald Howat, has pointed out that Wally Hammond did not find the social climate of professional football too congenial, it is unthinkable that he or, of course, Denis Compton - and there are other examples - would not have chosen to be full-time footballers and never played top-class cricket at all. It would be grossly unfair, given the dictates of economic life, to suggest that they might or should have done otherwise.

Sane and undemonstrative judges have said that Phil Neville was the best schoolboy cricketer they had ever seen. As he left school, just before his 16th birthday, it is reported that Lancashire were able to offer him not much more for the summer than Manchester United were prepared to pay him a week, that is, something in the region of £1500/£2000. Years on, and he was being paid £50000 a week and barely able to hold down a regular slot in the United side. It would call for a superhuman fixation on cricket for a teenager to opt for it in those circumstances.

That spectacular differentiation of income at the top of the two games, with a county outlay for staff and coaches of about an annual £1m meeting the salary of perhaps one high-ranking Premiership footballers, exemplifies the fundamental dissimilarity between the two sports. What follows from that is very critical. In cricket, the county clubs are in hock to the ECB. The counties receive subsistence doles to furnish the players they have developed to high standard for international duties and they become contracted England players, usually playing more first-class matches for the country than the club during a given year. The cynical might opine that the efficient course for a county to pursue would be the breeding of a squad of very good players who would play consistently for the county, eschewing the excellent ones, who would be grabbed for England. A county's best performers are now kidnapped - rather like W.E. Midwinter by W.G. Grace in 1878, from the Australians at Lord's, conveyed by cab to the Oval to play for Gloucestershire, although, self-evidently, that move was from country to county.

In football, the clubs remain almost condescendingly immune to centralised diktat. Envision the reaction of Alex Ferguson or Arsene Wenger did the FA demand the release of three or four players for an international match that coincided with a critical, nay, any, Premiership match. One might sell 60,000 tickets to those keen to witness their respective expressions of Caledonian wrath and Gallic despair. Oddly, almost counterfactually, it is the cricketing counties, established in the Victorian convention of the gentleman members' clubs with democratically elected committees, that have suffered such a loss of independence, not the football clubs, with their secondary roots in business origins and company law.

Thus it is that the biggest switch of the last 40 or so years is that, from a position nearer equity, the counties are now the Oliver Twists and the Premiership clubs the Dombey and Sons. The very existence of the Premiership is an example of that sort of bold fundamental change that is anathema to the world of cricket. Even when, breathlessly, two divisions were formed in the County Championship, it was with three relegated and three promoted out of groups of nine, rather as six or seven might be relegated from the football Premiership. This was presumably to avoid undue consolidation of the first and second-raters, while, of course, there was no third division to frighten the wits out of any lazybones in the second division and no likelihood of a brand-new evolution of, for instance, a NatWest Bank XI or SkyTV XI or Lashings XI. It is all so different from the ebullient Victorian era of experimentation and movement. With weak finances and a prudent disposition, there is the terrifying prospect of atrophy. If the sponsors withdrew and the TV screens went blank, cricket's life-support machines would be switched off.

Conversely, it is possible to make prophecies about the evolution of club football. For instance, the European Champions contest might become more structured over the next decade, with, perhaps, Manchester United, Chelsea and Arsenal included. Euro-league sides might then field 'reserve' sides in the Premiership, the rationalisation of a phenomenon already witnessed informally and sporadically, for instance, in Carling Cup games. Already, and it would be a useful parallel, an Atlantic league has been mooted for a couple of top clubs from the smaller North European countries (Scotland, Belgium, Holland, Denmark, Norway, Sweden, Iceland...) where the lack of localised competitive edge is unhelpful to the teams going forward to European club tournaments.

The biggest alteration, therefore, of the last half-century between the top levels of cricket and football has been financial. From a position of relative equity, in terms of income, wages and so on, a huge gap has opened. Lancashire's annual match receipts would barely pay the salary now of one of Manchester United's senior players. What happened?

The main explanation probably lies in changes within society itself. The essential difference between the two great sports represented by the two Old Traffords is in respect of cultural and social change. At the extremes, football is attractive because of its simplicity and cricket is attractive because of its complexity. Were the proverbial Martian, if not too weary from all the other demands on his time observing this and that facet of modern life, to be invited to both Old Traffords, the results are predictable. After four days at the one, he would still be wondering what the purpose was and how progress was recorded, although, if, as in H.G. Wells' *The War of the Worlds*, he was of advanced intellect, he might be able to explain to the laity the convolutions of the Duckworth/Lewis Method, after he had been persuaded it was not a form of contraception. After ten minutes at the other Old Trafford he would have comprehended that they were trying to get the pumpkin shaped object in one of the onion bags at either end. Adolf Hitler stiffly told C.B. Fry that Germans did not take to cricket because 'there are too many regulations'.

For many years I wondered bitterly why there were no football commentators who rose above the normal and suburban. Your Raymond Glendenning and Kenneth Wolstenholme were right enough, while now we are submitted to ex-players, full of obscure technical nit-picks and banal nicknames. The BBC had deployed in all other sports a reporter so apt that one came to believe that there was an Eng. Lit. expert in the sports department at Broadcasting House. A fastidious soul, he raided J.B. Priestley for rugby league and mixed Walter Scott and Dylan Thomas for rugby union correspondents. He found Trollopean whispering baritones for snooker and Damon Runyon prototypes for boxing. It was all so appropriate. The horse racing communicators looked like racehorses and the motor racing one sounded like a racing car. Complicated and profound, cricket was our litterateur's favourite game. He could serve up a fetching combine of Thomas Hardy and P.G. Wodehouse with a couple of fugitives from *Brideshead Revisited*. What a confection of delight! Yet, when it came to soccer, all was mundane.

It was many years before I was struck by the colossal truth that football is so simple that it needs no exposition on television and I apologise to football commentators for scolding them for not achieving the near impossible. Football may be beautiful, balletic, violent, dramatic, rhythmic, but, like a monumental ocean or a towering mountain, one needs little or no verbal enlargement or exegis.

This is the main reason why football is ubiquitous. It is the first art-form that has ever conquered the whole planet. Over 2bn people - 3% of all the human beings that have been born in 2m or so years of endeavour by the species - watched the last World Cup Final on television. Conversely, cricket suffers proportionately from being an elaborate and contemplative pastime in an era, certainly in Britain, of a quickened social tempo. There has been a shift away from the middlebrow, integrated audience for cricket, as for other similar cultural elements, in a period of multitudinous choice across a widening range of quick-fire options. In 1876 William Gladstone would address outdoor crowds of 12,000, with 'shouters' on the fringes to relay the message, for up to three hours on the vexed question of Turkish atrocities, an issue that did not actually affect everyday life. Tony Blair would be lucky to be allowed a sound bite on the meaningful issue of the Iraq War, plus maybe a facetious comment from an unfunny political diarist.

However, there is another possible reason for this mammoth change, one more connected to the fashion in which the two sports were exported. It has often been observed that cricket was an 'imperial' game, whilst football was an international sport. The swing in the centre of gravity of cricket to the sub-continent is highly significant. It is peculiar that, for all the weight of religious and administrative undertaking in the former colonies, it is cricket that is the indomitable survivor of Empire and, happily, the future of cricket is very much tied in with its popularity in Asia. In examining that development, it is, nonetheless, interesting to muse over the spread of the two games, both from a British base. Was it so predetermined that cricket would solely follow the flag, while football would conquer the world?

The consequences are important. The prestige, quality, interest and money that flow from European club football is substantial; it makes for a major difference with domestic first-class cricket, which is very domestic indeed and which is rarely tested competitively at external club level, as, for instance, by New South Wales or Transvaal. We live in a situation where there are four Test-playing countries in Asia and only one in Europe. The top English football clubs are tested in a way that the top English cricket clubs are not, with consequent effects on standards and, crucially, finances.

216

Now

When one considers the connections of great cities like Manchester with Europe as well as with the Commonwealth, the question arises of why the division between the lists of cricketing and footballing nations is so adamantly rigorous. It is true that these two marvellous diversions appeal to differing mind-sets, but those mental conditions are not incompatible and are very frequently found in the same individuals, in all those people who have taken the electric train, now the Metro, to Warwick Road, now Old Trafford, Station, in the summer to watch Lancashire and again in the winter, enduring the slightly longer stroll, to watch Manchester United.

Cricket scholars regarding French, Dutch and Flemish antecedents for cricket in medieval and early modern times cite etymological evidence. It is possible that these items, in reality, contributed to the widespread but highly localised incidence of folk-games throughout Western Europe, indeed everywhere. Club, ball and target amusements must have been very common, so that, on the face of it, continental Europe could have been as open to the development of cricket as England. Certainly the climate of Mediterranean Europe might have offered even more encouragement for an essentially summer game.

As the first industrialised and urbanised nation, Britain was also cast for the role of midwife of rationalised and unified sports. The Industrial Revolution included, as an important footnote, Edwin Budding's invention in 1830 of the cylinder mower, which, complementary to the British affection for the grassy park, fed that other love, the trim, perfectly striped lawn, what Walt Whitman called 'the handkerchief of the Lord', a necessary aspect of games like cricket and tennis.

Evolution was checked by a confluence of accidents of timing. There does seem to have been some cricket-oriented activity in France but the intervention of the Revolutionary and Napoleonic Wars acted as a barrier to any cross-Channel togetherness, so that, when English cricket became disciplined and mature in early Victorian times, it was too late. The moment had passed. Interestingly, a good-will cricket tour, involving the Duke of Leeds, then the foreign secretary, and the Duke of Dorset, then the ambassador in Paris, was abandoned because of the outbreak of the French Revolution in 1789. The team encountered the ambassador at Dover, as he himself fled from the insurrection. A refusal to tour Zimbabwe for political reasons is not, then, unprecedented.

It is also of interest that something of the same sort occurred in North America. The first international cricket match, indeed possibly the first international team encounter of any modern designation, took place in 1844 when Canada played the United States.

In the USA the dreadful effects of the American Civil War, plus some vestigial antagonism (for example, arising from the cotton blockade imposed by the Union) with the Old Country, and, importantly, the American desire to formulate a new and united nation in its own burnished image, spelt an end to much of American cricket. Baseball was heralded as the mainline national sport, even although the Philadelphia area remained a significant locus for cricket. Philadelphia beat the 1893 Australians, while their fast bowler, John Barton King, is numbered among the all-time greats.

Cricket, then, was bogged down rather by political and economic events, whereas football, making its move later in the century, when many more nations, in Europe and in South America, had adopted more ordered national formats and more industrial and urban habits, found the ground fertile for cultivation. It is significant that it was tradesmen, businessmen and returning visitors, rather than administrators and soldiers, who carried the footballing mission overseas. One further example is Guilherme Pinto Basto who, in 1884, returned to Portugal after completing his studies in England and introduced football to the nation that gave Eusebio to the world and Ronaldo to Manchester United. British sailors were in at the launch of Bilbao and British electricians were involved with the origins of Moscow Dynamo. It is worth remembering, too, that several of those initial attempts to form clubs in Europe coupled, as in England, cricket with football; A.C. Milan, started by those half a dozen Englishmen in 1899, is a case in point.

Historical ramifications assuredly had a hand in the differential distribution of football and cricket, but the suspicion remains that there was another critical distinction. At its simplest, football was viewed inclusively and cricket exclusively. Football did not carry so much ideological baggage as cricket; it was seen as a jolly winter diversion that might appeal to anyone and so it has proved. Cricket was regarded as a special feature of 'Englishry'. In 1945 Neville Cardus wrote that 'none except the people of England or of English-speaking countries has excelled at cricket...it somehow holds up the mirror to English nature.' A hundred years before *The Cricketer's Song* warbled ' 'Tis the king of Anglo-Saxon games - the type of our strength confessed/Where the charms of perils bravely dared inspires each manly breast', while the cricket antiquarian, Rev. James Pycroft wrote 'the game of cricket, philosophically considered, is a standing 'panegyric' to the English character'. John Mitford, writing in *The Gentlemen's Magazine* in 1833, asserted that 'cricket is the pride and privilege of the Englishman alone.'

The engagement of this dogma with imperial and Christian beliefs and practices constituted a faith in cricket as having some innate racial presence in the Anglo-Saxon, if not the Celtic, psyche. When, in turn, indigenous subjects in imperial possessions played cricket, not because they were born to it but, in part, either to compete with or to show their acceptance of Englishness, the notion of ethnic character was clumsily used to justify such wonders. We still hear of the subtlety of the Indian cricketer or of the exuberance of the West Indian cricketer. This explanation never quite resolves why, if Pakistanis and Barbadians are ethnically ready-made for cricket, Egyptians and Cubans are not. Here we touch yet again upon that thread of pro-natalist policies and creeds, with the supposition that the racial endowment of birth confers specific skills and interests. It is true that, as in England or the West Indies, people will play out the persona of what is currently in vogue as national character, but it bears negligible relation to genetic lineage.

It is about nurture, not nature. There is no inherent or inborn Australian or South African 'character' as such. Australians, West Indians and South Africans play cricket efficiently when and if they apply themselves in a well-organized and rigorously professional fashion. Located in a similar habitat and culture, any other human grouping could produce a number with the physical and mental capacity to succeed as cricketers. It is likely that the proponents of cricket did the game - and the world at large - a disservice by so tightly clutching to the imperial bosom the codes of a lovely sport. Cause and effect were reversed. It was a pathetic fallacy of pseudo-romantic eugenics.

Now

Although expatriates from England and commonwealth countries join with locally born friends to further the cause of cricket on the continent, it is difficult to close the historical gap and make good the loss of time and impetus. This leaves the English domestic game peculiarly isolated, even in an era of rapid global transit. There is no doubt that the infusion of European football has decidedly helped the profile of Premiership football. When next watching Manchester United play Bayern Munich or Athletico Bilbao, imagine the arcane possibility of Lancashire entertaining Bavaria or Catalonia at the other Old Trafford.

Finally, there came the dual news that Lancashire might leave Old Trafford and that, at the other Old Traffords, Manchester United might be taken over by Malcom Glazer, the American tycoon.

Tempted by a City of Manchester Council offer, as the poor old venue began to look a little woebegone, of a brand-new stadium, hard by Manchester City's splendid headquarters in north east Manchester, Lancashire are considering the first-ever move in the county's long history. After the enormous success of the Commonwealth games of 2002, and no more than a good walk from Piccadilly Gardens, in what was the old Bradford and Beswick area of Manchester, an architectural sonnet to sport is being composed, with cycling among the games already represented there. A Test match cricket ground would, of course, add something of a cachet to this sporting collection. To some, this project seems akin to subjecting the Vatican to the Babylonian Captivity, switching the Eiffel Tower to Berlin or shifting Lord's to Canary Wharf, while the more pragmatic wonder prudently about the possible unsteadiness of the income flow. The discussion continues, resembling the lovesick swain tearing the petals of the flower...'we should move; we shouldn't move'.

As for the takeover of the footballing Old Trafford, it is fascinating to observe the raw emotions roused. One understands that Malcolm Glazer, already holding a strong stock of United shares, was surprised at the intensity of suspicion among fans about his motive and whether, for instance, he intended to utilise the club as a monetary milch-cow for his other variegated enterprises. Those with close connections with any sports club were less amazed, comprehending the depth of sentiment that adherence to one's chosen heroes evokes. Perhaps the American has over-reached himself on this occasion and he appears, as of even date, to have lost some crucial legal and fiscal props.

Lancashire on the possible move; Manchester United on the possible change...writing the history of ongoing sports clubs is a bit like being a war correspondent in the middle of the Hundred Years War, knowing there is no end in sight. It is not a discrete study, like the biography of a dead statesman or the scrutiny of a long-finished military struggle. This sporting life goes on. As Henry Wadsworth Longfellow remarked, in addition to contributing versified profiles of Andy Flintoff:

Art is long, and Time is fleeting,
And our hearts, though stout and brave,
Still, like muffled drums are beating
Funeral marches to the grave.

Possibly in a hundred years time someone will be writing a history based on the proximity of the Manchester City and Lancashire grounds. I do hope Lancashire will have won the County Championship by then.

23.

Envoi; Keeping the Faith

THE ANNEX to the office of the Secretary of State for Education used to be lined with framed photographs of his or her predecessors, right back to Ellen Wilkinson, who was appointed Minister of Education in 1945. It was a profuse collection. The walls were practically covered from creamy ceiling to plush carpet. The job was often one of those middling posts, a brief respite for those scrambling up or sliding down what Benjamin Disraeli called the 'greasy pole' of politics, and there were dozens of them. It would have taken a political buff of immense anorakary, like a train spotter-cum-cricket memory man who knows how many railway miles W.G. Grace travelled, to recall them all.

40 years ago the incumbent was a Conservative politician by the name of David Eccles. There must have been one of those periodic bursts of breast beating about misbehaviour and values, because all the teacher training colleges were requested to hold a staff meeting to discuss the moral dimension in education. As the head of the history department, I was instructed to contribute and I inwardly groaned, knowing that the brand of humanist, tolerant, relativist pluralism I peddled was regarded as trendy and perilous by the righteously right-thinking right. So it proved. There was much said about the need to make children believe in Jesus and behave themselves and vice versa. Wondrously, my only allies were the members of the religious education department. They were very unhappy about religion being deployed as a means of social control. One said that the chief point about religion was whether it was true, not whether it worked, that is, in a functional way as cement for a crumbling society. Another said it was blasphemous to turn to religion just because the police force could not cope.

Their assertion that the basic question was about the existence or otherwise of a supernatural authority was unabashed and uncompromising. Although, over the eons, religious faiths have doubled up as usually authoritarian political credos, and as rationalisations for strict and often highly prejudicial ethical codes, this assertion pierced to the heart of the matter. One might, at least in any primary discussion, shelve what John Morley, disciple and biographer of the high churchman, W.E. Gladstone, but himself an agnostic, used to call 'ecclesiastical' affairs, in the literal connotation of having to do with the church buildings. He was, for instance, referring to churches anxious to build schools that they might receive the joint boons of state funding and captive clients, issues of more material than theological significance. Today he would point coolly both at the parents who genuflect at this or that altar to get their youngsters into a church school and at the clerical authorities that humour them.

From late teenage, drilled by and questioning of years of Sunday School attendance, I too had adopted his agnostic position, but not, I would like to think, given so positive an exemplar, in any negative, dithering, indecisive fashion. The 19th century doubters were not fence-sitting don't knows. The tough Victorian stance of T.H. Huxley, who coined the word 'a-gnostic', as in scepticism about the ability to have knowledge of 'gnosis' or spiritual mysteries, is a resolute position. In insisting that one cannot know finally of other than natural phenomena, of ultimately whether there is a God or not, this view maintains that, as there is nothing one can do about it either way, the ground is cleared to make the best, without spiritual prevarication, of the human condition with which we are presented.

Put another way, if there is an omnipotent Godhead, all-seeing and all-knowing, there is nothing left to free will or random choice, for all has been created and known of for all time with a complete omniscience. If there is something you can do about it, then the Godhead cannot be all-powerful. This was a problem over which many, among them the fathers of the Reformation, including Martin Luther, sweated long hours. In his majestic study of the Reformation, Diarmaid MacCulloch variously wrote of how Christianity was drawn toward 'the opposed affirmation of God's majesty as judge and of God's loving mercy as father…a logical conclusion of the (Lutheran) doctrine was the divine predestination of humanity to salvation or damnation…So our world and its history was a result of God's sovereign decision.' Seen in this light, 'God was the author of evil' as well as everything else. The Roman Catholic apologist, G.K. Chesterton, often used the metaphor of human souls remotely controlled, like the fish on the hook, enjoying the illusion of free play, of free will, in the water, only for 'a twitch of the hook' to reveal the fatal misapprehension. It is a metaphor that could well be applied to this fundamental question.

If all events are laid down forever more, one cannot surprise God. Manchester City could not surprise God, and, if they couldn't, it's God help the rest of us. Even if the creator is a blind jester, a being that starts the snowball rolling and then steps back, the kind of fateful providence implicit in the pessimistic novels and poems of Thomas Hardy, what is one to do but make the human best of it? The agnostic is liberated to pursue a humane and humanist agenda, forearmed with the knowledge that we are either completely free agents or as described by the limerick:

> There once was a man who said 'damn,
> I suddenly see what I am.
> I'm a creature that moves,
> In predestinate grooves;
> I'm not even a bus, I'm a tram.'

The metaphysics of buses and trams may seem a long way from the Metrolink carrying its passengers to the two Old Traffords. Few would deny that the great world confessions have wrought much that is good and much that is bad; an assessment that the latter has the more prevailed is but an opinion, but it happens to be mine. This is a robust position to adapt but, I trust, not an ungenerous one. It would be churlish as well as foolish not to recognise the profound and reverent depth of religious feeling and relief that has informed the thought and behaviour of humankind over the centuries. In the avant-garde view of a God who is 'interfused' with, not superior, to

222

human life, there is this same yearning for a goodly, moral imperative in a world wracked with badness. At the same time, and beyond private ties, most people seem to seek some emotional comfort, of the kind that religion has brought to many. Music and art, sometimes as expressions of religiosity, have something of the same function - and sport may, for some, have this purpose.

Let it be at once admitted that professional sport, as an emotional release, has its drawbacks. It might be castigated as, like religion in the Marxist critique, 'the opium of the people', doping the populace into somnolence about important political and social issues, as it pursues its capitalist jungle path. Hooliganism and xenophobia are rife, especially in football, with some clubs the focus for notorious 'firms', with noisome and racist links with the far right. The turmoil and bedlam anticipated for some football fixtures would probably be sufficient, were these judged to be political demonstrations or parades, to permit the police to have them banned under public order legislation. When Urs Meier, the Swiss referee, rightly (in my view) penalised John Terry and disallowed England's goal in the closing minutes of the European Championship quarter-final with Portugal in 2004, he received death threats and, courtesy of *The Sun*, 16,000 abusive e-mails. It is not all grace and light.

Denominational faiths, as with the Glasgow clubs, are identified with sporting concerns. Players in many sports obviously seek, in superstitious fashion, religious aid. On 6th March 2004 Steed Malbranque, the Fulham player, made the sign of the cross when Fulham won a penalty against Manchester United. Are we really to believe in an otherworldly dispensation in which the supreme being supports Fulham? Ruud van Nistelrooy then scored a penalty for Manchester United and passionately clutched the red shield on his shirt. There is no doubt in my mind of which was the more authentic - and the saner - expression of faith and attachment.

It must be freely admitted that having Manchester United and, on their glory days, Lancashire as one's conjoined creed is like backing the Church Triumphant and not the Church Persecuted. Knights Templar, not Martyrs, seize the emotions. However, as all true sports supporters recognise, these are life-long, non-severable ties. I recall a conversation with Brian Jackson, a charismatic education reformer of the 1960s and early 1970s, with whom I was much involved professionally and whose simple equation, 'socialism equals equality plus fun', is still very attractive. Discussing the renegade move of Labour Party members to set up the SDP, he made out the case for a heart-warming loyalty. 'You stick to the Labour Party through thick and thin', he said, 'it's like Huddersfield Town for me and Manchester United for you.'

The emotive relief of sporting affections has, of course, its ups and downs, as fans of Huddersfield Town might feelingly confirm. Certainly I never watch the television highlights of matches where Lancashire or Manchester United have been beaten, nor do I twist the knife more smartingly by reading newspaper accounts of such dismal proceedings. There is always another day. Until then, as the ancient drawing room ballad so insightfully had it, 'from sport to sport they hurry me to stifle my regret, and when they win a smile from me, they think that I forget.'

The infant, parochial, intense roots of this brand of worship mean that club transcends country. All passion spent, it is difficult to evoke the same admiration for the nation, about whose adventures the most effective sentiment one can summon forth is a neutral interest. In watching or reading about international cricket and football, one is torn between anxiety less one's heroes are injured in an alien cause (or, in the case of cricket, are absentees from their bona fide business) and fond desires that they might flourish. In an epoch of multinational recruitment, this leads to some mental confusion, as when watching Clive Lloyd, tightly embraced to the Lancastrian bosom, bat for the West Indies or Peter Schmeichel, adopted foster child of the Stretford End, keep goal for Denmark. In the 2004 European Championship one was faced with the logical cleft stick of Portugal, with Cristiano Ronaldo, versus Holland, with Ruud van Nistelrooy.

It is not a question of patriotism. I am as patriotic as the next person. I have voted in every national and local election since the age of 21, bar one Euro-election where, accompanied by the dog, I advanced on the polling station to explain to a startled clerk why I was positively abstaining. The dog seemed to understand. I was as outraged as were all sane thinking people when, in the 1980s and early 1990s, the public utilities that, along with every one else, I owned were summarily flogged off, in what Harold Macmillan, no Red he, icily described as the selling of the 'family silver'. The falling into privatised hands of the great natural asset of water was the one that especially angered me, but it is worth another mention of how cities, like Manchester, had in the heady days of local government bravely pioneered that branch of municipalisation, which did so much to offer the people decent educational, housing, transport, public health and other valued facilities.

I am a lover and user of the Welfare State and an adherent of the state education system and the National Health Service. Far from being a dark Bolshevik plot, the Welfare State was a term coined by the Oxford don, Alfred Zimmern in 1934, and popularised by Sir George Schuster and William Temple, Archbishop of Canterbury, as a counter to the 'Warfare' totalitarian states of fascist Germany, Italy and Spain and of Soviet Russia. They insisted that the ailing parliamentary democracies could build a genuine contract with their citizens, offering them a social code of protection from social ills, in the hope of preserving a strong, healthy, freedom-loving and peaceful nation-state. Sir William Beveridge, a classic liberal, was equally forceful on this theme of communal involvement, as his famous wartime report became the practical base of the post-war welfare settlement. Universalism was the key. It was the concept of comprehensive give and take; all should pay that all might benefit. Jose Harris, his biographer, confirms that William Beveridge believed that universalism, as well as creating wholesome social security, was 'desirable to foster social solidarity and feelings of identity'. He would doubtless have found a recent advertisement of a commercial health provider to supply a 'Personal Health Service' as gratuitously offensive, an inducement to civil selfishness and anti-patriotic to boot.

Patriotism, then, might be more seriously remarked as a civic ethic. What is one to make of those who travel as far as Portugal or Australia or the West Indies to support English sports teams, but who cannot cross the street to vote, that precious hard-fought shield against tyranny that the likes of Sandy Turnbull of Manchester United and Lancashire's Peter Eckersley died to protect? It is a muddled situation. We have a royal family that subscribes zealously to and purports to lead the state church, but who would not be seen dead, as consumers, inside a state school or state hospital, so the top patriotic model is itself very deficient. There are those who might croon *Swing Low, Sweet Chariot* at Twickenham on Saturday and send their children to fee-paying (let us eschew the mealy-mouthed euphemisms of 'private' or 'independent') schools on Monday, seek commercial medical care on Tuesday, dodge jury service on Wednesday and avoid tax payments on Thursday.

Obviously, that stern adjunction by no means applies to all of rugby's tuneful choristers, any more than the Barmy Army is exclusively manned by serial electoral abstainers. What one is attempting to do is to trace the line between the excesses of xenophobia, sporting and otherwise, and the serious precept of civil patriotism and, from that position, to indicate that the placing of sporting club before sporting country is not an altogether impure sentiment. At worst, there are several rather more basic aspects of life about which to wax patriotic, while a preference for these parochial sporting agencies that have offered such pleasure and emotional comfort over the lifespan do deserve some profound measure of affection.

In the 1960s there was esoteric discussion about who should inhabit the few nuclear shelters that had been constructed. Those in central and local government were firmly of the view that those in central and local government should use the shelters. It was perhaps consistent with their normal approach, namely, to remain as inaccessible to the general public underground as they were over ground. I penned an article at the time, arguing that, in the interests of preserving the best and most salient features of civilisation, the north-west shelter should be given over to the playing staffs of Manchester United and Lancashire County Cricket Club. It was written in what was dotingly hoped to be jestful satire, but I always had a sneaking feeling that I really believed it.

It is true that St Thomas Aquinas taught us, after the manner of Aristotle, that we must apprehend the misery of hell to taste fully the joy of Heaven. Thus there may be some impudent burlesque pointed in the direction of Yorkshire County Cricket Club and Manchester City by their friends at the two Old Traffords. There is no need for this to be either bloodthirsty or wrathful. Indeed, when Manchester City were relegated to the Second Division, and hiding the grins that naturally rose to every Red countenance, I solicitously telephoned one or two City fans of my acquaintance with timetable information about train services to some of the more obscure destinations to which their fallen heroes would now be dispatched. That some of the reaction was acidic, nay, unprintable, should not distract from the disinterested motives that prompted this kindly act.

As children, the late afternoon was marked by the arrival of the *Manchester Evening News*. My grandmother would pull me on her knee and, like all other local matriarchs, she first turned to the deaths column to study the obituaries as carefully as her husband, Harry, scrutinised the runners and riders on the racing pages. She taught me to read from this newsprint and I often wonder whether there were children, educated in this same macabre fashion, who grew up thinking Mancunians died in alphabetical order. In the summer we were instructed to turn to the late extra column on the back page, there to seek out the latest cricket scores. One was taught, not only to find how well Lancashire were doing, but how badly Yorkshire were doing. This particular theological tenet has, over the last quarter of a century, brought much rejoicing to the faithful. As Anthony

Trollope wrote, we are always able to bear the trials of our neighbours with equanimity. 'For what do we live,' uttered Mr Bennet in *Pride and Prejudice*, 'but to make sport for our neighbours, and laugh at them in our turn.'

What a paradox it all is! Lifelong commitment to sporting passions somehow manages to combine much that is important with much that is trivial. It is time to hang the shingle 'Dunintellectualisin' over the doorway and accept the unvarnished truth that, from the far distance of early childhood, an adoration of the two Old Traffords, and the two venerable clubs that adorn those grounds, has given rise to close on three score years and ten of a gratifying 'simple faith', Tennyson might have called it. So one continues to grasp the nettle of current joys. As Edward Fitzgerald wrote in his *The Rubaiyat of Omar Khayam*:

> *Ah, fill the cup - what book it to repeat*
> *If our time is slipping underneath our feet;*
> *Unborn tomorrow and dead yesterday,*
> *Why fret about them if today is sweet?*

Index of people

Index

232

Index

Index